The State, Class and Developmentalism in South Korea

This book problematises the statist underpinnings of the concept of the 'developmental state' in terms of both state–society and national–global relations, challenging the notion that the state is the agent of national development *qua* being autonomous from the domestic and global economies.

Presenting a thorough and comprehensive critical assessment of the extant approaches and theories of the Korean developmental state in particular, this book demonstrates that the existing literature, including Marxist critiques, only inadequately and partially challenges statism. It examines how statism reinforces and is reinforced by 'Third World Developmentalism', the idea that 'development' is in itself a positive goal and that a nationally autonomous mode of development should be promoted as a means of empowerment. In opposition, this book offers a critique of statism by constructing an alternative theoretical framework, extending Marx's concept of commodity fetishism to state–society and national–global relations.

Drawing on a new theoretical framework and significant Korean literature, *The State, Class and Developmentalism in South Korea* offers a novel historical interpretation and critique of the developmental state in the Korean context. As such, it will be useful to students and scholars of Asian studies, Development Studies and International Political Economy.

Hae-Yung Song works on political theory, development theory and the political economy of South Korea. She has taught at Warwick University and worked for the South Korean government in the areas of international relations and diplomacy. She currently teaches at Graduate School of International Studies, Korea University, Seoul, South Korea.

Routledge Advances in Korean Studies

38 Strategic, Policy and Social Innovation for a Post-Industrial Korea
Beyond the Miracle
Joon Nak Choi, Yong Suk Lee and Gi-Wook Shin

39 North Korea's Foreign Policy
The DPRK Part on the International Scene and Its Audiences
Lenka Caisova

40 Public Management in Korea
Performance Evaluation and Public Institutions
Edited by Soonae Park

41 Megacity Seoul
Urbanization and the Development of Modern South Korea
Yu-Min Joo

42 Korean Adoptees and Transnational Adoption
Embodiment and Emotion
Jessica Walton

43 Digital Development in Korea, Second Edition
Lessons for a Sustainable World
Myung Oh and James F. Larson

44 The State, Class and Developmentalism in South Korea
Development as Fetish
Hae-Yung Song

For more information about this series, please visit: www.routledge.com/asianstudies/series/SE0505

The State, Class and Developmentalism in South Korea

Development as Fetish

Hae-Yung Song

Routledge
Taylor & Francis Group
LONDON AND NEW YORK

First published 2020
by Routledge
2 Park Square, Milton Park, Abingdon, Oxon OX14 4RN

and by Routledge
52 Vanderbilt Avenue, New York, NY 10017

Routledge is an imprint of the Taylor & Francis Group, an informa business

First issued in paperback 2021

British Library Cataloguing-in-Publication Data
A catalogue record for this book is available from the British Library

Library of Congress Cataloging-in-Publication Data
Names: Song, Hae-Yung, author.
Title: The state, class and developmentalism in South Korea : development as fetish / Hae-Yung Song.
Identifiers: LCCN 2019028094 (print) | LCCN 2019028095 (ebook) | ISBN 9780367354725 (hardback) | ISBN 9780429342066 (ebook) | ISBN 9781000725636 (adobe pdf) | ISBN 9781000725773 (epub) | ISBN 9781000725704 (mobi)
Subjects: LCSH: Economic development—Political aspects—Korea (South) | Korea (South)—Politics and government—21st century. | Globalization—Political aspects—Korea (South) | Capitalism—Political aspects—Korea (South)
Classification: LCC HC467.965 .S645 2020 (print) | LCC HC467.965 (ebook) | DDC 338.95195—dc23
LC record available at https://lccn.loc.gov/2019028094
LC ebook record available at https://lccn.loc.gov/2019028095

ISBN: 978-0-367-35472-5 (hbk)
ISBN: 978-1-03-208767-2 (pbk)
ISBN: 978-0-429-34206-6 (ebk)

Typeset in Times New Roman
by codeMantra

Contents

Acknowledgements

I would like to thank my mother, In-Sook Lee, my partner Marcel Stoetzler and Ms. Barbara Fletchman-Smith for taking my book project as importantly as their own work and offering me invaluable support. I hope this book positively contributes to a new way of thinking about and acting on 'development'.

Introduction

The developmental state, 'Third World developmentalism' and the fetishism of national development

> ...a ruler full of the spirit of improvement is warranted in the use of any expedients that will attain an end, perhaps otherwise unattainable. Despotism is a legitimate mode of movement in dealing with barbarians, provided the end be their improvement and the means justified by actually effecting that end.
>
> (John Stuart Mill, On Liberty, Chapter 1)

This book provides a critique of the concept of the 'developmental state' as well as a critique of the extant critiques of the developmental state, with the primary focus being on South Korea (hereafter 'Korea'). Literature on the 'developmental state' has been growing since Chalmers Johnson first coined the term in 1982 with reference to the Japanese state in his book *MITI and the Japanese Miracle*, and there has been no shortage of critiques. Entering an area of study that had been heavily documented and researched, I will briefly set out in this introduction what motivated me to write this book and what contributions I hope to make to this much-vaunted-field of research.

While it is debatable whether the concept of the developmental state and the tenets around it constitute a theory, they have clearly dominated the discussions of post-Second World War East Asian industrialisation, widely considered to be the poster child for successful Third World development. Intensive debates have taken place over how and why Korea (and other East Asian economies) industrialised successfully and thereby moved away from the world-economic periphery when many other postcolonial countries did not, and how and to what extent the existence of a development-oriented state, namely the developmental state, has contributed to this 'success'.

To the extent that the concept of the developmental state was devised to explain what is seen as 'successful' development, it is grounded, from its inception, on what I call 'Third World developmentalism', the taken-for-granted idea that development itself is something to be desired and applauded. As discussed in Part I, most debates on the developmental state have been on who and what deserved most credit for the 'success' of East Asian industrialisation. In spite of otherwise opposed perspectives, all sides tended to share the presupposition that *more* development is desirable. 'Third World developmentalism' profoundly shaped the way in which development is understood both theoretically and politically. Above all, it limits the question of development to that of success or failure and instrumentalises it as to *how* this success can be emulated elsewhere. In so doing, it contributes to bypassing inquiries into *what* Third World development in fact is: *capitalist* development, essentially violent and brutal, arguably more so than the earlier processes of capitalist development that created what we commonly refer to as the 'developed world'.

'Third World developmentalism' has been enforced by the tendency for the developmental state to be used almost as shorthand for the rejection of neoclassical economics and thus came to carry the mantle of a politically progressive force. This is explained in part by the defensive position of heterodox economics and the left in general, which have been facing the ascendency of neoliberal ideology since the 1970s. Nevertheless, this tendency has produced a paradoxical situation in which broadly critical approaches, including development economics, (historical) institutionalism and Marxist critiques of neoliberalism, financial imperialism and the (post-) Washington Consensus, tend to exalt the developmental state as unproblematic, whose characteristics some liken to the Keynesian interventionist state. In fact, this favourable reception of the developmental state in liberal and left-wing scholarship in the West stands in sharp contrast to the way in which it has been perceived amongst the political left in Korea. The Park Chung-Hee regime (1961–79), as the principal embodiment of the Korean developmental state, was the main target of democratisation social forces and epitomised the political far right to the extent that many Korean public intellectuals saw it as 'fascist' (see Chapter 1).

This remarkable turnaround in the perception of the developmental state from representing the reactionary and far-right political forces in Korea to being the exalted driver of successful 'catch-up' national development can be accounted for, in the West, to some extent by Western scholars' bad conscience over the postcolonial countries: they might simply be too polite to make any harsh judgements on the developing countries' undemocratic political systems and instead positively value their economic achievements. It is not mere coincidence in this context that the authors that contributed most to forging the concept of the developmental state, Chalmers Johnson, Alice Amsden and Robert Wade, are also notable critics of the global (financial) institutions (International Monetary Fund, World Bank) and US imperialism on the ground that they encroach on the national autonomy of developing countries, thereby undermining their development prospects. The left-liberal advocates of the developmental state argue, at least implicitly, that successful development justifies authoritarianism or else that democracy in the developing countries needs to be judged according to its success in delivering economic development. The fact that they would hardly ever make such a proposition in the context of the West points to the implicit but deeply rooted presence in their thinking of what I call 'Third World developmentalism' (see Chapter 1).

This suggests that an adequate critique of the developmental state requires a critique of 'Third World developmentalism'. However, despite numerous critical assessments of the developmental state to date, the extant critiques have hardly addressed 'Third World developmentalism' as the core theoretical and political problem of the concept of the developmental state. One of the two main lines of critique of the developmental state primarily focusses on its authoritarian characteristics, social repression and the exclusion of labour from politics (e.g. Deyo 1987; Koo H 1987, 1993a, 1993b, 2001; Lee B-C 2003a; Ogle 1990, 2003b). Valid insights at the descriptive level notwithstanding, these critiques tend to limit the problem of the developmental state to the political realm rather than relate the extreme mode of societal control and labour discipline that characterise the developmental state to the requirements of 'catch-up' capitalist development itself. Without seeing the fundamental connection between the authoritarian state and capitalist development, capitalism being a system of exploitation that is necessarily expressed in a more intensive form in the context of the lower reaches of the capitalist world-economy's hierarchy, the authoritarian characteristics of the developmental state must seem accidental, or else unfortunate but necessary on the road to development, and liable to be corrected by democratisation and the extended participation of labour in politics. Consequently, critiques of the developmental state that focus on its authoritarianism often arrive at the view that the assumed positive aspects of the developmental state, such as its competency to deliver development, can be isolated from its authoritarianism and blended with democracy, a view that is epitomised in the term 'democratic developmental state' (see Beeson and Islam 2005; Robinson and White 1998).

Another line of critique of the developmental state has been offered by Marxist scholars. While Marxist critiques bring to the fore the essence of the developmental state in relation to class domination and exploitation, they tend to prioritise the question of how functional and instrumental the developmental state was in securing the interests of the capitalist class and the capitalist system (e.g. Cammack 2007; Chibber 1999, 2002, 2003, 2005; Hart-Landsberg 1989; Hart-Landsberg and Burkett 2000). Reflecting the general weaknesses of the instrumentalist-structuralist critiques of the capitalist state, which amount to what I call the 'class content' analysis of the state, these Marxist critics find the essence of the developmental state to be capitalist based on the fact that its autonomy is being restrained by the national bourgeoises or based on its brutality against labour. Failing to address the state as such as a political form of the capitalist societal totality, these Marxist critiques propose the view that the 'class content' of the state can be replaced, at least potentially, so that the state serves a social group other than the capitalists, such as labour, or another purpose, such as national development. In so doing, they arrive at an affirmative vision of the capitalist state itself, albeit unintentionally.

Even those very rare attempts to 'demystify' the concept of the developmental state by recourse to 'social form' critique that sees the state as the political form of capitalist social relations in their totality (e.g. Chang 2009) fail to inquire into the fact that the 'myth' about the developmental state is not only about its apparent autonomy from domestic social actors but also, just as much, about its alleged ability to achieve a nationally autonomous mode of development. The continued popularity of the concept of the developmental state and the incessant attempts by other actors in the periphery of the world system to emulate it stem from the fact that it is seen as the agent of successful 'catch-up' national development in the Third World.

The currently available Marxist critiques of the developmental state from both 'class content' and 'social form' perspectives have primarily engaged with the question concerning state-society and state-class relations at the *domestic* level: they hardly problematise another aspect of the concept of the developmental state – namely the notion that it is the main driver and agent of *national* development. Consequently, they tend to succumb to the conventional 'statist' approach in which the question about the transformation of the developmental state is posed in terms of whether the state remains intact or has been dismantled by the pressures of the global economy and whether it has shifted its orientation from the national to the global (see Chapters 4 and 5).

In this book I try to establish a more adequate theory and critique of the developmental state, particularly by addressing a lacuna within Marxist state theory in general and Marxist critiques of the developmental state in particular. I suggest that the 'statist' concept of the developmental state has two dimensions: namely the alleged autonomy of the state from the market or society at the domestic level, on the one hand, and the alleged autonomy of the state from the global economy as the agent of national development, on the other. Only when *both* of these dimensions are critiqued and theorised can an adequate theory of the developmental state be established.

I start this volume by discussing how the concept of the developmental state has been forged in the statist fashion from its inception, whereby not only the categories of the state and the market but also those of the national and the global have been juxtaposed as antithetical. I argue that these conceptual foundations are underpinned by 'Third World developmentalism' (Chapter 1). I also assess how this conceptual problem attached to the developmental state has been reinforced and reproduced by more nuanced approaches, such as (historical) institutionalism, and in the more recent debates on the transformation of the developmental state, including that on the 'hybrid' developmental state (Chapters 2 and 3). I then appraise two main approaches within Marxist state theory: namely 'class content' and 'social form critique', respectively, and how each of these traditions is reflected in the analyses of the developmental state (Chapters 4 and 5).

By identifying the limitations of existing Marxist critiques, I attempt to construct an alternative theoretical framework for the developmental state by extending Marx's critique of commodity fetishism and political economy, as set out in *Capital* and *Grundrisse*, to the question of the state and the global economy, or the nation-global relation. I derive the characteristics of the developmental state not only from its relation to society and class relations at the domestic level but in relation to its position in the world market and the timing of development in world time. My critique offers a theoretical framework that assesses the antithetical juxtaposition of the state and the market as state fetishism, on the one hand, and that of the national and the global as the fetishism of national development, on the other (Chapter 6).

While I attempt to construct a more adequate theory and critique of the developmental state on the basis of critical appraisals of various theories, my intention is neither to dismiss entirely these theories nor to collapse the differences that exist between them. Rather, my own theorisation of the developmental state is grounded on an eclectic approach, drawing on insights from each theory and synthesising them for the purpose of establishing a more adequate theory of the developmental state. I also apply Marx's critique of political economy to the ways in which I proceed with my analyses of the extant theories. I begin by discussing the relatively simple key tenets of the concept of the developmental state and gradually move into the critique of the more complex theories. This method aims to allow readers to prepare themselves progressively for the more complex theories and to continue following my journey towards an alternative theory of the developmental state.

The third part of the book offers a theoretically informed historical analysis of the social and economic history of modern Korea, considered the epitome of successful industrialisation during the post-Second World War period (Part III). In addition to historically verifying the theorisation of the developmental state set out in the earlier chapters, the historical analysis has three aims.

First, while there is no shortage of literature on Korean modern social and economic history, most literature, at least in the disciplinary context of Development Studies, finds the origins of the Korean developmental state either in Japanese colonialism (1910–45) or in the Park military regime (1961–79). As a counter-analysis to these dominant approaches, I date back the formation of the modern Korean state, in the context of Korea's integration into the world market, to the late nineteenth century. I demonstrate that the modern Korean state was formed as part and parcel of the global expansion of capitalist social relations, to which the reorganisation of the pre-existing political system into the international system of nation-states was integral.

Second, I offer a conceptually informed historical analysis of the formation of the modern Korean state, the origins of the developmental state and its transformation. In this respect, my approach is one of 'historical sociology' (see Abrams 1982; Adams et al. 2005; Calhoun 1996). One of the key propositions of historical sociology is the view that history cannot be relegated to a field concerned with the empirical as separate from other disciplines in the social sciences, such as sociology, that are supposedly concerned with concepts and theories: 'there is no distinction in principle between history and any of the other social sciences. The distinction is not that between theory and non-theory, but between the adequacy or inadequacy of the theory brought to bear' (Jones 1976: 296; see Giddens 1979).

Guided by my theoretical proposition that challenges the antithetical juxtaposition of the national and the global, and of structure and agency, I assess the *global social* origins of the Korean developmental state in the context of 'catching-up' development within the global relations of capitalism: I trace the ways in which *prima facie* external forces – imperialist inter-state competition in the late nineteenth century, Japanese colonialism and subsequent US army occupation – constituted integral parts of (*prima facie* domestic) class and social struggles. I discuss how they interacted with domestic class and social forces and the existing production structure, and at the same time transformed the social structure and class constellations, laying the material and historical conditions (the structure) which subsequent actors in turn strove to influence and transform (agency).

Third, I aim to contribute to expanding the general understanding of modern Korean social and economic history by incorporating a large amount of resources and materials available in Korean only and introducing debates and discussions that have taken place within Korea. This is not only to provide the perspectives of Korean historians and researchers but also to offer an historical analysis of the developmental state alternative to that of the 'Western' theorists of the developmental state and institutionalists that have dominated the interpretation of Korean development history outside of Korea.

Each theory and historical interpretation is motivated to convey certain political implications, and my critical-theoretical discussion of the developmental state and its history also come with political implications different from those of the extant approaches. Above all, my critique is intended to challenge the (usually unspoken) assumption that (capitalist) development is in itself desirable and that it can and should be attained in the most straightforward way possible, particularly in the context of the Third World. Viewed from the perspective offered in this book, 'state-led' and 'national' development does not constitute an alternative to 'market-led' and 'globally-oriented' development. Successful industrial development in the world-economic periphery merely represents other, often more brutal, modalities of capitalist exploitation as characteristic of the processes of 'catching-up' within the global system of capitalism: an extreme and destructive mode of human and physical mobilisation is intrinsic to capitalist 'catching-up' development in the hierarchical world system.

This understanding suggests that the question of development should shift from *how* and *why* it succeeds or fails, and how to achieve and augment developmental impact, to *what* development means in the capitalist world system and what it is for. Arguably, while much intellectual and political energy has been spent on questioning how to bring about and augment development, too little effort has been made to secure the emancipatory content of this development. I hope to contribute through this book to nothing less than a badly needed paradigm shift in the discourse of 'development'.

Part I

Forging, reinforcing and reproducing the statist concept of the developmental state

1 Antithesising the state and the market, and the national and the global

Forging the statist concept of the developmental state

With the rise of East Asia, especially the 'tiger economies' (Korea, Taiwan, Hong Kong and Singapore), as newly industrialising countries in the 1960s and the 1970s, intensive debate has taken place over the question of how and why these countries could move away from the world economic periphery more successfully than others.[1] In this chapter I assess how the concept of the 'developmental state' was formed and consolidated in a general effort to explain the rise of East Asia, on the one hand, and as a critical response to neoclassical explanations, on the other. I do so by looking at the main propositions of neoclassical economics and of key scholars of the developmental state paradigm, such as Chalmers Johnson, Robert Wade and Alice Amsden. I show how the process of establishing the concept of the developmental state was that of augmenting and maximising the role of the state *vis-à-vis* neoclassical economics' attempt to undervalue and minimise this role in development. I contend that while the key strength of the account of the successful rise of East Asia that is based on the concept of the developmental state lies in its explanation of the diverse development outcomes *within* the Third World or Developing World, the concept is g rounded on what I define as 'statism'. To the extent that the developmental state is defined in terms of its high level of autonomy over other social actors and as the promotor of national developmental against external influence, it posits *not only* state and market, *but also* state and global economy as antithetical categories, in which one side inevitably loses autonomy to the other. I describe the theoretical and political problems that result from the juxtaposition of these categories as antithetical, and discuss how the statist conceptualisation of the developmental state, in turn, conditions the ways in which social and economic forces (e.g. democratisation and the Asian financial crisis of 1997/98) are assessed either as external to the developmental state or in terms of the competition between the two sets of categories counterposed as antithetical.

Conceptualising the developmental state: maximising the developmental state

Insomuch as the concept of the developmental state was a critical response to or was initiated in an attempt to establish a vision alternative particularly to neoclassical economics' assessment of the successful industrialisation of East Asia, I will first of all, discuss some of the key arguments of neoclassical economics before moving on to the key contributors to the conceptualisation of the developmental state.

Neoclassical economics: minimising the role of the state in development

On the question of why and how East Asian economies developed more successfully than others in the world economic periphery, neoclassical economists presented the view that, although there were variations amongst them, these economies showed no or minimal distortion of the market. According to neoclassical economists, the low level of market distortion in East Asia, in particular in Korea and Taiwan, is evidenced by the adoption by these countries of export-oriented industrialisation strategies (EOI), which suggested an openness to the global economy. It was argued that in these countries, the normalisation of the exchange rate and the increase in the interest rate in the mid-1960s followed an initial stage of import substitution industrialisation (ISI) (Balassa 1988: S284).

In equating 'export-oriented' strategies with 'openness' or 'outwardness', neoclassical economists commonly carried out comparative assessments of a number of countries that adopted either ISI or EOI and the corresponding growth rates (Balassa 1980; Kruger 1978, 1980; Lal 1983; World Bank 1987). The conclusion typically drawn is that the more open an economy was, the higher the resulting economic growth was: 'growth performance has been more satisfactory under export promotion strategies than under import substitution strategies … there is little doubt about the link between export performance and growth rates' (Kruger 1980: 288–9). In a similar vein, after classifying 41 developing countries into 'strongly outward', 'moderately outward', 'moderately inward' and 'strongly inward' categories for the periods of 1963–1973 and 1973–1985, the *World Development Report* (1987) concluded that 'strongly outward' countries performed best, while 'strongly inward ones' performed worst. The correlation between EOI and economic growth identified by neoclassical economists is maintained on the grounds that EOI allowed the effective allocation of resources according to comparative advantage, overcoming the limited size of the domestic market and maximising specialisation (Balassa 1988: S280–1; see also Bhagwati 1978, 1988; Kruger 1978: ch. 12). This suggests that neoclassical economics is based on the belief that the world economy is an open system, leaving plenty of room for upward mobility insofar as market-conforming policies are implemented and markets are liberalised.

This optimistic neoclassical vision that the world economy does not pose a serious obstacle to Third World development is closely related to its view on state intervention in the economy. Alongside EOI strategies and economic liberalisation, neoclassical economists found additional, arguably more important, evidence of a low degree of market distortion in East Asia at the level of state intervention, which they argued was kept to a minimum, or was at least less pronounced than it was in other, less successful countries (Fei 1983: 34). In other words, according to neoclassical economics, as much as state intervention is counterproductive to development, it is *unnecessary*. With reference to the case of Korea, Balassa argues, for example, that the emergence of the exports of textiles and clothing occurred in response to (market) incentives rather than as a reaction to any particular government policy or statutory decision (Balassa 1988: S285). Even if government intervention is recognised, it is seen to have been reduced in subsequent years, and its main contribution is limited to the construction of a modern infrastructure and the provision of a stable system of incentives which aims at the elimination of administrative obstacles to exports (Balassa 1988: S285–7). Balassa (1998: S288) then concludes that '[t]he neutrality and stability of the incentive system, together with limited government intervention, well-functioning labor and capital markets, and reliance on private capital, thus appears to have been the main ingredients of successful economic performance in East Asia'. This amounts to what Chang calls 'self-cancelling state intervention', which suggests that various measures of state intervention cancelled each other out to produce a neutral incentive structure (Chang H-J 1993: 134; 1999: 2–3).

However, it is important to recognise that neoclassical economics' advocacy of free-market fundamentalism or reservations against state intervention has been expressed increasingly in a less direct form. One of the reasons for this was that it became difficult to propagate the benefits of free-market policies in the face of the failure of the stabilisation and structural adjustment programmes implemented in many developing countries on the recommendations of the World Bank and the International Monetary Fund (IMF) during the 1980s. Furthermore, it became hard to ignore that state interventionism was being credited with East Asia's rapid development by scholars like Alice Amsden and Robert Wade, which shall be discussed below. Consequently, state intervention was acknowledged, though to a limited extent, as a positive contributor to Third World development within neoclassical economist circles. One example of this was reflected in the World Bank report *The East Asian Miracle* (1993). In this controversial report, the World Bank indicated a shift in its attitude towards state intervention and stated that 'economic policy advice must be country-specific', and that 'their [Northeast Asian countries] success depended on the ability of governments to establish and monitor appropriate economic-performance criteria related to the interventions' (World Bank 1993: vi).

However, the World Bank's recognition of the diversity of country experiences and the significance of the role of government in development sits uneasily with the original neoclassical view. For instance, while the World Bank claimed to pay attention to the role of public policy and the particular institutional contexts within which policies were implemented in East

Asia, it also posited that 'some important government interventions in East Asia, such as Korea's promotion of chemicals and heavy industries, have had little apparent impact on industrial structure' (World Bank 1993: 9). State intervention was recognised positively to the extent that it offset other distortions, such as how import restrictions were compensated by export promotion (World Bank 1993: 22). According to the World Bank, an effective bureaucracy and a strong state led by technocrats, with what they described as 'deliberation councils', as in Japan and Korea, were favourable to development, as long as they helped to establish competition in the market, provided transparent rules to all participants and private sector groups, and created 'a business-friendly environment' that was 'generally hospitable to private investment' (World Bank 1993: 14).

> [V]ery rapid growth of the type experienced by Japan, the Four Tigers [Korea, Taiwan, Hong Kong and Singapore] … has at times benefited from careful policy interventions.… Unlike many other governments that attempted such interventions, HPAE [High-Performing Asian Economies] governments generally held costs within well-defined limits … interventions that became too costly or otherwise threatened stability were quickly modified or abandoned.
>
> (World Bank 1993: 24)

While the neoclassical vision of East Asian development as explained by the World Bank acknowledged the positive attributes of state interventionism as an aid to successful development, it also had a propensity to concomitantly minimise it. It did so by relegating the role of the state to a momentary function, which was not critical but rather coincidental to serving the market, which it did by 'getting the basics right' (World Bank 1993: 5). As one critic put it:

> [the] report makes an all-out effort to assert that East Asian economic success has nothing to do with government. If the government is to deserve any credit, it only does so because its myriad interventions … must have, by some magical coincidence, jelled into a neoclassical formulation.
>
> (Kwon 1994: 635)

The neoclassical view of the rapid growth of East Asian economies relies on specific conceptual underpinnings. It is constructed on the juxtaposition of the state with the market, and on the assumption that minimum intervention of the former in the latter equals minimum distortion of the market, which is an important precondition for successful development. While there was ambivalence on the role of government in East Asia to some degree, the view central to neoclassical economics is that state intervention was kept to a minimum and was momentary. This neoclassical reading has direct policy implications for other developing countries. If the successful development of East Asian economies is explained by the integration of those economies into the global economy through free trade and the liberalisation of their markets from state intervention in order for development and high growth to be achieved, other developing countries ought to pursue EOI as opposed to ISI, open themselves to international market competition and minimise state intervention or its reduction in the economy.

Against the market-centred neoclassical economists' interpretation of East Asia's successful development being based on the principle of 'the minimal state', an alternative vision, the essence of which was captured in the concept of the 'developmental state', was put forward by amongst others, Chalmers Johnson, Robert Wade and Alice Amsden. Work by each of these authors will be assessed, in turn.

Johnson's developmental state as social mobiliser

Chalmers Johnson was the first to coin the term 'developmental state' and arguably made for the first time a systematic attempt to explain the model of 'the developmental state' in the East Asian context (e.g. Woo-Cumings 1999a).[2] In his book *MITI and the Japanese Miracle: The Growth of Industrial Policy 1925–1975* (1982), Johnson describes how the effective implementation of industrial policies by the MITI (Ministry of International Trade and Industry) contributed to the rapid economic growth of Japan. His initial interest was limited to identifying particularly Japanese characteristics of capitalist development, on which he further elaborated in his book *Japan: Who Governs? The Rise of the Developmental State* (1995). He extended the application of the idea of the developmental state to both Korea and Taiwan in subsequent works (Johnson 1987; 1998). According to Johnson, 'the "developmental state" actually exists in time and space in East Asia and also exists as an abstract generalization about the essence of the East Asian examples. It is both particular and generalizable' (Johnson 1999: 43).

In his conceptualisation of the developmental state within the context of Japan, Johnson defines the specific characteristics of the Japanese economic developmental model as 'the state-guided capitalist developmental system' and 'a plan-rational economy with market-rational political institutions' (Johnson 1995: 29). According to him, the Japanese system is a unique combination of what he sees as two opposite and distinctive systems: on the one hand, an Anglo-American model; on the other, a socialist system. He maintains that the Japanese system differs from Anglo-American democracies, which he defines as 'regulatory states', where the state is primarily concerned with the forms and procedures of economic competition, without engaging in substantive matters (Johnson 1982: 308; 1987: 159; 1999: 37). At the same time, the Japanese system also diverges from socialist planned economies: it involves high levels of social goal-setting but without the known consequences of state socialism, such as inefficiency (Johnson 1995: 10). According to Johnson, this unique synthesis of two economic systems explains and is responsible for the successful industrialisation of Japan, where the goal of development was achieved 'without falling into the trap of authoritarian displacement of the market and private enterprise' (Johnson 1987: 164).

Johnson finds the origins of this distinctive model of Japanese economic development in its imperialist and wartime experiences, which he believes provided a strong impetus for development based on nationalism. His analysis shows that, for instance, both the Chinese communist revolution and Japanese economic development were motivated by what he describes as 'revolutionary nationalism', which he says was instigated as a matter of national survival in order to combat Western imperialism (Johnson 1999: 53–4; see also Woo-Cumings 1999a: 6). In addition, Johnson argues that since the Meiji Restoration in 1868, which he understood as a state-led campaign for modernisation, a particular model of state–society relations had been in place, where 'the state has always taken precedence over interests based on the economy, the society, or other private concerns' (Johnson 1995: 8). According to Johnson, the Japanese state, when equipped with institutional heritages of state-led modernisation under conditions where development was rendered a matter of national urgency, was able to mobilise its society more effectively towards the goal of national development, and gain national legitimacy by devoting itself to a widely believed-in revolutionary project of development (Johnson 1987: 140; see also Woo-Cumings 1999a: 7, 20). Similarly, in the cases of Korea and Taiwan, countries which had experienced colonialism, civil wars or the threat of war with North Korea and mainland China, respectively, effectuated economic nationalism, leading these countries to choose economic development as a strategy of national survival (Woo-Cumings 1999a: 7–9). In this manner, seeking the origins of the developmental state in the historical legacy of revolutionary nationalism in East Asia, Johnson assigns to the model of the developmental state as one of its core properties the state's ability to mobilise society for the overall goal of national development, and in this way the state becomes what I describe as the *social mobiliser* for development.

In an attempt to explain how the developmental state's role as the social mobiliser played out, Johnson examines the inner state structure of the Japanese state; that is, state bureaucracy on the one hand, and how it intervened in the economy on the other. First, he locates the efficacy of the Japanese political system for delivering economic development in what he calls 'soft authoritarianism', where bureaucrats or, in his terms, 'developmental elites', were granted great political power and insulated from electoral and judicial accountability (Johnson 1987: 140). He notes that through the separation of reigning and ruling – where politicians reign, and bureaucrats rule (Johnson 1995: 29) – bureaucrats could achieve a high level of autonomy from politicians, who are prone to seeking popular support in the short term rather than seeking to implement long-term developmental goals (Johnson 1987: 142, 151–2). At the same time, he argues, state elites were autonomous from private businesses, which created a system of 'public-private cooperation in which the state independently develops national goals' (Johnson 1987: 156), and the private sector operated under the overall guidance of a pilot-planning agency, the MITI. Johnson contends that this system worked positively for development as it reduced uncertainties and risks: the government plans and 'lay[s] out clearly what the elite's fixed-term goals are so that private enterprises and households can adjust to them with precision and over a definite period' (Johnson 1987: 142).

Johnson's conceptualisation of the developmental state had a significant influence on subsequent discussion of the subject, inspiring critics of neoclassical economics and laying the ground for the consolidation of the concept of the developmental state by other authors. While Johnson claimed that he did not intend to challenge the world of academic economics, his contention that the economic success of Japan was attributable to state-plan rationality and efficient bureaucrats distinguishes itself from the neoclassical argument that the positive aspects of the state in East Asia were absent or at best limited. The developmental state postulated by Johnson as *social mobiliser*, where the state presided over society, presented a counter-interpretation to the neoclassical view that the state was and should be subordinated to the market for successful development.

However, his view shows some degree of ambivalence not dissimilar to that of neoclassical economics, at least in the latter's recent version that favourably recognised the role of state guidance for development (see above). While Johnson assigns to the developmental state the role of social mobiliser, which implies its dominance over society at one level, he concomitantly maintains that the crucial task of the developmental state elites was 'to discover how, organizationally, to make its own developmental goals compatible with the market mechanism' (Johnson 1987: 140). He thus echoes the neoclassical doctrine when he states that an indispensable element in any model of the capitalist developmental state is 'the commitment by the political elites to "market-conforming" methods of intervention in the economy' (Johnson 1987: 141). Subsequently, this aspect was criticised by Wade and Amsden. In an endeavour to challenge the neoclassical model of state–market relations built on the primacy of the market over the state, and based upon Johnson's concept of the developmental state, Wade and Amsden carried out research which found that more responsibility than Johnson had acknowledged could be ascribed to the role of the state in development with reference to Taiwan and Korea.

Wade's developmental state that governs the market

Robert Wade, in his early anthropological study on state-directed rural modernisation in Korea (1983), demonstrated how pervasively the government intervened in the modernisation of the countryside and argued that 'the passive state' projected onto the Korean state by neoclassical economists was a myth. On the basis of further empirical studies on how the state could shape and determine development outcomes, particularly with reference to Taiwan, he developed a coherent conceptualisation of the active role of the state in development, which he labelled 'the governed market theory (GM theory)'.

In his book *Governing the Market* (1990), Wade differentiates his GM theory from what he categorises as 'the free market (FM) theory' and 'the simulated free market (SM) theory'. If FM theory refers to the views that attribute the industrial success of the East Asian economies to their reliance on a free market and no (or minimal) state interference, SM theory points to those perspectives that recognise the existence of positive state intervention but only to the extent that it offsets other distortions and eventually functions to stimulate a free market or free trade (Wade 1990: 22–4). Wade calls SM theory a variant of neoclassical theory because it offered little analysis of the nature of government intervention and placed primary causal weight on the character of the trade regime and efficient allocation of resources as opposed to production and capital accumulation (Wade 1990: 24–9). In this differentiation, he categorises Johnson's work under SM theory and points out its limitation because it 'says little about the nature of policies and their impact on industrial performance. Indeed, Johnson's institutional arrangements are for the most part as consistent with simulated free-market policies as with more directive ones' (Wade 1990: 26).

GM theory is thus distinguished by its emphasis on the role of the state, which goes far beyond SM theory, including Johnson's model. It points to certain patterns and degrees of state intervention in market processes that produced different production and investment outcomes, which would not have occurred with either a free-market economy or simulated free-market policies (Wade 1990: 26–7).

> A more tenable formulation [GM theory] is a synergistic connection between a public system and a mostly private market system, the outputs of each becoming inputs for the other, with the government setting rules and influencing decision-making in the private sector in line with its view of an appropriate industrial and trade profile for the economy.
>
> (Wade 1990: 5)

From the vantage point of GM theory, East Asian success is 'the result of a higher level and different composition of investment than in less successful countries. The difference in investment is due … to *government action* to constrain and accelerate the competitive process' (Wade 1990: 297; emphasis added). According to GM theory, the role of the state extends to 'steer[ing] the competitive process into higher-wage, higher-technology alternatives and away from short-term speculative or labor cost-reducing alternatives by means of *politically determined* constraints and rigged prices' (Wade 1990: 297; emphasis added). Wade highlights that the interventionist policies of East Asia were unique not only in terms of the degree of state interventionism but also in terms of the nature of the interventions, which 'distorted' market prices deliberately to induce market agents to invest in the desirable (strategic) sectors from a long-term national development perspective (Wade 1990: 29). Unlike FM and SM theories that emphasise the virtues of 'getting the prices right', meaning domestic prices being in line with international prices, 'the GM theory interprets superior East Asian performance as the result of … deliberately ge[tting] some prices "wrong" … and us[ing] non-price means to alter the behaviour of market agents' (Wade 1990: 29).

While Wade admits that not all policies adopted by East Asia fell into the category of GM policies, referring to the case of Taiwan, he argues that

> several kinds of evidence suggest that the Taiwanese government has exercised a significant amount of *big leadership* in some industries some of the time, meaning government initiatives on a large enough scale to make a sizable difference in investment and production patterns in the industry.
>
> (Wade 1990: 305; emphasis added)

Wade (1990: 304) also emphasises that the 'organizational arrangements for formulating and implementing industrial policies are such as to make plausible the claim that the government led the market in a coherent rather than ad hoc way'. Positing the state's 'big leadership role in leading the market' as a key to the successful industrialisation of East Asia, such as that in Japan, Korea and Taiwan, as opposed to that in other less successful countries, Wade draws the conclusion that

> [w]hat differentiates their efforts, above all, are a consistent and coordinated attentiveness to the problems and opportunities of particular industries, … and a state which is hard enough not only to produce sizable effects on the economy but also to control the direction of the effects.
>
> (1990: 343)

With this reasoning, Wade brings forward the existence of a 'hard' state as a key aspect of industrialisation in East Asia: one of the main reasons why it was able to avoid government failure caused by the fragility or abuse of public power is that 'East Asian states are relatively hard' (1990: 337). A 'hard' state is in effect synonymous with one autonomous from social actors to the extent that the degree of the state's 'hardness' is measured by how much it is 'centralized and relatively *insulated* from society' (1990: 337; emphasis added). Wade (1990: 337) understands that '[h]ard states are able not only to resist private demands but actively to shape the economy and society'.

Like Johnson, Wade incorporates an analysis of political structures and regime types of East Asian countries, with a view to explaining how the 'autonomy of the state' or the 'hard state' was ensured politically. Wade categorises Korea and Taiwan as 'authoritarian corporatism' while categorising Japan as having corporatism combined with both democratic and authoritarian features, equivalent to what Johnson called 'soft authoritarianism' (Wade 1990: 27). Characterising the political systems of East Asian countries as typically 'authoritarian and corporatist' rather than 'democratic and pluralist', Wade (1990: 27) holds that '[t]he corporatist and authoritarian political arrangements of East Asia have provided the basis for market guidance'. Authoritarianism conferred autonomy on a centralised bureaucracy with less or no direct political pressure from below, giving the state the space to coordinate industrial investment and to 'influence resource allocation in line with the long-term national interest' (Wade 1990: 29). Wade contends that

> in this kind of political regime [peculiar to East Asia], the bureaucracy can more easily demonstrate competence and remain 'clean', because it is *neither caught between and penetrated by struggling interest groups* nor subverted from above by the politics of rulers' survival.
>
> (Wade 1990: 339; emphasis added)

By characterising the states in East Asia in this manner, Wade adds a new dimension to the conceptualisation of the developmental state. While he shares the core proposition of Johnson, who postulated the developmental state as the social mobiliser for national development, Wade goes further and augments the role of the state in his assessment of industrialisation in East Asia. He understands that the role of the states in East Asia went beyond merely stimulating the market, as Johnson had postulated. In Wade's formula, the states undertook the role of 'big leadership' against investment actors (capitalists), whose investment decisions were made in response to the signals that the state purposefully generated through policies, which might appear 'wrong' from the perspective of the free-market rules. His GM theory thus imparts a higher degree of autonomy to the East Asian developmental state than either neoclassical economics or Johnson would acknowledge: the state's big leadership role was effective for delivering successful development because it was a 'hard state', enjoying a high level of policy autonomy against social forces, on the one hand, and political elites, on the other hand. These aspects that Wade brings forward in the concept of the developmental state in East Asia, namely the policy autonomy of state bureaucrats *vis-à-vis* capitalists and their ability to create the 'right' development outcomes (i.e. rapid growth) through implementing 'wrong' price policies, are shared with and further elaborated by Amsden.

Amsden's developmental state that disciplines capitalists

The primary focus of Alice Amsden's work has been on identifying positive correlations between the role of the state and economic development in 'late' or 'catch-up' development conditions (1997, 2001), with a special interest in Taiwan (1979, 1985) and Korea (1989, 1994). A common thread in her work is her challenge to the 'conventional explanations' offered by neoclassical economics and, especially, the World Bank, which she argues attempt to reduce the successful industrialisation of East Asia to a result of the adoption of free-market policies.

Reminiscent of Wade's critique, Amsden points out the limits of Johnson's approach. She argues that 'Johnson ... explored Japan's uniqueness from the political angle and saw the economic side of political economy as merely conforming to the traditional market norms' (Amsden 1989: 149). She claims that the role of the state in East Asia went beyond what neoclassical economists and Johnson depicted, and argues that the rapid industrialisation of East Asia was achieved by a deliberate distortion of free-market rules by the state or, as she describes it, by 'getting the prices wrong'. She elaborates this theme in her book *Asia's Next Giant* (1989) with reference to Korean industrialisation.

Amsden explains in her book why 'getting the prices wrong' produced the 'right' developmental outcomes by drawing attention to the particular nature of the *late* industrialisation that took place in the mid-twentieth century. She contrasts the conditions of late development with those of earlier periods such as those at the time of the first industrial revolution (eighteenth century) and those at the time of the second industrial revolution (nineteenth century). According to her, while the first industrial revolution occurred in England on the basis of *invention*, the second industrial revolution occurred in the United States and Germany on the basis of *innovation*. In contrast to these early industrialisations, late industrialisation in the mid-twentieth century is characterised as having occurred through *learning*, *borrowing* or *emulating* foreign technologies which were already in existence (Amsden 1989: 3–8, 1997: 469).[3] She states that 'the conquest of world markets in the mid-1960s, by late-industrializing countries on the *almost* exclusive basis of low wage rates represents a new phenomenon' (Amsden 1989: 18–9). She understands the peculiar aspects of the industrialisation of 'the rest' – countries outside the North Atlantic that underwent industrialisation after the Second World War – as follows:

> The rise of 'the rest' was one of the most phenomenal changes in the last half of the twentieth century. For the first time in history, backward countries industrialized *without proprietary innovations*. They caught up in industries requiring large amounts of technological capabilities without initially having advanced technological capabilities of their own. Late industrialization was a case of *pure learning*, meaning a total initial dependence on other countries' commercialized technology to establish modern industries. This dependence lent catching up its distinctive norm.
>
> (Amsden 2001: 2)

Amsden's identification of the particular conditions of late development as lacking endogenous technology suggests that late industrialisation did not come about without struggle and required different kinds of strategies: 'the waging of competition by dominant firms without the aid of a novel technology involves a very different struggle' (1990: 15). More precisely, late industrialisation has a distinctive disadvantage, originating from the lack or absence of original technology, to the extent that 'low wages were an insufficient condition for these [late industrialising] countries to gain international competitiveness' (Amsden 1990: 20). In this context, the countries of late industrialisation necessitated equally distinctive institutional arrangements and different degrees and kinds of state intervention. Amsden shows how in the context of the mid-twentieth century it was necessary to have increased government support: not only towards measures to protect infant industries but also to provide private investors with a battery of incentives, such as subsidies, tariff protection and financial incentives (Amsden 1989: 13).

Amsden verifies her argument with the case of Korean industrialisation by demonstrating how the specific requirements flowing from the conditions of late industrialisation were successfully met. She argues that the Korean case testifies to the fact that 'the government made most of the pivotal investment decisions. Instead of firms operating in a competitive market structure, they each operated with an extraordinary degree of market control, protected from foreign competition' (Amsden 1989: 139). This level of state intervention, she argues, gave the government the role of not merely a banker but also an entrepreneur, using the subsidy to decide what, when and how much to produce (Amsden 1989: 79–80, 143–4). Further, she explains that this degree of state intervention presupposed the deliberate decision by the state to 'get the prices wrong'. For instance, for the purpose of industrial expansion in a situation where there was a scarcity of resources, the Korean state introduced a system of multiple prices for loans: the state arranged long-term international credit for favoured firms or industries at rates far below those obtainable domestically or at a 'wrong' price (Amsden 1989: 144).

Comparably to Wade's 'hard state', according to Amsden, the key precondition to make 'getting the prices wrong' operate for the benefit of development lies in the existence of the state that dominates capitalists, or what she names the state that *disciplines* capitalists. Referring to the case of Korea, she argues that 'where Korea differs from most other late industrializing countries is in the *discipline* its state exercises over private firms' (Amsden 1989: 14; emphasis added). The characterisation of the Korean state as having disciplinary power over capitalists points to a particular relationship formed between the state and businesses, which Amsden describes as 'reciprocal'. The 'reciprocal' relationship is defined as the power of the state to set and enforce the performance standards that the *chaebol* (business conglomerates) have to meet in order to be provided with 'subsidies' and other forms of government support.

> The premise of late industrialization is a reciprocal relation between the state and the firm. This does not simply mean close cooperation, which is sometimes the way business-government relations in Korea and Japan are simplistically depicted. Nor does it simply mean that sometimes the government wields the carrot and at other, unrelated times, the stick. It means that in direct exchange for subsidies, the state exacts certain performance standards from firms.
>
> (Amsden 1989: 146)

Utilising the terms 'subsidy', 'getting the relative prices wrong' and 'reciprocal relations', Amsden makes a key contribution to forming and consolidating the concept of the developmental state. An important implication of her postulation is not only that it offers a vision alternative to the neoclassical concept of development, seen as 'a process of moving towards increasingly perfect markets' or 'an unqualified process of reducing market failures' (Amsden 1997: 470) – more importantly, it renders the distortion of the market not a momentary or accidental means to achieve development but the prerequisite for late industrialisation to succeed. Thus, Amsden's view provides a political and moral justification to state interventionism, particularly in the Third World: the distortion of the market is justified on the ground that late industrialising countries were in a disadvantageous position in the world market due to their relatively inferior technology and productivity. In so doing, Amsden assigns utmost importance to the state as the main agent in overcoming the hardship of late development and renders the developmental state, depicted as omnipotent, disciplinary and visionary, the most important factor that determines successful late industrialisation.

> What is clear is that, without a strong central authority, a necessary although not sufficient condition, little industrialization may be expected in 'backward' countries. Even getting relative prices 'right' according to textbook theory would require a state strong enough to battle whoever stood to suffer from a loss of government support.
>
> (Amsden 1989: 18)

Forging the statist concept of the developmental state

The significance of the conceptualisation of the developmental state by Johnson, Wade and Amsden in the context of the general theory of development cannot be overemphasised. Apart from the fact that it offers one of the most, if not the most, viable critiques of the neoclassical assessment of the industrialisation of East Asia, it also provides a view of development alternative to other main theories.

Despite different disciplinary origins, modernisation theory and neoclassical economics shared an optimistic attitude to 'catch-up' development, suggesting that there are no structural barriers to development in the global system and that 'lateness' does not constitute an unconquerable hurdle to the development of the periphery. On the other hand, some extreme versions of dependency theory (e.g. Frank 1979; see also Amin 1976) and 'post-development theory' (Escobar 1995: Rahnema and Bawtree 1997) offered a pessimistic vision of development, suggesting that the countries in the periphery are structurally blocked from developing as they are locked into the world economy in such a way that surplus from the periphery is transferred to the core.[4] In lieu of one-dimensional optimism or pessimism, the concept of the developmental state is based on the recognition of the barriers to development that emanate from 'lateness' in world historical-time. At the same time, it is grounded on the understanding that these barriers have been and can be overcome by inventing and implementing a range of development-inducing institutions, particularly when this is done by the state that plays the role of social mobiliser, governs the market and disciplines the capitalists for the goal of national development. Particularly, the concept has shown a key strength in accounting for increasingly diverging development trajectories *within* the Third World with reference to the rise of East Asia: the successful industrialisation of East Asia itself demonstrates that the developing world is characterised neither by a unilinearly successful 'catch-up' trajectory nor by underdevelopment.

The dual dimensions of statism in the concept of the developmental state

In spite of the significant contribution of the concept of the developmental state to the general theory of development, it is not free from weaknesses. Above all, the concept of the developmental state is grounded on what I describe as 'statism', which juxtaposes the state and the market, and the state and the global economy as antithetical categories. Each of these two dimensions can be assessed, in turn.

First, although the concept of the developmental state is initiated and consolidated against neoclassical economics, it mirrors rather than opposes the latter in terms of the ways in which the relationship between the state and the market is posed. As discussed, the conceptualisation of the developmental state was a process of *maximising* the role of the state in development as opposed to neoclassical economics' attempt to *minimise* it. In the same way that the market is posited by neoclassical economists to deliver optimal allocation of resources when it is left to be free from political interference, the developmental state is defined primarily in terms of its level of policy autonomy from and disciplinary power over market and private actors, i.e. how much it is able to implement development policies against and independently from the immediate requirements of the market and capitalist private interests. As much as neoclassical economists understand the market as a self-regulating mechanism neutral from social and power relations, it is implicit in the concept of the developmental state that the state can exist above and beyond sectoral interests and represent the interest of the general: the ideal developmental state is one standing above society and one that is strong enough to implement development policies against narrow (private) interests.

As neoclassical economics modified its perspective, to an extent, by recognising the positive role of state intervention in development, the theorists of the developmental state responded by further augmenting the role of the state vis-à-vis the market. Consequently, the initiation by Johnson, and subsequent efforts by Wade and Amsden to challenge neoclassical approaches by emphasising the crucial role of the state in development, arrives at the other end of the extreme: they replace the primacy of the market with that of the state and elevate the significance of the state to the point when development outcomes are dependent on whether there exists the developmental state. In this respect, neoclassical economics and the theorists of the developmental state, two seemingly opposing stances, diverge only in the matter of emphasis within the same conceptual framework in which the categories of the state and the market are juxtaposed as antithetical. Either one or the other is elevated as the cause of development, as long as both are antithesised.

Second, insofar as the high degree of policy autonomy of the developmental state is set against private interests as opposed to the general interest, which is *de facto* national development, the antithetical juxtaposition of the state and the market traverses that of the state and the global economy: the developmental state is understood as the agent of national development, the national being set against the external or the global. Johnson depicts the developmental state as the social mobiliser for national development or as a product of revolutionary nationalism as a reaction to and against 'Western imperialism'. Wade posits long-term development objectives in opposition to short-term profit maximising and equates development objectives with national development or national interest (Wade 1990: 29): he later accuses the rules of the international economic order of not giving 'more scope for different forms of *national* capitalisms to flourish' (Wade 2004: li; emphasis added). In this framework, the global economy is assumed to exist externally to a national economy; the global is posited antithetical to the national, while the state is the agent, or the pursuant, at least potentially, of national development.

The juxtaposition of the national and the global (the external) as antithetical is also evident in Amsden's work. She is in fact critical not only of neoclassical economics for projecting a unilinear vision of development by not recognising the specific difficulties that the developing countries are facing but also of other theories of development, such as dependency theory, for explaining development outcomes from the perspective of 'the external' or 'the exogenous'. On this ground, Amsden opposes approaches that seek the causes of East Asian industrialisation in 'external factors', such as the unequal structure of the world system and the needs of the Western core countries, as such approaches tend to undervalue the genuine aspect of Third World development based on technological upgrading (Amsden 1990: 8–12).[5] In this context, Amsden posits 'endogenous productive and social relations' as opposed to exogenous factors as the primary analytical category in deciphering the causes of East Asia's successful industrialisation (Amsden 1979: 342). These factors refer to a set of development-inducing institutions, such as an interventionist state; large diversified business groups; an abundant supply of competent salaried managers; and low-cost, well-educated labour (Amsden 1989: 8).

In summary, the central argument put forward by Johnson, Wade and Amsden through the concept of the developmental state is that, however disadvantageous late development may be, successful 'catch-up' development is possible. While recognising the hardship of late development, whether it was caused by the legacy of colonisation (Johnson) or the structural barriers of the world economy (Wade and Amsden), all these three authors believe that these difficult conditions that the developing countries face can be overcome. This view is built on the idea that development is determined not solely by external factors but by domestically motivated institutional inventions and implementations. It follows that development-inducing institutions are best fashioned domestically: there is no such thing as a universal policy that fits countries in different development conditions, and development is not pre-ordained by *external* world-systematic factors but is national entities' own making. In this context, the role of the state as the agent of national development is brought to the fore: the developmental state is defined not only in terms of its autonomy from domestic private actors but in terms of its ability to withstand 'external' influence too and turn this into the benefit of national development. In this way, the concept of the developmental state is to be understood within two dimensions: in terms of state-market relations, on the one hand, and of state-global economy (national-global) relations, on the other hand.

Development outside the question of capitalism

The statist underpinnings in the concept of the developmental state, positing state-market and state-global economy as antithetical categories, are not accidental and carry certain political and policy implications. First, in the framework of the developmental state, 'development' itself is placed outside the question of capitalism (Hart-Landsberg and Burkett 2001: 404).[6] What has been contested between neoclassical economists and the theorists of the developmental state is whether the state or the market is the key to successful industrial development. However, both shared the same starting point: the question of what factors allowed the rapid growth in Korea (East Asia). They took for granted the desirability of development itself. Put differently, the question central to the theorists of the developmental state is how and why East Asian economies industrialised faster than other countries while failing to ask what development, which is essentially *capitalist* development, actually means.

The displacement of the question of development from that of capitalism has important conceptual ramifications. On the one hand, the theorists of the developmental state have tended to ignore or downplay class contradictions and antagonism intrinsic to capitalist development. To be fair, Johnson, Wade and Amsden never assumed that development was a consensual and conflict-free process. However, to the extent that development is posited outside a critical inquiry into capitalism, the question of labour repression is either absent, or labour issues are dealt with in the context of asking how the particular labour relations within East Asian countries account for their high growth. Johnson states that 'the virtual absence of economically significant strikes in Japan…, a labor force that does not object to technological changes … are real comparative advantages in international economic competition' (Johnson 1987: 149). He continues to note that 'South Korea and Taiwan resemble Japan in their tranquil labor relations', and their 'higher labor turnover rates than Japan … have not posed a serious obstacle to high-speed growth' (Johnson 1987: 150; see also Johnson 1995: 31). Given the hyper-militancy in labour movements in Korea during the 1980s (see Koo H 1993b; Ogle 1990), this view not only demands historical verification – more importantly, it underscores the fact that Johnson considers labour as a factor of production or a source of comparative advantage within the framework whether or not it contributed to rapid growth.

A similar approach to labour is also found in Wade and Amsden. Wade even seems to deny the existence of class divisions in Taiwan by arguing that there was 'the absence of class-conscious or culturally disparate class division', and 'the ethnic division between mainlanders and islanders [in Taiwan] does not translate into a class division' (Wade 1990: 340). Similarly, in Amsden, labour is treated as a social group relating externally to capital and the state. She states that '[t]he relationship between developmentalism and democracy is complex, because reciprocity in the allocation of subsidies requires a strong state vis-à-vis business, not necessarily labor. What awaits systematic analysis is how much labor repression is critical for rapid growth' (Amsden 1989: 148). In short, Johnson, Wade and Amsden understand that the subordination of labour to capital or class division/conflict is a contingent factor rather than an integral part of capitalist development.

Relegating the issue of labour as external to capitalist development is closely related to the statist concept of the developmental state in which the apparent dichotomous relation between state and market is taken for granted. In the statist framework, social relations are reduced to the interactions and interrelations between presupposed separate and atomised units. The state is seen as an external entity that interacts with the economy and/or is understood in individualistic terms. The state emerges only as a group of state elites or policy makers who negotiate with other groups in society, such as business groups, who pursue their own interests on equal terms with other (interest-)groups. Thus, what are defined as characteristics of the developmental state, such as its being 'autonomous' and 'disciplinary', are derived from the apparent arm's-length personal relationships between the state bureaucrats and capitalists. Consequently, the form of the capitalist state that exists as an institution quasi-independent from the economy and capital accumulation is not grasped beyond the question of a power balance between state elites and individual capitalists.

As a consequence of placing class contradictions as contingent or external to capitalist development, the theorists of the developmental state assess the greater level of state intervention witnessed in late industrialisation in terms of differentials in national development *strategies*, not in terms of the *necessary* societal level of violent repression associated with (late) capitalist development. While the correlation between authoritarianism and late development will be further discussed in Part II, it suffices here to note that the theorists of the developmental state tend to reduce what are essential and universal aspects of capitalism and their manifestations in an intensive form in late development conditions, such as 'super-exploitation of labour', to strategic or national peculiarities.

For instance, Johnson says that 'the Japanese, Koreans, and Taiwanese have put together the political economy of capitalism in ways unprecedented in the West and with quite different trade-offs (greater performance but less political participation)' (Johnson 1987: 147). Likewise, comparing the United States and Korea, Amsden notes that while high wages are sufficient to motivate labour and ensure high productivity in the US, in Korea other measures were in place to achieve higher productivity, such as a shop-floor problem solving mechanism in quality-control circles and the successful repression of labour organisations or labour practices hostile to higher productivity (Amsden 1990: 26). In brief, Johnson and Amsden assess what others would consider as the alienation of labour from politics and an extreme mode of micro-level labour control as a different development strategy adopted at the national level.

Externalising political and economic forces from the developmental state

The conceptual and political vulnerabilities inherent in the statist concept of the developmental state manifested themselves in the discussions around the Asian financial crisis of 1997/98, which unleashed an unprecedented scale of political and economic upheaval in East Asia. Arguably, the Asian financial crisis was the turning point at which the discussion of the developmental state took on a new dimension, posing the question of whether the developmental state continued to be viable or was dismantled (see Chapters 3 and 4). As much as the developmental state was conceptualised largely as a critique of the neoclassical vision of East Asian development, the assessment of the Asian financial crisis by the theorists of the developmental state was also influenced by neoclassical economics. In what follows, I will first discuss key aspects of the neoclassical economics' view of the Asian financial crisis and then move on to the responses by the theorists of the developmental state.

One of the predominant neoclassical explanations of the origins of the crisis was government failure. According to them, excessive state intervention, which included the use of strategic trade and industrial policies, was the primary cause of the crisis as it had led to a 'moral hazard' as lenders extended credit to non-profitable (government-guaranteed) projects in the belief that they would be bailed out in the event of bankruptcy (Black and Black 1999; Krugman 2000). Neoclassical economists labelled the development model of East Asian countries as 'crony capitalism', where the misallocation of resources prevailed, with investment being made in sectors and industries according to government decisions or political motivations rather than efficiency or economic criteria (Baliño and Ubide 1999; Black and Black 1999; Cathie 1997; Krugman 2000). The conclusion is drawn from the Asian financial crisis that 'the greater the involvement of the government, the bigger the moral hazard problem whereby lending decisions did not reflect commercial risks' (Black and Black 1999: 44). On this ground, it is argued that 'a more liberalized Korea would have weathered the financial problems in the region, and at a lower economic and social cost, than the present financial and economic structure will be able to do' (Cathie 1997: 27).

A fundamental distrust in state interventionism is ingrained in this neoclassical interpretation, whose point is well expressed in the statement that '[j]ust as elephants cannot fly, not even badly, the government cannot manage ... the economy' (Black and Black 1999: 47). The neoclassical argument had unambiguous pro-market and anti-state policy implications: 'the only way to prevent further government failure ... is to remove the government from the market place' (Black and Black 1999: 47).[7] While not all neoclassical economists have advocated the government failure thesis, with some proposing accounts, such as macroeconomic mismanagement (McLeod and Garnaut 1998) and premature financial liberalisation unaccompanied by appropriate regulatory measures and monitoring practices (Furman and Stiglitz 1998; Radelet and Sachs 1998), even these 'moderate' versions problematised the viability of what was believed to be the East Asian development model characterised by heavy state intervention in the economy.

In defence of the developmental state against 'external' threats

Johnson, Wade and Amsden reacted to the neoclassical accusation of the East Asian developmental state model being 'crony capitalism' by externalising the causes of the financial crisis from the developmental state model and defending it or downplaying its contradictions. They commonly hold the view that the financial crisis was caused by the imposition of unfair rules by global institutions on otherwise well-functioning economies of East Asia.

Johnson (1998: 655) argues that 'crony capitalism was not the intent but a by-product of the structural characteristics of the Asian-type economies', and 'the current crisis was caused much more by under-regulation than by … an overly close relationship between businesses and the government' (1998: 654). However, according to Johnson, the pressure to undo regulation originated externally. He notes that Korea, 'in an attempt to follow the nagging of its patron, the United States, abolished the Economic Planning Board … and loosened virtually all controls over financial institutions' (Johnson 1998: 654). Similarly, Wade criticises what he describes as 'the Wall Street-Treasury-IMF complex' for imposing (financial) liberalisation on East Asian countries, which inevitably made them vulnerable to shocks that disturbed cash flows or supply of capital (Wade 1998a, 1998b; see also Wade and Veneroso 1998a, 1998b). Likewise, Amsden shares the view that the pressure on the developmental state model to change or dismantle came from the outside, primarily in the forms of liberalisation forces. She writes that 'the competitiveness problems of US industry in the 1980s were a major factor behind Washington's insistence that emerging economies open their markets' (Amsden 1997: 477).

Blaming 'unfair' external pressures for the causes of the crisis helped the theorists of the developmental state further avoid analysing fundamental (class) contradictions inherent in the developmental state model and societal structure itself. In fact, even before the financial crisis, Johnson extoled the Japanese state elite system by asserting that '[s]uch quasi-authoritarian political monopolies are disappointing to liberals, but it should be understood that they are ultimately legitimated not by their ideological pretensions … but by their results' (Johnson 1987: 143). Johnson states that although Japan experienced a financial bubble in the late 1980s and a subsequent recession, its economic performance was far superior to that of Western economies, especially in comparison to the United States (Johnson 1995: 8–9).

Similarly, Wade sees 'the developmental *virtues* of a hard or soft authoritarian state in corporatist relations with the private sector' in the state-business relations in Taiwan (Wade 1990: 29; emphasis added). He even applauds what others would consider a sign of 'clientelism', such as 'dense informal networks within the bureaucracy' based mainly on membership of elite universities, for 'low[ering] the transaction costs of supervision and cooperation (Wade 1990: 339). By the same token, Amsden depicts the regime of dictator Park Chung-Hee (1961–79) in Korea as 'relatively honest' because it was under pressure from the population, led by students who were less tolerant of the abuse of state power (Amsden 1989: 52, 148). Amsden even tries to redefine the concept of democracy by arguing that

> to the extent that the Korean government has disciplined business and has not allowed it to hold society to ransom with its investment decisions, Korea has extracted a measure of public accountability greater than that of many other late-, and even early-, industrializing countries.
> (Amsden 1990: 23)

The propensity of Johnson, Wade and Amsden to praise the developmental state model on the basis of its efficacy in delivering development, let alone problematising contradictions intrinsic to capitalist development, became further strengthened when they see the developmental state under attack or pressure to disintegrate. In this context, Wade goes as far as blaming democratisation for damaging the integrity of the developmental state and idealising the period of the developmental state as one where long-term and collective goals, as opposed to short-term private interests, prevailed:

> In Thailand and South Korea, new civilian democratic regimes corrupted the central policy-making technocracy and lost focus on national economic policies. Government-bank-collaboration came to be steered by the narrow and short-term interests of shifting coalitions. Their experience is bad news for the proposition that more competitive politics yield better policies.
>
> (Wade 1998a: 698)

This striking conclusion can also be explained by the problems associated with the statist underpinning of state-market and state-global economy relations. At one level, postulating democratisation externally to capitalist development stems from the fact that the developmental state is depicted as separable and immune from class and social struggles: social and political forces or democratisation and labour movements are seen as external factors that affect the state.

At another level, the justification of authoritarianism by the theorists of the developmental state in part originates from the fact that they understand the developmental state model as nationally distinctive. The reason that they are able to make claims that in the context of Western democracies can not be made openly, namely that authoritarianism or fascism was advantageous for economic development and should on such grounds be justified, comes from their understanding that authoritarianism in East Asia is a nationally specific political-cultural system: the repressive state and authoritarianism are seen as part of national variations associated with a distinctive development strategy.

In fact, it had long been contested in academic and public discussions in Korea how the contributions of the military authoritarian Park regime to economic growth ought to be evaluated. Many scholars addressed the Park regime's negative impacts not only at the level of economic but at societal and cultural levels (Baek N-C 2005; Cho H-Y 2005a, 2005b; Jeong H-K 1998; Kim S-H and Park S-H 2005; Lee B-C 2003a, 2003b; Lee K-I 1998; Shin Y-O 1998, 2002). Some even associated it with 'fascism' (Hong Y-K 2003; Lim J-H 2000; Sonn H-C 1989a, 1993).[8] Seen from the perspective of these Korean scholars, the theorists of the developmental state in effect provides justifications for a fascist regime.[9]

In this respect, the tendency to justify authoritarianism and the statist conceptualisation of the developmental state are mutually enforcing: the antithetical juxtaposition of state and market, and the national and the global underpins the notion that the developmental state is the agent of national development as opposed to narrow private (market) interest as well as to the external (global) threat. If the developmental state is to be defended, any challenge to it is to be posited as an external, negative, disintegrating force.

Conclusion

In this chapter, I have traced how the concept of the developmental state was formed and consolidated largely as a response to the neoclassical market-oriented assessments of the successful industrialisation of East Asia during the post-Second World War era. I have highlighted how neoclassical economists exhibited a propensity to minimise the role of the state in development and how this prompted critics to construct the concept of the developmental state by maximising the role of the state. By the same token, the more neoclassical theorists accommodated state interventionism in explaining the successful industrialisation of Korea and East Asia, the more critics counteracted this by assigning the state an even more significant role. Johnson, Wade and Amsden, as prominent critics of neoclassical views, constructed and furthered the concept of the developmental state as an entity independent and autonomous from capitalists and other social actors, on the one hand, and as the promoter of national development against the 'external' threat of global capitalism, on the other hand. In this perspective, the apparent detachment from market and society became a core property of the developmental state, and the existence of the developmental state emerges as the key factor that determines the success or failure of national development.

I have shown that although the concept of the developmental state was formulated and evolved as a critique of neoclassical approaches, it fundamentally shares with neoclassical views the conceptual dichotomy of state and market, and it is built on the statist notion that the state is and should be separable from the market. Statist underpinnings of the concept of the developmental state have deeper causes, stemming from the fact that the class implications and content of capitalist development are not seriously questioned. Without the notion of class contradictions intrinsic to capitalist development, the nature of the developmental state, which arises from the late development context, is relegated to a matter of national peculiarities. The two dimensions of the statist foundation of the developmental state, namely the antithetical juxtaposition of state and market, and that of the internal (the national) and the external (the global), are also expressed in the assessments of the Asian financial crisis of 1997/98. As much as the developmental state is seen as a self-contained entity that played a rational role above narrow private interests for the goal of national development, any perceived challenges to the integrity of the developmental states are seen as negative threats coming from the outside.

It is undisputable that the concept of the developmental state made a significant contribution to widening and deepening the understanding of development, in general, and industrialisation in East Asia, in particular. However, as much as it positions itself as a powerful strand or approach to development, as shall be seen, its influence on the subsequent debates is far-reaching. The statist framework of the developmental state built on the antithetical juxtaposition of state and market, and national and global is reinforced and reproduced in more nuanced approaches, such as (historical) institutionalism and more recent debates on the transformation of the developmental state, which will be discussed in the following chapters, in turn.

Notes

1 There is a large volume of literature on comparative studies of development in Latin America and East Asia. See Evans (1987, 1989, 1995), Gereffi and Wyman (1990), Gereffi and Fonda (1992), Haggard (1990), Hewitt et al. (1992) and Jerkins (1991, 1994).
2 As a political scientist, Johnson once confessed that he did not intend to forge a theory against neoclassical economics (1995: 34). However, apart from the fact that he first invented the term itself, to the extent that his work on the developmental state greatly inspired and influenced development economists such as Wade and Amsden, the two key contributors to the conceptualisation of the developmental state, Johnson's work should be the starting point.
3 Amsden locates Japan separately from Korea and Taiwan in terms of nature and patterns of development (state intervention) because Japan developed not only through learning but also, more importantly, through innovation (see Amsden 1989: 18–23 and ch. 3). Late industrialisation in Amsden (1989) refers to the countries that underwent industrialisation after the Second World War, i.e. 'later' than initial (nineteenth-century) late industrialisers.
4 While it is uncommon to associate dependency theory with the view of Frank, who held an 'extreme' version of pessimism about Third World development, the early scholars of dependency theory in Latin America (e.g. Furtado and Cardoso), whose work is less well known to Anglophone researchers, held more nuanced views and recognised the possibility of dependent development (see Fischer 2015).
5 Amsden criticised Lipietz's approach, for instance, for explaining the successful industrialisation of East Asia as the extension of the logic of Fordism in the core countries to the periphery in a form that is more labour intensive, which Lipietz calls 'bloody Taylorism' and 'peripheral Fordism'. While Amsden puts Lipietz in the theoretical tradition of dependency theory, Lipietz criticises dependency theory for being 'pessimistic functionalism', which holds a belief in the primacy of external causes without studying national social formation in its own right (see Lipietz 1971). Assessing the validity of Lipietz's claim is beyond the purview of this chapter.
6 Hart-Landsberg and Burkett (2001: 404) note that neoclassical economists and the developmental state theorists both embrace capitalism as the only effective means for achieving development. However, the framework that informs their own work is what they call 'a class perspective', which aims to illuminate 'the exploitative and contradictory nature of South Korea's growth trajectory' and 'anarchic market forces' (2001: 404). I take the view that Hart-Landsberg and

Burkett's approach falls into what I describe as 'class content' analysis as opposed to capitalist social form analysis. A critical assessment of Marxist discussions on the developmental state will be offered in Part II.

7 To the extent that neoclassical economists blame heavy state intervention for causing the misallocation of resources and imbalances leading to the crisis, they ironically support the thesis of the developmental state theorists that state interventionism during the period of the successful industrialisation had been prevalent, as in Wade and Amsden's formulations of 'the state governing the market' and 'the disciplinary state' (see Chang H-J 1999; Jayasuriya and Rosser 2001).

8 It is notable that Kohli stated that he initially thought of naming the Korean (developmental) state a neofascist state (2004: 10–11, fts. 14, 15).

9 The justification of the developmental state goes as far as to defend its high level of corruption. Neoclassical economists have been critical of state interventionism with the argument that the state is prone to corruption and rent-seeking behaviours as much as other individuals seeking to maximise their own interest. A critique had been made against such views, with reference to Korea, for instance, that a high level of corruption could co-exist with growth and can positively contribute to it. A rationale for such arguments is derived from the fact that in developing countries, where the conditions for development are different from developed countries, being riddled with imperfect market information and high levels of transaction costs, corruption and bribes can improve information flows, efficiency and the overall performance of a national economy (see Khan 1996, 2000, 2005).

2 Linking the state and the market

Reinforcing the statist concept of the developmental state'

In this chapter, I assess how institutionalist interpretations of industrialisation in East Asia, especially Korea, reinforced the statism that is inherent in the concept of the developmental state. The institutionalists I assess in this chapter include scholars from politics, sociology and economics backgrounds, such as Theda Skocpol, Peter Evans, Dietrich Rueschemeyer, Linda Weiss and Adrian Leftwich as well as Ha-Joon Chang and Byeong-Cheon Lee. In spite of divergences in their disciplinary backgrounds they share a common recognition that the state-market dichotomy is a conceptual problem in need of attention and propose a more nuanced conceptualisation of state-society relations. Above all, they emphasise not only that state and market are linked institutionally but also that the functioning of the market is in itself already a 'political' and 'historical' process. They also bring to the fore that the state exists *within* society and embrace categories hitherto considered to be outside the fields of mainstream economics and politics. In spite of the validity of these attempts, I contend that these broadly institutionalist approaches reinforce the statism inherent in the concept of the developmental state by inadequately theorising linkages between state and market. The state-market linkages postulated by institutionalism primarily refer to personal relationships between government officials (bureaucrats) and businesses. Within the framework of individualised relations between state and market, the emphasis on the linkages, rather than their dichotomy, has the effect of rendering capitalist social relations less antagonistic and more reconciliatory or harmonious than they actually are. I further show in this chapter how the institutionalist emphasis on individualised state-market linkages informs the way in which the causes of the Asian financial crisis of 1997/98 were analysed: namely primarily as a consequence of elite-level interactions in which state elites lost policy autonomy relative to capitalists.

Conceptualising the institutional linkages between state and market

The conceptualisation of the developmental state is grounded on juxtaposing the state and the market as antithetical categories, and postulating the former as standing above and autonomous from the latter, particularly in the case of private actors such as capitalists and businesses (see Chapter 1). In contrast, among other things, institutionalism in the context of assessing the successful industrialisation of East Asia is characterised by its attempt to go beyond the dichotomous view of state-market relations, on the one hand, and to provide a more adequate critique of neoclassical (market-centred) and other society-centred theories of development, on the other. In this section, I discuss the ways in which institutionalism has been adopted in the disciplines of (comparative) politics and economics in their conceptualisations of state-market relations and the developmental state.[1]

Institutional linkages in politics: historical institutionalism

Bringing the State Back In (BSBI) (1985), a co-edited book by Peter Evans, Dietrich Rueschemeyer and Theda Skocpol, is one of the key texts that endeavours to bridge the conceptual divide between state and society (market). BSBI is grounded on (comparative) historical institutionalism, an intellectual current which emerged from and became influential by incorporating 'new' institutionalism into comparative politics in the 1970s and the 1980s. Historical institutionalism can be characterised by its attempt to transcend two extreme trends of research orientation in politics: namely behaviourism, on the one hand, and structuralism ('old' institutionalism), on the other (Thelen and Steinmo 1992: 3–5). While the former attempted to explain political outcomes by looking at micro-level informal distributions of power, such as behaviours and interactions of individuals and groups, the latter was interested in formal attributes of policies, such as laws, rules and administrative structures (Thelen and Steinmo 1992: 3–4). Counter to both stances, new institutionalism moves away from the priorities of 'grand theorising', 'generalising' and 'homogenising' concepts, and instead places the primary research focus on specific comparative and historical research (Evans et al. 1985: 348). It focuses on intermediate-level variables, such as corporatist arrangements, policy networks and linkages between economic groups with the state bureaucracy and party structures. The significance of historical institutionalism thus lies in 'construct[ing] *analytic bridges*: between state-centred and society-centred analyses by looking at the institutional arrangements that structure relations between the two, and between grand theories that highlight broad cross-national regularities and narrower accounts of particular national cases' (Thelen and Steinmo 1992: 10; emphasis added).

Coming from the intellectual tradition of historical institutionalism that claims to bridge state-centred and society-centred analyses, the BSBI project was also initiated to transcend the limits of research orientations and dominant theories of the state in the US, which had hitherto been shaped by what Skocpol describes as 'society-dominated theories', by which she refers both to pluralist and neo-Marxist accounts. The BSBI authors argue that 'society-centred state theories' place their focus on social actors in society and see state policies as mere reflections of the demands or interests of the (dominant) social groups or classes, and the state's functions as subordinated to the structural requirements of society. Consequently, 'society-centred state theories' do not grant 'true autonomy' to the state (Evans et al. 1985: 347, 350; Skocpol 1985: 4–7). By the same token, Skocpol criticises the neo-Marxist theorisation of the capitalist state, particularly that of Poulantzas, which assigns the state relative autonomy but postulates it as determined eventually by the structural requirements of capitalist society (Skocpol 1979: 24–33).[2] However, the BSBI authors do not simply replace the primacy of society (or the market) with that of the state by bringing to the fore relational aspects of state-market relations: they refute 'either glorifying state power or overestimating its efficiency' as well as 'the old concatenation of the liberal critique of the state with a theoretical underestimation of the capacities of states be[ing] repeated in a mirror fashion' (Evans et al. 1985: 365).

> Bringing the state back in ... does not mean that old theoretical emphases should simply be turned on their heads: Studies of states alone are not to be substituted for concerns with classes or groups; nor are purely state-determinist arguments to be fashioned in the place of society-centred explanations ... a fully *relational* approach to states and societies is even more essential.
>
> (Skocpol 1985: 20; emphasis added)

The BSBI project carries important conceptual implications for state-society relations. Most of all, it is premised on the notion that institutional factors can shape both the objectives of political actors and the distribution of power among them in a given polity. For 'one feature typifying this new institutional perspective is its emphasis on ... the "relational characters" of institutions ... how a given institutional configuration shapes political *interactions*' (Thelen and Steinmo 1992: 6; emphasis in the original). It follows that 'more finely-tuned analyses must probe actual state organizations in relation to one another, in relation to past policy initiatives, and in relation to the domestic and transnational contexts of state activity' (Evans et al. 1985: 353).

From Evans's embedded autonomy to bringing politics and institutions back in

The relational view of state-market relations from the historical institutional perspective that has been applied to the analysis of the industrialisation of East Asia is most manifestly expressed in the title of Peter Evans's book *Embedded Autonomy* (1995). Evans writes that his approach is meant to offer 'an institutionalist alternative' to 'the political hegemony of "neoliberalism" and the theoretical hegemony of the "neo-utilitarian" vision'

(Evans 1995: 21). He praises the work of Amsden and Wade for contributing to the contemporary revival of institutionalist perspectives. In principle, Evans shares with developmental state theories the view that modern states play a crucial role in economic transformations and that state autonomy or the 'relative autonomy' of the state *vis-à-vis* social actors, in particular the dominant class, is a necessary (though not sufficient) condition for development (Evans 1995: 5; see also Rueschemeyer and Evans 1985: 44–6). However, as much as Evans (1995: 21) defies 'simplistic, asocial versions of neo-utilitarianism', i.e. the view that the state is utilised or captured by a dominant social group, he disavows 'sympathy for "statism" in the sense of utopian faith in the generic beneficence and efficacy of the state'. He argues that '[a] revival of open-ended faith in the state as a solution to the problem of underdevelopment is neither possible nor desirable' (Evans 1995: 22). As a theoretical solution, he (1995: 39) proposes that 'any comparative constitutional political economy of the state must offer a clear vision of both the state's internal structure and the character of state-society relations'.

Evans introduced two ideal types of states, namely the 'predatory' and the 'developmental' states, which are categorised according to variations in state structure and state-society relations (Evans 1995: 12, ch.3). The term 'predatory states' refers to those which have a great degree of autonomy from society but lack the ability to pursue and materialise developmental goals: '[p]redatory states extract at the expense of society, undercutting development', and 'lack the ability to prevent individual incumbents from pursuing their own goals', whereby 'individual maximization takes precedence over pursuit of collective goals' (Evans 1995: 12). According to Evans, a high degree of state autonomy cannot account for the developmental state alone. In order for the state to be developmental, while being autonomous from society and possessing an internal bureaucratic coherence, it needs to be 'embedded in a concrete set of social ties that binds the state to society and provides institutionalized channels for the continual negotiation and renegotiation of goals and policies' (Evans 1995: 12). In other words, '[o]nly when embeddedness and autonomy are joined together can a state be called developmental' (1995: 12). An archetype of the developmental state is epitomised as 'a rare beast with its tentacles reaching deep into the society while managing to keep its corporate integrity intact' (Woo-Cumings 1999a: 15).

State-society relations, formulated by Evans under the influence of the institutionalist relational perspective, therefore adds a new perspective on the concept of the developmental state. Evans et al. (1985: 353–4) understand that the combinations of various factors can potentially create various modes of state-social actor relations, in which state and society both enhance or decrease their strength concurrently. This understanding thus departs from 'an image of the state as an evermore self-aggrandizing juggernaut' (Rueschemeyer and Evans 1985: 49) and zero-sum state-society relations: namely that one gains power at the expense of the other sphere. Evans understands that the state is a contradictory body, being the representative of universal interests and simultaneously an instrument of domination and an arena of social conflicts under constant pressure from divergent social actors. It follows from this that state autonomy is defined relationally because '[s]tates are not generic. They vary dramatically in their internal structures and relations to society' (Evans 1995: 11), and 'the goals of state activities are not generated inside the state apparatus but dictated to it by the general interests of civil society' (Rueschemeyer and Evans 1985: 47). On this ground, Evans (1997: 80) argues that 'relations between the state and civil society are most productively thought of in terms of mutual empowerment or synergy'. While the theorists of the developmental state also addressed the relations between bureaucrats and businesses in defining the developmental state, as in Amsden's term 'reciprocal' relations (see Chapter 1), Evans engenders this aspect central to the definition of the developmental state, thereby shifting the focus from whether the state is autonomous from society to how much and in what way it is related to and embedded in society.

BSBI and 'embedded autonomy' influenced and informed subsequent discussions of the developmental state, particularly by those scholars who endeavoured to transcend 'simplistic distinctions between state, society and economy … in favour of more nuanced understandings of their relations … to see their continuous *interaction* and *mutual reshaping* into a variety of state forms' (Leftwich 2005: 594; emphasis added). In this context, having been inspired and influenced by the concept of 'embedded autonomy', some authors introduced comparable terms, such as 'reciprocal consent', 'organic independence' and 'governed interdependence', in an attempt to bring to the fore state-market linkages (Weiss 1998; Weiss and Hobson 1995). Similarly, Leftwich (1995) and Weiss (2003), paraphrasing BSBI, called for bringing 'politics' and 'domestic institutions', respectively, back in to address the importance of politics and institutions in explaining different development outcomes and the successful industrialisation of East Asia.

> [D]espite the power and autonomy of state bureaucrats, they have become embedded in a progressively dense web of ties with both non-state and other state actors (internal and external) through which the state has been able to co-ordinate the economy and implement developmental objectives.
>
> (Leftwich 1995: 408)

Weiss addresses 'institutionalised government-business cooperation' (formal and informal links with organised economic actors), alongside 'transformative goals' and 'a pilot agency', as one of the three essential ingredients of any developmental state (Weiss 2003: 247). In this framework, institutions are inclusive of formal and informal rules, norms, established procedures and conventions that govern individual behaviours (Leftwich 2005: 589; Weiss 1998: 246). The incorporation of non-economic factors and informal networks as constitutive of institutions is also closely related to an attempt to redefine or extend the boundaries of politics. For instance, Leftwich suggests that politics should be an all-encompassing concept, which consists of

> all the activities of co-operation, negotiation and conflict, within and between societies, whereby people go about organizing the use, production or distribution of human, natural and other resources in the course of the production and reproduction of their biological and social life.
>
> (Leftwich 2005: 591)

Therefore, when it is stressed that development is a political process, this means that it is 'embedded in, and mutually interacting with, a network of socioeconomic relationships' (Leftwich 2005: 574–5; see also Leftwich 2010).

Institutional linkages and economics: new institutional economics

If comparative historical institutionalism represents an endeavour to address state-market interrelatedness from the discipline of politics and sociology, new institutional economics (NIE) can be seen as a similar attempt made in the disciplinary context of economics. Since the term NIE was first coined by Oliver Williams in 1975, it has gradually become a prominent perspective within economics and has been linked to other social sciences approaches (Zimbauer 2001: 11–2). However, the boundary between old and new institutionalist economics has been disputed, and there is no uniform understanding of the meaning and significance of NIE (see Fine 2006a; Harriss et al. 1995; Zimbauer 2001). The rise of NIE and its growing prominence have often been understood as neoclassical economics' increased receptiveness to state interventionism, incorporating into their theory the idea of market failures and market imperfection caused by externalities such as information asymmetries and transaction costs. NIE has also been framed within the context of the emergence of the 'post-Washington Consensus', which pointed to a shift in thought in orthodox economics and concomitant changes in the development policy orientations of international development agencies such as the World Bank (Fine 2001; Fine et al. 2001).

First, NIE has brought increased attention to the fact that institutions are pivotal to the efficient functioning of markets (Zimbauer 2001), although the degree of emphasis varies amongst theorists. Second, social and political factors are consequently recognised as decisive for success in development, which render development a complex social process that involves more than a growth of per capita income and increase in consumption (Fine et al. 2001: xii). This means, for instance, that within the NIE framework, successful privatisation ought to be implemented within the appropriate socio-political, legal and economic environment beyond merely creating private ownership (Fine 2001: 10; see also Stiglitz 1999). In this context, NIE has helped renew interest in the role of the state, particularly in the context of developing countries where non-market institutions and market failure have been of particular importance, thereby acknowledging the ways in which institutions are constituted by politics and power (Harriss et al. 1995: 8–13). Some even go as far as arguing that '[i]nstitutions do not only encompass the formal and informal rules of the game but also the symbol system, cognitive scripts, and moral templates that provide the "frames of meaning" for guiding human action' (Hall and Tayler 1996: 948, as cited in Zimbauer 2001: 11). NIE can thus be seen as an endeavour to widen the horizons of economics and embrace more legal and political variables, such as rules and regulations, as well as ideas and ideologies in assessing development, matters which were traditionally considered to be lying outside the domain of mainstream economics (Harriss et al. 1995: 1–4).

Ha-Joon Chang's institutionalist political economy (IPE)

Institutionalist political economy (IPE), proposed by Ha-Joon Chang as an alternative to neoclassical or neoliberal political economy,[3] can be seen as one example of how the renewed interest in institutions in economics is translated into the interpretation of the developmental state based on a relational perspective on state-market relations.[4]

Chang points out that the main shortcoming of the neoclassical framework is that it inadequately conceptualises the state, the market and other institutions, and their interrelationships (Chang H-J 2002a: 542, 2003: 15). This is because it fails 'to base its discourse on a balanced and sophisticated theory of *the interrelationship* between the market and the state and other institutions' (2003: 15; emphasis added). On this ground, Chang introduces 'an alternative approach [IPE] that incorporates politics and institutions into its analytic core' (Chang H-J 2002a: 551): his approach is centred on the idea that 'the capitalist system is made up of a range of institutions, including markets as institutions of exchange, the firms as institutions of production, and the state as the creator and regulator of the institutions governing their *interrelationships*' (Chang H-J 2000: 14; emphasis added).

One of the points central to Chang's approach is that 'the market is ultimately a political construct' (2002a: 551). He problematises the neoclassical view that the market is a natural phenomenon that arises timelessly and independently of politics and institutional settings, and stresses that 'objective outcomes of "impersonal markets" are the results of certain political decisions about property rights, entitlements and prices' (Chang H-J 2000: 18). According to Chang, to the extent that 'the emergence of markets was almost always deliberately engineered by the state' (2000: 15), 'politics [should be seen] not as something alien and damaging to the market but as an integral part of its construction, operation and change' (2002a: 556). Likewise, Chang (1997: 718) writes that 'the boundaries of markets are determined not only by efficiency considerations but also by non-economic, or even "moral", considerations'. He gives a number of examples, such as child labour and slavery, where state regulations were viewed as a hindrance to the free market but have become a natural part of it, with participants internalising state regulations as inalienable elements of (free) market activities (Chang H-J 1997: 718, 2002a: 542–4). Through these examples he highlights that various factors, from economic and political to moral, come into play in determining the boundary between the market and an interventionist state, and stresses the changeability of the boundary itself in accordance with changes in institutions and rights-obligations structures (Chang H-J 2002a: 552).

Informed by and applying (new) institutional economics, Chang offers an analysis of the political economy of industrial policy in Korea and East Asia, and draws out the positive role of institutions, highlighting his analysis's implications for how to think about state-market relations. At one level his view is reminiscent of those of the theorists of the developmental state, particularly Amsden. Chang illustrates, in great detail, the depth and variety of interventionist measures that the industrial policy in East Asia, particularly Korea, deployed to facilitate industrialisation, such as artificially low interest rates, trade protection and subsidies to selected industries as well as various tax incentives offered to encourage certain types of investment (Chang H-J 1994: 307). Chang broadly accepts the view that the Korean developmental state enjoyed a high degree of autonomy *vis-à-vis* businesses, and that the former exercised the disciplinary power over the latter through control over financial resources and allocations, whereby policy-determined loans are granted to business groups only when they meet performance targets set by the state (Chang H-J 1993: 153, 1999: 5). However, at the same time, Chang argues that the state (and its level of autonomy) is constrained because various factors, such as 'the prevailing ideologies, institutions and political agenda of the society will set a limit to its innovativeness in the design of a coordination structure and of a conflict management system'. On the basis of this he contends that '[n]o state, however "strong" it may be, works with a clean slate and therefore is free from history' (Chang H-J 1994: 310).

The view that the state is contained by various societal factors relates to Chang's stress on the constitutive role of institutions that shape individuals' motivations themselves. Contrary to the neoclassical assumption that the state elites are prone to rent-seeking, and their intervention in the market results in inefficiency and distortion (Chang H-J 2002a: 553), he understands that the motivations and behaviours of individuals, including state personages, can be shaped by the institutions within which they operate (Chang H-J 1997: 722). 'This is not only because individuals often join public life with commitments to certain non-selfish values … but also because, operating in an explicitly "public" sphere of life, they end up internalising many "publicly oriented" values' (Chang H-J 2002a: 553–4). With this in mind, Chang finds the primary root of the Korean developmental state in institutional innovations initiated by political leadership. He states that 'the Korean state was … as much, if not more, an outcome of calculated political moves and institutional innovations as of historical conditions and culture' (Chang H-J 1993: 151).

Byeong-Cheon Lee's state in society

Another notable attempt to resolve the antithetical juxtaposition of the state and the market within the tradition of institutional economics is the placing of 'the state in society', as proposed by Byeong-Cheon Lee.[5] While Lee's work primarily focusses on the developmental state with reference to Korea, his approach underlines how a relational approach to state-market relations is applied to an analysis of the developmental state in the context of institutional economics.[6]

Lee's 'state in society' approach is initiated by the limits of the dominant literature on the developmental state in East Asia. He argues that the conceptualisation of the (Korean) developmental state by Johnson, Wade and Amsden takes the notion of 'state autonomy' for granted and enforces the flawed notion that the state exists outside and intervenes in society from above (Lee B-C 2003a: 114). In this respect, according to Lee, while these authors critique neoclassical economics as being based on 'market-centrism', they only replace it with 'state-centrism' (Lee B-C 2003b: 29). Lee also differentiates his approach from Evans's 'embedded autonomy' to the extent that the latter leaves unanswered the question of who disciplines the disciplinary state and how and why the state's being embedded in society did not result in outcomes detrimental to development (Lee B-C 2003a: 120, 2003b: 8–9): the state's embedded autonomy can mean mutually beneficial 'crony' relations formed between state elites and individual capitalists for their personal gains at the expense of broader societal goals (Lee B-C 2003a: 101, 118). Lee argues that both the developmental state theorists and Evans tend to one-sidedly take for granted the 'success side' of industrial development in Korea while disregarding its 'dark side', such as the lingering militaristic culture and environmental destruction that are associated with a blind pursuit of development under a state with a high level of autonomy (Lee B-C 2003a: 119).

On the basis of these limits of the dominant developmental state literature, Lee proposes 'state in society' as an alternative conceptual framework, which brings to the fore the idea that the state exists only within society as it is the embodiment of social power relations, and therefore 'the power and capacity of civil society and democracy should receive equal consideration with those of the state' (Lee B-C 2003b: 30). On the basis of the 'state in society' framework, Lee provides an answer to the question of why a high level of state autonomy and 'embedded autonomy' did not only lead to the individual enrichment of state and economic elites or to the formation of a rent-seeking predatory state. He argues that the Korean state was able to mobilise and channel the Korean masses' desire to escape from poverty for the goal of national development (2003b: 46–7). While development in Korea was characterised by 'growth first, distribution second', the fruits of rapid growth, such as extensive employment opportunities and a rapid rise in wages, provided workers with an incentive to tolerate hard working conditions and actively take part in the state-led national development project

(2003b: 50–1). In other words, what makes the Korean state a *developmental* state was not only its relative autonomy in economic management and the alliance between state elites and businesses but the support from the population for the goal of development: hence 'the state in society'.

Defining the Park Chung-Hee regime from 1961 to 1979 as a 'developmental dictatorship' (*Kaebal Tokchae*), Lee pays close attention to the specific international economic and geopolitical conditions that provided both opportunities and disadvantages for development, particularly for semi-sovereign countries like Korea (2003b: 31). According to him, on the one hand, as the Park regime came out of the postcolonial 'catch-up' context and ended up in competition with North Korea, it was able to mobilise the wider population for national development and combine it with Cold War anti-communism. On the other hand, as the Park regime undertook a semi-peripheral late industrialisation, its success was conditioned by its position in the international hierarchy as a junior partner of the US and Japan. The widened technological gap and development disparities between the industrialised countries and the world-economic periphery after the Second World War made it imperative for the Korean state to take on a more active entrepreneurial role in its pursuit of late industrialisation (Lee B-C 2003b: 61–2).

Having identified the international geopolitical conditions that are advantageous and disadvantageous for 'catch-up' development, Lee focusses on various institutional inventions and manoeuvres attributable to the rapid industrialisation of Korea: he assesses how advantages were maximised, while disadvantages were minimised. Key examples are the simultaneous pursuit of import substitution and export-led industrialisation policies, and a skilful combination of protectionism and openness to the global economy (Lee B-C 2003b: 47–8). While Lee shares with other institutionalists his emphasising institutional inventions as the main contributing factors to the successful industrialisation of Korea, his intention differs from the latter's as he addresses the point that successful industrialisation does not necessarily require an authoritarian political regime (Lee B-C 2003b: 51). Unlike Evans, Chang, Johnson, Wade and Amsden, who defend and exalt the developmental state or the Park government in the case of Korea (Chapter 1), Lee offers a critique of the Park regime, especially its turn to what he calls 'hard authoritarianism' in 1972, known as *Yushin* (the constitutional amendment that allowed Park to stay in power permanently). Lee contends that Korea could have adopted a more democratic and environmentally sustainable development path, at least after the initial phase of rapid industrialisation during the first ten years of the Park regime (Lee B-C 2003b: 62–5).

(New) Institutionalism, in the disciplinary contexts of both (political) sociology and economics, from BSBI, 'embedded autonomy' and Institutional Political Economy to the approach associated with the concept of 'the state in society', has brought the state to the fore as the key explanatory factor for the successful development of East Asia. Significantly, the state was theorised by this range of approaches not as autonomous but as related to, embedded or rooted in society. Expressed differently, in the institutional framework, the developmental state is characterised not only in terms of its high level of autonomy but also in terms of the (co-operative) relations which it formed with actors in the market or society. Therefore, the rapid development of the East Asian economies is attributed not to the presence of an autonomous state that intervened in the economy *per se* but to the ways in which the state and the market are related through interlocked networks of informal and formal institutions.

A relational perspective of state-market relations allows different types of states to be classified according to not only the *level* of their autonomy but *what kind of* autonomy they enjoy in relation to society. For instance, the relational approach is better able to account for a great level of divergence in development outcomes when there is little difference in the level of state autonomy: authoritarian governments in developing countries typically possess a high level of policy autonomy over society, but development outcomes differ. Furthermore, institutionalists tend to negate the neoclassical assumption (and neo-utilitarianism) that see individual behaviours being guided by egoism and instead underline the constitutive role of institutions in guiding and fashioning state behaviours: depending on within what institutional contexts state officials operate, they internalise different values. To be sure, Johnson, Wade and Amsden do not ignore these issues and engage with questions concerning state-business relations and the importance of development-inducing institutions. However, within the framework of institutionalist politics and economics, the core characteristic of the developmental state shifts from its autonomy from society and business actors to its relatedness to or embeddedness in society.

Superficial and external linkages between the state and the market

In spite of various valid points made by historical institutionalism and (new) institutional economics to provide a more nuanced theorisation of state-market relations in explaining the rapid industrialisation of East Asia, the state-market linkages proposed by institutionalists pose several conceptual and political problems.

Tension between state autonomy and state-market linkages

One of the conceptual problems of institutionalism lies in the ambiguity or confusion caused by the notion of 'state autonomy' on the one hand and its 'embeddedness in society' on the other. As discussed, BSBI is an attempt to provide a conceptual framework alternative to what its authors call the 'society-determined' understanding of the state, such as by neo-Marxists who emphasise the merely relative autonomy of the state. It is argued at the same time that BSBI is not meant to replace the primacy of the market with that of the state but to understand state-market relationally. It therefore remains unclear what the BSBI authors mean when they advocate 'true' autonomy against the neo-Marxists' 'relative autonomy' from immediate capitalist structural requirements and the interests of the dominant classes (Evans et al. 1985: 347, 350; Skocpol 1985: 4–7) while claiming at the same time not to displace the state completely from society.

A similar ambiguity is evident in Evans's characterisation of the state as both the representative of the general (public) interest and an instrument of domination: the developmental state is one in which general and national (developmental) goals override private interests (see above). However, it remains unquestioned what 'universal or public interests' are in comparison to private interests and how and by whom they are determined. Equally it is unclear how and why the state serves 'universal interests' (if it is possible at all to identify and achieve them), and how and why a greater degree of autonomy renders the state the representative of general (developmental) rather than narrow private interests. Evans and Rueschemeyer seek social and structural conditions leading to greater state autonomy, basing their argument on the assumption that greater state autonomy means more chances for development to succeed (Rueschemeyer and Evans 1985: 49). While the state's linkages to society is emphasised, the former's autonomy from the latter is also seen as a key factor for successful development. For instance, in searching for the main factors responsible for the different development outcomes in Latin America and the newly industrialising countries (NICs) in East Asia, Evans argues that '[i]n Latin America the state is a critical actor in the triple alliance, but … the interests of private capital predominate, … [while in] East Asian NICs … the state plays a more dominant role' (Evans 1987: 212).

Relatedly, while these authors recognise the importance of a well-functioning bureaucracy in determining the capacity of the state to intervene in the economy, the existence of development-oriented state managers is understood tautologically as the product of the state bureaucratic system itself. Rueschemeyer and Evans (1985: 53) hold that 'state managers having a perspective distinct from that of private members of the dominant class is their structural removal from concern with short-run profit considerations'. In other words, they 'find' that the state bureaucracy concerns itself with the 'general interest' after they have posited axiomatically that concern with the general interest is the essential characteristic of the state bureaucracy.

The same problem mars Chang's conception. He emphasises that society constrains the state in various ways (Chang H-J 1994: 310; see above) when he proposes Institutional Political Economy as an alternative perspective to neoclassical economics, but he also continuously refers to the notion of state autonomy as detached from market and society. His understanding of development is surely more sophisticated than neoclassical economics to the extent that he sees it as conflict-ridden, socially encompassing transformations. However, this recognition leads him to arrive at the statist view that 'the state, by definition, is the only agent which may represent the interest of the whole society' (Chang H-J 1994: 299). He argues that 'the co-existence of widespread interdependencies and private control of means of production [in capitalism] means that efficient structural change requires concerted efforts coordinated by the state' (Chang H-J 1994: 301).

To the extent that Chang posits development as a complex and multidimensional process, he understands that the *degree* to which the state exercises its alleged autonomy against, and immunity from, society becomes the crucial factor. This is because it is the (autonomous) state that can act as both conflict manager and coordinator with appropriate redistribution measures in order to ensure social cohesion and long-term productivity enhancement (Chang H-J 1994: 300–9). It is thus taken for granted that the state is 'the existence of an *exogenously* imposed impartial third party' (Chang H-J 1997: 722, ft. 1). As a consequence, Chang contends that '[state] autonomy *vis-à-vis* interest groups will determine how effectively it can institute a new property rights structure and manage conflicts in the way it wants' (Chang H J 1994: 310). In this manner, institutionalists' relational view offers a contradictory or at best ambiguous postulation on state-market relations: the developmental state is understood to be 'embedded' in or related to society on the one hand, but in order to be developmental it has to be 'autonomous' from society on the other.

Personal and individualised linkages

On a closer analysis, this problem follows from the fact that institutionalists tend to conceptualise state-market linkages primarily in terms of personal and individualised relations between economic and political elites. For instance, when Evans notes that his approach is influenced by institutionalists like Gerschenkron and Hirschman, he finds one of the most important insights of these authors in the idea that 'state-society relations, particularly those that link states and entrepreneurial elites, are as important as internal [bureaucratic] structures' (Evans 1995: 22). His 'embedded autonomy' points to 'a concrete set of connections that link the state intimately and aggressively to particular social groups with whom the state shares a joint project of transformation' (Evans 1995: 59). He (1995: 41) then argues that '[t]he whole idea of "joint projects" ... makes close ties to key social groups fundamental to [the state's] developmental efficacy'. Here key social groups are in effect businesses. Evans (1995: 41) reiterates that '[w]e are, after all, talking about capitalist societies in which neither investment nor production can be implemented without the cooperation of private actors'.

A focus on the elite and actor level of state-market linkages also characterises Chang's writings. For example, he finds the causes of the successful development outcomes engendered by states in East Asia and Scandinavia in the orientation of state elites: '[o]ne interesting commonality between the two groups of countries is the existence of a political and/or bureaucratic elite which had a stronger commitment to social goals such as industrialization and structural change' (Chang H-J 1994: 309). As a consequence, Chang exclusively focusses on the relation between the state and businesses (the *chaebol*) in his analysis of industrial policy in Korea (see Chang H-J 1993), and finds the linkages between the state and the market in various informal channels of influence on the business sector (Chang H-J 2000: 10). By the same token, Weiss derives from the historical analysis of the developmental state 'the importance of a political system which supports a shared project of economic transformation, where there is elite cohesion over core national goals, and where the economic bureaucracy is given sufficient scope to take initiatives and act effectively' (Weiss 2003: 247).

As a consequence of state-market relations' being primarily understood as an elite level of interaction, the question around labour is broadly absent in the institutionalist framework. Otherwise, it is considered as a secondary factor in determining the level of state autonomy after the relation between the state and the dominant class, as in Rueschemeyer and Evans (1985: 60–5), or as one question amongst those that need to be dealt with as part of 'conflict management', as in Chang (1994: 310, 2003: 46–7). Even if Lee defines labour repression as a key characteristic of the Korean developmental state regime, he regards labour as having willingly taken part in the project of national development (Lee B-C 2003b: 50–1). The fact that the question of labour is ignored or treated as secondary by the institutionalists is not only indicative of the fact that their primary focus is on elite-level personal interactions. More fundamentally, labour, in the institutionalist setting, is a factor contingent to development or a matter associated with management. This reflects the view that as much as state and market relations are personalised, labour is seen as a distinct interest group that interacts with or competes against other private actors. To be fair, the institutionalists discussed in this chapter do not posit development as a process free from oppression and conflicts. Nevertheless, as much as they do not problematise development itself as *capitalist* development, or as far as they place the question of development outside a critical inquiry into the nature of capitalist society, labour does not constitute an intrinsic element of the totality of capitalist social relations.

The absence of a critique of capitalist development or the placement of successful industrialisation, at least potentially, outside of capitalist contradictions makes Lee's assessment of the Korean developmental state more similar than dissimilar to other institutionalist understandings assessed in this chapter. His call for a 'balanced' evaluation of the Park regime, taking into account its negative and positive aspects, in fact reinforces the statist antithetical juxtaposition of the state and the market. His critique suggests that an alternative path to development, namely 'development based on democracy', would have been possible. However, in so doing, he renders the relations between authoritarianism and late industrialisation accidental: he suggests that social and labour discipline imposed by an authoritarian regime was extrinsic to 'successful catch-up' development rather than intrinsic to capitalist development in general and particularly in the context of late development within the hierarchical global economy. Lee fails to notice that a developing country that competes in the world market as a producer of low-end manufacturing goods based on low wages presupposes super-exploitation and a highly disciplinary labour regime. While the issue will be further discussed in Part II, here it suffices to say that Lee in effect limits the problems of the Park regime to the political realm, pointing to military dictatorship and authoritarianism: development as an achievement is separable from its negative aspects, such as authoritarianism. To the extent that it is suggested that the undemocratic political system is primarily responsible for labour repression, this, in this context, is understood to be external or potentially external to capitalist development.[7]

De-politicising and de-historicising the political

To the degree that institutionalism posits state-market linkages mainly as individualised ties, the institutionalist conceptualisation of the political reinforces statism. Chang and Leftwich's argument that the functioning of the market is determined by political and non-economic (ideological and cultural) factors is grounded on the fact that it is the state that sets up the terms of market entry and the boundaries of what legitimate market activities are (see above). From this perspective, the market is seen to be of a political nature primarily because it requires and presupposes the state. In other words, 'the political' primarily points to state affairs and state intervention in the market: it is assumed that if the state intervenes in the economy with more regulations, it is 'linked' to the market; if it intervenes in the economy with fewer regulations, it becomes 'de-linked' from the market and thus less political; if and when it permits certain market transactions as legitimate, the boundaries of the free-market shift. In this formulation, the state-market linkages are contingent and arbitrary as the intervention of the state in the economy appears to be a choice that the state, as an actor, can make (or refuses or fails to make). Consequently, the institutionalists maintain and reinforce the statist framework of the developmental state paradigm by assessing different kinds of state, interventionist or otherwise, by the degree to which they intervene in the market and with what policies. For instance, Leftwich (1995: 404) distinguishes different modes of state intervention depending on whether they are 'parametric' (framework setting) or 'pervasive' (substantive involvement).

Narrowing the question of how political the market is to the extent to which it is determined by state regulations has the effect of 'depoliticising' the concept of the political. While Evans, Leftwich, Chang and Lee stress the dynamic character of institutions and the extent to which they determine the boundaries of the free market, they do not historicise the institutions themselves in relation to capitalism: although they argue that individual motivations and behaviours are shaped by the institutional environments within which they operate, and that the historical legacies of institutions ('path dependency') influence social and economic changes and policy outcomes, they avoid asking why these institutions exist in a particular form in the first place. In order for institutions, their history and their politics to be understood adequately, they need to be discussed with reference to the capitalist mode of production that gives rise to the historically specific (capitalist) *forms* of these institutions themselves.

To illustrate this point, the question of what things or services count as marketable within a market cannot be separated from the question of what a commodity is and how a mode of production operates that is entirely dedicated to the production and exchange of commodities. This involves far more fundamental issues than the institutionalists' concern with how states institute certain rules and regulations on markets (which they seem to presuppose as already existing). Formal regulations and informal norms, including property, contract laws and mutual trust, which institutionalists take as the starting points of their inquiries, arise historically in accordance with the necessity to guide individual behaviours: for instance, to ensure smooth transactions of the exchange of equivalent quantities of 'labour power' and 'wages'. The existence of such institutions (rules and regulations) presupposes the existence of a historically specific mode of production and social relations: namely (in the modern context) the capitalist mode of production, wherein commodity production and exchange relations are generalised, and a majority of the population sell labour power as a commodity on the labour market as their only way to secure access to subsistence.

By the same token, corporate organisational structures, to which institutionalists pay a great degree of attention, cannot be fully explained without reference to the fundamental causes and drives of their existence, which emanate from the dynamism of the capitalist mode of production. Private firms are compelled to be efficient and productive by the innovation and reorganisation of production techniques as a matter of survival as they operate in cut-throat competition inbuilt in the capitalist system. This, in turn, has class implications because 'efficiency' and 'productivity' in capitalism are measured from the perspective of capital accumulation and valorisation: '[t]he only worker who is productive is one who produces surplus-value for the capitalist, or in other words contributes towards the self-valorisation of capital' (Marx 1976: 644). Seen in this way, institutions themselves are embodiments of class content not only because they serve the interests of some at the expense of others but because their existence itself is conditioned by historically specific forms of production and social relations.

As far as institutionalists assess institutions outside of historically specific capitalist social relations, their primary focus on the 'intermediate level of institutions' and refusal of 'grand theorising' results in their escaping the truly relevant political questions. They bypass inquiries such as why institutions exist in certain forms in particular periods and locations and whose interests they serve (the class content of institutions). Expressed differently, in the institutional theorising of state-society relations, 'the social conditions that make possible the emergence of the institution of generalised market exchange, such as class structure, and access to the means of production, remain a closed book' (Fine et al. 2001: xii).

Rendering capitalist social relations harmonious & bringing statism back in

With scant attention to the historically specific form of capitalist institutions and their functions in relation to the reproduction of capitalist social relations, the institutionalists' embracing of non-economic (e.g. political and moral) aspects of economic relations furnishes the developmental state with moral justification on the basis of the allegedly public nature of state elites.

For instance, refuting the simplistic dichotomy of a zero-sum relation between state and market or society, the BSBI authors emphasise that the relation between the state and the market actors (capitalists) could constitute a 'win-win' situation whereby 'state autonomy and the power of social groups can increase … together' (Evans et al. 1985: 353). For this reason, they call 'vulgar Weberian perspectives' the view that 'the increased ability of a bureaucratic state to realize internally generated goals supposedly reduces the power of all societal groups' (Evans et al. 1985: 353). They also argue that 'the presence of powerful social actors, specifically transnational corporations, has stimulated the growth of autonomous states with capacities for economic intervention in many Third World countries' (Evans et al. 1985: 353).

Similarly, Evans's embedded autonomy of the developmental state renders positive the close relations between state bureaucrats and business actors, which, according to some, amounts to 'crony capitalism'. He (1995: 41) contends that '[t]he presence of organized social groups with something to gain from transformation enhances the prospect of sustaining a transformative bureaucratic state'. With an emphasis on the constitutive role of institutions in shaping and influencing individuals' behaviours and motivations, Chang provides a moral justification to state elites by arguing that 'we should acknowledge that there is no need for selfish motivations to dominate our behaviour in the public sphere of the state, where non-selfish values are institutionally emphasised and therefore the actors internalise many such values' (Chang H-J 2002a: 555). Lee's 'state in society' approach praises the state's ability to mobilise public aspirations for national development, defining the Korean developmental dictatorship as one in which the alliance between state elites and the *chaebol* functioned productively because of public consent (Lee B-C 2003b: 46–7). Woo-Cumings (1999a: 20) succinctly summarises this point: 'the power of the developmental state grows both out of the barrel of the gun and its ability to convince the population of its political, economic, and moral mandate'.

The portrayal of the developmental state as one which promoted national development consensually (or with less coercion) and through co-operation with social actors (businesses) is not only questionable from a historical perspective (at least with reference to Korea, where social and labour struggles on a massive scale characterised the period of rapid industrialisation; see Part III); more crucially, it presents the developmental state as if it achieved successful industrialisation on moral grounds, thereby downplaying violence and conflicts inherent in capitalist development. In so doing, in the institutionalist framework, capitalist development under the developmental state is rendered, at least potentially, a conflict-free harmonious process.

Consequently, rather unsurprisingly, institutionalists eventually bring back statism, the idea that the autonomous state was the key agent for national development, but impart strengthened moral justifications to the developmental state beyond its technical competency in delivering development. Calling for 'bringing politics back in', Leftwich concludes that 'politics [should] be in command' because 'without an effective state, there is likely to be little growth and even less poverty reduction' (Leftwich 2005: 595). Chang stresses the idea that, despite the institutional diversity among capitalist societies, 'the fact remains that all successful developmental efforts involved substantial state intervention' (Chang H-J 2002a: 548), and 'there is virtually no country ... which achieved the status of an industrialized country without at least some periods of heavy state involvement in the development effort' (Chang H-J 2000: 16).[8]

In summary, institutionalism in the context of development theory and the discourse on the developmental state is significant in that it rightly recognises and brings to the fore the antithetical juxtaposition of state and market that underpins the concept of the developmental state as the centre of inquiry. However, its endeavour to challenge neoclassical economics and society-centred theories of the state by linking state and market reinforces the statist conception of the developmental state. The institutionalist emphasis on state-market linkages primarily points to close personal relations between state elites and capitalists, the latter representing the market or indeed society. In so doing, institutionalism fortifies the idea that the autonomous state is the main agent of national development: the existence of a state that stands above or external to society is a prerequisite for successful development and determines development outcomes. If the earlier conceptualisation of the developmental state praises its high level of state autonomy or even authoritarianism on the basis of necessary conflicts emanating from resistance to social and economic actors in the process of development, within the institutionalist framework, state-market relations assume the appearance of harmonious relationships. To the extent that the linkages between state and market, and the formers' embeddedness in the latter are understood to be effected by co-operation between political and economic elites and supported by popular consent to national development, capitalist development is rendered less contradictory and more reconciliatory.[9] In so doing, the institutionalist recognition of development as a political and multidimensional process not only solidifies the statist concept of the developmental state but also treats it in a more affirmative fashion.

Institutionalist accounts of the Asian financial crisis and the transformation of the developmental state

The conceptual problematic of institutionalism discussed above translates into its assessment of the transformation of the developmental state, a subject that has been debated intensely since the Asian financial crisis of 1997/98. Some of the institutionalists discussed in the chapter actively engaged in the debate about the causes of the Asian financial crisis of 1997/98 and its impact on the developmental state. In what follows, I will discuss how the conceptual limitations of institutionalism are reflected in its appraisal of the financial crisis and its relations to the developmental state.

Loss of state autonomy vis-à-vis business actors

To the extent that the institutionalist approach is based on recognising the positive role of the state in development, like the theorists of the developmental state, the institutionalists discussed above oppose the neoclassical interpretation of the Asian financial crisis of 1997/98. For instance, challenging the neoclassical proposition that state interventionism, particularly industrial policy and an insufficient degree of liberalisation, caused the financial crisis of 1997/98 (see Chapter 1), Chang argues (1999: 28) that 'it was actually the *demise* of industrial policy, rather than its continuation, that was one major factor behind the current crisis in Korea'. Weiss (2003: 251) also notes that the crisis was a result not of the persistence of Korea's state-guided development model but of '[s]tate withdrawal from industrial policy'. Even equating the demise of industrial policy to that of the developmental state itself, Weiss maintains that '[d]ismantling [of the state-guided development model] ... left Korea more vulnerable to economic turmoil and paved the way for global flows to wreck their havoc [on the Korean economy]' (Weiss 2003: 251). In the institutionalist framework, therefore, what neoclassical economists believe were key contributors to the crisis, such as ill-managed financial liberalisation and uncoordinated and excessive investments by the private sector, or 'crony relations' between the state and the *chaebol*, were not characteristics inherent in the developmental state model. Rather these were symptoms that surfaced as a *result* of the dismantlement of institutions central to the developmental state, such as the Economic Planning Board and the state-controlled financial system (see Chang H-J 1998: 1559; Chang H-J et al. 1998: 739; Lee Y-H 2000).

As for the question of why industrial policy and key state-governed development institutions were abolished, however, the institutionalists discussed in this chapter tend to diverge from Johnson, Amsden and Wade, who found the answer in 'external' liberalisation pressure coming from global institutions and the US's having lost their competitiveness in the world market (see Chapter 1). Reflecting the fact that institutionalists tend to see state-market linkages in terms of personal relations between state bureaucrats and business elites *within* national society, they put the emphasis on 'domestic' rather than 'external' variables: they trace the demise of industrial policy or the developmental state through changes in state-businesses relations. Chang et al. (1998: 745) write that the demise of industrial policy reflects 'the rise of neo-Liberal ideology and the growing power of the *chaebols* (conglomerates), which now hankered for greater freedom in their investment decision-making'. Relatedly, Weiss suggests that the increasingly powerful and independent position of the *chaebol vis-à-vis* the state explains the shift in the orientations of bureaucrats and development policies. She holds that 'the momentum for change was primarily *domestic-political in origin*, long preceding external pressures for financial liberalization in the 1990s' (Weiss 2000: 22; emphasis added). The growing contradictions within the developmental model were the result of the dynamic that 'the chaebol, in their continuing quest for diversification and expansion, had become financially "over-enmeshed" in the DS [the developmental state], while in their structure and ambition they had grown more and more independent of it' (Weiss 2003: 250).

The institutionalists' primary focus on internal dimensions is limited again to elite-level interactions between state bureaucrats (policy makers) and capitalists. The dismantling of key developmental institutions is seen primarily in terms of changes in policy and elite orientation. Illustratively, having 'examined the forces behind the policy changes that led to the crisis', Chang (1998: 745) concludes that 'policy failures certainly have to take a large portion of the blame'. Chang et al. (1998: 744) similarly assert that 'had it not been for the ill-designed financial liberalisation policy and the demise of industrial policy that led to over-investment, high corporate debt in Korea would not have produced a crisis'. Weiss states that '[d]ismantling had been driven by reformist-minded bureaucrats who viewed state retreat from industrial finance (and thus industrial policy) as the solution to the government-business impasse' (2003: 250). Insofar as the changes in the developmental state are seen as a result of the increase in the power of the *chaebol* relative to that of the state and/or the changes in the orientation of policy makers, the institutionalist interpretation betrays the statist concept of the developmental state: its demise is judged primarily by whether the state is able to discipline and direct the *chaebol* for the goal of national development. In other words, changes in the nature of the state are traced within the statist framework of whether or not individual state bureaucrats or policy makers have lost or gained policy autonomy.

It is indisputable that institutionalist analyses shed light on the fact that the financial crisis of 1997/98, particularly in the context of Korea, reflected a deeper power dynamic between the government and businesses than that which external pressure towards liberalisation posed. Nevertheless, there is little explanation offered of the fundamental economic and societal causes that conditioned the changes in the power balance between the two in the first place. As a consequence, changes in policy orientation appear to be more of an accidental and arbitrary outcome. While institutionalists and the theorists of the developmental state diverge in this respect in prioritising domestic variables and external forces respectively, they both *externalise* capitalist class contradictions in their explanations of the crisis. Expressed differently, whether the crisis is caused by external pressures towards liberalisation, as in the theorists of the development state, or by the loss of state dominance against businesses, as in the institutionalist theorising, the theorists of the developmental states and the institutionalists both see it as caused by factors external to the developmental state: the developmental state in itself is posited as immune from the contradictions of capitalist development.

From the state-market dichotomy to the production-finance dichotomy

The tendency of the institutionalists to downplay capitalist contradictions and conflicts inherent in East Asian development leads them to depict the developmental state as a 'superior alternative to the Anglo-Saxon variety of capitalism' (Chang H-J 1994: 310). The institutionalist imaginary of a non-contradictory form of capitalist social relations leads to their tendency to magnify the positive characteristics of the developmental state when neoclassical economists and others present it as the main cause of the financial crisis.[10] For example, the developmental state is depicted as based on 'generalistic' state-business links, whilst the dismantlement of the developmental state underpins a shift towards 'particularistic' (or 'cronyistic') ones (Chang H-J et al. 1998: 741). Similarly, it is argued that industrial policy in East Asia allowed 'coordinated investment' and thereby 'managed competition' as opposed to 'wasteful competition' (Chang H-J 1999: 7–9).

The institutionalist tendency to posit the developmental state as a superior system, in turn, produces a propensity to exaggerate the antagonism between productive and financial capital. Chang and Yoo (1999: 1) conclude from their comparative study of previous foreign debt crises of Korea that 'the 1997 crisis is distinguished from the previous economic crises ... most importantly in the way it has been managed in the interests of the financial rentier class, rather than of industrial capitalists'. They also argue that the financial crisis is distinct from other crises in its management in its abolition of 'the traditional anti-finance/pro-industry stance of the Korean government' (Chang H-J and Yoo C-G 1999: 23). According to Chang and Yoo, the strong capital controls that characterised the Korean financial system underlined the ability of the Korean state to carry out tight monitoring (via state-owned banks) to ensure that the recipients of policy loans, particularly the *chaebol*, used them efficiently. On the basis of this reasoning, they differentiate the era that characterises the developmental state and that following it according to the extent to which the state was able to direct the *chaebol* in the interest of 'industrial production' rather than 'rentier interests'. They thus project negative growth prospects of the Korean economy as long as financial interests dominate because this means that 'short-term' and 'shareholder' interests, as opposed to 'long-term' and 'productive' ones, are likely to prevail (Chang H-J and Yoo C-G 1999: 27–31; see also Crotty 2000, 2002; Lee et al. 2002).

Positing industrial and financial capital as antithetical and declaring the former to be superior or more desirable leaves crucial questions unanswered.[11] More fundamental questions that need to be addressed are what drove the *chaebol* to accumulate an unsustainable level of corporate debts at a particular time; why they resorted to short-term borrowing to an historically unprecedented degree, given that periodic crises are intrinsic to the capitalist dynamic; and how and why the *chaebol* were able to access international financial markets. As shall be shown in Chapter 9, these questions can be answered more adequately when the financial crisis is analysed through the lens of how global capitalist contradictions in general, on the one hand, and intensive social and class struggle, a product of very rapid industrialisation, on the other, intensified the pressure on the competitiveness of Korean capital, and how this, in turn, magnified the contradictions of the developmental state model.

Restating statism: the developmental state mark II

Insofar as they see the financial crisis as having been caused by factors external to the developmental state, institutionalists tend to be optimistic about its future prospects. They believe in its continued validity, even in the context of post-'catch-up' industrialisation, and argue that the developmental state should and could be reconstructed. For instance, challenging the view that industrial policy has become less feasible in East Asia, Chang (1999:360) reiterates that 'there is no direct causal link between economic development and the rise of the private sector, on the one hand, and between the rise of the private sector and the demise of industrial policy, on the other hand'. He continues to argue that

> if there is a democratic consensus on it … industrial policy can be even more effectively implemented, given that every policy requires for its long-term success some degree of consent by those who are going to be affected by it.
>
> (Chang H-J 1999: 33)

Some institutionalists even hold that globalisation and liberalisation necessitate and even augment the role and capacity of the state (Mosley 2005; Weiss

2000, 2005). This is because there is no automatic or irreversible 'eclipse' of the (developmental) state by external or globalisation forces (Evans 1997, 2008a, 2008b) for globalisation, which they see as an external economic force, is filtered through domestic institutions, primarily state institutions (Weiss 2000, 2005). Weiss writes that 'the impact of the Asian crisis has not been *to disengage* the state from the economy *even further*, but rather *to bring it back in* – in a number of new and significant ways' (Weiss 2003: 256; emphasis in the original). Likewise, Evans states that 'state capacity will have an even greater role to play in societal success in the coming century than it did in the last century' (Evans 2008a: 3).

The institutionalist proposition that the developmental state can be reconfigured first reveals that it assesses the capitalist state primarily in terms of dismantling and erecting certain institutions. Second, it highlights that in the institutionalist framework, the global economy is considered as the background before which the national economies operate and from which national elites can benefit for national development purposes. This downplays what I would like to call the 'structure-like' constraints of capitalism as a global system that condition the development prospect of the developing countries.[12] For instance, while recognising that the use of interventionist measures by developing countries is restrained by today's international trade system governed by the World Trade Organisation (WTO), Chang and Weiss suggest that there is still room for developing countries to manoeuvre using the loopholes of and opportunities offered by the system (Chang H-J 1999: 22–4; Weiss 2005: 348–9). Evans (1995: 8) states that 'in a globalized economy where most value is added at several removes from natural resources, the global division of labour presents itself as an opportunity for agency, not just an exogenous constraint'. He adds that '[i]n a world of constructed comparative advantage … [s]tate involvement must be taken as one of the socioeconomic determinants of what niches a country ends up occupying in the international division of labour' (Evans 1995: 9–10). Similarly, Lee understands that the integration of a national economy into the global economy can be selectively and strategically managed on a national level, and that Korea is a case where external constraints had been successfully overcome by relevant policy and institutional innovations (Lee B-C 2003b: 31; see above). Consequently, while he is critical of personalised relationships between the state and the *chaebol* (crony capitalism), which he argues are responsible for causing the financial crisis and the 'irresponsible capitalism' of post-crisis Korea (Lee B-C 2005), he believes that with new policy innovations, a more egalitarian and democratic mode of development will be possible.

This understanding, at one level, underscores once again that the institutionalist emphasis on the state-market linkages end up limiting the problems of the developmental state model to the realm of politics: the negative aspects of the developmental state, such as authoritarianism, can be delineated while retaining its positive aspects, such as its capabilities to deliver successful economic development. At another level, this highlights that the institutionalist state-market linkages reinforce rather than overcome the statist concept of the developmental state: the state is seen as the actor that determines development outcomes insofar as it is able to (re)attain its autonomy from other social actors and insofar as it maintains its capacity to utilise the (external) global economy to the advantage of national (productive) development. In the institutionalist framework, as much as in the theories of the developmental state, the antithetical juxtaposition of state and market, and between national and global, are retained, and thereby the idea that the state that is autonomous from both spheres is the agent of 'national' development is reinforced.

Conclusion

In this chapter, I have critically appraised the core premises of institutionalism through a selected number of key authors from the disciplines of politics (historical institutionalism) and economics (NIE). While acknowledging the conceptual advancements made by institutionalists in the discussions of the developmental state, which proposes a relational perspective on state-society relations, I have addressed the limits of the institutional linkages. The institutionalist conception of the state as 'autonomous' from and simultaneously 'embedded' in society generates conceptual ambiguities. The political nature of the market is recognised only to the extent that the state intervenes in the latter, which limits the concept of the political to state affairs and policies. The state-market linkages are in effect personalised elite-level interactions and ties formed between state officials and businesses. Consequently, while the market and the state are posited as interlinked institutionally, the historicity of institutions themselves is not inquired into, and the questions of the class content and form of the capitalist state are bypassed. To the extent that the state's connectedness to and embeddedness in society are emphasised without addressing the capitalist class contradictions inherent in capitalist development, the institutionalist framework makes capitalist social relations appear less contradictory and more harmonious.

Reflecting these conceptual weaknesses, institutionalists offer elite- and policy-centred analyses of the Asian financial crisis of 1997/98 and its impacts on the (Korean) developmental state. They tend to seek the causes of the crisis in the policy failures of state elites who mistakenly bought into neoliberal ideology and in the loss of the state's grip on private capitalists and the financial system. As much as this understanding 'de-historicises' the 'system-like' world-systematic constraints, geopolitical and societal conditions that gave rise to the developmental state, it is unable to explain the deeper structural and societal causes beyond elite-level interactions. To the degree that the transformation of the developmental state is caused by the dismantlement of a set of institutions, institutionalists suggest that the developmental state can be resurrected through institutional changes and remain resilient against external (globalisation) forces. This would mean that the institutionalist endeavour to offer a more sophisticated theory based on state-market linkages would eventually remain statist. The institutionalists uphold and reinforce the view that the developmental state is autonomous from private actors and is capable of exploiting external forces to its advantage, that is, for national development.

In the following chapter, I will discuss how much and to what extent the statist concept of the developmental state sets the framework of a variety of discussions, including contemporary Marxist critiques of neoliberalism, the discourse on the transformation of the developmental state and the arguments of those who support moving 'beyond the developmental state'.

Notes

1 While this chapter focusses on how the general institutionalist understanding of state-market relations is reflected in its assessments of the developmental state in East Asia, the relatedness of state and market is also emphasised in the more general disciplinary context of International Political Economy (see Strange 1988). Polanyi (1957) is one of the classical points of reference for the critique of traditional economics that assesses the market as a self-contained entity separated from politics and who emphasises how economies are embedded in society and culture.

2 Phillips (2005) also categorises Marxist state theories as 'society-centred' or 'economy-determined'. For a Marxist critique of Skocpol and BSBI, see Cammack (1989). Conceptual issues related to the capitalist state and the limits of current Marxist analyses of the capitalist state, including those by Cammack and Poulantzas, are discussed in Part II.

3 While Chang's critique is directed towards both 'neoliberalism' and 'neoclassical economics', and uses the two terms interchangeably, the term 'neoliberalism' is more encompassing (having political as well as economic implications) than neoclassical economics. Chang writes that 'neo-liberalism emerged out of an "unholy alliance" between neoclassical economics, which provided most of the analytical tools, and what we may call the Austrian-libertarian tradition, which provided the political and moral philosophy' (Chang H-J 2002a: 540).

4 While Chang claims that his approach is closer to 'Old Institutional Economics' than to 'New Institutional Economics' (Chang H-J 2002a: 551–2), given that the spectrum of NIE is broad, his view can legitimately be located within the general inclination of institutional economics to recognise institutions as prerequisites for the existence and operation of political and economic organisations, and as an encompassing category that includes non-economic (political) constituents. Further, in an earlier article, he claims to analyse the political economy of the industrial policy of Korea 'using some recent developments in economic theory such as the New Institutional Economics' (Chang H-J 1993: 131).

5 All translations from Lee's work from Korean to English, as cited in this chapter, are mine.

6 Koo H (1993a, 1993b) and Migdal (1994) also proposed an approach comparable to 'the state in society' from the disciplinary backgrounds of sociology and politics. For instance, Koo, who specialises in the formation of the Korean working class and labour movements, proposes a broadened conception of civil society against what he calls 'the East Asian literature'. He defines civil society as constituting 'market and non-market spheres of social relations, comprising a

multitude of "market-regulated, privately controlled, or voluntarily organized" activities' and encompassing 'a complex of ideological and cultural relations, spiritual and intellectual life, and political expressions of those relations' (Koo H 1993a: 7). Under this broadened notion of civil society, he argues that '[m] odern Korean history demonstrates *complex, dialectic relationships* between the state and civil society, far more dynamic and conflict-ridden than is usually assumed in the literature' (Koo H 1993a: 4; emphasis added).

7 The idea of a 'democratic developmental state' can be found in Beeson and Islam (2005), Robinson and White (1998).

8 Chang also traces historically various protectionist and industrial policies adopted by most industrialised countries during (and after) early industrialisation, not only by late developers such as Germany and Japan but by those like Britain and the US that are often wrongly perceived as having based their development trajectory on free market policies (see Chang H-J 2002b).

9 This argument is comparable to Fine's critique of the 'post-Washington Consensus'. Fine (2001: 10) argues that 'the virtues of the market and its opposition to the state are replaced by a balance between the two'.

10 The accusation that the developmental state and its 'crony' relations with business (the *chaebol*) caused the crisis was made not only by neoclassical economists but also by democrats and left-wing social activists in Korea. The question of how the developmental state model based on the close relations between the state and the *chaebol* conditioned and imparted particular meanings to democratisation in Korea will be discussed in Part III.

11 Marxist scholars tend to emphasise the symbiotic relations between production and financial capital, although adherence to this theoretical proposition is not necessarily expressed coherently in politics: some Marxists, for example, endorse and promote (Keynesian) state control on finance. For Marxist discussions on this subject, see Marx (1956: part I, 1959: part V), Harvey (1982: chs. 3, 9, 10), Itoh and Lapavitsas (1999), Evans (2004), Fine and Saad-Filho (2004: chs. 4, 13). Marxist reception of the developmental state in the context of critiquing neoliberalism will be discussed in Chapter 3.

12 Recognising the structural constraints of global capitalism on developing countries does not automatically mean adhering to the argument of dependency theory that in order for Third World development to occur, countries in the 'periphery' should delink themselves from the world economy. Rather the recognition of 'structure-like' world-systematic constraints for development points to the dual dynamics of global capitalism, which are expansionary but at the same time highly polarising. This issue will be discussed in more detail in Part II. For the classical texts on 'dependency theory' and the 'unequal exchange thesis' see Frank (1979) and Emmanuel (1972). For a summary see Brewer (1980: chs.7, 9).

3 Old assumptions in new debates

Reproducing the statist concept of the developmental state

In this chapter, I discuss how the statist concept of the developmental state has continued to set the framework for subsequent discussions. Democratisation, the Asian financial crisis of 1997/98 and the neoliberal reforms that followed rapid industrialisation in East Asia stimulated debates about whether the developmental state still remains intact or has been dismantled. Subsequently, the global financial crisis of 2007/08 added more complexity to the debate when the credibility of free-market ideology propagated by global development institutions and the Anglo-Saxon neoliberal development model seemed to have been undermined, and state intervention appeared to remain strong or to have been revived. I identify two strands of these recent debates and critically assess them, in turn. One strand is the debate concerning the transformation of the developmental state, which addresses the question of whether the developmental state remains intact or has been transformed or 'hybridised'. This debate focusses on how much and to what extent the East Asian states retain characteristics of both the (interventionist) developmental state and (market-centred) neoliberalism. The second strand I examine is closely related to critiques of neoliberalism and the (post-) Washington Consensus, in which context the East Asian developmental state is actively reinstituted as an alternative to the neoliberal development model. I show that in spite of divergences in intellectual backgrounds and political motivations, these discussions reproduce the statist concept of the developmental state. The new debates base their arguments on whether or not the state dominates the economy and how much external or internal social force it is able to withstand. Antagonism between state and market, and between the national and the global, is taking precedence over the class antagonism between capital and labour and the contradictions of capitalist development, to which the developmental state, as a *capitalist* state, is integral.

The debate on the transformation of the developmental state

Reflecting the fact that the East Asian developmental state has been the centre of discussion amongst opposing political and intellectual traditions in explaining the rapid industrialisation of the region, the question of the transformation of the developmental state has also been intensively debated. As industrialisation was followed by democratisation, the Asian financial crisis of 1997/98 and economic liberalisation reforms, many scholars from diverse disciplinary and political backgrounds have come to raise the question of whether the developmental state remains intact or has been dismantled. As discussed in the previous chapters, the theorists of the developmental state and institutionalists have directly or indirectly taken part in the debate either by externalising the political and economic challenges from the developmental state or by reiterating its continued viability. The first phase of the debate on the transformation of the developmental state was advanced by critics of the institutionalist approach. Subsequently, the debate about the East Asian developmental state took on another dimension in line with the global financial crisis of 2007/08: the question of the transformation of the developmental state developed into a debate on the newly 'hybrid' developmental state.

Developmental vs. regulatory (neoliberal) state

As discussed in Chapter 2, institutionalists see the Asian financial crisis as the result of the policy failures of state elites who mistakenly bought into neoliberal ideology and caused the loss of the state's grip on private capitalists and the financial system. To the extent that institutionalists understand that this loss of the policy autonomy of the developmental state can be temporary as a result of the dismantlement of a set of institutions, they tend to hold the view that the developmental state can be reconstructed through institutional modifications and remain resilient against external (globalisation) forces. Jayasuriya (2001, 2005) and Pirie (2005, 2006, 2008) challenge this institutionalist view. Their key arguments in contrast to institutionalism can be summarised in three aspects.

First, if institutionalists are optimistic about the continued viability of the developmental state, Jayasuriya and Pirie hold that the Korean developmental state has metamorphosed irreversibly into a different kind of state, which they call 'regulatory state' and 'neoliberal state', respectively.[1] The transformation of the Korean *dirigiste* state into a regulatory or neoliberal state is argued for with regard to the changes in the relationship between the government and technocratic institutions, and to legal and institutional reforms undertaken, particularly in the financial sector. Pirie and Jayasuriya point out, as the signs of these changes, financial sector reform, such as the enforcement of central bank independence (the BOK Act); the creation of independent financial regulatory bodies, such as the Financial Supervisory Commission (FSC) and Financial Supervisory Agency (FSA); and a series of organisational reforms within the state apparatus and the adoption of global financial regulatory standard measures (Jayasuriya 2005: 384–5; Pirie 2005: 31–8). According to Jayasuriya and Pirie, these reforms underline an important shift in the orientations and functions of the Korean state.

> Korea went, almost overnight, from having a system of financial and monetary governance that left all major decisions in the hands of politicians, to one in which all key day-to-day decisions are made by autonomous bureaucrats – or, to put it another way, from institutional structures that supported interventionist policies to new structures that seek to embed the principles of the contemporary neoliberal order deep within the Korean state.
>
> (Pirie 2005: 38)

Second, if institutionalists argue that the financial crisis and the subsequent reforms had domestic origins, Jayasuriya and Pirie attribute the ultimate causes of the crisis and the transformation of the developmental state to structural changes in the global economy. These changes include the rise of the global financial market, the third industrial revolution and shifts in global production structures (Pirie 2005: 28, 2006: 50–3). According to Pirie, the third industrial revolution and new technological developments increased the cost of Research and Development (R&D) and accelerated the internationalisation (de-nationalisation) of production processes. These developments altered the imperatives of firms: in order to remain competitive, high technology firms increasingly sought to have access to global capital and equity markets, and to embed themselves within transnational technological networks (Pirie 2005: 28–9). These new developments in the global economy, in turn, imposed a different set of demands, beyond promoting large, nationally based firms, on 'the traditional developmental *dirigiste* Korean state' (Pirie 2005: 29–30, 2006: 51). Pirie (2005: 29) contends that 'the state comes under intense pressure to secure the confidence of global markets by reconfiguring institutional structures and policies to guarantee the integrity of the currency and the sanctity of the market order'. Likewise, Jayasuriya brings to the fore changes in the global political economy, particularly global finance as the key driver of the transformation of the state. He notes that 'the transformation of the global order and the globalisation of finance ... facilitated the emergence of changed concepts of statehood' (Jayasuriya 2005: 383–4). According to Jayasuriya and Pirie, the rise of a regulatory or neoliberal state is a response to these new demands, emanating from the changes in the global political economy.

> [T]he virtuous cycle of the East Asian political economy has become a particularly vicious cycle plunging these economies into deep crisis. But it needs to be clearly acknowledged that the crisis is not a result of policy error but rather a result of deep-seated structural changes in the international political economy.
>
> (Jayasuriya 2001: 109)

Third, Pirie and Jayasuriya's regulatory or neoliberal state intends to go beyond the institutionalist understanding of the state that is '[t]rapped within an unhelpful binary of strong and weak states' (Jayasuriya 2005: 381). Pirie (2005: 36) contends that 'the effective neoliberal state is a strong regulatory state'. In a similar vein, Jayasuriya (2005: 382) maintains that 'the crucial transformation in East Asia is from the developmental to the regulatory state, not the weakening or otherwise of the capacity of the strong state'. Therefore, according to Pirie and Jayasuriya, neoliberal projects point not to the retreat of the state but to 'the creation of a "new" state which seeks to support the functioning of market disciplines and the commodification of ever greater areas of social and economic life' (Pirie 2005: 27). Market prioritisation as the essence of neoliberalism only works with strong legal institutions, and the neoliberal state is not the same as the minimal state (Pirie 2005: 26). On the basis of this, Jayasuriya (2001: 102) argues that a central focus should be on how 'state forms (not just state power) are embedded within the particular sets of global structures ... how state structures are being reconfigured in the new global political economy'.

From magnifying the newness of the state to returning to institutionalism

Pirie and Jayasuriya's emphasis on the global economy as a force that transforms and restructures the developmental state appears to be in opposition to the institutionalist proposition that the state remains resilient against globalisation and even augments it relevance (see Chapter 2). However, a closer examination of Jayasuriya and Pirie suggests that they share rather than depart from the institutionalist framework.

First of all, Jayasuriya and Pirie return time and again to the statist concept of the developmental state to justify their argument that the developmental state is demised. They differentiate between the developmental state and the regulatory (neoliberal) state according to whether or not the state is committed to serving the national (industrial) development led by the state as opposed to the global economy. In other words, what they question is the continued viability of the developmental state, not the statist concept of the developmental state itself. Put in Pirie's own words, 'the old state-led developmental project [was] based upon "controlled" interaction with the global economy' (Pirie 2006: 53), and 'the [developmental] state was in a position to directly discipline major firms' (2006: 54) and geared toward developing 'independent exporting capacity/industrial self-sufficiency' (2006: 67). Jayasuriya (2005: 383) also notes that 'the globalisation of finance rendered problematic the very notion of "national" economic development that was so central to the evolution of the developmental state'. In this understanding, the statist concept of the developmental state is taken as given: the state and the market, and the national and the global are juxtaposed as antithetical categories.

While sharing the statist framework, the fact that Jayasuriya and Pirie refer to the global economy as the main driver of the changes in the functions of the state and its internal structures reveals these authors' limitations, which differ from those of institutionalism. Although Pirie and Jayasuriya continuously reference the structural changes in the global economy, in their assessment, globalisation itself remains unexplained beyond the deregulation of financial markets and technological advancements: there is no sustained inquiry into what actually drives these technical changes and creates the globalisation impulse. Globalisation is primarily understood, in technical terms, as a force that operates separately from the capitalist dynamic and class contradictions, and/or as a power that puts pressure on the state to change its orientation from the outside.[2] In other words, Jayasuriya and Pirie tend to conceive of state-global relations rather mechanically: heightening capital mobility (the global financial market) compels the state to adjust its inner structure in a way that is more 'congruent with a more globalised political economy' (Jayasuriya 2005: 384). Pirie argues that the reconfiguration of the structures of the Korean state is driven by the change in the global economy 'to meet the dictates of the new global order' (Pirie 2005: 26). Similarly, Jayasuriya states that '[t]he emerging complexity of the global political economy … limits the capacity of the state', and 'domestic stability … is now achieved through [the state's] credible commitment to, or compliance with, policies directed toward ensuring confidence of international markets' (Jayasuriya 2001: 101). In this framework, the global economy is posited not only as *external* to the state but as a force exerting its power over the state *newly*, something to which the state adjusts or transforms itself in line with its changing structures and needs.

Positing the global economy as external to and overwhelming the state in a new way, Pirie and Jayasuriya oppose institutionalism by magnifying discontinuities between the developmental state and its successor. In so doing, they make the rather implausible presupposition that the developmental state, before it turned into a neoliberal or regulatory state, was outside of global capitalist relations and not concerned with strengthening market discipline or extending commodification. For instance, Pirie identifies neoliberalism with a process 'essentially involv[ing] the creation of a "new" state which seeks to support the functioning of market discipline and the commodification of ever greater areas of social and economic life' (Pirie 2005: 27). Jayasuriya (2005: 384) understands the transformation in the nature of the global political economy as a process of creating 'frameworks of public authority that were more congruent with a more globalised political economy'.

Pirie and Jayasuriya seem to imply that the developmental state was not conforming to the logic of the market and the interests of individual capitalists, on the one hand, and the global economy, on the other. Stated differently, they seem to suggest that the developmental state was nationally oriented and thus remained outside the global economy, and that the economy under the developmental state was not capitalist, existing outside of commodified social relations as well as the global economy. As long as state elites appear to dominate market actors, the developmental state is seen to be free from market imperatives, while the new regulatory or neoliberal state is conceived to be functioning for the market and following the global rather than the national development logic.

Basing their arguments on a statist conception of state-market and state-global economy relations, no less than institutionalists, Jayasuriya and Pirie resort to a policy- and elite-centred analysis. For instance, while Jayasuriya (2005: 383) argues that 'state transformation ... is always a socially constituted and dynamic process', his actual analysis of state transformation in Korea includes only changes in economic governance, the organisation of political authority and new forms of social contracts (such as health care).

Similarly, Pirie locates the primary causes of the transformation of the developmental state in elite interactions at the domestic level: groups within the Korean bureaucratic circles that had long favoured neoliberal policies gained leverage over conservatives, as the financial crisis provided them with credibility and a rationale for restructuring and reforms (Pirie 2005: 26, 2006: 58).[3] To be fair, this elite-level analysis is descriptively valid, but it needed to be contextualised within capitalist contradictions and the intensive social and class struggles that took place towards the financial crisis of 1997/98. Jeong notes that Pirie's analysis of the Korean economic 'miracle' lacks any Marxist analysis of class relations, although Pirie self-identifies as a Marxist (Jeong S-J 2009: 253–4).[4]

In brief, Pirie and Jayasuriya engage in the question of the transformation of the developmental state and make a valid attempt to offer a vision alternative to the institutionalist approach by bringing to the fore the structural force of change imposed on the developmental state. Some important insights notwithstanding, their assessments of the transformation of the developmental state hardly transcend the institutionalist framework. Although these authors rightly recognise that the neoliberal project does not necessarily imply the retreat of the state, they assess the transformation of the developmental state in terms of how much it changes its orientation from the national to the global in accordance with the global economy posited as external to it. Furthermore, Jayasuriya and Pirie assess the integration of the national economy into the global economy as a matter of what policies are adopted and how rational and forceful state elites are in pursuing their aims. In so doing, they not only fail to offer a viable critique of institutionalism by taking the statist concept of the developmental state itself as given but contribute to reproducing it.

The hybrid developmental state: from the neo-developmental to the post-developmental state

The debate on the developmental state further evolved, especially after the global financial crisis of 2007/08. While liberalisation reforms intensified after the Asian financial crisis, the states in East Asia responded proactively during the global financial crisis, and their heavy involvement in the economy was noticeable in certain sectors. Accordingly, the debate on the transformation of the developmental state has taken on a new dimension. Instead of looking into a clean break between the developmental state and its successor, more recent discussions recognise the coexistence of what are believed to be the core characteristics of the developmental state with those of neoliberalism, hence the 'hybridity' of the resulting form of state. In the new debate, which I call the 'hybrid' developmental state debate, the main focus shifts from *whether or not* the East Asian states are still developmental to *how much and to what extent* they are developmental and which aspects between the two distinctive ideal types are prevalent. Given the immense literature available on these questions, I will focus on the approaches and authors that represent the respective key positions.

The first key proposition in the debate on the hybridity of the East Asian states places the greatest emphasis on the enduring features of the developmental state, characterising the contemporary East Asian states as more developmental than neoliberal. One of the key rationales that supports this line of argument is the 'path-dependency' thesis. Richard Stubbs, one of its key advocates, acknowledges that '[e]ach of the East Asian societies has ... developed a mix of state structures and policies that reflect both developmental and neo-liberal philosophies' (Stubbs 2011: 163). However, according to Stubbs, 'in no way can it [the developmental state] be said to be totally disappearing', and 'convergence of East Asian political economies on the US [neoliberal] economic model is not likely' (Stubbs 2009: 15). He bases this argument on the assumption that 'ideas and institutions have a "stickiness" or resilience, usually referred to as "path dependency" ... that continue to be influential in terms of policy making after the circumstances that elevated them to prominence have changed' (Stubbs 2009: 9). Stubbs (2011: 159) thus argues that globalisation can promote the continuity of the developmental state and that '[t]he Great Recession has bolstered the legitimacy of the developmental state coalitions, away from the structures and policies promoted by the neo-liberal coalition'. On the basis of these reasonings, he (2011: 163) envisages that 'many key developmental state structures, policies, and indeed, ideas survive and will remain very much part of the political economy of East Asia well into the future'.

Another key proposition in the debate recognises the enduring characteristics of the developmental state in East Asia but puts more emphasis on changes that it has undergone than Stubbs and others (e.g. Hayashi 2010) would be ready to acknowledge. This position is shared by authors such as David Hundt, Tomas Kalinowski and Yin-wah Chu, all of whom put forward their respective arguments with respect to Korea.[5] For instance, Hundt contends that even if it is usually taken as a case of successful neoliberal reform, there is 'a much stronger degree of continuity with the pre-crisis period'. This is due to the fact that the 'pressing need to overcome the economic crisis became a powerful new rationale for a continuation of state leadership' (Hundt 2015: 467), and '[n]eoliberalism … has offered the Korean state a new set of rhetorical tools with which to justify its hold on power' (Hundt 2015: 470). Hundt suggests thinking of neoliberalism 'as an environment condition to which states adapt with various degrees of success' and concludes that '[i]n the case of Korea, neoliberalism has not fundamentally transformed the developmental state' (2015: 470). However, he equally recognises important changes that have taken place since the Asian financial crisis and the global financial crisis: state intervention has become less effective, and industrial policy has been practiced on a reduced scale and has moved away from 'purely nationalist ends' in terms of its orientation (Hundt 2014: 509–11). In order to make the point that the developmental state has adopted new forms of assistance to industry but with less transformative impact on the economy than before, Hundt defines the contemporary Korean state as a 'degraded developmental state'.

Kalinowski also comes up with a new label for the post-crisis Korean state: 'neo-developmental state'. He understands that the rapid recovery of the Korean economy from the Asian financial crisis was thanks to the '"traditional strengths" of the pre-crisis developmental state, resting on export orientation and strong state capacity' (Kalinowski 2008: 447). However, he argues that this large scale of state interventionism amounts to 'the last stage of the developmental state in Korea' (2008: 447). This is because there have been significant changes in state-business relations and in the nature of state intervention which render the restoring of the old developmental state implausible. Kalinowski (2008: 450) notes that 'state interventions [after the crisis] are becoming less and less strategic and more and more reactive, mitigating the economic and social costs of market-reoriented reforms'. He therefore argues that 'any attempt to return to an old-style developmental state has to fail, because it would require getting the *chaebol* back under the control of the state' (Kalinowski 2008: 450). According to Kalinowski, while industrial policies have not been abolished, the Korean state's industrial policy has transformed from macro-economic planning to micro-interventionism. Further, while the Korean government's fiscal spending in response to the global financial crisis is much greater than that of liberal market economies (e.g. the US) and European neo-corporatist states (e.g. Germany and the Nordic welfare states), the government, instead of forcing companies to reinvest their profits, spends its own funds to support companies, particularly Small and Medium-sized Enterprises (SMEs) (2015: 258). On the basis of this analysis, Kalinowski (2015: 258) concludes that 'increased government spending, industrial policies and export promotion do not indicate a return of the "old developmental state" but rather signal the transformation to a "neo-developmental state"'.

Another account similar to Kalinowski's is offered by Yin-wah Chu (2009). Chu challenges the view that the East Asian developmental state has succumbed to the forces of globalisation but acknowledges at the same time the ways in which its developmental role has undergone significant changes.

Scrutinising Korean government policy and its manner of intervention, particularly in the information technology sector, Chu (2009: 296–7) concludes that 'the Korean state continues to play a developmental role', and '[s]tate elites … continue to believe that … it is imperative for the state to assume leadership in matters of national economic development'. However, there has been a major shift since 'the implementation of government initiatives no longer relies on the threat of coercion or the provision of cheap bank loans' (Chu 2009: 297). In an attempt to capture the continuities and discontinuities of the developmental state legacy, yet not overemphasise 'the weight of institutional path dependency … to the neglect of Korea's ongoing politico-economic transformation', Chu (2009: 298) proposes a new term for the contemporary Korean state: namely, 'a reconfigured developmental state'.

If Hundt, Kalinowski and Chu assess the hybridity of the contemporary East Asian states, particularly the Korean state, from a perspective that stresses the prevalence of the characteristics of the developmental state over its counter-ideal type of a 'neoliberal state', another key argument in the debate understands the contemporary East Asian states as more neoliberal than developmental. For example, Iain Pirie, moving away from his earlier argument that the Korean state has transformed itself into a neoliberal state (see above), argues that 'this [neoliberal transformalist] concept of a decisive neoliberal shift fails to capture the full complexity of the contemporary Korean political economy' (Pirie 2012b: 366). He recognises that the 2008 global financial crisis weakened the global hegemony of neoliberalism, and 'it reinforced certain features of Korean industrial policy that directly challenge neo-liberal principles and further undermined (the already highly compromised independence) of the Bank of Korea' (Pirie 2012a: 418). From this, Pirie (2012a: 418) argues that 'the Korean state cannot be seen as either pursuing a coherent neo-liberal programme or systematically seeking to reserve key neo-liberal (market opening) reforms.'

While not ignoring sectoral differences in the level of endurance of 'developmentalism', Pirie gravitates towards the view that neoliberalism prevails over developmentalism. Tracing changes in the role of investment in Korea and Taiwan, he argues that 'the allocation of capital and capital-relations have been largely marketised … meaning that the essential elements of the neo-liberal project are in place' (2018: 141). Pirie (2018: 139) concludes that 'contemporary Korea and Taiwan cannot be defined as developmental states' because 'the structural conditions for the existence of a developmental state … has been eroded by the transition from an environment of capital shortage to capital surplus'. He finally arrives at the conclusion that the contemporary Korean and Taiwanese states 'maintain a greater commitment to industrial and credit activism than other neo-liberal states', but their pattern has shifted to 'selective intervention within a marketised/depoliticised economy' (Pirie 2018: 141). On this ground, he proposes the new term 'post-developmental state' to better capture the essence of the contemporary Korean and Taiwanese states.

Apart from these key authors, there are numerous other researchers and scholars who have engaged in the debate on the transformation of the developmental state.[6] Defining the contemporary Korean state has also been one of the key subjects of debate amongst Korean scholars in recent years (for a summary see Park S-Y 2015). To introduce a few, Joo-Hyoung Ji (2009, 2013) holds that the Korean state has shifted from the 'authoritarian developmental state' to the 'neoliberal state' and argues that neoliberalism in Korea is characterised not by the retreat of the state but by 'the intervention by technocrats'. Sang-Woo Yoon (2009) defines the Korean characteristics of neoliberalism as 'developmental neoliberalisation' based on the idea that neoliberal policies, such as the deregulation of financial institutions and foreign investment, are used for developmental goals, such as high growth and export. Referring to the Lee Myung-Bak government's (2008–13) active involvement in and promotion of development policies in the construction sector, which was paralleled by radical deregulation and privatisation, Myeong-Rae Cho (2008) characterised it as a 'neoliberal developmental state'. Some authors, like Don Moon and Jin-Young Chung (2014), even reject the term 'hybrid', given that every state in transition entails both developmental and neoliberal characteristics. For this reason, they propose that the focus should be on the most essential characteristics and argue that the Korean state has shifted to a neoliberal state, given fundamental changes in state-finance-firm relations.[7]

Old assumptions in new debates

The discussion of the transformation of the developmental state sheds light on various changes taking place in East Asia, especially since the Asian financial crisis and the global financial crisis. Furthermore, assessing the different degrees of the 'hybridity' of developmental and neoliberal elements rather than seeking a clean break between the two can be seen as an effort to capture the complexity of the political and economic transformations taking place in the countries that had been characterised as 'developmental states'. Important empirical insights and merits notwithstanding, the recent and ongoing discussions of the 'hybridity' of the developmental state shows yet again how much the statist framework set by the early theorists of the developmental state and institutionalists informs the ways in which the transformation of the developmental state is assessed.

As the present discussion of the transformation of the developmental state has shown, there is disagreement over the degree of its recent 'hybridity', but there is consensus on the statist assumptions attached to the concept of the developmental state itself. No matter how much the characteristics of the developmental state are seen to be retained or not, the reference point from which the transformation of the developmental state is assessed is the statist framework, in which state and market, and state and global economy are set as antithetical categories in a 'zero-sum' relationship.

For instance, while Stubbs insists that the developmental state legacy is resilient, he holds that globalisation does erode it: '[t]he Cold War became less of a dominant factor in global affairs as the forces of globalization took over' (Stubbs 2009: 10). This 'fallout from the end of the Cold War tends to undermine the independence of the bureaucracy' as well as 'the expressions of nationalism and the priority given to security during the Cold War' (Stubbs 2009: 10). Similarly, Kalinowski forges the argument that the developmental state has transformed into a 'neo-developmental state' on the ground that 'the effectiveness of technocratic policies is declining', and the 'decline of technocratic capacity is linked to ... declining state autonomy' (Kalinowski 2015: 261). Even Pirie, who claims to oppose Stubbs, displays the same statist assumption attached to the developmental state when he notes that '[n]eoliberal reform need not necessarily be understood to mark the end of industrial policy. Rather, it simply means an end to policies of shielding firms from, or managing integration into, world markets' (Pirie 2012b: 371). In short, even if the degree of the hybridity of the developmental state is contested, what guides this discussion is how much the state is able and willing to shield itself from the economy or from capitalists (the *chaebol*, in the case of Korea), on the one hand, and from the global economic forces, on the other, thereby making itself able to pursue the goal of national and industrial development.

While statism underlies the debate on the 'hybridity' of the developmental state, it manifests itself now in a manner that differs from earlier debates. Unlike the theorists of the developmental state and institutionalists who are politically committed to the developmental state, those engaged in the debate on the 'hybridity' of the developmental state do not necessarily endorse either the developmental or the neoliberal state as superior to the other. However, if the original concept of the developmental state was established in conversation with and through active engagement with competing intellectual traditions regarding state-market and state-global economy relations, as seen in Chapters 1 and 2, the new debate tends to bypass concept-driven inquiry. Instead, it is preoccupied with the question of how much the developmental state retains its core characteristics and how to best *describe* the balance between developmental and neoliberal elements.

As there could exist numerous levels of 'hybridity' in the continuum with the developmental state at one end and the neoliberal state at the opposite end, there has been a proliferation of new terms attempting to define contemporary East Asian states, from 'neo-developmental state', 'degraded developmental state' and 'reconfigured developmental state' to 'post-developmental state'. In this context, the developmental state model is juxtaposed with the neoliberal model, and these two models are treated as the only viable ideal-type economic development models.[8] This way of framing the question of the transformation of the developmental state has important political implications, independent of and in opposition to the intention of those engaged in the debate: it reduces the question of development to a combination or oscillation between these two stylised models, thereby confining the political imagination to a binary choice between them.

To the extent that those engaged in the 'hybridity' debate emphasise the compatibility of the developmental and neoliberal elements, they (unintendedly) reduce the difference between these heretofore contested views to a level that is increasingly meaningless and insignificant. The more the 'hybridity' is emphasised, the less obvious the differences between the competing views become. Pirie himself acknowledges this point when he states that '[m]any of the policies [seen] as key evidence of the renewal of the developmental state could as easily be defined as converging with actually existing neoliberalism' (Pirie 2012b: 372).

In reaction to this 'assimilation' or 'blurring' effect, those engaged in the debate show the propensity to exaggerate the differences that exist between the characteristics of the developmental and the neoliberal state, which might appear to be trivial to others. For instance, Chu finds a sign of the 'reconfigured developmental state' in the fact that instead of government leadership involving only top-down imposition of the government's will, it 'now also includes wide-ranging consultations, arbitration of differences, and the making of controversial decisions when necessary' (Chu 2009: 297). Kalinowski finds evidence of the rise of a 'neo-developmental state' in the shift in the orientation of industrial policy from 'making winners' to 'picking winners' (Kalinowski 2015: 260) and in the fact that 'the state … is less strategic, and less associated with "midwifery" than with a "nursing" function – feeding the losers of market reforms and cleaning up the mess when markets get out of control' (Kalinowski 2008: 450). Hundt detects a sign of the decline of the developmental state element in the fact that industrial policy results 'in "finetuning" rather than … [direct] forms of intervention' (Hundt 2014: 507). Pirie differentiates the developmental state from the 'post-developmental state' based on whether 'pursuit of industrial policy is *the* primary objective of the state … [or] it is simply an important objective' (Pirie 2018: 139; emphasis in the original). As a consequence of schematising (minor) differences between the two economic models, these authors hardly ask the more fundamental question as to what *unifies* the two models in spite of their apparent differences. To put this differently, what is lacking in the debate on the 'hybridity' of the contemporary developmental state is an inquiry into the *capitalist* state and its form of existence within the capitalist world-system before it is defined as developmental, neoliberal or otherwise.

Another problematic of the 'hybrid' developmental state debate becomes apparent in its approach to the 'path-dependency' thesis. It is not only Stubbs who finds the enduring characteristics of the developmental state in 'institutional stickiness' or 'path-dependency'. Kalinowski, who argues that the return to the old developmental state would not be possible, notes that 'the specific character of fiscal policies [after the global financial crisis] can largely be explained by the path dependency of East Asian developmental state capitalism' (Kalinowski 2015: 246). Pirie (2018: 141), who asserts that the 'developmental state is dead', resorts to the 'path-dependency' thesis to justify his new term 'post-developmental state', noting that in 'Korea and Taiwan contemporary systems of governance reflect the impact of substantial neo-liberal reform and the importance of path-dependency' (Pirie 2018: 150). By the same token, Hundt, who claims that the original developmental state has been 'degraded', believes that 'the developmental state … is a permanent feature of East Asian political economy' (Hundt 2014: 501). These supposedly contrary perspectives have in common that they explain institutional elements associated with the developmental state but resistant to change via 'path-dependency'.

However, this way of explicating the resilience of the developmental state is questionable not least because its central argument, that the legacy of past ideas and institutions interacts with and influences the present, is most banal. More importantly, the reasons for 'path-dependency' itself, the societal origins and class foundations that make certain institutions form, dominate and persist, are not accounted for. For example, Kalinowski finds the reason for 'a lack of vision and political support for an alternative to the utopian US-style market system and the anachronistic state-centred approaches of the past' in the fact that 'Korea has experience neither with a democratically controlled interventionist state nor with a redistributive welfare state' (Kalinowski 2008: 460). Pirie (2018: 151) also finds the main cause for '[l]ow levels of independent union membership, the de-legitimisation of social democratic parties and the underdevelopment of welfare systems in contemporary Korea and Taiwan' in 'their histories as developmental states'. To be fair, these authors intend to offer a critical assessment of contemporary Korean and Taiwanese societies, but their reasoning is based on a circular argument: they explain the developmental state legacy through that legacy itself.

To put this differently, paraphrasing Rosenberg's critique of 'globalisation theory' (2000: 3), they short-circuit *explanans* and *explanandum*: instead of seeing 'path-dependency' as the emerging outcome of a historical process that needs to be explained, they posit 'path-dependency' (the developmental state legacy) as its own explanation. This not only reveals that the debate of 'hybridity' is flawed from a logical standpoint; more critically, it has the effect of erasing the historical and societal origins of the developmental state and rendering it immune from societal and historical dynamics. In so doing it solidifies the statist characterisation of the developmental state even further, grounding it on a permanent basis.

In summary, subsequent to the first phase of the debate on the transformation of the developmental state based on the question of whether the developmental state remains intact or has been dismantled, discussions of the developmental state have evolved into the debate on the 'hybridity' of the developmental state. Accordingly, instead of suggesting a clean break between the developmental state and its successor, in the new debate, the focus has shifted to how 'hybrid' the East Asian states have become. In spite of some valid empirical insights, the debate about 'hybridity' also shows, as much as the first phase of the debate, how deeply the statist conception of the developmental state is taken as given in the assessment of the transformation of the developmental state. Moreover, preoccupied with the apparent differences between the two schematised economic development models, the debate bypasses the most fundamental aspect that unifies the two ideal-type state models juxtaposed as antithetical in the debate, that is, the *capitalist* nature of the state.

Reinstituting the developmental state in critiques of neoliberalism

Besides those who argue for the neoliberal transformation of the developmental state and those engaged in the 'hybrid' developmental state debate who are *not* politically devoted to the developmental state, there is another group of contributors to these discussions who purposefully aim to reinstitute the developmental state as an alternative to a neoliberal (market-led) development model. This tendency is most evident in contemporary Marxists' critiques of neoliberalism and the '(post-) Washington consensus'. The rise of neoliberalism as a dominant ideology has been a subject of intensive debate amongst Marxist scholars, particularly with reference to the structural crisis, the end of the so-called 'Golden Age' towards the end of the 1960s and the concomitant attack on and retreat from the welfare state (Armstrong et al. 1991; Clarke 1988; Harvey 2005; Saad-Filho and Johnston 2005). Recognising the complexity of and immense literature available on this topic, I will focus here on how the statist concept of the developmental state is unproblematically adopted by some Marxist scholars, especially in the context of critiquing neoliberalism, financial imperialism and the (post-) Washington Consensus.

Good vs. bad capitalism

One of the main approaches that can be identified in Marxists' discussions relating to the developmental state is to casually take for granted its established statist assumptions. For instance, Robert Brenner (1998), in his analysis of the causes of the structural crisis in major economies, such as the US, Germany and Japan during 1950–98, bases his references to East Asian industrialisation solely on works by Amsden and Wade. While arguing that the increased entry of East Asian economies, such as Korea, Taiwan, Singapore and Hong Kong, into manufacturing exacerbated the overproduction/overcapacity problem, he adopts the conventional statist view that '[t]he export-dependence of the East Asian statist "organised capitalisms" reached extraordinary proportions and was one of the central foundations of their ability so rapidly to raise productivity' (Brenner 1998: 150). Consequently, rather than analysing these states in terms of class contradictions associated with capitalist development, Brenner is more attentive to how 'the East Asian states made sure not only to provide public goods at high levels ... but also to deliver, through a combination of repression and material gains, relatively "cooperative" labour forces' (Brenner 1998: 150).

Another, arguably more common, position within Marxist critiques of neoliberalism in relation to the developmental state is to actively defend the perceived peculiarities of the developmental state and the corresponding development trajectory against forces such as neoliberalism or imperialism that are deemed to disintegrate them. For instance, William Tabb, in his assessment of the Asian financial crisis, holds that when the financial crisis hit East Asia, 'Asia's political insider capitalists are forced to surrender ownership and control to them [international capital] as condition for any rescue' (Tabb 1998: 36). In this account, post-crisis reforms and liberalisation are seen to be driven by external forces and under pressure from the US and the IMF. Tabb states that 'Korea has granted foreign investors control over Korean companies and banks, something it had steadfastly refused until forced to its knees by the financial crisis' (Tabb 1998: 37). Likewise, Bello explains the 'miracle of Korea' through its dependence on 'local financial resources extracted through a rigorous system of taxation plus profits derived from the sale of goods to a protected domestic market and to foreign markets opened by an aggressive mercantilist strategy' rather than foreign capital (Bello 1998). Bello and Cunningham then defend the alleged state-led and nationalist policies adopted in Korea. For example, they describe its economy as 'the NIC [Newly Industrialised Countries] *par excellence*' and 'as a "command capitalist" regime, where the state built up industry not only by putting into place trade and investment regimes favouring domestic enterprises but also engaging in production itself, with singular success' (Bello and Cunningham 1994: 446). In this understanding, the state-global economy relations are posited as internal-external relations, and Korean development prior to the financial crisis is conceived as internally (nationally) oriented and protected by the state against the external.

Some authors, such as Stephen Gill, go as far as arguing that the Asian financial crisis was part of a US strategy to dismantle the East Asian model or 'shift away from state capitalism towards a free market system based on investor interests and the maximization of shareholder value' (Gills 1999: 3). In this formulation, Gill emphasises divergences 'between Anglo American and [East Asian] state capitalist models' (1999: 4) and portrays the latter as 'dedicated capital systems' whereby 'the government generally has tended to negotiate adjustments amongst affected groups ("stakeholders") within society, including workers ... with the help of business networks' (Gill 1999: 4–5).

The same tendency to demarcate different models of capitalist social formations and to posit one variation as more desirable than others is also found in the work of Peter Gowan. In his critique of the alleged US dominance of the global financial system, Gowan (2004: 17) argues that US financial imperialism pressed other countries, particularly Japan and other East Asian countries, to 'adopt corporate governance systems that are stock market based and oriented to "shareholder value"'. Positing US imperialism as a disintegrating force of the developmental state model, Gowan applauds what are deemed to be the peculiarities of East Asian economies. Referring to Japan, he notes that the 'pattern of Japanese capitalist expansion has been different in the 1980s and 1990s simply because Japanese capitalism has been far more genuinely *productive* as a *national* capitalist system than the capitalisms of the Atlantic world' (Gowan 1999: 127; emphasis added).

Similarly, David Harvey segments different kinds of capitalist development in his critique of neoliberalism.[9] Basing his analysis of the Korean developmental state on the main contributors to the statist conceptualisation of the East Asian states, such as Wade and Veneroso (1998a) and Woo-Cumings (2003), Harvey applauds the export-led success stories of Japan, West Germany and the Asian 'tigers' in the 1980s as opposed to those of countries such as the US and the UK that experienced economic difficulty after taking a more strongly neoliberal path. On the basis of this, he states that it 'was hard not to conclude that the West German and Asian "regimes" of accumulation were deserving of emulation' (Harvey 2005: 89). Similarly, even if he notes that 'independent unions were weak and rates of labour exploitation were high' he portrays 'the tight relationship between corporations and banks in Japan' as 'felicitous' because they 'generated an astonishing export-led growth performance in the 1980s' (Harvey 2005: 89).

Harvey's presentation of state-led capitalist development as preferable to other types resonates with his distinction between 'hegemony-based US imperialism' (1945–70) and 'neoliberal US imperialism' (1970–2000). The first period is characterised by accumulation of capital through expanded reproduction, when 'profits were reinvested in growth as well as in new technologies, fixed capital, and extensive infrastructural improvements' (Harvey 2003: 57). In contrast, neoliberal imperialism corresponds to the era of financial volatility and speculation detached from production, turning to a violently predatory mode of capital accumulation that is 'accumulation by dispossession' (see also Harvey 1982: Ch. 13, 2003: 137–82). Consequently, his vision of an alternative to the new imperialism is the return to a 'benevolent' form of capitalism, alongside what he calls 'more [state] interventionist and redistributive lines' on a domestic level and what he calls 'New Deal' imperialism on a global level (Harvey 2003: 209).

The developmental state against the (post-) Washington Consensus

Much like the Marxist critiques of neoliberalism and financial imperialism, Ben Fine, a vocal critic of neoclassical orthodoxy, finds in the developmental state aspects that are more progressive than market-dominant and World Bank-dictated development. While neoclassical economics has softened its free-market stance, becoming more receptive to the idea of market failure and state intervention, a tendency usually dubbed 'post-Washington Consensus' as opposed to 'Washington Consensus', Fine argues that there are more continuities than differences between the two (Fine 2001, 2006a, 2013; see also Chapter 1; Andreoni and Chang 2017). According to Fine, in spite of its increased receptiveness to state interventionism, the 'post-Washington Consensus' or the 'new structural economics' (e.g. Lin 2017) still fail to fully acknowledge the positive role of the state in development (see Fine 2013).

Therefore, Fine's problem with the 'post-Washington Consensus' has to do with the fact that the term 'the developmental state' is unrecognised in new development discourses, and the World Bank's newly exploited concept of 'social capital' is used as 'a device to outflank and marginalise adoption of the developmental state in the shift to the Washington Consensus to the post-Washington Consensus' (Fine 2013: 1; see also Fine 2006b). Fine (2013: 2) finds '[t]he limited influence of the DSP [Developmental State Paradigm] … all the more unfortunate in light of the responses to the global crisis'. He thus laments that 'the developmental state has with few exceptions failed to emerge as a prominent alternative as a response to, or in anticipation of, the crisis' (Fine 2013: 2), and that 'the Developmental State Paradigm (DSP) has been diluted, eroded and induced to be complicit with the new structural economics' (Fine 2013: 29). Arguing that the DSP's 'failure has had much more to do with the stranglehold that neoliberalism has exerted over this field of study' (Fine 2013: 2), what Fine calls for in the name of moving 'beyond the developmental state' (Fine et al. 2013) is in fact its renewal and expansion.[10] He searches for ways to revive the DSP by overcoming its limits so that it can be applied both to the examples of success and failure of development, and beyond its narrow focus on state-industry relations. In other words, Fine actively seeks to reinstitute it as an alternative to neoliberal orthodoxy or the '(post)-Washington Consensus'.

A review of contemporary Marxist discussions of neoliberalism, financial imperialism and the (post-) Washington Consensus in light of a critique of statism shows how the statist presuppositions attached to the concept of the developmental state have been taken for granted more often than they have been problematised. In some Marxist critiques of neoliberalism and neoclassical economics, the notion that the developmental state is autonomous from social actors has become the touchstone of assessments of what followed subsequently. Capitalism is divided according to its different orientations or organisations, for instance, whether it is geared towards production or finance, national or global, and state or market, and one side of these pairs of concepts is favoured over the other. Neoliberalism is defined as the market taking over the state and the external domain overriding internal (developmental) priorities. The 'post-Washington Consensus' is criticised for marginalising the 'developmental state' and thereby undermining development prospects both in developed and developing countries.

Within this framework, the more neoliberalism and neoclassical orthodoxy is criticised, the more the (interventionist) developmental state appears to represent a mode of development that is more national, more productive or growth-inducing and less contradictory than what was to follow it. In so doing, the Marxists examined in this section not only take the statist presupposition of the developmental state for granted, but they become active defenders. As an effect, they neglect the conflict- and contradiction-ridden capitalist development of which the developmental state is an intrinsic part while celebrating its ability to plan and achieve (national) development. It is not mere coincidence that the Marxists appraised in this chapter and the theorists of the developmental state converge into critiquing US imperialism (see Amsden 2007; Johnson 2004; Wade 2006): both groups of scholars have become advocates of the developmental state in the name of production-centred, nationally oriented capitalism. This insensitivity to the capitalist contradictions of the developmental state is in part related to the way in which these authors understand capitalist contradictions. Most Marxist scholars discussed in this section, from Brenner, Tabb, Gill, and Gowan to Harvey, commonly find the causes of capitalist crisis in overproduction. Once it is posited that the fundamental structural problems of capitalism lie in overproduction, caused by uncoordinated production, 'organised (state) capitalism' is likely to be considered superior to 'market-led less organised capitalism'. In this context, the state is likely to be seen as the agent that can resolve or mitigate the problem of overproduction rather than as an embodiment or part of the contradictions of capitalist social and production relations.

Conclusion

This chapter has discussed how pervasively the statist concept of the developmental state is adapted and reproduced in the debates on its transformation, on the one hand, and in Marxist critiques of neoliberalism and the (post-) Washington Consensus, on the other.

Jayasuriya and Pirie's challenge to institutionalism and the 'hybrid' developmental state debate show that the ultimate reference point that guides these new discussions is the statist concept. The discussions revolve around the question of how much and to what extent the state intervenes in the economy, and how much it replaces or keeps its autonomy and its national orientation intact against the forces of the market and the global economy. On the other hand, some Marxist critiques of neoliberalism and neoclassical orthodoxy juxtapose production with finance capitalism; national with global capitalism; and, by implication, good with bad capitalism, in which the developmental state represents the former of these bipolar categories. While coming from different intellectual traditions and political intentions, both sets of discussions relating to the developmental state examined in this chapter fail to conceptualise the state as an integral aspect of, or as the political form of, the totality of capitalist social relations. Once this is unrecognised or inadequately conceptualised, the transformation of the developmental state is reduced to the oscillation between the two schematised economic developmental models.

From a critical appraisal of an extensive range of literature on the developmental state undertaken in Part I, some important insights and lessons can be drawn in highlighting what a theoretical framework alternative to the statist conceptualisation of the developmental state should entail. Above all, the review of the dominant literature on the subject underscores the fact that the statist concept has two dimensions: the developmental state is seen as autonomous from the (domestic) economy, on the one hand, and from the global economy, on the other. In other words, within the idea of the policy autonomy of the developmental state, it is implicit that it is the agent of national development, serving general as opposed to private interests: the statist concept of the developmental state as autonomous from the economy is intertwined with the idea of its autonomy from the external or the global. It can be derived from this that without locating the state as a political form of capitalist social relations, and at the same time resolving the dichotomy between the national and the global, any scholarly discussions are likely to dichotomise the state and the market, the internal and the external, and the national and the global as antithetical categories, and reduce the question of development to the oscillations between these two categories.

On the basis of these insights drawn out from the critique of statism in Part I, I will now embark on constructing an alternative theoretical framework in Part II.

Notes

1 Pirie's view seems to have changed over the years, especially after the global financial crisis of 2007/08. His early work tends to emphasise the rise of a new Korean state, implying a break from its old *dirigisme*, while his later work tends to argue a more moderate view on the transformation of the Korean state. His later work will be discussed below.

2 While there is much literature on globalisation, relevant literature concerning the current subject can be broadly divided into two positions. The first position emphasises the diminishing significance of the state, as argued by 'globalisation enthusiasts' such as Scholte (2000) and Held and McGrew (2000). The other position, that of 'sceptics' of globalisation, tends to stress the enduring power of the state or policy autonomy *vis-à-vis* the global economy. This latter view is also broadly upheld by what is referred to as 'institutionalism' in this volume (see Chapter 2). For critiques of the view that globalisation undermines the state, see Barrow (2005) and Rosenberg (2000).

3 Pirie's elite-centred view is also evident when he argues that the long-term recession of the Japanese economy is due to the inability (or unwillingness) of Japanese state (elites) to adapt fully to global structural change (Pirie 2005: 39).

4 Pirie tends to emphasise the stability rather than the contradictions of the neoliberal regime of accumulation in Korea: he writes that 'contemporary Korea is fundamentally a *strong* neoliberal economy' or 'a *stable* neoliberal regime of accumulation' after structural problems associated with the Asian financial crisis were resolved (Pirie 2008: 149, 198: emphasis added). He further asserts that the move to the neoliberal model is 'a *logical* attempt to secure Korea's position

as a site of accumulation within a rapidly changing global economy' and 'a *rational* response to structural changes in the global economy' (Pirie 2005: 25). From these, some classify his work as 'right-wing' (Moon and Chung 2014: 139) or liberal (Hundt 2015: 467). Jeong (2009: 254) also points out that Pirie explains the causes of the development of the Korean economy from institutional legacies of Japanese colonialism, which is 'the most reactionary version of the developmental state theory'. This seems to come, in part, from the fact that Pirie is influenced by Kolhi (1997, 1999, 2004) or related work without assessing competing historical analyses and their different political implications. There is much literature on this topic that is highly controversial in Korea and beyond (see, for example, Booth and Deng 2017; Lee B-C 2011; Yi M-Y 1997). The debate on the relation between Japanese colonialism and capitalist development in Korea (and its former colonies) will be discussed in Chapter 7.

5 For a similar debate, specifically on Taiwan, see Haggard and Zheng (2012) and Wong (2005), and on Japan and China see Beeson (2009).

6 For instance, while not proposing a new term, Wai-chung Yeung (2017: 84) assesses the transformation of the developmental state in terms of changes in intensity: 'evolved from strong home states nurturing weak domestic firms in their early decades of industrialisation … to relatively weakened home states focusing on facilitating globally competitive national firms'.

7 While the Korean scholars' debate on the transformation of the developmental state is on par with the one taking place amongst Western scholars, they tend to be more attentive to the social consequences of the transition, particularly the casualisation of the labour market and the authoritarian character of 'democratic' governments. In this chapter, my critique will focus on the literature published in English.

8 To be more precise, Kalinowski (2015: 245–7) discusses more than two ideal types of states. He differentiates the East Asian state-model from the liberal, (neo-)corporatist or welfare states in the West. However, in this formulation, capitalist development is reduced to a few ideal-type models, particularly along the West and the East. His discussion of 'varieties of capitalism' is concerned with how much the East Asian model converges into or diverges from the models identified as prevailing in the West.

9 Harvey also draws extensively on Chibber (2003), who understands state-capital relations in individualist terms between state elites and capitalists. Limits of Chibber's work will be discussed in Chapter 4.

10 A more systematic attempt has been made to explore the applicability of 'Developmental States beyond East Asia' in a Special Issue of *Third World Quarterly* (2018). This issue precisely aims to 'directly engag[e] the "transferability" debate: that is, the extent to which the developmental state (DS) model(s) can be adapted beyond East Asia's geographical, socio-political and historical conditions to provide alternative ways of doing development in the Global South' (Nem Singh and Ovadia 2018: 1034). Its primary concern lies in *how* the success story of 'catch-up' development in East Asia can be reproduced while taking the success itself for granted.

Part II

Theorising the developmental state beyond statism

4 Traditional Marxist theories of the state as class content analysis and their application to the Korean developmental state

In this and the subsequent two chapters that constitute Part II, I will construct an alternative theorisation of the developmental state beyond statism. As it primarily originates from the fact that development is posited outside a critique of capitalism, an alternative framework requires bringing the questions of *capitalist* development and the *capitalist* state to the fore. In this regard, assessing Marxist theories of the capitalist state is necessarily a starting point. As a first step, I identify and critically review two approaches to the capitalist state within the Marxist tradition. One, more traditional, perspective is what I call the 'class *content* analysis' of the capitalist state, which finds its essence in its function or role servicing the interests of the capitalist class (instrumentalism), or helping maintain the capitalist mode of production structurally (structuralism), two positions which were famously expressed in the Miliband-Poulantzas debate in the late 1960s and early 1970s. In this chapter, I discuss the key premises of the Miliband-Poulantzas debate and how the instrumentalist and structuralist accounts are reflected in discussions of the (Korean) developmental state in the works of Vivek Chibber, Paul Cammack and other Marxists. I contend that, key strengths and important insights notwithstanding, 'class content analysis' fails to grasp the historically specific *capitalist form* or character of the (modern) state as well as the fact that the (modern) state is the political *form* of capitalist society and, as a result, fundamentally shares the mainstream (statist) framework, in which the dichotomous appearance of state and market is either taken for granted or inadequately theorised in relation to the capitalist mode of production. In Chapter 5, I will assess an alternative Marxist tradition, which I call the 'social *form* critique', that addresses the historically specific *form* of the state in capitalism beyond and in addition to its class *content*, and how this approach has been applied to the Korean developmental state. The critical appraisal of these two main Marxist strands of theorising the capitalist state and their reflections in the discourse on the developmental state will be the base on which my attempt to theorise the developmental state without succumbing to statism will be constructed in Chapter 6.

The class content analysis of the capitalist state

As discussed in Part I, the statist conceptualisation of the developmental state as autonomous from the (global) economy and neutral in terms of class interests flows from the fact that capitalist development itself remains unproblematised. The starting point of a challenge to statism thus involves bringing to the fore the question of the state in relation to capitalist development, a process in which class contradictions and antagonism are inherent. Scholars working within the Marxist tradition have addressed the questions of the capitalist state extensively; the central theme of Marxist discussions of the capitalist state has been how to conceptualise the essence of the state in relation to the dynamics and requirements of capitalism as a system of class domination.

However, these discussions have been neither uniform nor uncontentious.[1] While Marx's plan to elaborate a coherent theory of the state did not materialise, he and Engels analysed the capitalist state in instrumental terms, stating that it is an instrument that serves the interests of the bourgeoisie. This proposition was famously expressed in *The Communist Manifesto* (1985 [1848]): the 'executive of the modern State is but a committee for managing the common affairs of the whole bourgeoisie' (Marx and Engels 1985: 82). On the other hand, a view that assesses the state in relation to and as a reflection of struggles between different social classes could be drawn from Marx's writings, such as *The Class Struggles in France* (1850) and *The Eighteenth Brumaire of Louis Bonaparte* (1852).[2] In these works, complex interplays between various political, ideological (religious) and social forces as well as within and between fractions of social classes were brought to light in assessing the 1848 revolution and the coup by Louis Bonaparte in France, respectively. The rise of Bonapartism, a dictatorship or an 'autonomous' form of the state, is analysed with reference to class struggle and a particular class power balance in which neither bourgeoisie nor other classes were dominant, especially when the former was divided and faced challenges from various factions of other classes. Marx's analyses of these historical events are rich in detail and sophisticated in capturing various dimensions at play in the real world. Yet the very richness of these writings, incorporating various aspects of social struggles, makes it difficult to pin down their theoretical stance on the state (Abrams 1992: ch. 3; Knuttila and Kubik 2001: 98–9; see also Miliband 1965: 1; Poulantzas 1969: 67–8, 1976: 80). Arguably, Marx and Engels's works that address different levels of complexity rather than presenting a systematic theory of the state developed largely into either an approach that emphasises the instrumental functions of the state for the capitalist class (instrumentalism) or one that assesses the capitalist state in terms of its structural functions, i.e. the maintenance of capitalism as a whole.

Instrumentalist-structuralist accounts of the capitalist state

The Miliband-Poulantzas debate that took place in the late 1960s and early 1970s has been regarded as one of the key instances of Marxist discussions on the capitalist state based on instrumentalist-structuralist accounts.[3] The core proposition by Ralph Miliband is to address the capitalist state as '"the instrument" of a ruling class so designated by virtue of its ownership or control – or both – of the main means of economic activity' (Miliband 1983: 58). 'The state in ... class societies is primarily and inevitably the guardian and protector of the economic interests which are dominant in them. Its "real" purpose is to ensure their continued predominance, not to prevent it' (Miliband 1969: 22). Referring to Marx's concept of the Bonapartist state, Miliband argues that Marx's point is 'however independent it may have been *politically* from any given class, [it] remains, and cannot in a class society but remain, the protector of an economically and socially dominant class' (Miliband 1965: 285; emphasis in the original).

Nicos Poulantzas criticises Miliband for equating the capitalist state with the interests of individual agents and their motives. He emphasises that the essence of the capitalist state cannot be understood in terms of its instrumental role for the dominant class, or 'the State as Thing', whereby 'the dominant classes absorb the State by emptying it of its own specific power' (Poulantzas 1976: 74). Poulantzas argues that

> Miliband has [difficulties] in comprehending social classes and the State as *objective structures*, and their relations as an *objective system of regular connections*, a structure and a system whose agents, 'men', are in the words of Marx, 'bearers' of it.
>
> (Poulantzas 1969: 70; emphasis in the original)

According to Poulantzas,

> Miliband constantly gives the impression that for him social classes or 'groups' are in some way reducible to *inter-personal relations*, that the State is reducible to inter-personal relations of the members of the diverse 'groups' that constitute the State apparatus.
>
> (Poulantzas 1969: 70; emphasis in the original)

Poulantzas differentiates the concept of 'state power' from 'state apparatus' (1976: 72–3). This distinction points to the fact that if 'state power' refers to the capacity of a social class to realise its objective interests through the state apparatus, it cannot be reducible to the state apparatus (governmental institutions) and state personnel. In other words, state officials are constrained to act on behalf of capital not because they are, as a group, the same as the economically dominant classes or because they are personally affiliated with them but because the state is 'objectively' and 'structurally' capitalist (see also Barrow 1993: 58, ch. 2). On the basis of this reasoning, Poulantzas (1976: 73) 'refuse[s] to account for the relative autonomy of the State in terms of the group made up of the agents of the State and in terms of the specific power of this group'.

> The relation between the bourgeois class and the State is an objective relation. This means that if the *function* of the State in a determinate social formation and the *interests* of the dominant class in this formation *coincide*, it is by reason of the system itself: the direct participation of the members of the ruling class in the State apparatus is not the *cause* but the *effect*, and moreover a chance and contingent one, of this objective coincidence.
> (Poulantzas 1969: 73; emphasis in the original)

Poulantzas grounds his 'structuralist account' on the fact that

> the capitalist State has its own institutional specificity (separation of the political and the economic) which renders it irreducible to an immediate and direct expression of the strict 'economic-corporate' interests (Gramsci) of this or that class or fraction of the power bloc, and that it must represent the political unity.
> (Poulantzas 1976: 73).

He thus defines the state as 'the instance that maintains cohesion of a social formation and which reproduces the conditions of production of a social system by maintaining class domination' (Poulantzas 1969: 77). According to him, the fact that the state is able to function as the unifier of varying fractions of classes, thereby safeguarding the reproduction of the *overall* capitalist system, is precisely because it is autonomous from the interest of the dominant class. In Poulantzas's own words, the 'State can only truly serve the ruling class in so far as it is relatively autonomous from the diverse fractions of this class, precisely in order to be able to organize the hegemony of the whole of this class' (Poulantzas 1969: 74).

Miliband, in turn, accuses Poulantzas of falling into 'a structural super-determinism, which makes impossible a truly realistic consideration of the dialectical relationship between the State and "the system"' (Miliband 1970: 57). According to him, Poulantzas's

> *exclusive* stress on 'objective relations' suggests … that … the structural constraints of the system are so absolutely compelling as to turn those who run the state into the merest functionaries and executants of policies imposed upon them by 'the system'.
> (1970: 57; emphasis in the original)

Miliband asserts that one of the dangers of Poulantzas's structural determinism is to erase or underestimate the important 'differences between a state ruled by bourgeois constitutionalists, whether conservative or social-democrat, and one ruled by, say Fascists' (Miliband 1970: 58). Furthermore, the fact that Poulantzas conflates state power and class power, namely stating that the institutions of the state do not have any power as it is social classes that exert power through the state apparatus (see above), enforces an (extreme version of) the instrumentalist view which 'subvert[s] the very concept of relative autonomy itself' (Miliband 1973: 87). Miliband (1970: 57) holds that while the state operates as the guardian and protector of the economic interests of the dominant class, 'within this "problematic", ... the state élite is involved in a far more complex relationship with "the system", and with society as a whole than Poulantzas's scheme allows'.

Although the debate between Miliband and Poulantzas has typically been dubbed the instrumentalist-structuralist debate, both modified their respective positions and narrowed the gaps over the course of it (Knuttila and Kubik 2000: 124; Poulantzas 1976: 76). Miliband replied to Poulantzas's criticism by arguing that he did not deny 'objective' aspects of the capitalist system imposed on the ruling class: 'I repeatedly note how government and bureaucracy, irrespective of social origin, class situation and even ideological dispositions, are subject to the structural constraints of the system' (Miliband 1970: 57). Miliband later made this point more explicit by distinguishing between 'the state autonomously acting *on behalf of* the ruling class, and its action *at the behest* of that class' (Miliband 1983: 58; emphasis in the original). On this basis, he reiterated that '[w]hat I was rejecting there was the crude view of the state as a mere "instrument" of the ruling class obediently acting at its dictation' (Miliband 1983: 58). In his later work, he addressed time and again the 'relative autonomy' of the state as the central aspect of Marxist theories of the capitalist state. He eventually arrived at a point not far from where Poulantzas stands:

> The state is indeed a class state, the state of the 'ruling class'. But it enjoys a high degree of autonomy and independence in the manner of its operation as a class state, and indeed *must* have that high degree of autonomy and independence if it is to act as a class state. ... This notion of the relative autonomy of the state forms an important part of the Marxist theory of the state.
>
> (Miliband 1977: 74; emphasis in the original)

Poulantzas, on the other hand, admitted his own previous affiliation with structuralism and formalism, for which he had been criticised most prominently by Laclau (1975). In an endeavour to overcome the limits of his own work, Poulantzas proposed that 'the State should be seen (as should capital, according to Marx) as a relation, or more precisely as the condensate of a relation of power between struggling classes' (Poulantzas 1976: 74). He (1976: 82) stated that 'the class division of society necessarily means class struggle, for we cannot speak of classes without speaking of the class struggle'. Along the same line, he brought forward the concept of 'conjuncture' to address the fact that varying state forms are outcomes brought about by class struggle. On this ground, he deliberately refused to provide a definite answer to the question of the relative autonomy of the state. To the extent that 'the term "relative" ... refers to the relationship between State and dominant classes … to the class struggle within each social formation and to its corresponding State forms' (Poulantzas 1976: 72), they cannot be assessed independently of class struggle.

> True, the very principles of the Marxist theory of the State lay down the general negative limits of this [state] autonomy. The (capitalist) State, in the long run, can only correspond to the political interests of the dominant class or classes … Yet, within these limits, the degree, the extent, the forms, etc. (*how* relative, and *how is it* relative) of the relative autonomy of the State can only be examined … with reference to a given capitalist State, and to the precise *conjuncture* of the corresponding class struggle.
>
> (Poulantzas 1976: 72; emphasis in the original)

While the weaknesses of Miliband and Poulantzas's instrumentalist and structuralist approaches will be discussed below, it is indisputable that they have made important contributions to the general understanding of the *capitalist* state. Miliband and Poulantzas's point of departure is how to conceptualise the role and function of the state in a society characterised by class division and domination. Above all, they call into question the mainstream, liberal view of the state, in which it is assumed to be an entity that is neutral in terms of class interests or embodying the general and public interests. They problematise the view that the capitalist state is the rational agent standing opposite to society or that state policies are reflections of diverse interest groups seeking to maximise their interests by influencing the state on equal terms.[4] In so doing, they bring to the fore the capital-serving functions as the core essence of the capitalist state, whether it is seen to benefit the capitalist class (the ruling class) or to maintain the capitalist system as a whole.

Miliband and Poulantzas also provide an avenue from which to challenge the ways in which the statist literature on the developmental state claims that its supposed autonomy derives from personal relationships between state bureaucrats and individual capitalists (see Part I). Miliband and Poulantzas advance the view that the state's ultimate functions for the benefit of the capitalist class and the capitalist system do *not* point to the coincidence of interests between individual capitalists and state executives at an immediate level. Viewed from the perspectives of Miliband and Poulantzas, while conflicts between and amongst capitalists and state executives accruing from different interests do occur, they do not alter the fundamental fact that the state is constrained and compelled to function for the ruling class and the capitalist system.

Seen from the concept of the 'relative autonomy' of the state postulated by Miliband and Poulantzas, particularly the latter, the state's detachment from the immediate interests of the (economically) dominant class is precisely what allows it to serve the interest of the dominant class: the necessity for the state to be autonomous from the dominant classes arises from the reality of a society that is divided by class. The fact that the state's being autonomous from a particular fraction of class or a social group is what enables it to safeguard the capitalist system as a whole. In fact, Poulantzas and Miliband critique any approach that takes the apparent state autonomy at face value. The former criticises seeing 'the State as Subject' for being an approach that considers the autonomy of the State 'as absolute, by being reduced to its "own will"', in the form of the rationalizing instance of civil society, and is incarnated in the power of the group that concretely represents this rationality/power (bureaucracy, élites)' (Poulantzas 1976: 74). Similarly, Miliband's critique of Skocpol's theory of the state, which he refers to as 'the model of the "state for itself"' (Miliband 1983: 66), can also be read as a critique of the institutionalist view of the state:

> [T]here are things which the state wants and does, and which are very irksome to the dominant class: but this is a very different matter from there being a fundamental conflict between them. Moreover, if such a conflict between them did occur, the state would in all likelihood be acting in ways that would favour some other class or classes. In other words, a new partnership would have been created; or the state would be acting, for whatever reason, in favour of a class or classes without any such partnership having been established. In neither case would the state be 'neutral' or acting solely 'for itself'.
>
> (Miliband 1983: 66–7)

One-dimensional critique of the capitalist state

Despite the significance of Miliband and Poulantzas's approaches in bringing to the fore the capital-serving function of the capitalist state, their views fall short of offering a theoretical framework alternative to the existing liberal (pluralist) approaches and the statist concept of the developmental state.

While the capital-serving function of the state constitutes one of its essential characteristics, Miliband and Poulantzas focus primarily on what I propose to call its class *content* as opposed to its social *form*. By drawing attention mainly to state functions' being intrinsically linked to the interests of capitalists or the capitalist system, the class content analysis bypasses a fundamental question, that is, the particular manner in which the class content of the capitalist state is expressed, or the *form* of the state that exists as a sphere or 'instance', in Poulantzas's terms, detached from other spheres, such as the economic. Addressed differently, even if Poulantzas sees the separation of the political and the economic as an institutional specificity of the capitalist state, this separation itself is not adequately explained or historicised in relation to the capitalist mode of production: while he refers to capitalism as an 'objective' structure, he fails to ask why it takes this form or why it expresses itself as an 'objective' structure standing *externally* to individuals. To the extent that they fail to seriously inquire into the historically specific form of the state in capitalism as existing and appearing as an entity presiding outside and above the economic and society, or to question the dichotomous mode of the existence of the political and the economic itself, Miliband and Poulantzas, contrary to their intentions and claims, remain beholden to the mainstream liberal theoretical framework.

First, Miliband and Poulantzas understand the domination of capital in terms of the domination of a class or social group that possesses more economic resources than other groups. However, pre-capitalist societies were divided by class and characterised by class domination; the fact that the capitalist state serves the interests of the dominant class in a class society (the capitalists in capitalism) does not point to the specifically capitalist aspect of the capitalist state. To be sure, Miliband and Poulantzas address the 'asymmetry' in the level of material endowment between social groups, thereby differentiating themselves from mainstream approaches that presuppose the same and equal level of influence over and access to the state enjoyed by and available to diverse social groups. Nevertheless, their perspectives likewise reduce capitalist contradictions and class antagonism to conflicts over material resources between social groups. This suggests that their view of class domination is more about inequality, namely the unequal distribution of material resources between social groups, rather than the contradictions intrinsic to the capitalist mode of production itself. For this reason, Clarke points out that Poulantzas's assessment is closer to what he calls 'bourgeois sociology' in that it finds the domination of capital at the level of 'social interaction' but not at the level of the relations of production (Clarke 1977: 3). Miliband and Poulantzas's critique of the capitalist state is therefore bound to arrive at a moralistic critique of capitalism based on the claim that 'the structure is characterised by the dominance of one or a number of classes over other classes' (Clarke 1977: 19). Class content analysis alone is unable to grasp the historically specific form of the capitalist state and capitalist form of class domination fully. Moishe Postone addresses the limits of assessing capitalist contradictions, primarily in terms of class domination, as follows:

> While class analysis remains basic to the Marxist critical project, the analysis of value, surplus value, and capital as *social forms* cannot be fully grasped in terms of class categories. A Marxist analysis that remains limited to consideration of class entails a serious sociological reduction of the Marxian critique.
>
> (Postone 1993: 153, ft. 87; emphasis added)

Second, Miliband and Poulantzas's key concept of 'relative autonomy of the state' illustrates another key instance of their affiliation with the mainstream framework. As discussed above, the idea that the state is 'relatively' autonomous from the dominant class is central to both authors' assessments as they intend to transcend mainstream liberal approaches as well as what they conceive of as the problem of orthodox Marxism: namely 'economic determinism' (Miliband 1983: 63; Poulantzas 1976: 67). However, they fail to ask why categories such as the economic, the political and the ideological assume the form of quasi-independent and autonomous spheres in capitalism in the first place. Insofar as these categories are taken as givens, rather than seen as specific forms taken by capitalist social relations, the connections between them are bound to be external or superficial. For instance, the connection is achieved either by emphasising the interaction between the categories that are presupposed to be autonomous or by rendering them as co-determinants of the mode of production. Onto this essentially mainstream theoretical account, what are conceived as 'Marxist elements' are simply added: namely positing the economic as the ultimate determinant 'in the last resort'.

> [O]ur ... conception of 'instances' (economic, political, ideological) ... are both specific and autonomous with respect to each other, and whose interaction produces the mode of production – determined by the economic in the last resort, but in which another instance may play the dominant rôle.
>
> (Poulantzas 1976: 77)

To the extent that Miliband and Poulantzas take as given the apparent dichotomy of state and economy or assume the autonomous existence of various social categories, they end up privileging the sphere of the economic over other categories, resurrecting the 'economic determinism' which they had intended to rectify. Against such approaches that attempt to transcend 'economism' by rendering non-economic spheres autonomous from the economic, Etienne Balibar formulated the following eloquent critique:

> [W]hat is called the critique of economism is most often undertaken in the name of a claim that the political sphere and the state are autonomous, either in relation to the sphere of the market economy or in relation to the class struggle itself, which comes down practically to reintroducing the liberal dualism (state/civil society, politics/economics) which Marx criticized so tellingly.
>
> (Balibar 1991: 3)

Failing to address the capitalist state in terms of the peculiarities of capitalist social form, Miliband and Poulantzas's theory of the capitalist state eventually arrives at a functionalist view that is not dissimilar from pluralism. Miliband argues in his later work that the state *must* be autonomous in order to act as a class state (see above). Poulantzas similarly explains the relative autonomy of the state, or the detachment of the state from other spheres, based on the fact that it *needs* to function as a political unifier: the state functions to maintain the cohesion of a social power bloc under the hegemony of a class or faction and to intervene to ensure the reproduction of the overall system (Poulantzas 1976: 75). Accordingly, its detachment from the economy or the dominant class is enforced by the systemic necessity to function as a class state. An explanation that derives the nature of an object from its own inherent necessity is tautological, however.

Seen from Miliband's instrumentalist perspective, the state is capitalist as it serves the interests of the ruling class: what makes it capitalist is the dominant class occupying and exploiting it. To be sure, the dominant class in capitalism is likely to be capitalist, but this theoretical perspective implies that the state *can* serve any class that is dominant, including, potentially, the working class. This view is mirrored in Miliband's contention that 'state power in a post-capitalist society is not in conflict with [working] class power, but its essential complement' (Miliband 1983: 68). In other words, if the state is presented as an instrument to realise the interests of the dominant class, it can be emptied of its contents and turned into an instrument to realise the interests of *other* classes, including the working class.[5]

Similarly, viewed from the perspective of Poulantzas's structuralism, the state is capitalist because the system it functions to safeguard is capitalist. When Poulantzas stresses that the state is a 'condensation of a relation of power between struggling classes' (1976: 74) and 'a factor for the establishment of the unstable equilibrium of compromises [between classes]' (1976: 71), he is in fact projecting the view that the state merely mirrors the results of class struggle, implying that the state itself is (at least potentially) dispossessed of a particular class orientation. To the extent that the essential aspect of the state is its function for the whole, as in Miliband's approach, it is implied that the state could function also for a non-capitalist system: the state in itself is independent of the historically specific capitalist social form. This fundamentally uncritical view of the state is also expressed when Poulantzas argues that the state should be seen as a relation as much as capital (see above), which suggests that the state was hitherto seen as external to capital or could be external to capital. This formulation is not far from the pluralist account that recognises conflicts between social groups in society and yet sees the state as the base of social harmony not because it is able to eliminate conflicts but because it is accepted as the arena of legitimate political conflict (Holloway and Picciotto 1978: 12–3; Knuttila and Kubik 2000: 88–1). For this reason, Clarke argues that Poulantzas's intellectual base is closer to 'social functionalism' than to Marxism.

> Poulantzas's concept of the social structure is essentially indistinguishable from that of social functionalism. The definition of the structure, the specification of its levels and their functions, require no reference to Marxist concepts of any kind. The Marxist claims of the theory depend entirely on the claims of the theory of class which is superimposed on

> the theory of social structure. The state, for example, is a specific institution which has specific functions to perform in relation to the whole ... the state continues to be class state because the social formation whose unity it maintains is a social formation in which a particular class is dominant. In maintaining the unity of society, therefore, the state is at the same time maintaining the dominance of the dominant class.
>
> (Clarke 1977: 13)

In summary, the class content analysis appraised thus far offers only a partial critique of the capitalist state. Despite the fact that Miliband and Poulantzas advance crucial insights that problematise mainstream approaches and could potentially provide a critique of the statist concept of the developmental state by placing the essence of the capitalist state in relation to class domination, they do not probe adequately into the particular form of class domination in capitalism and the particular form of the political, which exists in capitalism as a supra-individual power juxtaposed to the economic sphere. As a result, Miliband and Poulantzas resort to the notion of the relative autonomy of the state to transcend 'economism' by juxtaposing the political to the economic. Instead of historicising the categories of the political and the economic as elements of a historically specific form of society, that is, capitalist society, they take them for granted and leave unquestioned the fact that the state and the economy appear to exist as distinctive spheres. Consequently, the class content analysis supports, at least implicitly, political projects that instrumentalise the state to overcome the class contradictions of capitalism. It fails to problematise the existence of the state as such and as the expression of specifically *capitalist* class domination.

The class content analysis of the developmental state

Despite these crucial limitations of the instrumental-structural accounts of the capitalist state, they continue to inform subsequent Marxist discussions. Notable Marxist scholars that have attempted to analyse the (Korean) developmental state from the instrumental and structuralist perspectives are Vivek Chibber, Paul Cammack, Martin Hart-Landsberg and Paul Burkett. In this section, I will assess these authors' work, in turn, particularly focussing on Chibber and Cammack, and how their discussions of the developmental state and its transformation reflect the class content analysis of the Marxist theory of the capitalist state.

The challenge to the autonomous developmental state

The initial questions that Chibber raises in relation to the developmental state are not so different from the theorists of the developmental state and institutionalists. For instance, he asks how and why Korea succeeded in industrialisation, while other developing countries, particularly India, failed to achieve the same level of development, in spite of efforts made for state-building and policy implementations similar to those made by Korea (Chibber 1999: 309). Chibber also shares the proposition with developmental state theories that the Korean developmental state possessed an unusual capacity that was absent in other developing countries, that is, the state's disciplinary power over private firms and its ability to formulate and implement development and industrial policies in a coherent fashion (Chibber 1999: 310–1, 2003: 7). However, he goes further than the early developmental state theorists by asking under what conditions the Korean state was able to assume such power over capitalists or what he calls the 'national bourgeoisie'.

Chibber understands that in both Korea and India the national bourgeoisie demanded state protection and subsidies, and that both states introduced similar policy measures for the goal of national development. However, because Korea was successful, while India was not, he seeks the explanatory factor for Korean development beyond what he calls 'supply-side' explanations (Chibber 1999: 336). According to Chibber, the dominant literature on the Korean developmental state is characterised by 'statist' or 'supply-side' approaches and has placed the primary focus on the overriding power of the state over the capitalists' own proclivities: this literature has focussed exclusively on the state as the supplier of loans and policies designed to overcome the backwardness of local industries (Chibber 1999: 311, 336). On the basis of this, Chibber (2003: 9) offers a 'demand-side' explanation for Korean development by looking at the state's relation with societal actors. He argues that 'the analytical focus, therefore, needs to shift from an exclusive focus on the state to a consideration of its relations with local classes' (Chibber 2003: 23; see also 1999: 313).

Chibber holds that the introduction of certain development policies did not itself provide sufficient conditions for the state to exercise disciplinary and monitoring power that the Korean state uniquely possessed *vis-à-vis* private enterprises. If Korea's rapid industrialisation was attributable to the existence of the disciplinary state, what allowed the state to punish and reward national entrepreneurs according to the latter's performance was a switch of development strategy to export-led industrialisation (ELI) from import-substitution industrialisation (ISI) in the early 1960s (Chibber 2003: 32, 39). The reason was that while the national bourgeoisie under an ISI strategy tends to shelter from external competition and resist their states' attempts to implement ELI, those under an ELI strategy are compelled to innovate new technology in the face of global market competition, thus relying on state guidance (Chibber 2005: 149–51). Being exposed to global competition with the adoption of an ELI strategy, it was in the interest of the Korean bourgeoisie to support and cooperate with state managers (Chibber 2003: 29). Chibber argues that '[i]t was not that the Koreans first built a developmental state, which then herded local capitalists onto the new accumulation strategy'; 'it was the launching of ELI that provided the basis for building a developmental state' (Chibber 1999: 312).

On the question of why the Korean state could shift its development strategy to ELI and thereby direct the national bourgeoisie under its command, Chibber answers that this was due to a unique opportunity offered by Japanese capital. Japanese exporting firms increasingly saw Korea as a new site of production and formed partnerships with Korean producers from the early 1960s, providing the latter with extensive sales and marketing networks in addition to private loans made available on favourable terms by Japan (Chibber 2003: 43, 2005: 158). Being 'blessed with the happy accident of falling within the ambit of Japanese capital's emerging accumulation strategy' (Chibber 1999: 337), Korean capital enthusiastically embraced ELI, having 'garnered for itself a unique window to foreign markets through entering into an alliance with Japanese capital' (1999: 329). Chibber (1999: 323) contends that 'the turn to ELI was not imposed on Korean capitalists but was arrived at consensually; indeed, there was even pressure from business to initiate it', and it 'was consonant with the emerging orientation of this class'.

From the fact that the switch to ELI depended upon how leading capitalists reacted, Chibber argues that contrary to the portrayals of the theorists of the developmental state and institutionalism, the Korean developmental state could not have imposed its own agenda on the capitalist class, regardless of the latter's perception of its interests (Chibber 1999: 316–20). He thereby highlights how crucial and determinant it was for the state to obtain a consensus or support from national capitalists in realising national development successfully. Furthermore, referring to a number of historical incidents, Chibber demonstrates how much the Korean developmental state (in the period of the military Park regime) was restrained by local capitalists in pursing development strategies (Chibber 1999: 317–23). In his words, 'far from being a "senior partner", it had to work within the constraints of business pressure' (Chibber 1999: 324).

> [T]he new strategy that did emerge in Korea – export-led industrialisation – was just such as a 'pact' between the state and its bourgeoisie. It was not foisted onto business by the new regime; to the contrary, it was pushed by business itself.
>
> (Chibber 1999: 337)

Chibber's analysis is significant in calling into question one of the core premises of the statist concept of the developmental state: the idea that it was autonomous from and exerted disciplinary power over capitalists. By bringing to the fore the idea that the Korean developmental state was restrained by and aligned with the interests of the national bourgeoise, he challenges what are conceived of as the defining characteristics of the developmental state. This challenge to the notion of the autonomous state amounts to a class content analysis of the developmental state: the revelation that the developmental state was a creation pushed for by local capitalists, and that its successful operation for the goal of national development was made possible by the latter's consent, is another way of stating that the developmental state functioned as an instrument servicing the capitalist class.

From critiquing the state for having been captured by the national bourgeoisie to exalting a community-serving state

While it is beyond dispute that Chibber's reworking of the statist literature has important merits in countering the 'autonomous state' thesis, the core component of the statist concept of the developmental state, his assessment of the Korean developmental state, suffers the vulnerabilities generic to the class content analysis of the capitalist state, on the one hand, and those specific to the ways in which he posits the relation between the state and the national bourgeoisie, on the other. The problems of Chibber's analysis can be assessed in several respects.

First, while questioning the notion of state autonomy *vis-à-vis* the capitalist class, Chibber assesses divergent development outcomes primarily with reference to what types of relations – whether conflictual or consensual – are formed between the state and the national bourgeoisie. This way of assessing the success and failure of development shares with rather than opposes the statist framework. Although the emphasis differs in terms of who dominates and determines development outcomes between state elites and national capitalists, Chibber, no less than the theorists of the developmental state and institutionalists, reduces state-economy as well as state-society relations to actor-level relations between state elites and individual capitalists. Consequently, he hardly ever raises the question of labour.

The absence of the question of labour in Chibber's assessment has deeper origins. Even if he addresses the autonomy of the state being limited by the capitalist class, his understanding of capital is based on the mainstream liberal framework in which society is constituted by the sum of social relations between atomised individuals and social groups. Capital is personalised and perceived as 'the capitalists', i.e. one of several interest groups seeking to maximise their own interests. Insofar as state-capital relations are understood in this way, the power of capital is measured primarily by how effectively capitalists influence or capture state elites for their interests, and labour is only seen as constituting another (weak) interest group, relegated to secondary *vis-à-vis* more influential groups (e.g. the capitalists). As discussed above, this approach amounts to what Clarke refers to as 'bourgeoisie sociology' in which the 'dominance of capital is explained as the dominance of a social group endowed with a disproportionate share of material resources' (Clarke 1977: 3). In this understanding, class contradictions inherent in capitalist development disappear and are replaced by conflicts over divergent interests between distinct social groups. When labour oppression arises as an issue at all, it is seen as contingent at the actor level. For instance, Chibber explains the marginalisation and demobilisation of labour as an outcome of the actions of political elites who wanted to 'gain the confidence of their business classes' and believed that 'the active and hegemonic members of the "modernizing bloc" would be the state and capital, the natural partners in the venture' (2005: 162).

Chibber's framework based on an individualistic account of state-capital relations equally conditions his assessment of 'the eventual demise of the developmental state, and its replacement by neoliberalism' (Chibber 2005: 148). As much as he explains the origins of the Korean developmental state through the support that the national bourgeoisie paid to state managers, he finds the driving force for the transformation or the dismantlement of the developmental state primarily in conflicts between state elites and the national bourgeoisie, and the growing power of the latter over the former. Relatedly, the cause of the Asian financial crisis is explained by the dismantlement of the institutional arrangement that had prevailed under the developmental state, brought about in accordance with the new demands of capitalists. In his supposedly 'Marxist' analysis, there hardly exists any consideration of the contradiction of capitalist development and class antagonism between capital and labour.

> An exceptionally united capitalist class had, by the early 1990s, outgrown its need for state support as a condition for export success. The partnership that had supported the developmental state therefore dissolved, and the chaebol began calling for a dismantling of the planning apparatus ... The old apparatus had fallen into disrepair much earlier under the pressure of the chaebol, and it was in fact its prior dismantling that brought on the crisis.
>
> (Chibber 2005: 163)

Chibber's assessment of the causes of the Asian financial crisis does not diverge from that of the institutionalists, who find such causes in the shift in power relations between state managers and capitalists (the *chaebol*) (see Chapter 2). More importantly, in the context of this chapter, Chibber's understanding of the capitalist state is grounded in a variant of instrumentalism: as much as the developmental state had been created under the pressure of capitalists, its dismantlement was caused by the changing needs of the latter. Chibber in fact problematises the instrumentalist view of the capitalist state, arguing that it fails to take into account conflicts or tensions between the state and the national bourgeoisie. From his perspective, therefore, overcoming an instrumentalist account means to 'allow for some independence of the state from capital', whereby 'the conflicts surrounding developmentalism become less mysterious', and the 'very fact of the state's relative autonomy meant that its powers were not under the direct control of the national bourgeoisie' (Chibber 2005: 161). In other words, Chibber believes that acknowledging 'the state's genuine, albeit limited, independence from their [capitalist] control' is a way to move beyond an instrumentalist view of the capitalist state (2005: 161). He thus challenges as instrumentalism a version that even Miliband would have rejected as too crude (see above). His inadequate challenge to instrumentalism only demonstrates that his supposedly 'superior' approach is merely a restatement of the concept of 'relative autonomy', which does little to resolve the apparent dichotomy of the state and the economy.

Another problematic aspect of Chibber's assessment of the developmental state is that he critiques capitalists rather than capitalism. According to this assessment, reminiscent of Miliband's, the capitalist state is capitalist to the extent that capitalists utilise it to their advantage and to serve their interests: Chibber exposes the class content of the developmental state only to the extent that it is captured or dominated by self-serving capitalists.

> The point worth noting is that even in Korea, where there was some kind of business support for a national development project, indeed, where this partnership with capital was crucial to the projects' success, capitalists remained in the alliance only so long as state intervention was a central precondition to their profitability.
>
> (Chibber 2005: 163)

Chibber's criticism of capitalists is closely related to his challenge to what he calls the 'myth', held by some Marxists, that national capitalists support industrialisation, and political elites and national capitalists are therefore national allies (2005: 160). However, his critique of the capitalist state on the ground that it is captured and exploited by an egoistic bourgeoisie is in sharp contrast to his uncritical view of the state itself. To the extent that Chibber sees the success of the state's (national development) project as dependent on how cooperative the capitalists are, he renders the state immune from capitalist contradictions. In other words, while he criticises the national bourgeoisie for prioritising their narrow interests, he has a favourable view of state managers. For instance, the main source of resistance to building strong and supple policy apparatuses, crucial for rapid industrialisation in the South, came from the national bourgeoisie (Chibber 2005: 148–9). Along the same line, he asserts that capitalists prevented development from occurring, stating that the 'problem [of implementing ISI] was not resistance from [state] *planners*, but from *firms*' (Chibber 2005: 157; emphasis in the original). He goes on to say that '[o]pposition to strengthening the policy apparatus thus did not need to come from bureaucrats or from landed classes – it issued from the very agent the policies were meant to favour [that is, the national bourgeoisie]' (Chibber 2005: 149).[6] Chibber's emphasis on 'the possibility for real conflict between the two central actors of the developmentalist drama, state managers and the national bourgeoisie', is part of his argument that the latter are to blame for being a major hindrance to development (Chibber 2005: 149).

Projecting the view that the state managers' genuine interest in (national) development is only frustrated by the national bourgeoisie, Chibber finally arrives at a conclusion that hardly differs from the statist conception of the developmental state. He holds that a socially beneficial mode of development serving the interests of the 'community' was possible during the post-Second World War period when the state dominated the national bourgeoisie. In contrast, the current shift towards a less desirable mode of development that serves the interests of 'private' capitalists was caused by the weakening of the state.

> The weakness of state planning apparatuses thus played a critical role in the unravelling of national development projects in the 1980s. ... The aims of industrial policy in the post-war period can be understood as a sort of implicit contract: public funds would be funnelled to firms in the short term, on the understanding that the state would, in exchange, hold them accountable to certain performance standards. So over the medium term, the community would gain from the initial coddling of local capitalists. But with states left weak and fractured, the equation was reversed. Capitalists were able to initiate a half-century long primitive accumulation, socializing their risks and losses, while privately appropriating the gains ... at an enormous cost to the public.
>
> (Chibber 2005: 157)

Beyond merely restating the statist proposition, Chibber's view can be seen to have more politically conservative implications. As shown in the passage above, he calls what social scientists usually refer to as 'society' 'the community'. If the theorists of the developmental state and institutionalists defend the developmental state on the basis that it is more rational than society as it sits above the latter, Chibber's critique of the capitalist class is linked to his uncritical view of the state as a servant of the interests of 'the community', that is, national development, or 'the nation'. The primary role of the state is to serve the (national) 'community'. This uncritical vision of national development is in part explained by the fact that Chibber's assessment of the capitalist state is confined to a class content analysis: only insofar as the state is able to discipline and direct the national bourgeoisie it functions for the benefit of the nation rather than for that of the capitalists.

A critique of the repressive developmental state

Paul Cammack's critique of Chibber's assessment of the developmental state and of Weberian state theories represents another key example of class content analysis, albeit from a functionalist angle. In this section, I will critically appraise how his general functionalist perspective on the capitalist state informs his critique of Chibber as well as his assessment of the Korean developmental state.

While Cammack's criticism of Chibber has several dimensions, one of the key points is that the latter is uncritical of capitalist development in Korea:

'Korea is presented without qualification as the success story that contrasts with India's failure', and 'he takes no account of Korea's repressive labour regime' (2007: 1–2). Cammack holds that due to the absence of a critique of capitalism, Chibber 'comes to the Korean case with a set of assumptions drawn from institutionalist debates', whose accounts 'typically pay little attention to class struggle, or the links between exploitation, accumulation, and legitimation' (Cammack 2007: 12). Consequently, according to Cammack, Chibber makes 'it impossible to understand the "capitalist developmental state" or the alliance between the state and business' (2007: 2). Cammack stresses that 'the East Asian developmental state was pre-eminently a *capitalist* developmental state' (2007: 4; emphasis in the original).

Another issue Cammack discusses is that Chibber poses the question of the capitalist state in instrumentalist terms and reduces state-capital relations to relations between actual individuals (Cammack 2007: 12). From Cammack's point of view, Chibber reduces capitalist interests 'to the interests of *actually existing capitalists*' and, as a result, 'falls into an instrumentalist trap; and he compounds the error … by imaging such an actually existing capitalist class in Korea, independent of the state in the sense that it has its own accumulation model already in place' (Cammack 2007: 12; emphasis in the original). As a consequence, 'he cannot grasp the logic of the capitalist developmental state in Korea' (Cammack 2007: 12). According to Cammack, Chibber's depiction of the domestic capitalist class, which has the upper hand over the state, comes from his reliance on an extreme version of the 'statist literature' that emphasises the weakness of the capitalist class in Korea (Cammack 2007: 7).

Cammack's critique of Chibber makes highly valid points, which resonate with my own critique of him. However, Cammack's view also suffers the limitations typically shown in instrumentalist and functionalist accounts. First, his understanding of the '*capitalist* developmental state' primarily refers to its overt mode of labour repression. To put this differently, he finds the essence of the *capitalist* developmental state in its brutality towards and disciplining of labour or, in his words, in 'its creation and disciplining of an exploitable proletariat' (Cammack 2007: 4).

> Chibber glosses entirely over this central feature of the Korean developmental state – the repressive regime instituted after 1961 through which labour was politically excluded, policed by the intelligence services, faced with intimidation and physical repression, and subjected to unparalleled levels of exploitation in the workplace. The squeezing of a new proletariat out of the countryside, the corralling of mostly female workers in dormitories alongside sites of production, the regime of exceptionally long working days and limited holidays and the enormous differentials between male and female wages are massively documented, yet play no part in his analysis.
>
> (Cammack 2007: 3)

While Cammack illuminates one of the key features of the developmental state that not only Chibber but the theorists of the developmental state and some Marxist critics of neoliberalism either ignore or underrate, this way of posing the capitalist essence of the developmental state does not differentiate itself from non-Marxist (liberal) approaches. While the connection between an overtly oppressive mode of political rule and capitalism is one of the relevant questions to be raised, an equally compelling question is how and why democracy or other less overtly oppressive modes of political rule coexist with the capitalist form of class domination. In fact, numerous liberal, non-Marxist sociologists and labour activists have addressed labour repression and the exclusion of labour from politics as a key characteristic of the developmental state (see Deyo 1987; Koo H 1987, 1993a, 1993b, 2001; Ogle 1990). Cammack himself draws on these authors to address the brutality of the developmental state.

By construing the *capitalist* essence of the developmental state primarily as its role and function in oppressing and disciplining labour, Cammack does not go beyond an analysis of the class content of the developmental state, and its form of existence as a quasi-independent entity and a specific social form remains unexplored. As a consequence, Cammack is unable to provide an adequate analysis of the continuity of the Korean state as a capitalist state, even after it ceases to be an authoritarian military regime, and its exercise of overt coercion is diminished in line with democratisation and the growth of the labour movement from the mid-1980s onward. Cammack ends up assessing the transformation or dismantlement of the developmental state in a way that does not differ much from Chibber's. While Cammack criticises Chibber for referring to the institutionalist literature uncritically, in discussing the transformation of the developmental state, he himself restates the institutionalist claim that 'the Korean state itself fell prey to "bureaucratic paralysis" or "capitalist rent-seeking"' (Cammack 2007: 2).

Moreover, although Cammack rightly points out that Chibber holds an uncritical view of capitalist development in Korea, Cammack's assessment of the origins of the labour-repressive regime of the Korean developmental state is also problematic inasmuch as he seems to attribute it to the Japanese colonial legacy. He writes that the repressive labour regime was 'inaugurated under Japanese rule and perfected under Park' (Cammack 2007: 3). On this basis, he reproaches Chibber for 'miss[ing] both the link to Japanese colonial rule (to which Park himself was a living monument), and the roots of the repressive labour regime' (Cammack 2007: 10). Relatedly, quoting from Cumings, he states that several features of Japan's 1930s political economy reappeared in Korea and Taiwan later, including militarisation and harsh repression of labour, and notes that 'labour repression is the *only* social legacy of Japanese colonialism to which Haggard, Kang and Moon will admit. If there was ever a case of consensus, this is it' (Cammack 2007: 4; emphasis in the original).[7]

While Cammack's assessment has some merit in critiquing the repressive labour regime under Park, it contains the misleading implication that labour repression under the Korean developmental state was owed to Japanese colonialism rather than to capitalist development (primitive accumulation).[8] This suggests either that Japanese colonialism was external and accidental to capitalist development in Korea or that a form of endogenous capitalist development in Korea could have occurred without repressing labour, both of which are questionable theoretically and cannot be supported historically (see Part III). It is in fact highly implausible that capitalist development, particularly in the context of 'catch-up' development in the lower end of the world-economic hierarchy, could have occurred without 'super exploitation of labour', i.e. low wages and extremely long working hours. A simple historical observation illustrates this. The Rhee government (1948–60) that was in office before the Park government (the developmental state regime) was as anti-communist and labour-repressive as the latter, if not more, even if Rhee himself had been academically trained in the US (George Washington, Harvard and Princeton Universities) and was vehemently anti-Japanese.[9]

From critiquing the capital-serving developmental state to endorsing organised capitalism

Cammack's limited critique of Chibber and his own inadequate assessment of the developmental state are rooted in his general view of the capitalist state. His review article (1989) of *Bringing the State Back In* (BSBI) (1985) and related neo-Weberian state theories, and his more recent article 'The Governance of Global Capitalism: A New Materialist Perspective' (2003), underscore his general perspective of the capitalist state as one that does not go beyond a class-content and essentially functionalist framework. In fact, Cammack himself states that his aim is not 'to advance a more sophisticated notion of Marxist views of the state than is reflected in current distinctions between instrumental and structuralist perspectives' (Cammack 1989: 289).

He points out that the BSBI authors 'distort the legacy of Marxist and neo-Marxist writing on the state' (Cammack 1989: 265). He grounds this critique on the fact that they 'present "state" and "society" as separate polar opposites, denying in practice the presence of classes and class struggle within the state' (Cammack 1989: 263). Similarly, Cammack criticises Skocpol for 'drawing a false contrast between the "society-centred" perspective of classical Marxism, and the "state-centred" perspective' (Cammack 1989: 289). He believes that 'the central preoccupation of Marxists and neo-Marxists alike [is] with class, and in this connection with the relationship *between* class forces and the state' (Cammack 1989: 265; emphasis in the original). According to Cammack, 'a genuinely Marxist perspective' is one 'in which state and social classes are seen as inter-related' as opposed to 'one in which "the state" confronts "civil society"' (Cammack 1989: 282). In short, what he proposes as an alternative to the BSBI perspective is a conceptualisation of the state as an arena of class struggle: 'the state is differentially penetrated by conflicting classes, and incorporates, reflects and affects the struggle between them' (Cammack 1989: 289).

In spite of the fact that Cammack rightly problematises the BSBI author's conceptual dichotomy between 'the state' and 'society', his 'Marxist vision' centred on the relation between the state and classes is more similar than dissimilar to the liberal-pluralist approach. While the language might differ, as the term 'class' is more often utilised by Marxists, pluralist accounts also construe the state as the object of the varying interest groups trying to maximise their interests. Furthermore, the fact that the state is a condensation of class struggle does not say much about the specific forms this takes in capitalism or the form of the political in capitalism. This is due to the fact that Cammack fails to question why society and the state assume 'separate' and 'distinct' forms, and why class struggles in capitalism are fought through and within the state. In other words, his inquiry takes for granted the capitalist form of the modern state and focusses on how the state serves to maintain the interests of the dominant class or the capitalist system, or else, reflects class struggles, which is what I refer to as the 'class content' of the state.[10]

As Cammack, like Miliband, Poulantzas and Chibber, fails to analyse the *forms* of capitalist social relations he reiterates the mantra of 'the relative autonomy of the state' as an alternative to Weberian state theories or the approach of the BSBI authors. He defines the relative autonomy of the state as 'the capacity of political institutions to stand at a distance from capitalist interests as they exist at any particular moment in time'. He argues that 'the state acts, at times against the short-run interests of even dominant capitalists, to secure the long-term survival of the system as a whole' (Cammack 1989: 270). He argues that this function of the state is a structural necessity of capitalism as there are a variety of competing capitalist interests in any society.

> The *need* for it [relative autonomy] follows from the gap between the character of existing capitalist interests on the one hand, and the presumed optimum configuration to secure competitiveness in the world market on the other (the logic of *accumulation/realisation*), and from the constant imperatives to reproduce the hegemony of the bourgeoisie over the proletariat, ... The social and political mechanisms through which both accumulation and legitimation are secured are crucially underpinned by economic compulsion sedulously maintained by the 'relatively autonomous' state.
>
> (Cammack 2003: 41–2; emphasis in the original)

As the passage above highlights, Cammack's understanding of the relative autonomy of the state echoes the Poulantzasian functionalist account: in order to secure the capitalist system as a whole, the state *needs to be* relatively autonomous; the functional necessity emanating from a society divided by classes gives rise to a form of state that is separate and autonomous from that same society (see above). While functionalist accounts have merit in exposing the class content of the capitalist state and its functions for the capitalist system, functionalism does not differ fundamentally from the approach presented by the BSBI authors. As Cammack himself recognised, there is a fine line between the concept of 'relative autonomy' proposed by Marxists such as Miliband and Poulantzas and that of 'true autonomy' put forward by Skocpol in opposition to them (Cammack 1989: 269). In a similar context, Hugo Radice also points out that 'the concept of the "relative autonomy" of the state – the idea most firmly associated with Poulantzas' own work – is in practice impossible to distinguish from the "essential autonomy" that he disavows' (Radice 2008: 1161).[11]

Finally, the limits of the class content analysis of the developmental state can be further addressed with reference to Paul Burkett and Martin Hart-Landsberg. These authors offer formidable Marxist critique of capitalist development in Korea and East Asia (Burkett and Hart-Landsberg 1996; Hart-Landsberg 1993, 2004). Although they have not engaged directly with the question of the capitalist state, they problematised the main two approaches to industrialisation in Korea, i.e. free-market and statist approaches (Hart-Landsberg and Burkett 2001). Hart-Landsberg and Burkett correctly argue that even if these free-market and statist approaches differ in their assessments of the importance and desirability of industrial policy, 'both embrace capitalism as the only effective means for achieving development' (Hart-Landsberg and Burkett 2001: 404).

Nevertheless, the framework that informs their work is what they call 'a class perspective', which aims to illuminate 'the exploitative and contradictory nature of South Korea's growth trajectory'. The concept of 'contradiction' refers here to the exploitation of labour and 'anarchic market forces' (Hart-Landsberg and Burkett 2001: 404). As a consequence, they tend to promote *organised* capitalism as an alternative or, in their own words, 'the replacement of anarchic market forces with cooperative-democratic decision-making mechanisms' and 'worker/community-led socialization of the chaebol and the government bodies' as a solution in the context of post-Asian crisis Korea (Hart-Landsberg and Burkett 2001: 404).

Undoubtedly, Hart-Landsberg and Burkett's critique of capitalist development in Korea and East Asia is more thorough and concrete than most approaches discussed in this volume. However, as discussed above and in Chapter 3 in relation to Marxist critiques of neoliberalism, once the primary capitalist contradiction is seen to emanate from 'unequal' market relations, distribution (property ownership) or the anarchic nature of the market, the state is likely to be seen as a means to resolve these 'contradictions' of capitalism through a 'fairer' distribution of resources or a restoration of 'order' to the market. This ultimately leads to an affirmative view of the capitalist state, which is evident when Hart-Landsberg and Burkett reiterate Leo

Panitch's proposition that 'what is needed for truly progressive change ... is 'a "transformation of the state" into a "state whose functions are not tied to guaranteeing the economic res *publica* for capitalism"' (Panitch 1994: 87, as cited in Burkett and Hart-Landsberg 1996: 81). In other words, Hart-Landsberg and Burkett imply that fundamental societal change can be delivered at the level of the political (i.e. by changing the function of the state), and the state can function for purposes other than serving the interests of capitalists or capitalism. This again underscores the fact that insofar as the question of the capitalist state is posed primarily in terms of its capital-serving content or function, the state is viewed, at least potentially, as immune from capitalist contradictions rather than as the political expression of the capitalist societal totality.

Conclusion

As the first step to construct a theoretical framework for the developmental state beyond statism, I have identified two different perspectives on the capitalist state within the Marxist tradition, namely 'class content analysis' and 'social form critique'. In this chapter I have focussed on the former.

I have appraised the key aspects of the class content analysis, or instrumentalist-functionalist accounts of the capitalist state in general, and how they are applied to assessing the (Korean) developmental state. I argued that class content analysis has helped advance the theory of the *capitalist* state by unpacking its servicing role and function for the dominant class and the capitalist system. However, the way it poses the question of the capitalist state is limited by its inability to differentiate itself fundamentally from the mainstream liberal framework (pluralism). This is because, in the framework of class content analysis, the state attains capitalist content only when it is occupied by the capitalist class or serves the interest of the capitalist system as a whole. It is implied in this formulation that the state itself is an entity that could (at least potentially) be neutral in terms of class orientation and whose content could be changed and replaced depending on which group of society, be it capitalists or workers, seizes and utilises it to its advantage or when society turns non-capitalist. These conceptual limits of class content analysis are also reflected in the analyses of the developmental state by Chibber and Cammack. These authors reduce the question of the capitalist state to how much state autonomy under the developmental state was constrained by local capitalists (Chibber) and how brutal and functional the Korean developmental state was in repressing labour (Cammack).

Having highlighted the strengths and limitations of Marxist state theory that focusses primarily on the class content of the capitalist state and its reflections on the analyses of the developmental state, in the following chapter, I will discuss another tradition of Marxist state theory whose central concern lies in addressing the social *form* of the capitalist mode of production and how it has been applied to the analysis of the (Korean) developmental state.

Notes

1 For a detailed discussion on Marxist theories of the state, see Barrow (1993), Jessop (1990), Clarke (1991), Knuttila and Kubik (2001: chs. 5, 6).

2 A similar work by Engels is *The Peasant War in Germany* (1850). For an analysis of Marx and Engels's historical analyses of class struggles from a methodological viewpoint, see Abrams (1982: ch. 3).

3 Miliband and Poulantzas's approaches cannot be delineated sharply along the lines of instrumentalism and structuralism. Neither of them denies instrumentalist or structuralist aspects of the capitalist state, and they modified their respective positions over the course of the debate. This aspect will be further discussed below. For discussions on instrumentalist and structuralist accounts within the Marxist tradition, see Laclau (1975), Clarke (1977, 1991: 18–22), Barrow (1993: chs.1, 2), Jessop (1990: 29–30) and Radice (2008: 1161).

4 Miliband's book *The State in Capitalist Society* (1969) was precisely aimed at challenging 'pluralism'. For discussions on 'pluralism' see Knuttila and Kubik (2001: ch. 4) and Held (1987: ch. 6).

5 Relatedly, Lenin's assessment of the state can be classified as one of class content analysis. He argues in *State and Revolution* that 'the state is an organ of class *domination*, an organ for *oppression* of one class by another; its aim is the creation of "order", which legalises and perpetuates this oppression by moderating the collisions between the classes' (Lenin 1990: 9).

6 Chibber's advocacy of 'bureaucratic rationality' and the internal coherence of the bureaucratic system as the key factors for 'successful' national development are also evident in Chibber (2002).

7 Haggard, Kang and Moon (1997) critiqued the 'colonial modernity' thesis proposed by Kohli (1994): namely that Japanese colonialism was decisive for the post-War high-growth economic development of Korea. Cammack argues here that even these authors who oppose the 'colonial modernity' thesis would agree to the colonial origins of labour repression.

8 Cammack's view that the repressive labour regime under Park was owed to the Japanese colonial legacy appears to take a critical stance against Japanese colonialism. However, this view resembles how Kohli and Pirie explain the 'successful' industrialisation of Korea through the (institutional) legacy of Japanese colonialism. A critical assessment of the debate on Japanese colonial legacy and its influence on Korean capitalism will be made in Chapter 7.

9 A historical analysis of primitive accumulation in Korea from the late nineteenth century and a comparative analysis of the Rhee and the Park governments are the subjects of Chapters 7 and 8.

10 For the bourgeois-liberal origins of the categories of 'class' and 'class struggle', see Stoetzler (2004: 264–5).

11 Cammack's functionalism also manifests itself in his application of the 'relative autonomy' thesis to an analysis of global governance. He argues that 'IMF-World Bank should enjoy relative autonomy from even the most powerful national governments' (2003: 55): the IMF and the World Bank attain and perform a role equivalent to the state at the global level for global capitalism. The question of national-global relations, or of the relation between the nation-state and the global economy, is the subject of Chapter 6.

5 An alternative Marxist theory of the state

Social form critique and its application to the Korean developmental state

As a second step towards the theorisation of the developmental state beyond statism, in this chapter, I will assess the key propositions and debates around 'social form critique' by looking at the classic contribution by the Soviet theorist Evgeny Pashukanis in the 1920s, the so-called 'German state derivation debate' of the 1970s and the British *Open Marxism* discussion in the 1990s. The most distinctive and crucial contribution of the tradition of 'social form critique' lies in the fact that it brings to the fore the historically specific *form* of the political in capitalism beyond and in addition to its *function* for the dominant class and the capitalist system. It explains the origins and characteristics of the specific form of the state in relation to the capitalist mode of production whose historical specificity lies in the production of wealth in the form of value (in the specific Marxian sense of the word). Viewed from social form critique, the state is the political form or expression of capitalist social relations in their totality, in which individuals are related as exchangers of commodities (values), in particular the commodity labour power, which means that in capitalist society, relations between individuals are mediated by 'abstract labour', i.e. labour under the perspective of its being productive of value. Significant conceptual advancement notwithstanding, the social form critique is limited in that its primary focus is on the 'derivation' of the state and its form from the concept of capital, which makes it susceptible to being understood as a theory operating exclusively at the level of the 'logic' of capital separated from 'historical', empirically observable class struggles, that is, at the level of state-society relations within a particular (national) social formation. This tendency is apparent in the assessment of the Korean developmental state by Dae-oup Chang. Apart from the fact that Chang's assessment contradicts a core premise of social form critique by implausibly postulating that working-class struggle *in and of itself* constitutes a movement against capital, his analysis primarily problematises the contradictions of capitalist development in Korea in terms of state-society relations through class struggle at the *domestic* level, leaving unexamined the other aspect of the statist conception: namely that the state is presented as the agent of national development by being autonomous from or even antithetical to the global.

The social form critique of the capitalist state

While the class content analysis of the capitalist state brings to light its function for the dominant class and the capitalist system, it falls short of providing a coherent alternative theoretical framework because it fails to examine the form of the state seriously or question why the state appears to stand outside the economic and other societal spheres. In contrast to class content analysis, 'social form critique' prioritises inquiry into the historically specific form of the existence of social relations in the context of the capitalist mode of production.[1]

Pashukanis and the form of the capitalist state

The most prominent scholar who brought to the fore the notion of the modern state as the social form of capitalist society is the Soviet legal theorist Evgeny Pashukanis. His work elucidates the main difference between class content analysis and social form critique. His book *Law and Marxism: A General Theory* (1989[1924]) was written more against contemporary Soviet legal theorists than against bourgeois thinkers, and pointed out the shortcomings of the former in spite of their intention to offer a critique of law in capitalism. If many of his contemporaries aimed to reveal the class determinants of law, namely how it corresponds to and safeguards the interests of the ruling class, Pashukanis probed into the fact that law is a social form in bourgeois society, posing the question of why 'this society itself appears as an endless chain of legal relations' (1989: 85): he asks why individuals in capitalism are seen to be the bearers of private egoist interests and exist as legal subjects, whereby 'all economic life is to be built on the principle of agreement between autonomous wills' (Pashukanis 1989: 103).

According to Pashukanis, those that analyse bourgeois state and law in terms of their service to the interests of the ruling class can 'uncover the class *content* concealed within legal forms, but do not explain why this content assumes that particular *form*' (Pashukanis 1989: 84; emphasis added). Viewed from Pashukanis's perspective, the question of the functions of the state and that of its form are different, and the latter constitutes the starting point of Marx's inquiry into capitalist social relations, including the state. Therefore, assessing the state, and likewise the legal and ideological apparatus, in terms of how they serve the interests of the ruling class, helps explain the *content* of class rule but not how and why they arose in a specific *form*. In Pashukanis's words, 'the conscious exploitation of ideological forms [by the ruling class] is … something separate from their emergence, which usually occurs independently of people's will' (1989: 140).

> Incidentally, if the bourgeoisie is politically, that is, by its state power, 'maintaining injustice in property relations'… *it is not creating it.* The 'injustice in property relations' which is determined by the modern

> division of labour, the modern form of exchange, competition, concentration, etc., *by no means arises from the political rule of the bourgeois class*, but vice versa, the political rule of the bourgeois class arises from these modern relations of production which bourgeois economists proclaim to be necessary and eternal laws.
>
> (Marx 1976: 319, as cited in Pashukanis 1989: 92; emphasis by Pashukanis)

Pashukanis argues that the question of the capitalist state should be posed not in terms of whose interests it serves or what function it performs for the system but in terms of its social *form* and social constitution, including the separation of state and economy itself. The question here is why the capitalist state assumes a form of existence as separate from the economic. According to Pashukanis, the idea of linking or merging the public and the private, or the political and the economic, can only arise when these two categories are assumed to be separate from each other in the first place (1989: 105).

> [W]hy does class rule not remain what it is, the factual subjugation of one section of the population by the other? Why does it assume the form of official state rule, or – which is the same thing – why does the machinery of state coercion not come into being as the private machinery of the ruling class; why does it detach itself from the ruling class and take on the form of an impersonal apparatus of public power, separate from society?
>
> (Pashukanis 1989: 139)

Pashukanis finds the material conditions that give rise to a particular social form itself from given relations of production or property relations (1989: 91). For him, capitalist production relations are historically specific in that they constitute 'a society of commodity-owners first and foremost', and thereby 'social relations in the production process assume a reified form in that the products of labour are related to each other as values' (Pashukanis 1989: 111). In the capitalist mode of production, wherein commodity production is generalised, the relation between the exploiting and the exploited is expressed in the form of 'equal' and 'independent' individual commodity exchangers. 'Just as in the commodity, … the concrete types of human labour are dissolved into abstract human labour as the creator of value' (Pashukanis 1989: 113). In the social formation in which 'the exploitative relation exists formally as relationship between two "autonomous" and "equal" owners of commodities, political power can take on the form of public authority' (Pashukanis 1989: 141). Expressed differently, '[t]o the extent that society represents a market [where individuals meet as exchangers of commodities], the machinery of state is actually manifested as an impersonal collective will, as the rule of law, and so on' (Pashukanis 1989: 143). As rephrased by Gerstenberger, the state 'comes forward as the guarantor of the (legal) regulation of exchange relationships, it formally withdraws from society and at the same time becomes the state of society as a whole' (Gerstenberger 1978: 156).

> Effective power acquires a markedly juridical, public character, as soon as relations arise in addition to and independently of it, in connection with the act of exchange, that is to say, private relations par excellence. By appearing as a guarantor, authority becomes social and public, an authority representing the impersonal interest of the system.
>
> (Pashukanis 1989: 137)

The fact that the state appears to be detached from the economic as the external guardian ensuring and guaranteeing the interests of society as a whole is engendered by the material conditions of capitalist production relations themselves. The historicisation of the form of capitalist social relations in this manner also denotes a historically specific form of class domination in capitalism: it expresses itself in the form of an 'indirect', 'impersonal' and 'abstract' force as opposed to that of the direct and personal subjugation of the exploited by the exploiters characteristic of pre-capitalist (e.g. feudal) social relations. '[C]lass domination in modern society is mediated by the rule of law and the modern state' (Arthur 1989: 16). The specific form of capitalist social relations and class domination in distinction from earlier periods, such as during slavery and serfdom, points to the fact that even

> coercion cannot appear [in the society based on commodity production] in undisguised form as a simple act of expediency. It has to appear rather as coercion emanating from an abstract collective person, exercised not in the interest of the individual from whom it emanates ... but in the interest of all parties to legal transactions.
>
> (Pashukanis 1989: 143)

In summary, according to the social form analysis of the capitalist state following Pashukanis, it takes the form of an entity embodying formal, official and impersonal rules, detached from the economic arena of direct exploitation. This is what characterises the specificity of the capitalist state and the capitalist mode of class domination. One of Pashukanis's most distinctive contributions to the general theory of the state and law is that he inquires into their form, or mode of existence, beyond their servicing functions for the dominant class. His perspective differs from class content analysis that sees that 'the form of law is essentially neutral and can be filled with a given class content according to the will of the dominant class' (Arthur 1989: 29). This understanding also carries a political implication different from that implied in class content analysis: to the extent that the form of the state arises from the historically specific capitalist production relations, it cannot be transposed to a post-capitalist society. Seen from the perspective of

Pashukanis, the 'withering away of certain categories of bourgeois law ... in no way implies their replacement by new categories of proletarian law', but it will 'mean the withering away of law altogether, that is to say the disappearance of the juridical factor from social relations' (Pashukanis 1989: 61).[2]

From the state derivation debate to open Marxism: critiques of structural functionalism

The question of capitalist social form central to Pashukanis has been carried forward as the guiding framework of what came to be known as the '(German) state derivation debate'. The group of those who engaged in and shared the theoretical stance of the 'state derivation debate' overlaps with that of the participants in the Conference of Socialist Economists (CSE) in the late 1960s and early 1970s in the UK, and those who contributed to three edited volumes titled *Open Marxism* published in the early 1990s.[3] In discussing the core propositions of social form critique following Pashukanis, I will focus on a selected number of key authors, including John Holloway, Sol Picciotto, Werner Bonefeld, Simon Clarke and Heide Gerstenberger.

The 'state derivation debate' refers to an intellectual development in Marxist theory of the state initiated in West Germany in the 1960s. As the term suggests, its primary aim was to 'derive the state as a political form from the nature of the capitalist relations of production', and this was understood 'as a first step towards constructing a materialist theory of the capitalist state' (Holloway and Picciotto 1978: 2). The contributors to the state derivation debate focussed on the question of social form because 'to ask about the form of the state is to raise the question of its historical specificity: the existence of the state as a thing separated from society is peculiar to capitalism' (Holloway 1994: 29). Acknowledging the intellectual influence of Pashukanis on the state derivation debate, the participants of the debate understood that it is the social relations of the capitalist mode of production that have given rise to the forms of the economic and the political (Clarke 1977: 13; Holloway 1994: 27; Holloway and Picciotto 1977: 78–9, 1978: 18). The scholars of the state derivation debate thus pose the question of the relation between the economic and the political not in terms of how the economic base determines the political superstructure or how much the latter is autonomous from the former. Instead, they ask, 'what is it about social relations in bourgeois society that makes them appear in separate forms as economic relations and political relations?' (Holloway and Picciotto 1978: 18). Gerstenberger puts this question more specifically for the state: '[w]hy does the state change its form in the bourgeois epoch? Why does it become, in form, the state of society in the whole?' (1978: 155).

While there is a significant degree of divergence amongst the contributors to the 'state derivation debate', as shall be discussed below, they commonly see both categories, the political and the economic, as separations-in-unity rather than prioritise one category over the other or try to link them by stressing their intensive interaction. As the contributors to the debate understand the forms of the political and the economic to exist within the totality of capitalist social relations, they criticise extant Marxist discussions for failing to see the inner connection between them. For instance, Holloway and Picciotto critically assess the two dominant Marxist theories of the state, which they call 'economic determinism' on the one hand and 'politicism' on the other: the former explains the actions of the state directly from the requirements of capital, considered to operate in the realm of the economic, and the latter insists on, often as a reaction to the former, 'the autonomy of the state' (see also Clarke 1977, 1992; Gerstenberger 1978, 1992). Differentiating their approach from these two approaches, Holloway and Picciotto argue that a materialist theory of the state is 'not to develop "political concepts" to complement the set of "economic concepts", but to develop the concepts of *Capital* in the critique not only of the economic but also of the political form of social relations' (Holloway and Picciotto 1978: 4).

Holloway and Picciotto extend their critique to another common propensity apparent amongst Marxists, that is, positing capital accumulation as an economic phenomenon and class struggle as a political one. According to them, with the question of social form ignored or not seriously inquired into, capitalist contradictions have often been seen to emanate from the economic logic of capital accumulation, while class struggle has been seen to be a political process (Holloway and Picciotto 1978: 11–2). They contend that class struggle does not merely provide a mediating link between the economic base and the political superstructure; rather 'the economic and the political [are] separate forms of the *single* class struggle, a single class struggle informed and bounded by the exigencies of capital accumulation' (Holloway and Picciotto 1977: 92; emphasis added). On this ground, they call into question the tendency, shared amongst Marxist scholars from Miliband and Poulantzas to Gramsci as well as the Neo-Ricardians, to dichotomise economic and political crises as if they were separable from each other. Holloway and Picciotto (1977: 92) hold that the 'crisis (i.e. the periodic crisis of capitalism) is neither an economic nor a political crisis: it is a crisis of the capital relation, a crisis made inevitable by the inherent contradictions of that relation'.

For Holloway and Picciotto, and for most contributors to the 'state derivation debate', capitalist social relations entail intrinsic contradictions as they are based on the appropriation of surplus value as the dominant form of exploitation. The fact that capital accumulation is dependent on the appropriation of surplus labour, particularly its increasing reliance on relative as opposed to absolute surplus value, tends to expel living labour, the producer of value, from the production process (e.g. through automisation), whose contradiction expresses itself as a tendency for the organic composition of capital to rise and the rate of profit to fall (Holloway and Picciotto 1977: 91).[4] This tendency cannot be understood as one operating in the realm of the economic but itself constitutes and is constituted by class struggle to the extent that it involves capital's incessant attempts to reproduce the conditions of its own existence by restructuring production relations as well as political organisations. This understanding suggests that class antagonism between capital and labour, class struggle, is inherent in the capital relation; hence there is no separation between economic structure and political class struggle. To put this succinctly, 'capitalist development is ... itself a process of class struggle' (Holloway and Picciotto 1978: 22).

The emphasis on the unity of structure and agency in class struggle and the critique of a concept of structure as supposedly external to human agency is central to the initiative of the three volumes of *Open Marxism*. Defining their own approach as 'dialectical/critical (that is "open") Marxism' as opposed to structural Marxism (e.g. Althusser and Poulantzas), the contributors to *Open Marxism* reiterate the essence of Pashukanis's argument and the 'state derivation debate' but place further emphasis on the dynamic character of the capitalist totality: 'dialectical and critical Marxism ... see the separation between the "economic" and the "political" as a difference subsisting within, and constituted by, an active unity' (Bonefeld et al. 1992: xv). According to the editors of *Open Marxism*, the question of (social) form refers to the mode of existence of capitalist social relations: namely the aspect that something exists only in and through the form(s) it takes (this is different from the more colloquial sense of the word 'forms', similar to 'types', such as in the notion of 'fascist' or 'authoritarian' forms of the state). Putting the question of social form in this manner, Bonefeld et al. problematise and aim to transcend the dichotomy between the economic and the political, structure and agency, and the abstract and the specific: 'the generic [must be seen] as inherent in the specific, and the abstract as inherent in the concrete' (Bonefeld et al. 1992: xvi).

> 'Openness', here, refers not just to a programme of empirical research ... but to the openness of Marxist categories themselves. This openness appears in, for instance, a dialectic of subject and object, of form and content, of theory and practice, of the constitution and reconstitutions of categories in and through the development, always crisis-ridden, of a social world.
>
> (Bonefeld et al. 1992: xi)

Amongst the contributors to *Open Marxism*, Bonefeld brings forward the question of 'social form' in his critique of the prominent Marxist state theorists or discussions prevalent in the 1970s and 1980s, from Poulantzas and the debate on (post-) Fordism (e.g. Jessop) to the state derivation debate (e.g. Hirsch). Defining Marx's methodology as 'substantive abstraction' as opposed to 'abstract materialism', Bonefeld opposes any theoretical tendencies that reduce social forms to objective laws or structures within and against which human agency acts. For this reason, he holds that Jessop's work on post-Fordism, based on 'the periodisation of the capitalist state form according to the changing forms of accumulation', is a variant of Poulantzasian structuralism. This is because it 'theorises [accumulation] crisis as a structural dysfunctionality' and assumes a 'corresponding, and hence functional, relation between mode of accumulation and regulative forms of the state' (Bonefeld 1992: 97; see also Clarke 1992; Holloway and Picciotto 1978: 27–8). Similarly, Bonefeld points out the weaknesses of Hirsch's approach insofar as the latter holds the dualism of structure and agency (class struggle) whereby objective laws of capitalist development are juxtaposed to class struggle. According to Bonefeld, in Hirsch's schema, the action of subjects and classes is seen as operating *within* the framework of its general law; as a result, class struggle is subordinated to a predetermined, objectively given, development of capitalism (Bonefeld 1992: 95; see also Bonefeld 1987; Holloway 1988). For Bonefeld, 'substantive abstraction' means tracing out 'the inner connection of social phenomena, an inner connection which constitutes social phenomena and their relation to each other as modes of existence of this very inner connection' (Bonefeld 1992: 104).

> Contrary to these [Jessop and Hirsch's] approaches to the state … 'structures' are modes of existence of the class antagonism of capital and labour. The 'laws of capitalist development' are nothing else than the movement of the class struggle. The 'laws of capitalist development' are an abstraction in action, a historical reality, a process and a movement of the process of labour within capital.
>
> (Bonefeld 1992: 98)

Social form critique advanced by the 'state derivation debate' and *Open Marxism* following Pashukanis is significant in that it historicises the mode of the existence of the political and the economic, and assesses state-economy relations as separation-in-unity and unity-in-separation. It takes the category of capital as the starting point of understanding the dynamics of social and political development, and posits the state as the political form of and a constituent of the totality of capitalist social relations. It explains the mode of existence of the state as a separable and quasi-independent entity from the other equally parcelised unit, 'the economic', in relation to the specific nature of capitalist production relations or the value-form of social relations. In so doing, it provides a theoretical framework alternative not only to liberal but to Marxist approaches that either argue that the separation arises from the functional necessity of capital (instrumentalist-functionalist accounts) or juxtapose state-led to market-oriented development and elevate the former as superior to the latter (institutionalism and Marxist critiques of neoliberalism).

Another distinctive aspect of the 'state derivation debate' and *Open Marxism* is that they relate the specifics of capitalist social relations to those of class domination in capitalism. In the capitalist mode of production, in which individuals are predominantly connected to each other as exchangers of commodities, the relation between the exploiting and the exploited assumes the form of 'equal' and 'voluntary' (legal) agreements between individuals. In this social foundation, the 'mode of existence of the state inheres in the historical tendency towards the expanded social organisation of social reproduction in terms of law' (Bonefeld 1992: 117). Seen in this way, 'formal freedom and equality … is the mode of the existence of exploitation' in capitalism (Bonefeld 1992: 116). This suggests that categories, such as 'the political' and 'the economic' that assume the form of separate spheres, independent of each other, each operating with its own laws, are historically specific to the capitalist mode of production, to which class antagonism between capital and labour is intrinsic. In other words, the 'state is not a state in capitalist society, but rather a moment of the class antagonism of capital and labour' (Bonefeld 1992: 113).

The state being theorised as a political expression of capitalist totality, social form critique has political implications that differ from those implicit in class content analysis. If the particular mode of the political is derived from capital, this highlights the fact that the critique of capital is inseparable from that of fragmented forms of capitalist social relations. Viewed from the perspective of social form critique, then, the capitalist state is capitalist not because of its capital-serving functions, as implied in class content analysis, but because it is an expression, or form, of the capitalist totality. This understanding suggests that the growth of state activity, for instance Keynesianism, indicates a mere shift *within* the form of capitalist domination rather than a shift *away* from capitalist domination. This is because the 'difficulties of capital accumulation arise not from capitalist anarchy but from the capital relation itself; even if capital could "organize" itself through the state, the basic contradiction of capitalist accumulation would remain' (Holloway and Picciotto 1977: 95; see also Clarke 1988). It follows that a critique of the state necessitates that of the entirety of capitalist social relations: 'production relations or relations of exploitation are neither economic nor political … the task of Marxist theory is precisely to criticize and transcend these forms' (Holloway and Picciotto 1978: 178, ft. 3).

Problems and ambiguities of social form critique

Despite the fact that social form critique offers valuable insights beyond liberal as well as functionalist-Marxist accounts of the state, it is not without weaknesses and particularly falls short of providing an adequate theoretical framework for the developmental state. The fact that social form critique addresses the state at the most fundamental level, namely *what it is* rather than what it does and what it is *for*, is arguably the most distinctive aspect that makes it differ from other approaches. However, this strength also constitutes its vulnerability. As diversity *within* the state derivation debate indicates, there is much disagreement beyond the general proposition that the state is the political form of capitalist social relations (see Holloway and Picciotto 1978: 15–30). Particularly, there is a great degree of ambiguity concerning issues such as the relation between the state form and its class content (or its functions for class domination), structure and agency (class struggle), and the state and the global (world market).

In fact, the relation between the state form and its class content has never been ignored in social form critique.[5] For instance, while Pashukanis's focus is on the question of why the state in capitalism takes the form of a social and public authority representing the impersonal interest of the system, he also acknowledges that the capitalist state as a class state cannot merely be reduced to the abstract guarantee of the conditions of exchange according to value: '[i]n historical reality, the "constitutional state", … the state standing above society is only realised as its own opposite, as a "committee for managing the common affairs of the whole bourgeoisie"' (Marx and Engels [The Communist Manifesto] 1969: 110–1, as cited in Pashukanis 1989: 146–7, ft.18). Reminiscent of the instrumental and functionalist approach to the capitalist state, Pashukanis understands that the state detached from the economic serves the interest of capitalists: 'class society is not only a market where autonomous owners of commodities meet, but is at the same time the battlefield of a bitter class war, where the machinery of state represents a very powerful weapon [for the bourgeoisie]' (Pashukanis 1989: 149–50). Similarly, he recognises that individuals in concrete situations are bound by multiple ties of mutual dependence, beyond those of appropriation and alienation: 'the state consists of the struggle between various political forces, between classes, parties, all manners of groups' (Pashukanis 1989: 147). Above all, he suggests that a particular form of the capitalist state that is in tune with its ideal representation, namely the 'constitutional state', is not automatically given with the rise of capitalism, nor is its endurance guaranteed. He hints that class rule in capitalism can be expressed in a more naked or overt manner, depending on the particular conditions of class struggle: what prevents the capitalist state from resorting to a more overt mode of domination is the power balance between classes. Pashukanis (1989: 150) thus states that when the bourgeoisie are met by an 'extraordinary sharpening of the class struggle', they are 'forced to discard the mask of the constitutional state altogether, revealing the nature of state power as the organised power of one class over the other'.

This view is also implied in Gerstenberger's emphasis on history. She traces the actual historical processes of Europe's political, economic and ideological transition to capitalism, and argues that 'capitalism is the result of historical processes in the course of which capitalist class relations were constituted and made dominant' (Gerstenberger 1992: 152). She notes that the rise of less overt modes of class domination based on 'equal rights of citizens do not form a functional necessity of capitalist exploitation' (Gerstenberger 1992: 171). To the extent that 'the naked force … lurks behind the form of [state] appearance', 'it is not definitely settled that the capitalist mode of production *requires* formal equality, universal suffrage and democratic structures' (Gerstenberger 1978: 149–50: emphasis in the original). According to this understanding, the form of the state detached from individual capitalists' interests does not come about 'automatically'; it is not naturally given by the logic of capital. By the same token, as discussed above, Holloway and Picciotto, Bonefeld and Clarke's critiques of functional structuralism can be understood as the same endeavour to refute the ossification of social form as structure external to concrete historical processes: '[s]ocial form has no existence separate from concrete historical development' (Bonefeld 1992: 105). This highlights the fact that social form critique, at least in principle, does not operate only at the level of 'capital logic' and that its primary focus on the delineation of the specificity of the capitalist state form does not mean that it disregards its class content or capital-serving functions.

However, ambiguities and contradictory tendencies remain in social form critics' assessments of the relation between the state form and its class content. If Pashukanis only touched upon these issues crudely, the contributors to the 'state derivation debate' and *Open Marxism*, in their opposition to reducing social form critique to an analysis of logical structure detached from history, tend to emphasise the concreteness of history and class struggle. This proposition leads them to underestimate or ignore 'structure like historical patterns' of the capitalist dynamic operating at the global level. For instance, when Gerstenberger stresses that the formation of capitalist class relations is a result of historical processes arising from the pre-existing political structures and practices (e.g. the *ancien régime*) (1992: 158–61), she notes that there are 'vast differences in these historical processes which led to the dominance of capitalist class relations in those societies in which capitalism developed indigenously'. She adds that the differences are even greater in 'those societies where capitalism was introduced by colonial or imperialist forms of domination' (Gerstenberger 1992: 152).

While Gerstenberger's view has merit as a critique of the separation between logical and historical analyses, first, it brings up the question of whether capitalist development in any given society, even England, can be assessed 'indigenously'. In fact, this understanding, at least implicitly, presupposes a 'national society' as a given unit.[6] Second, even if she seems to imply that there is a common factor or mechanism that separates societies of 'indigenous' capitalist development from those where capitalism came about due to colonialism or imperialism, she does not specify *which* differences there existed and why and how they were produced. As a result, her sensitivity to concrete historical processes concerning the rise of capitalist class relations renders the patterned unfolding of the capitalist dynamic that can be identified beyond national variations accidental and contingent. Expressed differently, her approach is unable to account for certain historical patterns discernible at the global level which are crucial for the theorisation of the state in the world-economic periphery, e.g. the developmental state: the pattern most relevant in this context is that, the later capitalist development takes place in terms of world time, the stronger the compulsion for the state to intervene in the economy and for development to take a 'national' form in the name of overcoming 'backwardness' (see Chapter 6 for further discussion). If almost all modern states exist as, or aspire to become, nation-states, and most of them have built their modern states through and under the influence of 'exogenous' powers, regardless of the varying degrees of intensity and the different outcomes of class struggle, then there is a *structural* tendency that generates such convergence that needs to be explained: if contingency repeats itself, it becomes a structure or at least a structure-like pattern. In short, Gerstenberger's interest in liberating history from the logic of capital, combined with her implicitly nation-focussed approach, has the effect of ignoring 'structure-like historical patterns' operating at the global level that mediate and condition the content and outcomes of class struggle at the level of the national social formation itself.

A similar kind of ambiguity concerning the relation between social form and class content, and structure and agency in class struggle, can be found in the works of Holloway and Picciotto and Bonefeld, albeit differently from Gerstenberger.[7] In fact, these authors' assessments of these issues are in themselves not wrong and provide important insights missing from most Marxist theories. Above all, they assess the question of the relation between social form and class struggle dialectically by bringing to the fore the contradictory dynamic of capitalism. While stressing class struggle as the motor of history in their critiques of functionalist structuralism, their understanding of it differs from that prevalent in class content analysis. For example, Holloway and Picciotto differentiate the form of class struggle and class struggle in general: while 'all hitherto existing society is the history of class struggle', 'the *form* of class antagonism has a central role in determining the dynamic of that struggle' (1978: 12; emphasis in the original). This underscores the fact that some form of class struggle in a generic sense may have characterised all of human history, but the historically specific form of class struggle *in capitalist society* is conditioned and determined by the specific form of capitalist exploitation based on the appropriation of surplus value. In their analysis, Holloway and Picciotto draw attention to the historically specific *forms* of class struggle in capitalism and to the contradictory and dialectical nature of class struggle, that is, 'the nature of the *constraints* and the *impetus* arising from that form' (Holloway and Picciotto 1978: 29; emphasis added).[8] A similar insight can be found in Bonefeld's work. His argument for the unity of theory and history, and structure and agency, intends to emphasise the dynamic character of capitalist social relations based on class antagonism: '[t]here is no movement outside social antagonism' (Bonefeld 1992: 102). The contradictory movement of capitalism points to the fact that labour exists *in* and *against* capital: 'the contradictory existence of the working class is manifest in its antithesis to capital's command and in its existence as a moment of social reproduction in the form of capital' (Bonefeld 1992: 102).

These valuable and distinctive insights notwithstanding, the social form critique on its own is not able to explain which aspects of which labour struggles promise to transcend rather than be integrated into capital. In the same vein, this highly general theory cannot explain why labour has historically tended to exist *in* rather than *against* capital. These questions, though relevant universally across capitalist societies, are particularly pertinent in the context of the world-economic periphery, where most social and working-class struggles have called for the realisation of liberal values (e.g. fair wage levels, improving working conditions) rather than the transcendence of the capitalist mode of production. As shall be discussed in the context of the Korean case in Part III, the mode of Korean working-class struggles in the 1980s was militant, but its primary goals were limited to achieving political democratisation (e.g. direct presidential elections) and 'fairness' in the workplace. This Korean experience seems to suggest that 'catch-up' development that demands an extreme level of mobilisation of human and natural resources, typically performed by an authoritarian state conditioned by a country's place in the world-economic hierarchy, structurally patterns, if not determines, the intensity and content of the working-class struggle itself. Furthermore, to the extent that 'catch-up' development takes place in the form of 'nation-building' in the context of de-colonisation, 'catch-up' development is expressed as an anti-imperialist and nationalist movement. I argue, therefore, that the construction of an alternative theory of the developmental state makes it necessary to pay attention to 'structure-like historical patterns' that operate at the global level.

The social form critique discussed in this chapter is strongly opposed to any tendencies to 'close' history to a pre-determined structure (hence 'open' Marxism). In this sense, it emerged as a critical reaction to structuralism and functionalism, which were the dominant Marxist theories of the state in the 1970s and 1980s in Western Europe. This leads it, though, in spite of arguing for the unity of structure and history, to underestimate and dismiss anything 'structural' as it tends to equate 'structure' with 'determinism'. 'Open Marxist' theory has attempted to overcome structuralism by emphasising class struggle: openness in history is attained by asserting the primacy of agents against structure.[9] Rather ironically, this leads to an ahistorical element in the theorisation of capitalism: the commitment to and interest in the practical negation of the structure-like features of capitalism prevents these theorists from examining how capitalism operates as a structure and how and why it reproduces itself.

The social form critique as applied to the developmental state

Social form critique has hardly been discussed outside a relatively small circle of Marxist theorists, partly, perhaps, because its orientation is limited, albeit relevant and important, to the fundamental aspects of capitalist social relations: namely the mode of existence of the political and the economic.

In this context, Dae-oup Chang's assessment of the Korean developmental state under the framework of what he calls 'value reading' is a rare attempt to analyse it from the perspective of social form critique.

The 'value reading' of the developmental state

Chang starts, similarly to Chibber and Cammack, critiquing the dominant literature on the Korean developmental state, that is, the statist or what he calls 'neo-institutionalist' view that the Korean state was autonomous from the dominant group in society and thus neutral in terms of class interests (Chang D-O 2009: ch. 2).[10] However, Chang goes further by arguing that it is a 'myth' that the Korean developmental state was autonomous and that this mystification stems from the fundamental limits of the statist understanding of state-capital relations. A key weakness of the statist literature lies, according to Chang, in the fact that it assesses

> the relations between the capitalist state and other societal forces, such as capital, in an a-historical way in which the state and capital appear merely as different sets of individual social actors, without regard to the nature of the capitalist state in relation to *particularly* capitalist social relations.
>
> (Chang D-O 2009: 27; emphasis in the original)

In addition to the statist approaches to the developmental state, Chang also addresses the inadequacy of what he calls 'the essentialist and structuralist accounts' of orthodox Marxist theories of the capitalist state, which I refer to as 'class content analysis' (see Chapter 4). For Chang, both accounts are built on the 'spatial separation of spheres [i.e. the political and the economic]' and ignore the fact that this 'separation … [is] a specific mode of manifestation of capitalist social relations through which those relations are fetishised into forms of independent entities, including the political state' (Chang D-O 2009: 35). In transcending the statist view based on the thesis of state autonomy as well as the essentialist and structuralist views of the capitalist state, Chang proposes, as an alternative conceptual framework, Marx's critique of capitalist social forms or else an interpretation of the capitalist state in terms of the category of value, which he calls the 'value-reading of the capitalist state' (Chang D-O 2009: 35).

According to Chang, '[Marx's] critique of the labour theory of value is … a critique of the naturalistic conceptualisation of the categories of capitalist society' (Chang D-O 2009: 35). Marx's theory of value reveals the origins of the mysterious, abstract forms of social domination in capitalism, that is, the relations of commodity production and exchange whereby 'the individual's labour becomes a part of social labour in the form of exchange-value and money' (Chang D-O 2008: 37). Thus, 'value is the mode of existence of labour, the human activity in capitalist social relations and, at the same time, the form in and through which the specific social relations appear and exist' (Chang D-O 2009: 37). Chang argues that 'the areas and categories of social interconnection, including the state … [are] … forms of the totality, modes of existence of capitalist social relations' (2009: 35), and 'the state… [is] the *specific mode of manifestation* of capitalist social domination' (2009: 30; emphasis in the original).

To the extent that Chang probes into the capitalist state and its specific form of existence, he shares his starting point with the 'state derivation debate'. He sees it as an 'attempt to relate the particular form of the capitalist state in the context of Marx's critique of the abstract nature of the reproduction of relations of commodity production' (Chang D-O 2009: 44). While basing his critique on the question of capitalist social form, he critically engages with the 'state derivation debate', particularly with those that he believes undervalue the role of working-class struggle in the formation of the 'state form'. For instance, Chang argues, Müller and Neusüss (1978) fail to offer an 'explanation of the essential relations between class struggle and the state in deriving the state-form' (Chang D-O 2009: 47). According to Chang, these authors assess the limit of the self-reproduction of the capitalist relations in terms of the self-destruction of capital itself rather than in terms of class struggle constructed by the working class: the authors assume, according to Chang, that labour is passive and subordinated to capital (2009: 47).

The centrality of class struggle to deriving the state form and animating the capitalist dynamic is further stressed in Chang's critique of a text by Blanke, Jürgens and Kastendiek (1978), who, from Chang's perspective, separate the aspect of the 'coerciveness of class domination' (the subjective aspect) and the 'abstractness of capitalist domination' (the 'material-abstract' aspect). Chang contends that these two aspects of capitalist domination must be seen as '*the continual movement of inversion between those two aspects*, i.e. the fact that the inherently coercive relations appear continually in the form of a material-abstract form of relations' (Chang D-O 2009: 48–9: emphasis in the original). He writes that the 'coercive force does not find a place *outside* of the value relations but *it is in there*, i.e. in the movement from the coercive nature to the abstract form through value-forms' (Chang D-O 2009: 49: emphasis in the original). He emphasises that capitalist social relations are characterised by continual inversion, or fetishisation, a process whereby the social relations become and appear to be relations between things, and the coercive nature of capitalist social relations is inverted into mutual contractual relations between equal individuals. This inversion, however, constantly encounters the counter-movements to the inversion: namely de-fetishisation through the class struggle between labour and capital; the counter-tendencies against the inversion (i.e. de-fetishisation) are inherent in the value-form of social relations.

> … the immanent limits of the movement of inversion of the social relations finally appear in the concrete forms of 'class struggles' between a wage labourer working at various points of surplus value creation and a capitalist … The class struggle between labourers and capitalists now

> express [sic] the *immanent limits* of the very inversion. In this sense, the necessity of the state cannot logically be given to the state but is what has been acquired in and through the development of class struggle.
> (Chang D-O 2009: 51: emphasis in the original)

Chang concludes from this that the law of value is not 'a law imposing a purely abstract rule on the passive working class' but 'a law manifesting its intrinsic contradiction in the class struggle' (2009: 54). He holds that the form of the state separated from civil society is a theoretical (hypothetical) moment of the inversion, which can only be realised historically through the concrete class struggle (Chang D-O 2009: 50–4). On this basis, he puts forward his key proposition that 'it is only possible to look at state formation as *a form-formation process* in the development of the capitalist relation as a totality through the development of class struggle' (Chang D-O 2009: 58). Having set this proposition as the guiding framework of his analysis, Chang traces the form-formation and form-transformation of the Korean state through the development of class struggle from the period of Japanese colonialism to the post-Asian financial crisis of 1997/98.

Bringing class struggle back in, leaving 'catch-up development' out

Chang's 'value-reading' of the developmental state makes the important point that the capitalist state must be seen as a complementary-but-differentiated moment of the capital relation. This view throws light onto the fact that mainstream state theories, including statist forms of Marxist theory, take the autonomous *appearance* of the state for its *nature* without understanding its being a dimension of the capitalist social totality. Furthermore, Chang engages with one of the key problems of the 'state derivation debate', that is, the tendency of social form critique to be confined to a logical analysis of categories detached from history. His proposal to assess 'state formation as a form-formation process through the development of class struggle' is precisely an endeavour to impart a dynamic and history-sensitive perspective to social form critique.

In spite of these valuable points, Chang's analysis entails many ambiguities and falls short of offering an alternative perspective beyond the statist theorists. First, while he argues that fetishisation *and* de-fetishisation are equally intrinsic to the value-form of capitalist social relations, he accuses Müller and Neusüss of finding the limits to capital not in the development of class struggle but in the self-destructive nature of capital itself. This seems to suggest that Chang sees class struggle as a force of de-fetishisation, posing a limit to the capitalist inversion of social relations to mysterious and abstract value-forms. In this context, he assesses working-class struggle *in and of itself* as a movement against capital that poses a limit to capital from the *outside*: he posits working-class struggles as constituting the countermovement to fetishisation, as *extrinsic* to the category of capital.

This conceptualisation of the relation between capital and labour raises the question of whether and in what cases any working-class movements constitute movements against capital. For instance, it begs the question whether the working-class struggles in Korea in the 1970s and 1980s, though increasingly well-organised and militant, primarily demanding 'higher wages and establishment of unions', as Chang puts it (2009: 98), can be seen as a movement against capital. Chang's understanding of capital-labour relations contradicts one of the principal aspects of the 'state derivation debate' and *Open Marxism*: namely to challenge the very dualism of structure and class struggle. The scholars of the social form critique, including Clarke, Holloway, Picciotto and Bonefeld, all emphasise that the dynamic character of the capitalist contradiction lies in the fact that labour exists *in and against* capital: labour movements struggle for the conditions of labour's own reproduction, which is at the same time the reproduction of capital. Class struggle is constrained by but at the same time attains impetus from the capital relation of whose dynamic it is constitutive. Chang, however, assigns working-class movements and activism a privileged status in challenging and overcoming fetishised (value-form) social relations. This view is in effect a 'workerist' critique of structural Marxism that places the primacy of working-class struggles over the 'structural' constraints of capital. By proposing a critique of one tradition of traditional Marxism (structuralism) from the standpoint of another (workerism), both of which the 'state derivation debate' had set out to challenge, Chang offers a rather flattened, non-dialectical theorisation. His claim of 'bringing class struggle back in' (2001) makes little sense when class struggle is constitutive of capital in the first place.

Second, Chang offers only an unconvincing critique of the 'state derivation debate'. He criticises a range of contributors to this debate for failing to grasp the unity of the 'coerciveness of [concrete] class domination' and the 'abstractness of [formal] capitalist domination' within the capitalist form, or 'value-form', of social relations. However, as discussed above, the dialectic of form and class content of the capitalist state, or the relation between its apparent detachment from society and its capitalist-serving coercive character, has been central to the 'state derivation debate', albeit with varying degrees of emphasis by different authors. As seen above, while Pashukanis sought to identify the historically specific form of capitalist social relations in a society of generalised commodity and value production, he located, albeit not systematically, the question of social form in relation to its class content (coercion). In fact, the 'state derivation debate' is initiated precisely to explain why the state as a *class state* in capitalism takes the form of impersonal *abstract* authority and why even coercion is exercised in the form of serving the *general* interest as opposed to serving private interests. Chang's critique is directed at a particularly formalistic interpretation of the 'state derivation debate', which has been acknowledged and problematised within the original debate itself (see above).

The ambiguities inherent in Chang's general understanding of the relation between capital and class struggle are also reflected in his assessment of the Korean state as a 'form-formation process' that emerges in and through class struggles. This view generates confusion in terms of what he means by 'form'. As seen above, Bonefeld et al. (1992) distinguished the concept of form (in the Hegelian-Marxist sense) as 'mode of existence' (e.g. 'the political' and 'the economic' as forms – modes of existence – of modern society, i.e. the forms in which the latter exists) and that of form (in the positivistic sense) as a subset, or species, of a more general category, or genus (e.g. the fascist and the liberal-constitutional states as particular forms of 'the modern state' in general). Chang seldom clarifies his use of these concepts and tends to use them interchangeably. On the one hand, he engages in the question of social form and emphasises time and again how the capitalist state has been 'mystified' or 'fetishised' as autonomous from society and labour, and how the relations of exploitation are mystified as those of equality. On the other hand, he refers to the developmental state as a specific form of the state, as a species of something more general. Conflating these two dimensions of the concept, he directly applies his critique of social form to that of the developmental state. In this analysis, there is no difference between the autonomy of the state as *the political form* of capitalist relations and that of the developmental state as *a specific kind of* capitalist state.

This collapsing of the two levels of analysis of the state in part comes from Chang's national-centred approach, ignoring the relation between the (fetishistic) characteristics of the developmental state and 'catch-up' development in the context of the hierarchical world-system. He assesses the 'state-form formation process' through class struggle within the given national social formation: state-form formation is assumed to be taxonomically comparable on equal terms, state by state. This position derives from Chang's failure to distinguish between the 'formation' (i.e. the historical constitution or emergence) of the modern state as the political form, or *mode of existence*, of modern, bourgeois society, and the 'formation', or emergence, of this or that particular form or *kind* of modern state, such as the developmental state.

For sure, Chang does not ignore the global and regional contexts (e.g. Japanese colonialism, US occupation and the Cold War) within which capitalist development in Korea took place (see Chang D-O 2009: 69). However, he hardly goes beyond claiming that all nation-states are related to each other and that they are part and parcel of global social relations: he does not inquire into *how* they are related and what implications the differentiated and hierarchical organisation of the world economy hold for specific contradictions and the mode of class struggle in the countries of 'catch-up' development in the context of the world-economic periphery. Chang himself acknowledges that his critique of the Korean state deals with 'inter-state political relations or global capitalist system … merely as contexts of capitalist development in Korea' (Chang D-O 2009: 168, fn. 4). He then justifies his domestic-centred perspective on the grounds that 'the global capital relations come to exist as national relations only through mediation of the development of the national class struggles within and over the existing social relations' (Chang D-O 2009: 69).

As a consequence, Chang is not able to fully grasp the specific nature of the 'mystification' of the developmental state. The mystification of the developmental state by the statist literature concerns not only its supposedly high level of autonomy from society *per se* but also, and arguably more importantly, the supposition that its alleged autonomy chiefly contributed to successful *national* development. As seen in Part I, the term 'developmental state' itself was introduced to denote a state deemed to be effective and successful in delivering national development in the world-economic periphery. The developmental state is exalted by Johnson, Wade and Asmden, institutionalists and Marxist critics of neoliberalism not only because of the 'myth' that it is autonomous from society but also because of the second 'myth' that it delivered 'nationally-oriented' development in the Third World. Even if Chang recognises the Korean developmental state's nationalist discourse, he hardly pursues this aspect as part of his critique of state fetishism. In this respect, he only offers, at best, a partial critique of statism: he limits his critique to the one dimension that the state is presented as autonomous from society and class struggles at the domestic level, leaving unquestioned the other dimension of the statist conception that the state is the agent of national development by being autonomous from the global economy, or else, as an agent that puts up a resistance to the intrusions of global capitalism.

As Chang limits his critique of statism to the dimension of state-society relations, his analysis fails to challenge the antithetical juxtaposition of the national and the global inherent in the discourse on the developmental state. While he sees the Asian financial crisis of 1997/98 as having been caused by the 'upsurge of the working class's challenge' to state and capital, he also sees it as having been caused by the 'growing involvement of Korean capitals into the crisis-ridden development of global capitalism' (2009: 8). This assessment tends to downplay the fact that capitalist development in Korea was part of the global totality of capitalist relations *from its inception*. Specific contradictions emanating from 'catch-up development' do not feature as factors that might have conditioned and mediated the magnitude of the crisis itself as well as the contents, limits and outcomes of working-class struggles in Korea (see Part III). As a result, when Chang accuses Jayasuriya (2000, 2001) of not adequately theorising the relation between globalisation and the state, he likewise remains trapped in a conceptual framework in which the national is juxtaposed as antithetical to the global. He argues that 'in order to understand properly the transition of the national states in the context of globalisation, it is also important to explain why and how national patterns of coordination of economic management have been undermined' (2009: 63–4). Chang arrives here at the conventional, nationalistic argument that the transformation of the developmental state is one in which its national orientation is undermined by globalisation. In a simple reversal, he replaces Jayasuriya's notion of the primacy of the global economy over the state with the primacy of domestic labour-capital relations over the global economy.

Conclusion

As the second step towards the construction of a theoretical framework that transcends the statist concept of the developmental state, in this chapter, I have critically reviewed an alternative perspective on the capitalist state within the Marxist tradition, 'social form critique', as opposed to what I described in the previous chapter as 'class content analysis'.

In contrast to class content analysis, which focusses on the capital-servicing functions of the capitalist state, as discussed, social form critique inquires into why the state takes the form of an entity or sphere separate from the economic and as a public as opposed to private authority, and why class domination is expressed not in the form of personal subjugation but in the form of an impersonal, formal and abstract force. The question of social form was most explicitly posed by Pashukanis and developed further by 'the state derivation debate' and *Open Marxism*. I have shown that social form critique offers an important starting point from which statism is challenged. Above all, it elucidates that the conceptual separation between the state and the economy arises from the historically specific production relations of capitalism, wherein individuals are related as commodity exchangers, and relations between individuals are mediated by abstract labour. Social form critique sheds light not only on the fact that taking for granted the apparent separation between state and economy and the forms in which they appear is fetishism, but on where this fetishised notion itself arises from: the specificity of the generalised commodity production relations.

While social form critique allows a fundamental critique of the capitalist state as a form of the totality of capitalist social relations, it is not without its ambiguities. Its focus on what the state is, and its form being derived from the nature of capital, makes it susceptible to being understood as a theory operating at the level of the 'logic' of capital separated from 'historical' class struggle. Furthermore, reflecting the political and intellectual climate of the period when structural-functionalism was predominant, some social form scholars have shown an inclination to place the primacy on agency (class struggle) over structure, in spite of their own core argument that labour exists *against* as well as *within* capital. Consequently, there is a lack of serious consideration of 'structure-like historical patterns' of capitalist development operational at the global level, which I contend are crucial to the theorisation of the developmental state.

These limits entailed in social form critique are apparent in Chang's approach in a more augmented fashion. While he attempts to provide a critique of the Korean developmental state from the perspective of social form critique, he takes on, as the object of his critique, a highly formalised interpretation of capital within the 'state derivation debate' and attempts to rectify it by putting class struggle centre-stage. Moreover, his approach lacks a systematic assessment of the question of 'catch-up' development, which is crucial to countering the statist conceptualisation of the developmental state, whose advocates see it as autonomous not only from domestic class relations but also from the global economy. Largely ignoring the specific contradictions emanating from 'catch-up' development, Chang reduces the developmental state to a mere national variant of the modern state, mediated and determined by *domestic* class struggles, by which he narrowly refers to working-class struggles. In so doing, while he criticises the statist notion of the state-market dichotomy and the notion of state autonomy, he leaves unquestioned the antithetical juxtaposition of the national to the global, or the internal to the external that underpinned the postulation by theorists of the developmental state and institutionalists of the state as *the* agent of national development.

Having identified the limitations of two key strands of Marxist state theory and their reflections in the analyses of the developmental state in the previous and current chapters, in the following chapter, I will propose an alternative theorisation of the developmental state beyond statism.

Notes

1 The term 'social form critique' is chosen to emphasise its concern with forms or modes of expression of capitalist social relations, such as the political (the state) and the economic, in distinction from a concern with, for instance, different particular forms of the capitalist state, such as the constitutional state or the fascist state. Some use the synonymous term 'form analytical approach' (see Starosta 2004: 45).

2 Pashukanis's critique of the state and law has been criticised for denying the value of democracy or liberal institutions. For instance, Robert Fine points out that Pashukanis's 'over-criticial view of law' eventually supported the bureaucratisation of the Soviet state. According to such criticism, his struggle for new forms of law and state was subordinated to a struggle for *less* law, and the withering away of law meant, in effect, the subordination of legal forms of the state to the state's other forms, in particular to the bureaucracy. As a consequence, according to Fine, Pashukanis lost sight of the democratic nature of Marx's critique of the state and ended up accepting Stalin's view (see Fine 2002: 155–69). Though not directly addressed against Pashukanis, there is a view that socialism (post-capitalism) should be built on existing democratic mechanisms to check the abuse of state power. Socialism is then understood as the full realisation of democracy (the radicalisation of democracy). For such a view see Wood (1995).

3 In this chapter, I primarily base my discussion of 'the state derivation debate' on the contributions in *State and Capital: A Marxist Debate*, edited by Holloway and Picciotto (1978).

4 According to Marx, 'capitalist production is not merely production of commodities, it is essentially the production of surplus-value'; hence, 'the labourer produces, not for himself, but for capital'. Capitalist labour thus consists of

necessary labour and surplus labour: the former points to an equivalent for the value of his labour-power, and the latter points to the value appropriated by capital beyond the former.

> In order to prolong the surplus-labour, the necessary labour is shortened by methods whereby the equivalent for the wages is produced in less time. The production of absolute surplus-value turns exclusively upon the length of the working-day; the production of relative surplus value, revolutionises out and out the technical processes of labour, and the composition of society (Marx 1967: 477).

The relative as opposed to the absolute surplus value extraction results in the organic composition of capital to rise, namely the ratio of the value of the *materials* and *fixed costs* (constant capital) embodied in production of a commodity (automation) to the value of the *labour-power* (variable capital) used in making it, for instance, through the introduction of new machinery.

5 Arthur says that the 'most difficult point in Pashukanis' argument is his handling of form and content' (1989: 29).

6 This question relates to one of the most contested debates within Marxist scholarship. One instance is the 'Brenner debate' (see Brenner 1977), which took place over the question of whether the expansion of the market through intensifying trade linkages, or the establishment of new social relations of production, caused the rise of capitalism. I take the view that Brenner's definition of capitalist class relations based on free wage labourers, implicitly imagined within the confinement of national social formation, is too restricting to be historically valid (see Song 2015; Chapter 7)

7 A key difference between Gerstenberger, on the one hand, and Holloway, Picciotto and Bonefeld, on the other, is how they theorise the relation between the nation-state and the global economy. The latter authors take the view that capitalist social relations are a global totality, whereby the nation-states subsist in and through the world market, rather than that the sum of the nation-states constitute the global (see the next chapter for these authors' discussions of the 'national-global' relation).

8 Gerstenberger argues (1992: 168) that

> [t]hrough the elimination of estates (the - more or less - institutionalised form of the generalisation of personal domination), class relations were - so to speak - structurally set free. Class struggle thus came to be the form of motion of society.

9 This tendency seems to be most apparent in Bonefeld's critique of Postone (1993, 2004) for being structuralist or for offering a *theory* rather than a *critique* of capital (Bonefeld 2004b: 122). While Bonefeld's argument itself is valid, I think his critique of Postone is rather ill-placed, given that Postone's approach has fundamental similarities to his own approach. For instance, Postone's argument that 'the Marxian critique is a critique of labor in capitalism, rather than merely a critique of labor's exploitation and mode of social distribution' (1993: 124) is in tune with Bonefeld's claim that 'Marxism is neither a theory of oppression/domination nor an economic theory, but a theory of the contradictions of social reality … I shall refer to the social relations of production in terms of the presence of labour *within* capital' (1992: 104; emphasis added).

10 Chang does not differentiate between the two approaches I assessed separately as 'developmental state theorists', such as Johnson, Wade and Amsden (see Chapter 1), and 'institutionalists', such as Skocpol and Evans (the authors of *Bringing the State Back In*) (see Chapter 2).

6 Theorising the developmental state beyond statism

A critique of the fetishism of national development

In this chapter, on the basis of the critical appraisal of class content analysis, social form critique and their respective reflections on the extant analyses of the developmental state carried out in the last two chapters, I attempt to establish a theoretical framework of the developmental state that transcends statism. I have shown in the previous chapters that while the question of the relation between the national and the global is of the utmost importance in constructing a theory of the developmental state beyond statism, it is either ignored or under-explored by the Marxist critics of the developmental state. The aim of this chapter is to theorise the developmental state by addressing the national-global relation with regard to 'catch-up development' *within* the framework of social form critique. First, I assess works of key scholars from the social form critique tradition (the state derivation debate and *Open Marxism*), such as von Braunmühl, Holloway and Bonefeld, who have engaged most directly with the question of the national-global relation. I argue that one of the key strengths of these authors lies in the fact that they make a methodological break from most approaches by placing the primacy on the totality over individual instances or constituents. They hold that capitalist social relations exist as a global totality, and the nation-state subsists in and through the world market. However, I also argue that these authors' framework is insufficient for developing a coherent analysis of the relation between the state and 'catch-up' development, which is crucial for the theorisation of the developmental state beyond statism: they pay scant attention to the *specific* manner in which the global totality manifests itself or else *how* the nation-state subsists in and through the world market. They seldom engage at any length in the question of the uneven and hierarchical dynamic of the global economy and the interstate system but rather focus on the early capitalist development of Europe (von Braunmühl) or address state-global economy relations at a highly conceptual level (Holloway and Bonefeld). In order to overcome these limits, in the second part of the chapter, I extend Marx's method of the critique of political economy to a critique of statism and theorise the developmental state in light of a critique of the fetishism of national development.

The developmental state and the question of the relation between the national and the global

Marxist state theory in general distinguishes itself from mainstream (liberal) theory in that it poses the question of the state in relation to class domination and exploitation. However, when it comes to the question of the relation of the national and the global, or the state-global economy relation, it is less distinguishable from mainstream theory to the extent that both tend to take as given society as nationally contained and antithetical to the global. As seen in Chapters 4 and 5, this tendency is also evident in Marxist assessments of the (Korean) developmental state, as seen in Chibber, Cammack Burkett and Hart-Landsberg and Chang.

To be fair, these Marxist critics of the developmental state never ignored the global contexts in their analyses. Nevertheless, despite significant differences amongst these authors in theorising the *capitalist* state, they share a commonality in that they posit the global as the *external* background within which *national* development and class struggle take place.[1] They hardly discuss the question of the national-global relation systematically at the level of theory, namely concerning the state existing as a nation-state within the interstate system and the world market: there has been no serious attempt to relate this question to the characteristics of the developmental state. As a consequence, in spite of their important contributions to challenging the statist assumption that the state is neutral and autonomous from class interests, the Marxist critics of the developmental state commonly fail to problematise adequately the notion that the state is the main agent of national development as being autonomous from the global. The inadequate level of theorisation of the national-global relation of these Marxist approaches also manifests itself in the fact that they either fall back into the statist framework when they assess the transformation of the developmental state or are unable to counter the reproduction of the statist concept of the developmental state in recent debates: they tend to adopt unproblematically the framework in which the transformation of the developmental state is assessed in terms of whether or not its orientation has moved from the national to the global and how much it is able to sustain its integrity against the global, posited as external to the national (see Chapters 4 and 5). However, to the extent that the statist understanding of the allegedly autonomous developmental state lies not only in its relation to the economy but in its relation to the global economy or the world market, posited as the external to a (national) social formation, the question of the national-global relation should be part of a critique of statism.

In what follows, I will discuss the ways in which the national-global relation is assessed within social form critique by looking at the works of key authors such as von Braunmühl, Holloway and Bonefeld. Social form critique, conceptualising the state as the political form of the capitalist social totality, is theoretically more rigorous in comparison not only to mainstream liberal state theories but also to instrumentalist and structuralist Marxist accounts of the capitalist state. Analysing the capitalist state from the standpoint of the social form of capitalist production relations offers the base from which a critique of statism can be constructed. The aim of the following section is to identify the strengths and limitations of social form critique concerning the question of the national-global relation, whereupon I will discuss ways in which to fortify and complement it.

Social form critique and the relation of the national to the global

Arguably, the national-global relation has not been central to social form critique. A critic of the 'state derivation debate' argued that insofar as the question concerning the relation between the nation-state and the global economy remains unresolved, the theory of the capitalist state is confined to the state-society relation within a single nation-state (Barker 1978). In a similar vein, recognising that the question of the state that exists as a nation-state in the international system is one of the lacunas of Marxist state theory, von Braunmühl (1978) addressed most directly the question in the context of the 'state derivation debate'.

In her discussion of the seemingly contradictory movements between *internationally* operating capitals and the continued intervention of states in the reproduction of *national* capitals, von Braunmühl opposes the commonly held view that the so-called 'internationalisation' of capital results from the process in which 'a national capital which was once essentially internal in scope reproduces itself externally to a growing extent and thus produces imperialism' (1978: 160). von Braunmühl rejects this dominant view as it posits the contemporary state as the political representative of *national* capitals, thereby retaining a 'methodological procedure which focuses on the national capital and its state' (1978: 161). She turns the perspective the other way round: instead of seeing the internationalisation of accumulation as a 'spill-over' of national capital into the external international arena, as a result of which a nationally bound state acts in conformity with international standards, she posits the totality of the international system, or the world market, as the unit of analysis. She places therewith the methodological primacy on the totality over individual instances.

> An international system is not the sum of many states, but on the contrary the international system consists of many nation states. The world market is not constituted by many national economies concentrated together, rather the world market is organized in the form of many national economies as its integral components.... Similarly the influence of the internationalization of capital accumulation cannot be understood if it is thought of as an external factor acting upon national statehood and the actions of the nation state, but must be conceived of as a process taking effect within the national economy as part of the world market.
>
> (von Braunmühl 1978: 162)

Citing from Marx's *Grundrisse* that the 'tendency to create the world market is directly given in the concept of capital itself' (Marx 1973: 408), and that the world market is the place 'in which production is posited as totality together with all its moments' (Marx 1973: 227), von Braunmühl (1978: 163) argues that the world market 'becomes the sphere of a global context of production and exchange in which capital is in the process of constituting itself as historical real world capital'. She holds that over the course of the process of the accumulation or valorisation of capital itself, 'the unity of the divided complexes of reproduction (i.e. national capitals) ... coheres increasingly to become a real, unified, global complex of reproduction' (von Braunmühl 1978: 165). To the extent that this development arises from the valorisation of capital itself and that it marks a new historical and concrete form of appearance of the unity of capital, the 'analysis of the movements of capital must start from the level of that unity within which capital movement actually takes place' (1978: 165). From this she argues that as much as the movement of capital and the law of value are to be analysed at the world-market level, 'the derivation and determination of the form of the *bourgeois state* must [also] be introduced in this dimension' (1978: 165; emphasis in the original).

> The world market must be seen as an international, state-organized and specifically structured, all-encompassing effective international context of competition, within which statehood arises and consolidates itself and states form their characteristic economic, social and political structure.
>
> (von Braunmühl 1978: 167)

On this ground, von Braunmühl brings to the fore the world-market determination of the form of the capitalist state and maintains that 'the form of the bourgeois nation state cannot be derived from the merely internal dimensions of a commodity producing class society alone' (von Braunmühl 1978: 166). For her, deriving the form of the state as a political expression of the capitalist mode of production at the level of the single state is inadequate: 'it is not just a question of the derivation of the state in general, but of the derivation of the specific political organization of the world market in many states' (von Braunmühl 1978: 166). Expressed differently, the form of the state is derived from capital not only as a political entity separate from the economy but as a nation-state within the multi-state system wherein interstate competition is intrinsic: the capitalist state exists not only in the form of an entity quasi-independent from the economy but in the form of the nation-state in the interstate system whereby each state relates competitively to all others.

Von Braunmühl describes the origins of the current interstate system, consisting of a plurality of nation-states, as the historical outcome of a complex interplay between pre-existing forms of class domination and the specifically modern, capitalist form of class domination: the capitalist mode of production came into being within pre-existing bounded territories, where authority and competition prevailed (von Braunmühl 1978: 173). With the rise of the capitalist mode of production, the previously existing class domination was reproduced in an altered form, namely being practiced through the mechanism of market relations, while the pre-existing political authority is reproduced in the form of the bourgeois nation-state (von Braunmühl 1978: 173–4). The establishment of the capitalist mode of production generated a new competitive dynamic between the pre-existent, territorially bound authorities: in order to maintain her power, the ruler is compelled to secure its material base, i.e. the capitalist mode of production within her territory.

Equally, the arrival of the capitalist mode of production redefines the role and function of political authorities: the territorial boundaries increasingly lose their purely political character, and the pre-existing structure of political power takes up new functions as 'the objective vehicle of the capitalist mode of production' (von Braunmühl 1978: 174) or, in Marx's words, the administrative executive of 'the historical dissolution process and as the makers of the conditions for the existence of capital' (Marx 1973: 507). In this

> transformation of pre-existing territorial boundaries into the bourgeois nation state as political form of organization a necessary basis for the operation of capital, the world market retains its characteristic principle of organization, the general realization of which reflects the penetration of capitalist relations of production.
>
> (von Braunmühl 1978: 172)

In this manner, von Braunmühl identifies the origins of the current interstate system with the beginning of the process, in which the capitalist mode of production altered the economic content of the pre-existing political structures. This is important because it suggests that the modern bourgeois nation-state form within the competitive interstate system is the expression of *both* the continuities of the class domination that had been characteristic of all previous forms of society and the rise of the new form of *capitalist* class domination: the 'existence of a state apparatus is in itself the admission by a society that its reproduction is organized along the dimension of domination, that it is a class society' (von Braunmühl 1978: 173).

While von Braunmühl engaged with the question of the national-global relation in the context of the 'state derivation debate' in the 1970s, Holloway and Bonefeld did so in the context of the more recent globalisation debate. As discussed in Chapter 3, discussions on globalisation have, to a large extent, been framed in terms of a zero-sum relation between the nation-state and the global economy, that is, the former either loses or retains its autonomy *vis-à-vis* the latter: globalisation has often been seen as a process of 'deterritorialisation' emerging from the allegedly hitherto national form of economic and social organisation built on 'territorial' principles. Holloway and Bonefeld, similarly to von Braunmühl, address the issue of the national-global relation, especially against this proposition.

Holloway (1994) opposes the view that the global nature of capitalist social relations is a result of the recent internationalisation or globalisation of capital. In problematising this popular view, he acknowledges the inadequacy of social form critique, which is primarily concerned with the question of 'statehood' and 'the political', abstracted from the fact that the state exists only in the form of a multiplicity of states: the conception that the state is a form of social relations says nothing about its existence in the nation-state form (Holloway 1994: 29–30). In an attempt to overcome this limit, Holloway makes a distinction between the question of the political and that of the nation-state. Concerning the latter, he argues that 'the "totality of capitalist social relations" is a global (world-wide) totality' and that the nature of the capitalist relation of exploitation has been inherently global from its inception (Holloway 1994: 30). He derives the global totality of capitalist social relations from the nature of capitalist exploitation, which has no spatial bounds: capital is indifferent to specific geographical locations and specific individuals; while exploitation exists in space, the space is undefined and contingent. According to Holloway, to the extent that the political is a moment of the totality of capitalist social relations, and the totality of capitalist social relations is a global totality, each national state is a moment of a global relation which is expressed not in the existence of a global state but in the existence of a multiplicity of apparently autonomous, territorially distinctive national states (Holloway 1994: 30–1).

> The freeing of the worker from a particular exploiter, the freeing of the exploiter from a particular group of workers, implied the establishment of social relations in which geographical location was absolutely contingent, in which capital could, and did, flow all over the world. The destruction of personal bondage was also the destruction of geographical constraint. The lord-turned-capitalist may or may not know where his money is being used for the exploitation of labour: that is in any case irrelevant, since all capital shares in the exploitation of all labour through the equalisation of the rate of profit through competition. ... The absolute contingency of space is epitomised in the existence of capital as money.
>
> (Holloway 1994: 30–1)

Similarly, Bonefeld and Burnham discuss the question of the nation-state and the global economy, particularly in the context of debating the neo-Gramscian perspective (Bieler and Morton 2003; Bieler et al. 2006; Bonefeld 2000, 2004a, 2006, 2008; Bruff 2009; Burnham 1991, 1994, 1997, 2001). The neo-Gramscian notion of the 'internationalisation of the state' has become an important metaphor in globalisation literature that indicates how the state has undergone transformation in terms of its functions and apparatus in conjunction with globalisation (Cox 1996; see also Panitch 1994). Problematising the implication inherent in the concept of the 'internationalisation of the state' that it shifts its functions and orientations from the national to the global according to supposedly new needs of globalising capital, Bonefeld argues, in line with von Braunmühl, that the totality, the world market, should be given methodological precedence over individual instances or 'national economies'.

> [A]ll and everything subsists not only in relation to the world market, but fundamentally, in and through the world market. Marx' critique of political economy points … towards the world market as the proper mode of existence and movement of the capital relation. … It [the world market] is the presupposition and result of the reproduction of capitalist social relations. … This suggests that the world market is not the sum of many states and their 'national economies', but it is instead the condition through which exists [sic] the inter-national relations between states.
>
> (Bonefeld 2006: 49–50)

Bonefeld, however, goes further than merely reiterating that capital is a global totality. He analyses the world market in light of a critique of commodity fetishism, problematising its social constitution. He asks 'why humanity exists as a mere personification or agent of abstract laws' (Bonefeld 2000: 48) and argues that the objective law-like existence of the world market is enforced by commodity fetishism and the value form of social relations. The world market is the universal existence of the fetishism of the commodity as 'the most developed form of individual interconnectedness and interdependence' (Bonefeld 2000: 43). To the extent that the world market stands for the totality of bourgeois social relations and the basis of the productive practice of all individuals as alienated individuals, it expresses itself in the form of 'independent' and 'abstract' forces that lie beyond the control of individuals (Bonefeld 2000: 43–4). If the point of Marx's critique of political economy is to disclose the social constitutions of the value form as relations of exploitation, the world market that appears to be the objective law external to human relations must be seen not as the global expansion of capital as a thing but as the social constitution of the universality of the class antagonism between capital and labour (Bonefeld 2000: 48–51).

One of the key strengths and distinctive aspects of the social form critique concerning the question of the national-global relation lies in the fact that it places the methodological primacy on the totality (the whole) rather than on individual components. According to von Braunmühl, Holloway and Bonefeld, the world market is not the sum of the national economies but the condition and at the same time outcome of the reproduction of capitalist social relations, in and through which the nation-states subsist: the world market organises and gives a particular meaning and function to political organisations in the multiple nation-state form. By postulating the state-global economy relations in this way, the scholars from the social form critique tradition assessed above offer a formidable counter-view against theories and approaches that tend to take the nation-state as a self-contained entity that (at least potentially) can move from the national to the global depending on the needs of capital and the orientation of ruling elites. From the perspective of social form critique, particularly Bonefeld's, positing the world market or the global economy as an objective force that exists externally to capitalist social relations, which are in effect inherently global and of which the state is a constituent political form, is fetishism.

A global totality of capitalist social relations devoid of uneven and hierarchical development

Despite the important insights provided by the scholars of social form critique concerning the national-global relation, their perspective is not entirely without blind spots. The emphasis on the global totality of capitalist social relations leads Holloway and Bonefeld to focus on the general aspects of the dynamics of (global) capital across nation-states. They correctly point out that being subject to the imperatives of capital accumulation, every nation-state is compelled to compete to secure more global surplus value within their respective territories (Bonefeld et al. 1995: 11; Bonefeld and Holloway 1995). However, they pay scant attention to the fact that each nation-state is located in a different position in the hierarchical global system, as a result of which it possesses different material and political resources for accessing global surplus value. Although differences in the ways in which nation-states relate to global capital are not entirely ignored (Holloway 1994: 37), there is no sustained inquiry into what differences there are and how and through which mechanisms they are (re)produced. The question of the hierarchy or power-asymmetric relations operating within the global economy and the interstate system, or the distinction between the developed ('rich') and the developing ('poor') countries, is not considered in a sustained manner. In other words, the totality of global capitalist social relations is derived primarily from the highly general fact that all nation-states, without exception, are part and parcel of the totality of global capitalist social relations (Holloway 1994: 32) or that all nation-states subsist in and through the world market (Bonefeld 2006: 49–50).

The fact that capitalist social relations are the global totality or, similarly, the proposition by Marx and Engels (1985: 83) that 'the need of a constantly expanding market for its products chases the bourgeoisie over the whole surface of the global. It must nestle everywhere, settle everywhere, and establish connexions everywhere', do not in themselves explain the *unevenness* and the *hierarchical* organisation of 'national' economies within the interstate system and the world market. In other words, to the extent that the social form critique focusses on deciphering the highly general aspects of capitalist social relations, it is relatively indifferent to how the uneven and hierarchical movement of global capitalism gives rise to specific political dynamics in societies in the 'lower end' of the world market or how the positioning and timing of development condition the ways in which class struggles are mediated and expressed in social formations of 'catch-up' development. These questions are central to understanding the nature of the state as it arises in the Third World, such as the developmental state and the specific manner in which the fetishism of the developmental state manifests itself, not only as the state's imagined autonomy from society but as the autonomous agent for *national* development *vis-à-vis* the global economy.

Compared to Holloway and Bonefeld, von Braunmühl shows greater sensitivity to the actual historical processes of the formation of the interstate system within the world market and touches more directly on the issues that I believe are crucial to the theorisation of the developmental state. She accurately grasps via the cases of France and Prussia (Germany) that primitive accumulation took place in the forms of 'forced accumulation' or through the formation of nationally determined centres of capital accumulation mediated through the state. From this, she hints at a correlation between the level of endurance of pre-capitalist relations and the state-mediated acceleration of capital accumulation: the role of the state implanting capitalist production relations has to do with the level of 'backwardness'. From this she makes the important point that 'class relations and the relations of the state apparatus to society bear in a specific manner the imprint of that country's position on the world market' (von Braunmühl 1978: 171). In so doing, she offers an avenue with which to analyse, *within* social form critique, the specific role that the states in 'catch-up' development are assigned to as the 'vehicle of the capitalist mode of production' under the 'world market compulsion'. However, she does not develop this insight into a more systematic analysis of the relation between state interventionism and 'catch-up' development beyond the early period of capitalist development in Europe. Her focus is primarily on the interstate rivalry and imperialism of what she calls 'metropolitan areas', such as England, France, Germany and the US. In her uniquely inspiring but only essay-length contribution, she uses terms such as imperialism and colonialism in a cursory manner, and due to her focus on the 'metropolitan' countries, she does not develop the specific characteristics and manifestations of 'forced accumulation' in the Third World or the context during and after de-colonisation.

By addressing the limits of social form critique concerning the national-global relation, my aim is to advance and strengthen its insights with a view to constructing a theory of the developmental state beyond statism. Phrased differently, my aim is not to challenge but to complement Bonefeld's claim that 'the national economies subsist in and through the world market' (2000: 37) by bringing to the fore *the hierarchical and uneven ways* in which national economies subsist in and through the world market, which animate the specific political and economic dynamic in the world-economic periphery and give rise to aspirations to build a developmental state.

Towards a theory of the developmental state beyond statism

Having identified the strengths as well as the limitations of social form critique in its assessment of the relation between the national and the global with a view to constructing a theory of the developmental state beyond statism *within* social form critique, I aim to extend Marx's critique of political economy in two ways. First, I pose the question of the statist concept of the developmental state within his framework of the critique of commodity fetishism: I look for the global social origins of the statist concept of the developmental state itself, i.e. I try to explain and historicise rather than merely dismiss this particular fetishism. Second, guided by Marx's proposition in *Grundrisse* that 'the concrete is concrete because it is the concentration of many determinations' (1973: 101), I incorporate the categories of world-system analysis (e.g. 'historical capitalism' and 'core-periphery relations') as determinants that illuminate the specific ways in which the totality of global capital relations is constituted.

Framing the question of statism within Marx's critique of commodity fetishism

The central theme of Marx's main theoretical work, *Capital*, is to identify the historically specific form of wealth in the context of the capitalist mode of production: here, wealth takes the form of an accumulation of commodities. Commodities have use value, i.e. some form of utility, but in commodity exchange their specific utilities are abstracted, and they are reduced to quantities of the abstract, homogeneous denominator of all commodities, whatever they are in the concrete, that is, abstract labour or value (like the commodity, labour also has, in capitalism, a dual nature: concrete labour is labour under the perspective of its producing concretely useful things, while abstract labour is labour under the perspective of its producing exchange values). As discussed before, the scholars of social form critique commonly find the historically specific character of capitalist social relations in the production and appropriation of value, whereby the products of labour exist as commodities, and most social mediation takes place through the exchange of commodities. However, capitalist society is historically specific not only in the fact that it is a society first and foremost of commodity (value) production: the commodity-form of social relations is also peculiar in that it expresses and at the same time veils its social constitution. It creates the effect that value, in spite of being a historically determined *social* category, appears as a thing: 'relations between persons are *really* thing-like rather than social, and relations between things are *really* social rather than thing-like' (Stoetzler 2017: 108–9: emphasis in the original). It also gives rise to the fetishistic notion that the historically specific social characteristics of the commodity-form appear to be transhistorical or emanate from the inner nature of the commodity itself. As Postone (1993: 134) puts it, '[o]ne particularity of capitalist society, which makes its analysis so difficult, is that this society has an essence, objectified as value, which is veiled by its form of appearance'. Marx's endeavour was therefore to show how 'the "laws of motion" of the social formation are veiled on the level of immediate empirical reality' (Postone 1993: 135).

> The mysterious character of the commodity-form consists therefore simply in the fact that the commodity reflects the social characteristics of men's own labour as objective characteristics of the products of labour themselves, as the socio-natural properties of these things. Hence it also reflects the social relation of the producers to the sum total of labour as a social relation between objects, a relation which exists *apart from* and *outside* the producers. Through this substitution, the products of labour become commodities, sensuous things which are at the same time supra-sensible or social. ... the commodity-form, and the value-relation of the products of labour within which it appears, have absolutely no connection with the physical nature of the commodity and the material [*dinglich*] relations arising out of this. It is nothing but the definite social relation between men themselves which assumes here, for them, the fantastic form of a relation between things.
>
> (Marx 1976: 164–5; emphasis added)

Marx's critique of the commodity fetish intends not only to *describe* the fact that the fundamental nature of capitalist society takes a mysterious appearance but to *explain why* it does so. To put this differently, the importance of his critique of political economy lies not merely in proving that classical political economists and vulgar economists eternalise the capitalist form of social relations on the basis of categories drawn from surface phenomena (e.g. prices, profits and rents); more importantly, Marx's critique attempts to *explain* the origins, or the material conditions, of the mysterious, fetishistic or illusionary appearance of capitalist social forms from the peculiarity of the value and commodity forms themselves. In Postone's words, an adequate analysis

> must not only show *that* abstract human labor has a social character; it must also investigate the historically specific social relations that underlie value in order to explain *why* those relations appear and, therefore, are presented by Marx, as being physiological–as transhistorical, natural, and thus historically empty.
>
> (Postone 1993: 145; emphasis in the original)

> Whence, then, arises the enigmatic character of the product of labour, so soon as it assumes the form of commodities? Clearly from this form itself. The equality of all sorts of human labour is expressed objectively by their products all being equally values; the measure of the expenditure of labour-power by the duration of that expenditure, takes the form of the quantity of value of the products of labour; and finally, the mutual relations of the producers, within which the social character of their labour affirms itself, take the form of a social relation between the products.
>
> (Marx 1967: 76–7)

Extending Marx's critique of commodity fetishism and complementing social form critique for the purpose of a theorisation of the developmental state beyond statism, I propose that a critique of statism be framed within Marx's critique of commodity fetishism: rather than merely arguing that statism amounts to fetishism as it takes the apparent autonomy of the state as given, the critique has to explain which social conditions give rise to such fetishism. In other words, the question should be: what specific characteristics of the capitalist mode of production give rise to the statist notion that the state is (in the sense of 'actually appears as') the embodiment of the general interest, or the driver of *national* development, against narrow private domestic (class) interests as well as against the *external* world market. Framing the question of statism in this manner complements Bonefeld's critique of world-market fetishism: the question of the world market as a fetish should be posed in its two aspects, not only as an apparently autonomously existing entity but also as an entity apparently *antithetical* to the apparently autonomously existing series of national economies.

My proposal to probe into the origins of the fetishism of the statist concept of the developmental state can radically re-frame the critical discussion of the developmental state. As shown in the previous chapters, the statist notion that the developmental state is autonomous from the domestic economy and the global economy has been continuously reproduced across various approaches to date. Recent debates on the transformation or the supposed 'hybridity' of the developmental state are limited to arguments about how much and to what extent its autonomy from groups and classes in society is retained and to what extent its 'nationally' oriented policy stance has been able to withstand 'external' global forces. Similarly, as seen in the attempts to extend the 'developmental state beyond East Asia', taking the characteristics of the East Asian developmental state as nationally determined, there have been numerous endeavours to build autonomous states similar to the East Asian developmental state as a way to warrant 'successful' development in underdeveloped and undeveloped countries (see Chapter 3). In these contexts, it is important to be able to demonstrate that it is the globally dominant capitalist order itself that continuously reproduces statist notion that an allegedly autonomous state can determine development outcomes, particularly in the context of the Third World. Only when the social origins of statism are explained and theorised is it possible to establish a fundamental critique of the statist concept of the developmental state.

Extending Marx's critique of political economy and concretising the concrete

Having extended Marx's critique of commodity fetishism to the question of statism, I will in the following section revisit his critique of political economy, as laid out in *Grundrisse*, and seek to further concretise the concrete (i.e. the capitalist totality) by incorporating key categories taken from 'world-system analysis'.

Marx contrasts in *Grundrisse* the conventional method adopted by the political economists of the Enlightenment period and subsequently by economics to his own method of the critique of political economy. Marx (1973: 100) writes that the former start with the real and the concrete, or 'the living whole', and 'conclude by discovering through analysis a small number of determinant, abstract, general relations such as division of labour, money, value, etc'. To this he contrasts 'a more scientifically correct method':

> as soon as these individual moments had more or less firmly been established and abstracted, there began the economic systems, which ascended from the simple relations, such as labour, division of labour, need, exchange value, to the level of the state exchange between nations and the world market.
>
> (Marx 1973: 100–1)

What Marx is getting at here is that the abstract is *not* an end result of abstracting from concreteness, as it is often conventionally understood; conversely, the concrete becomes concrete with more abstractions as 'a rich totality with many more determinations and relations' (1973: 100). As Marx succinctly puts it, the 'concrete is concrete because it is the concentration of many determinations, hence unity of the diverse' (1973: 101). He therefore holds that what appears to be the simplest abstract category presupposes the fullest development of the capitalist system: 'the appearance of exchange value as a simple point of departure upon the surface presupposes the whole system of bourgeois production' (*Grundrisse*, German edition: 907, as cited in von Braunmühl 1978: 162).

> As a rule, the most general abstractions arise only in the midst of the richest possible concrete development, where one thing appears as common to many, to all. Then it ceases to be thinkable in a particular form alone. ... The simplest abstraction, then, which modern economics places at the head of its discussions, and which expresses an

> immeasurably ancient relation valid in all forms of society, nevertheless achieves practical truth as an abstraction only as a category of the most modern society.
>
> (Marx 1973: 104–5)

Marx's method of political economy, discussed in *Grundrisse*, has important methodological implications due to its challenge to the juxtaposition of the concrete and the abstract, and the concrete and the concept (thinking), as antithetical: 'the method of rising from the abstract to the concrete is only the way in which thought appropriates the concrete, reproduces it as the concrete in the mind' (1973: 101). Particularly for the purpose of this chapter, I draw on Marx's method, in which epistemological advancement can be made by incorporating new determinants (abstractions) in line with the evolving concrete itself: the capitalist mode of production that is analysed by Marx in *Capital* in terms of abstractions based on observations made in the nineteenth century needs to be examined at a richly concrete historical level. On the basis of this reasoning, as an attempt to further concretise the concrete, or to grasp the specific manner in which the global totality of capitalist social relations exists and constitutes itself, I incorporate some key categories introduced by world-system analysis into social form critique in an attempt to identify the 'structure-like' features of capitalism as a global system. This is intended to explicate points addressed only fleetingly by social form scholars and, at the same time, appraise world-system analysis within the framework of social form critique.[2]

World-system analysis has specific conceptual limitations.[3] It has been accused by Marxists, most famously by Brenner (1977), of being 'neo-Smithian'.[4] Brenner argues that world-system analysis defines capitalism in terms of exchange relations and 'confuses markets/trade/commercial relations with the social relations of capitalist production' (Song H-Y 2015: 3). According to Brenner, to the extent that world-system analysis finds the origins of capitalism in trade rather than production relations whose historical specificity lies in the commodification of labour power as 'free' wage labour, it is grounded on 'an ahistorical, non-class concept of the division of labour' (Brenner 1997: 56; see Chapter 7). A key limitation of world-system analysis does indeed lie in its failure to engage in the question of social form and the 'value-form' of capitalist social relations (which is also true of Brenner's work). In addition, world-system analysis and closely related dependency theory were also criticised by social form critique scholars for prioritising the bipolarity between core and periphery, and the exploitation of the latter by the former rather than that of labour by capital as the fundamental contradiction of capitalism (Holloway 1994: 35; Radice 2008: 1165–6; von Braunmühl 1978: 161).[5]

Its limitations notwithstanding, there are important points of contact between social form critique, particularly the work of von Braunmühl, and those of world-system analysis, such as Wallerstein and Chase-Dunn.[6]

However, in seeking to incorporate certain categories developed by world-system analysis into social form critique, I do *not* intend to discuss world-system analysis at the level of a general theory of capitalism. In fact, Wallerstein himself deliberately calls his approach 'world-system analysis' rather than a 'theory' (Wallerstein 2004). As Chase-Dunn (1981: 21) puts it, the 'world-system perspective has not been formalized as a theory of capitalist development, and indeed some of its proponents seem hesitant to move in this direction'. I shall focus primarily on the world-system analysis's elucidation of the enduring 'structure-like' patterns of historical development of capitalism at the global level, which I see as important for a more systematic analysis of the global social origins of the statist concept of the developmental state.

'Structure-like' patterns of capitalist development

World-system analysis's point of departure is the totality rather than its components, that is, the world-system, a view that is in tune with what Bonefeld emphasises as the core premises of Marx (and Engels) on the world market as well as with von Braunmühl and other key contributors to *Open Marxism*, such as Holloway and Clarke (see Bonefeld 2008: 67–8). Starting from the world-system as the totality of capitalist relations, the authors of world-system analysis point out that a distinctive aspect of the 'capitalist world-economy' lies in the fact that it is overlaid by a multicentric system as opposed to a 'world-empire' characterised by a single overarching state apparatus. In other words, within the concept of the 'capitalist world-economy', the political system of capitalism is not the state as a single unit but the larger state-system (Chase-Dunn 1981: 25; see also Wallerstein 1996: 57). The 'capitalist mode of production exhibits a single logic in which both political-military power and the appropriation of surplus value through production and sale on the world market play an integrated role' (Chase-Dunn 1981: 20–1). To the extent that 'capitalist world-economy' is defined as a term inclusive of interstate geopolitical rivalry, it is implied that the state system, state building and geopolitics are the political side of, rather than independent from, the capitalist mode of production.

> Note the hyphen in world-system and its two subcategories, world-economies and world-empires. Putting in the hyphen was intended to underline that we are talking not about systems, economies, empires *of the* (whole) world, but about systems, economies, empires *that are* a world (but quite possibly, and indeed usually, not encompassing the entire globe). … It says that in 'world-system' we are dealing with a spatial/temporal zone which cuts across many political and cultural units, one that represents an integrated zone of activity and institutions, which obey certain systematic rule.
>
> (Wallerstein 2004: 16–7: emphasis in the original)

By conceptualising the capitalist world-economy in this manner, world-system analysis brings to the fore what I call the enduring 'structure-like' patterns of capitalist development as a global system through the concepts of 'historical capitalism' and 'core-periphery' relations. One of the key characteristics of the capitalist world-economy that these concepts try to capture is that capitalism 'was from the beginning an affair of the world-economy and not of nation-states' (Wallersten 1975: 19), and it has been 'imperialistic' from its inception in two respects. First, it is imperialistic in the sense that the rise of the capitalist mode of production was historically not a process bounded and explained by proletarianisation on a domestic level but a global process involving the subjugation of weaker states by stronger states (i.e. colonisation) and geopolitical conflicts (Bergesen 1984; Chase-Dunn 1981: 30). Second, it is imperialistic to the degree that 'it constitutes a hierarchical division of labour between core areas and peripheral areas' (Chase-Dunn 1981: 19).

The category of core-(semiperiphery)-periphery implies that the 'catch-up' dynamic is not only inherent to the capitalist world-system but expressed in the form of interstate competition. While many scholars from different intellectual traditions have noticed the correlation between heavy state interventionism and 'backwardness' (see below), namely the tendency for state interventionism to intensify the 'later' development that takes place in world time, world-system analysis assesses this tendency as intrinsic to the operation of the capitalist world-economy and is attentive to its mode of expression as interstate rivalry over other territories. Therefore, to the authors of world-system analysis, European seventeenth- and eighteenth-century absolutism amounts to an early form of state capitalism in contrast to the view that absolutism is an expression of feudal reorganisation in the face of the crisis of feudalism in Western Europe in the seventeenth century (e.g. Anderson 1974). In the context of 'the growth of commodity production and the emergent core-periphery relations of labour between East and West Europe', the 'mercantilist international policy and state-sponsored development of crucial sectors of production' were 'variants of state capitalism appropriate to the first epoch of the expansion of the capitalist world-economy' (Chase-Dunn 1981: 29). Similarly, 'the creation of "national" barriers – generally mercantilism – has historically been a defensive mechanism of capitalists located in states which are on a level below the high point of strength in the system' (Wallerstein 1979: 19): erecting 'national' barriers is understood to be the major tool of (semi)-peripheral countries seeking to climb the ladder of the world-economy hierarchy. In this context, the USSR's mercantilist semi-withdrawal from the world-economy was viewed as an attempt from a state in the semiperiphery to move up to the core (Wallerstein 1979: 29–31). The creation of 'national' barriers through mercantilist or protectionist measures taken by the state is seen as one of the original features of the capitalist world-economy: it is a defensive mechanism typically deployed by (semi-) peripheral states to narrow the gap with or compete with core countries in the world system (Wallerstein 1979: 19–20).[7]

Another 'structure-like' pattern of capitalist development that the category of the 'core-periphery' relation captures is the fact that the dynamics within the capitalist world-economy, such as industrialisation in the periphery, are not merely a result of the contingent movements of global capital, which are supposedly boundless and indifferent to specific geographical locations as suggested by Holloway (see above). Industrialisation, particularly in the context of the world-economic periphery, has not been a random process, not only because it has always been concentrated on certain locations, typically in core areas or the developed countries (Wallerstein 1974)[8] and determined by geopolitical factors (e.g. the Cold War), but also because it has hardly altered the enduring systematic patterns of the hierarchies, disparities and inequalities (unequal exchange) of the capitalist world-economy. The history of capitalism is characterised by certain 'structure-like' features: the 'successful' transition from the world-economic periphery to the core through technological advancement has been the exception rather than the norm, and even if industrialisation in the periphery did occur it has not altered the hierarchical structure of the world-system or narrowed the level of inequalities between core and periphery. For instance, although manufacturing-based industrialisation has taken place in the last few decades in the developing countries, it has not contributed to narrowing income gaps between rich and poor countries. Silver and Arrighi (2001: 12) note, based on World Bank data, that while the industrialisation gap between the countries of high-income strata and those of the middle- and low-income strata narrowed throughout the 1980s and 1990s, this has contributed to more *widening* than narrowing of the income gap.[9] They conclude that the 'spread of industrialization effects ... resulted more in the downgrading of industrial activities in the value-added hierarchy of the world-economy than in the upgrading of the low- and middle-income economies that were becoming more industrial' (Silver and Arrighi 2001: 12; see also Arrighi et al. 2003).[10]

According to world-system analysis (and dependency theory), there are various mechanisms in operation that enforce polarising tendencies between the core (the developed) and the periphery (the developing), such as unequal exchange, unilateral transfer of labour, i.e. forced immigration (slavery and 'voluntary' emigration of workers), and unilateral transfer of capital, i.e. the extortion of monetary instruments from colonies and capital flight (Arrighi 1990: 12–4; see also Amin 1976, 1978).[11] Similarly, studies carried out within the framework of world-system analysis highlight the fact that industrialisation in the periphery (semi-periphery) has been susceptible to severe competition challenges from other peripheral states in the world market due to its specialising in low-end manufacturing industries and has (thus) been more prone to political and economic crises (see, for instance, Arrighi 1990; Arrighi and Drangel 1996; Gills et al. 1993; Martin 1990; McGowan 1981; Wallerstein 1996). This suggests that the core-periphery relations have implications not only for the prospect of economic development but for the content and intensity of socio-political struggles.

In summary, having identified the limitations of social form critique in relation to the question of the national-global relation, I have extended Marx's critique of commodity fetishism and his critique of political economy outlined in *Grundrisse*, respectively. On the one hand, by extending the question of statism within his critique of commodity fetishism I quested for the (global social) origins of the statist concept of the developmental state rather than merely dismissing it. On the other hand, by following his method in the critique of political economy that the concrete becomes concrete only through rich determinations, I incorporated categories developed by world-system analysis as key determinates of the concrete. While world-system analysis does not form a coherent theory of capitalism, its scholars, as examined in this chapter, have paid close attention to the actual and historical development of capitalism as a global system (which is why Wallerstein designates the object of his research 'historical capitalism'), which brings to light what I call the 'structure-like' patterns of capitalist development operational at the global level.

Theorising the developmental state beyond statism

In this final section, on the basis of the critical appraisal of social form critique with respect to the question of the national-global relation, and by extending Marx's critique of commodity fetishism and political economy as a way of complementing the limits of social form critique, I will formulate a theoretical framework for the developmental state beyond statism in light of a critique of the fetishism of national development.

The state, 'catch-up' and national development

The theorists of the developmental state, institutionalists and Marxists have commonly recognised the correlation between state interventionism and 'catch-up' or 'late' development. For instance, Lenin (2010[1916]) and Hilferding's (2007[1910]) notions of 'monopoly capital' and 'finance capital' can be understood as an attempt to capture the historical tendency for state intervention to increase in the context of 'late development'. This is due to the fact that these terms, formulated in the early twentieth century, reflect the rise of particular patterns of capitalist conflicts, expressed as interstate rivalries (i.e. imperialism) between core nation-states in Western Europe, whereby the states protect oligarchic businesses or even merge with them. They mirror the perception that a particular type of state emerged in the context of 'late development' (in Germany) that intervened in and controlled a large portion of productive and financial (banking) industries, together with the heightening tendency of the state to take the initiative in industrial planning and directing (see Brewer 1980: Chs. 4, 5). Along the same lines, the correlation between 'economic backwardness' and stronger doses of state intervention (and big banks) was famously noted in Gerschenkron (1962). The tendency of the state to take a penetrating role in the economy is seen to intensify in development *later* than that of Germany and Japan: Korea and Taiwan are notable examples. As seen with the theorists of the developmental state, amongst others, Amsden formulated her theory of development and introduced the concept of the 'disciplinary state' on the basis of specifying the conditions peculiar to 'late development', particularly those *later* than *late* development: namely the post-Second World War period (see Chapter 1).

However, the intensifying tendencies of state interventionism in 'catch-up' or 'late' development contexts have been either discussed primarily at the descriptive level on a country-by-country comparative basis (e.g. Gerschenkron) or referenced to stress the state's instrumental function for dominant (monopoly) capital primarily in Europe (e.g. Hilferding) or as the basis for the justification of (further) state interventionism in the Third World (e.g. Amsden). Seen from the perspective of social form critique complemented by furthering Marx's methods of political economy, the 'catch-up' drive can be theorised as an intrinsic characteristic of global capitalist development and 'national' development as the universal form through which the 'catch-up' drive expresses itself.

While degree, timing, process and outcome of development differ in each social formation (hence, 'uneven development'), the 'catch-up' drive is generative of a capitalist dynamic and a universal feature of capitalism. With the Industrial Revolution in England in the eighteenth century, a new world-systemic dynamism was generated, compelling countries industrialising later than England to 'catch-up' with the forerunner. In fact, the compulsion to 'catch-up' presupposes the existence of discrepancies or unevenness of development at the global level, and the industrial/nonindustrial or developed/backward contrast itself is a perception arising from a phenomenon specific to the historical dynamics of capitalism as a global system. World-system analysis even offers the view that mercantilism that prevailed before the rise of industrial capitalism is an early form of state capitalism that emerged to compete in the hierarchical capitalist world-system. To restate this in Marx's terms, just as the 'tendency to create the world market is directly given in the concept of capital itself' (Marx 1973: 408), the 'catch-up' drive is innate to capital itself and has unfolded historically as a system of interstate competition conditioned by the pre-existing political struggles between territorially bound authorities.

While the 'catch-up' aspiration is intrinsic to capitalism as a global system, it manifests itself as the desire to achieve *national* development. For instance, the preoccupation of the elites in the US and Germany in the eighteenth and nineteenth centuries with 'catching-up' with the then industrial powerhouse of England was expressed as a quest to protect *national* industries by using state interventionism through tariffs on imported goods, subsidising imports of raw materials and infant industry protection, as evidenced in the work of Henry Carey, Alexander Hamilton and Friedrich List (see also Chang H-J 2002b). In the context of East Asia, without exception, the political elites and intellectuals of Japan, China and Korea pondered, at the turn of the twentieth century, how to overcome 'backwardness' and embrace modernity in order not to become victims of colonialism, in response to which they constructed highly racialised and ethno-centric nationalisms (Dikötter 1997; Lie 2001: 111–41; Shin 2006: part I). Further, modernisation movements in China and Korea in the early and mid-twentieth century were typically expressed as calls for protecting and nurturing national industries and national capitalists against Japanese capital. In fact, as seen in Chapter 1, the theorists of the developmental state, particularly Johnson (1999: 53–4), acknowledged that in the context of capitalist development in East Asia there was an extreme degree of mass mobilisation under nationalist discourses, which he calls 'revolutionary nationalism', although these are hardly critically assessed.

The very desire to 'catch-up' with other advanced countries emanates from a system that creates an unprecedented scale of social upheaval, uneven development, interstate rivalry, colonisation and polarisation at the global level (see also Berman 1982). Added to this, world system analysis's observation that the capitalist world-economy has been 'imperialistic' from its inception can explicate why development in the world-economic periphery takes a more strongly nationalist form of development to the extent that national development is taken even as part of anti-imperialist and national security strategies. Marx already hinted at the fact that the states' role as the 'makers of the conditions for the existence of capital' is conditioned by and associated with 'backwardness' (Marx 1973: 507). On similar ground, von Braunmühl (1978: 171) noted that 'class relations and the relations of the state apparatus to society bear in a specific manner the imprint of that country's position on the world market'. Extending these further, using the insight from world-system analysis, it can be suggested that to the degree that capitalism as a global system is 'imperialistic' in its origin and nature (i.e. the dominance of more developed countries over less developed ones) and that nationalism in the periphery is, to a large part, a product or response to imperialist expansion particularly, the fact that 'catch-up' development takes an intensely nationalistic form is induced by the imperialistic nature of the capitalist world-system itself.

The national is the form through which global capitalism exists and subsists: capital is inherently global not only in its operation but also in its *form*. This is comparable to the fact that class struggles in capitalism are typically, and universally, expressed as demands for equality and in the form of claims on surplus value. Likewise, the uneven and hierarchical movement of capital not only generates the 'catch-up' compulsion but also conditions the form of its expression, that is, national development, often as part of anti-imperialist struggle and 'nation-building'. In short, the aspiration to 'catch-up' with more industrialised countries is a historically specific dynamic that characterises the modern world, and national development is the form that 'catch-up' development takes in capitalism as a global system. The national-global relation that the theorists of the developmental state and many later scholars considered to be antithetical is in fact one of mutual constitution: the national is a universal form through which global capitalism subsists and expresses itself.

A critique of the national development fetish

The statist concept of the developmental state as autonomous from society and the global economy is induced by the perception of an historical pattern of development that there had been a growing tendency for a particular type of state, committed to *national* development, to rise in 'backward' economies. The particular pattern of capitalist development caused by the uneven and hierarchical dynamics of capitalism compel the state to try to overcome backwardness under conditions of 'catch-up' development, which constitutes the material conditions from which the statist notion that the state is the main agent of national development emerges. In this respect, the developmental state is a type of state that is far more general than a mere national variant as the theorists of the developmental state and institutionalists suggest, and more specific than the generic concept of the capitalist state that social form critique implies (e.g. Chang D-O). It is a *particular type of the capitalist state* that emerges in 'catch-up' processes as a by-product of the uneven development of capitalism and the hierarchical world-system.

This theory, in turn, implies that as long as the capitalist world-system exists, it will persistently generate the drive to 'catch up', and *attempts* to mobilise the 'catch-up' energy in the form of state-driven national development, regardless of development outcome, will continue to be a defining feature of the ways in which Third World development is sought. In fact, the continued popularity of the developmental state discourse in the international community and the recent discussions on 'going beyond the developmental state beyond East Asia' precisely express such attempts (see Chapter 3).

However, although the *aspiration* to 'catch up' through the good offices of an omnipotent, visionary, autonomous and nationally oriented state – the idealised imago of the developmental state – is continuously generated by the uneven and hierarchical dynamics of global capitalism itself, its actual *realisation* is not induced by domestic-level policy, as argued by the advocates of the developmental state; in fact, the epithet 'developmental state' is, like a title of honour, only given to state apparatuses in societies that have already been seen to have *achieved* successful 'catch-up' development. As seen through the lens of world-system analysis, there are 'structure-like' patterns of polarisation and various mechanisms at the world-market level that make 'successful' development in the periphery hard to achieve: the success of development in the world-economic periphery is less dependent on decisions made at the national level than it is on those made elsewhere, as this success largely depends on capitalist investment and technology from the core countries. As shall be discussed more fully in Part III, the so-called 'economic miracle' of East Asian countries in the post-Second World War period was largely mediated by world-market level competition, expressed as an interstate rivalry between the powerful states (the Cold War) that worked against the grain of 'polarisation'. The case of South Korea demonstrates that a fairly inconspicuous authoritarian military government was given a chance to become a 'developmental state' only when the US granted Korean firms the exceptional opportunity to receive Japanese declining industries and upgrade their technology through various forms of assistance and procurement contracts in the context of the Cold War (Cumings 1984; Fischer 2018; Glassman 2016; Glassman and Choi 2014; see Chapter 8).

Now the statist concept of the developmental state can be critiqued in light of what I call *the critique of the national development fetish*. To the degree that Marx's critique of commodity fetishism not only deciphers the material and social origin of its fetishistic appearance but reveals the 'concealing' effect of the commodity-form of social relations, I rearticulate his critique of the commodity fetish in the context of a critique of the statist notion of the developmental state. Even though the uneven and hierarchical capitalist dynamics lay the conditions for the statist notion to arise by enforcing states in 'catch-up development' to act as the promoters of national development, it *appears* that the development orientation of the developmental state originates from the nature of the state itself. Even though *in reality* the particular positioning and timing of development within the world-market condition the failure and success of development, an autonomous and effective (developmental) state appears to be the main driver and determinant of the outcomes of national development. Even though the developmental state embodies class contradictions emanating from 'late capitalist development', it appears that the characteristics of the developmental state are the product of national-level policy choices (typically taken by national elites) and national distinctiveness.

The notion of national development led by the autonomous developmental state also amounts to *national development fetishism* to the extent that it essentially neutralises its class content or its capital-serving function by presenting this in a class-neutral national form. With the help of the framework proposed in this chapter, Marx's critique of Friedrich List can be interpreted as a critique of the class content of the developmental state as a capitalist state.[12] Against List (2005[1841]), who argued for protectionism and a national industrial policy *vis-à-vis* liberal political economy in the nineteenth century in the name of the enhancement of the productive forces of Germany and the promotion of national development, Marx (1845) wrote the following:

> Since the bourgeois now hopes to become rich mainly through 'protective tariffs' and since protective tariffs can enrich him only insofar as

> no longer Englishmen, but the German bourgeois himself, will *exploit fellow-countrymen*, indeed exploit them even more than they were exploited from abroad, and since protective tariffs demand a sacrifice of exchange values from the consumers ... the industrial bourgeois has therefore to prove that, far from hankering after material goods, he wants nothing else but the sacrifice of exchange values, material goods, for a spiritual essence. Fundamentally, therefore, it is solely a matter of *self-sacrifice*, of *asceticism*, of Christian *grandeur of the soul*. It is pure accident that A makes the sacrifice, but B puts the sacrifice in his pocket.

Paraphrasing Marx's critique within the framework developed in this chapter, 'the rationale for state protectionism' and 'sacrificing' exchange values (by forfeiting the right to buy cheap on a free world market) in the name of the larger good of developing the productive forces of the nation reflect the 'backwardness' of an economy within the capitalist world-system. This, in turn, conditions the manner in which the class character of the state manifests itself in its claim to be concerned with improving national productive forces rather than serving narrow capitalist class interests. The fact that development assumes the form of class-neutral national development led by an impartial and autonomous state in effect entails a class content. This is because it primarily involves protecting the national bourgeoisie from competition from more advanced bourgeoisies and granting the national bourgeoisie the freedom to exploit domestic labour, typically in the form of 'super-exploitation', e.g. long working hours and low wages in the conditions of 'late' development in the hierarchical world-economy. Seen from the perspective of a critique of national development fetishism, what is usually considered 'successful' capitalist development in the periphery is in fact a case of brutal and intensive capitalist exploitation. To restate this in Marx's terms, in the same manner in which surface phenomena (price, rent and profit) express and veil an essence (value) in Marx's critique of political economy, national development is the form that both expresses and veils the class content of global capitalism.

Towards a critique of the Korean developmental state

The benefits of the alternative theoretical framework proposed above can be summarised as follows. First, it allows a conceptual critique of statism as well as an analysis of 'catch-up' or 'late' development in terms of class content and form of capitalist contradictions. At a conceptual level, it permits, on the one hand, an understanding of the fundamental aspects of the capitalist state as derived from capitalist social relations. It puts into perspective the discussions of whether the state or the market is dominant by assessing the state as a political form of social relations in capitalism and seeing the social relations of capitalism as separation-in-unity. On the other hand, it enables us to capture the specificity of the developmental state beyond its particular national variations. Its appearing to stand above capital for the purpose of pursing national development stems from the fact that it is 'compelled' to play the role of enforcing capitalist plan rationality in the context of 'catch-up' development in the hierarchical capitalist world-economy. This understanding allows us to assess the Korean developmental state as *a particular capitalist state* that practised capitalist rationality as a form of delivering 'national development' in a social formation where capitalist social and production relations were absent or immature. As shall be fully analysed in the subsequent chapters, the fact that the Korean developmental state was built on the extreme mobilisation of nationalist ideology and a super-repressive labour regime with reference to the goal of achieving national development is not merely accidental or due to a lack of democratic culture and history. The more a state is forced to eliminate societal barriers to capital accumulation under the conditions of a low level of development of capitalist social and production relations, the more likely this state will emerge and function as an entity appearing to be autonomous from society. It will act (i.e. 'actually appear') as the embodiment of capital rationality by carrying out this function in the form of national development.

The theoretical framework proposed in this chapter also offers a more systematic way of linking the contradictions of capitalist development in Korea to 'catch-up' development. It explains why 'late development' produces and necessitates authoritarian and development-obsessed types of state (the developmental state), and sheds light on the role and function of the developmental state not only as a capitalist state but as a state that has to produce the conditions of capitalism itself. Furthermore, it permits a fresh perspective on the questions of why labour and democratisation struggles in the periphery express themselves in violent and militant forms but lack in substantive contents in democracy,[13] and why economic crises tend to have more adverse impacts on the population and create more adjustment problems in the periphery than they do in core countries. These matters, amongst others, can be understood as not merely contingent but emanating from the capitalist social form as well as world-system constraints. In this manner, the new theoretical framework proposed here opens up novel ways to address the issues of Third World development not only in economic terms but also in societal and political terms, particularly concerning the limitations of their democratic character (see Chapters 9 and 10).

However, the emphasis on the constraints emanating from capitalist social form and the 'structure-like' capitalist dynamic is not meant to suggest that the position of the economy in the global hierarchy and the timing of development *automatically* determine the rise and fall of the developmental state and development outcomes. While the impulse to capitalist development came in the form of 'external' forces and was enforced by colonisation by Japan and the Cold War, the rise of the developmental state, at least with reference to Korea, characterised as standing above particular societal and class interests, was made possible and mediated through incessant class struggles. The Korean state was able to fulfil the 'mission' to enforce capitalist plan rationality over society only after the labour movement was effectively exterminated, first by the Japanese colonial power, then by the Korean Civil War and finally by anti-communist governments sponsored by the US. Furthermore, the 'effectiveness' of the developmental state was maintained through continuous and permanent class struggles from above, which imposed social and labour discipline.

Class struggles here are to be analysed at the world-market level in three respects. First, the country's position in the world market conditions the way in which the state relates to society, which has important ramifications on class relations. Second, what are normally seen as 'external' forces, such as Japanese colonisation and US intervention, have always acted with a clear class orientation and thereby constituted a dynamic constituent of 'domestic' class struggle. Third, insofar as 'catch-up' development necessitates an authoritarian state compelled to lay the conditions of capitalist social relations, the content and substance of class struggle is likely to be expressed in the form of demands for democratisation by movements against (military) dictatorship and for political rights. The gist of this chapter is my proposition that the *specific ways* in which class contradictions are inscribed into the Korean state, its class form and content, are conditioned and mediated by its position in the hierarchical world market and the temporal context of its push to development. The timing of development and the location of the Korean economy within the world market generate the compulsion to 'catch up' itself, condition the rise of a particular type of state and mediate the manner and substance in which class struggles are expressed.

Conclusion

As an endeavour to build a theory of the developmental state beyond statism, in Part II, I categorised Marxist theories of the state into two traditions: namely class content analysis and social form critique. I then critically assessed them, in turn, focussing on how these two traditions are reflected in the assessments of the Korean developmental state (Chapters 4 and 5). By identifying the conceptual strengths as well as weaknesses of social form critique, particularly regarding the national-global relation, I extended Marx's critique of commodity fetishism to the question of statism, on the one hand, and his critique of political economy, as outlined in *Grundrisse*, on the other. I sought to explain the global social origins of statism and identify 'structure-like' patterns of global capitalist development that give rise to the fetishism of statism itself.

While my theorisation of the developmental state aims to overcome one of the lacunas in Marxist state theory, it conveys political implications different from most approaches discussed in this volume. Viewed from the theoretical perspective proposed in this chapter, the formation of the modern state in the form of multiple bourgeois nation-states was integral to the process in which capitalism established itself as the dominant mode of production at the world-market level. It follows that the national is the manner through which global capitalism expresses itself. It is thus not antithetical to the global, which means that the state does not at some point stop being national-oriented and begin being global-oriented: it has always been global-oriented *qua* being national. From the perspective of the critique of the developmental state offered in this chapter, the statist argument that Third World development requires the autonomous and development-oriented state only testifies to the fact that successful and rapid 'catch-up' development requires extreme social mobilisation led by a coercive state. There is no 'successful' Third World development in the current capitalist world-system that can be attained without subjugating humans and their environment to intensive and violent processes of (primitive) capital accumulation.

The theoretical framework I have developed in this chapter as an alternative to the statist concept of the developmental state will guide the historical analysis of the Korean state in the subsequent chapters and will, in turn, I hope, be vindicated by it.

Notes

1 Cammack attempts to analyse, if not theorise, the state-global economy relation, though not in relation to the developmental state. However, he mechanically applies the relative autonomy thesis to an analysis of global capitalism. He holds that '[Marxist] references should be treated as resources for thinking about relative autonomy in a genuinely global capitalist system' and proposes that 'relative autonomy should be thought about at both *national* and *global* levels' (Cammack 2003: 42; emphasis in the original; see also Chapter 4). Cammack's assessment of the state-global economy relation reaffirms his general view of the functionalist account of the capitalist state: he explains the current state and global governance institutions using the functional requirements of the capitalist system.

2 In some of my previous work (Song H-Y 2011, 2013b) I attempted to 'synthesise' world-system analysis as a historical approach with social form critique as an abstract theory. By contrast, in this monograph, guided by Marx's method in the critique of political economy, I try to go beyond my previous approach by incorporating key categories (abstractions) of world-system analysis in order to render comprehension of the concrete whole (the global totality of capitalist relations) more concrete. If my previous work is based on 'externally' linking the two approaches, my current attempt is to integrate world-system analysis more organically within the methodology of Marx's critique of political economy.

3 This chapter draws on 'world-system analysis' literature highly selectively, consulting primarily the works of Wallerstein (1979, 1984, 1995, 1996, 2004), Chase-Dunn (1981), Bergesen (1984) and Arrighi (1990).

4 For a critique of Wallerstein from a Weberian perspective, see Skocpol (1977). For a critique of Brenner from a perspective of world-system analysis, see Bergesen (1984). For a more recent discussion of Frank in relation to the capitalist transition question, see Bergeson (2015) and Song H-Y (2015).

5 It can also be argued that prioritising the enduring global inequality and underdevelopment in the world economic periphery caused by 'imperialistic' capitalism has led some dependency theorists to endorse and affirm nationalistic development policies (autarky) of the periphery, and praise the industrialisation

of China as an outcome of its pursuing a development path different from a capitalist path (Arrighi 2007) or outside of contemporary financial globalisation (Amin 2013).

6 Chase-Dunn, one of the key scholars within world-system analysis, notes that 'von Braunmühl has done the most interesting work at the conceptual level to integrate specifically the role of the larger state system with the operation of the world market within a framework of basic Marxist concepts' (1981: 20, fn. 2).

7 Bonefeld (2000: 41) also depicts protectionism as amounting merely to a measure of defence *within* free trade.

8 For instance, even if foreign direct investment has been 'globalised' for the last few decades, as of 2011 the greatest number of flows are concentrated in the core countries, like the US and Europe, receiving 14.8 and 27.8 per cent respectively, while China received 8.1 per cent, and Brazil, Russia and India collectively received only 10 per cent (UNCTAD 2012, as cited in Hardy 2013).

9 Wade (2010) has also demonstrated empirically that the global system has shown a remarkable level of 'stability', with little mobility between the four income categories of countries in 1960–78 and 1978–2000 – the majority of the countries in either the highest or the lowest income groups remained in the same income category, and the middle two categories showed more *downward* than upward trends. Wade uses this evidence to support state interventionism in development.

10 This issue can be related to a more recent discussion on the question of how significant the 'rising powers' (such as China and the BRICS) are in challenging the US-centred hegemony. While some hastily conclude that this signals the 'end of peripheries', the rise of the 'post-American world' or the emergence of the 'post-Western world' (see Stuenkel 2016; Zakaria 2011), some argue that the significance of the 'rising powers' has been exaggerated and the discourse of the 'rising powers' conceals the enduring global imbalances and deepening US-hegemony (see Fisher 2018).

11 Arguably, the unpopularity of world-system analysis and dependency theory amongst the left is to some extent explained by the pessimism of their vision concerning the chances of Third World development: world-system analysis's scepticism about this frustrates the rationale for and belief in the effectiveness of development (aid) agencies and industries, which may reduce its attractiveness for many leftists in the core countries who make their living in the 'development industry'.

12 For a discussion of List in the contemporary context, see Shaefedin (2005) and Selwyn (2009).

13 Arrighi (1990: 26) notes that leaving aside the special cases of Hong Kong, Israel and South Africa, 92.6 per cent of the total population belonging to the semiperiphery have experienced some kind of authoritarianism, in the form of either fascist, bureaucratic-authoritarian or military rule. Similarly, Gills et al. (1993) show, through a comparative study of democratisation in varying countries in the periphery and semi-periphery in the 1970s and 1980s, that democracy in these countries, including Korea, was characterised by a common pattern of 'low intensity democracy': democratisation in these countries proved to be limited to procedural aspects of formal democracy.

Part III

The global and social origins of the Korean developmental state and its transformation

7 The rise of the modern Korean state

Capitalism by imperialism and capitalism from above

This chapter traces the rise of the modern Korean state by examining primitive accumulation processes before and after de-colonisation from Japan in 1945. If the state is the political form of capitalist social relations, the modern Korean state should be analysed as integral to the development of capitalist social relations, to which intensive class struggles are intrinsic. However, capitalist development in Korea was a global process from its inception: while the transition to capitalism itself was inherently a global process because it was part and parcel of capitalism's fundamental systemic dynamism, Korea's integration into the capitalist world economy in the late nineteenth century took place under the influence of and under pressure from external powers, such as China (under the Qing dynasty), Japan and Russia, all vying to become the regional hegemon, followed by eventual annexation by Japan in 1910 and the US occupation after the Second World War. In tracing the global and social origins of the early modern Korean state, I will first contextualise the question of the capitalist transition and the formation of the modern Korean state within what I identify as key approaches to primitive accumulation in general and to Korean modernisation more specifically. Second, I will assess three periods that are crucial to the formation of the modern Korean state: the integration of Korea, under the Yi (Chosŭn) Dynasty, into the capitalist world economy in the late nineteenth century; the first stage of primitive accumulation under Japanese colonialism from 1910 to 1945; and the second stage of primitive accumulation under US occupation after 1945. I will first show how the failure of the Yi state to defend itself against imperialist powers and carry out modernising reforms in response to the social forces from below (the Peasant War of 1894 and the *Tonghak* movement) coincided with and opened the door for colonisation by Japan. Second, I will discuss how Japanese colonial policy took decisive turns when its own 'catch-up' drive met intensive social and class struggles in metropolitan Japan and colonial Korea. Third, I will trace how Koreans' aspirations to build a society based on the socialist and communist ideals that prevailed after national independence fainted in the process of land reform and the disposal of the Japanese-held properties under the US occupation. Finally, I will show how a highly militarised state dominating society emerged and became consolidated through an intensive class war (the Korean War) and the defeat of the left with the help of the US occupation authority, which laid the ground for *partial* conditions for the rise of the developmental state.

Primitive accumulation and modern state building

In assessing the formation of the modern Korean state, I will bring to the fore capitalist development and state-building as an inherently global process to which class and social struggles are integral. While I formulated the theory of the developmental state beyond statism in Part II, in this section, with a view to setting out a more concise conceptual guide to an historical analysis of the rise of the modern Korean state and its attributes, I will elaborate my own approach within the context of and in opposition to what I identify as several influential approaches to primitive accumulation in general, and the ongoing debate on the relations between Korean modernisation and Japanese colonial legacy.

Global vs. national perspectives on capitalist accumulation

The question of primitive accumulation concerns how the capitalist relations of production were historically established. Delineating the capitalist mode of production historically and assessing its genesis has been one of the key issues within Marxist scholarship. Marx defined primitive accumulation as

> the process which takes away from the labourer the possession of his means of production; a process that transforms, on the one hand, the social means of subsistence and of production into capital, on the other, the immediate producers into wage-labourers.
>
> (Marx 1967: 668)

Marx added that the 'expropriation of the agricultural producer, of the peasants, from soil, is the basis of the whole process', and the 'history of this expropriation, in different countries, assumes different aspects, and runs through its various phases in different orders of succession, and at different periods' (Marx 1967: 669–70). To the degree that his historical assessment of primitive accumulation in *Capital* focusses on the case of England and indicates manifold ways in which it can unfold in different social formations, arguably, his comments on this matter have often been understood as suggesting that primitive accumulation can be assessed at the national level.

For instance, Brenner finds the characteristics of capitalism first and foremost in the '"self-transformation" of class relations from serfdom to free wage labour', which set in motion an historically unique capitalist dynamic separate from previous epochs, that is, compelling the enhancement of labour productivity by way of innovation (Brenner 1977: 38) or, in Marx's terms, by relative rather than absolute surplus extraction (Marx 1967: 476–85; see Chapter 6). According to Brenner, what differentiates capitalism from pre-capitalist modes of production lies in its systematic tendency towards unprecedented economic development

> for the first time through increases of labour productivity ... without necessarily having to resort to methods of increasing absolute surplus labour ... i.e. the extension of the working day, the intensification of work, and the decrease in the standard of living of the labour force.
>
> (Brenner 1977: 30)

For this reason, he criticises world-system analysis (particularly Wallerstein) for conflating market, trade and exchange relations with capitalist production relations. Brenner argues that 'the rise of trade is not at the *origin* of a dynamic of development because trade cannot determine the transformation of class relations of production' (1977: 38; emphasis in the original).

To the extent that Brenner finds the essence of capitalism in its production relations as opposed to market (exchange) relations (e.g. the expansion of the world market and the global division of labour), he tends to assume that the social relations of capitalist production are nationally contained or determined (Bergesen 1984; Song H-Y 2015). Relatedly, his focus on class relations and class struggle at the national level tends to prioritise 'the role of contingent interactions among different elites and classes', often at the expense of what appear to be actor-less structural processes operating at the global level (Hung 2008: 570). Marx however hints that the origins of capitalism are to be assessed in a longer and broader perspective beyond whether or not and how much the creation of 'free labour' or the commodification of labour proceeded (Marx 1967: 669). He finds the base of the capitalist mode of production in the expansion of foreign trade, which, in turn, compels the progress of the capitalist mode of production and the further expansion of the (world) market (Marx 1959: 237). According to this view, capitalist production and market (exchange) relations are inextricably related and mutually constituted, a point that Marx expresses by stating that the 'tendency to create the world market is directly given in the concept of capital itself' (Marx 1973: 408; see Chapter 6).

Brenner's narrow definition of capitalist transition, measured by the degree to which labour is converted into 'free labour', is unable to account for the continued existence of 'non-capitalist labour' not only at the early stages of capitalist development but in highly industrialised countries, even today, most evidently in forms of 'semi-waged labour' performed by many migrant workers (e.g. family-run businesses) and women's domestic labour. The persistent existence of 'non-wage labour' is *not* always the lack of capitalist development but is enforced by the advancement of capitalist development as it often benefits capital as non- or partially paid labour (Wallerstein 1996).

This tendency is most prominent in the colonial context, where pre-modern social relations are reproduced and solidified to serve the interests of the capitalist colonisers. This underscores the inadequacy of a nationally centred assessment of the capitalist transition, particularly in the context of the world-economic periphery. As shall be shown, the class relations in colonial Korea were conditioned and determined by the needs of Japanese capital and inextricably linked to the class struggles and relations in metropolitan Japan.

Another key Marxist contribution that attempts to assess different trajectories to capitalist transition as determined by differentiated class constellations at national levels can be found in Lenin's concept of the two types of bourgeois agrarian evolution – the revolutionary, democratic path involving the break-up of feudal landed property with peasant capitalism developing from below, namely, 'the American path', versus the conservative path of preserving land monopoly, whereby feudal landlords themselves developed into capitalists while using their erstwhile serfs as hired labour, that is, 'the Prussian path' (Lenin 1907; see also Patnaik 2005: 85). Applying Lenin's concepts, Byres (1996) further analyses two different paths: namely 'capitalism from above', as in 'the Prussian path', and 'capitalism from below', as in 'the American path', respectively. According to Byres, the former is characterised by a low degree of peasant differentiation and a strong presence of authoritarian *Junkers*, who became capitalist farmers, whereby capitalist transition sprang from 'above', namely from a landlord class allied with the state (Byres 1991: 22–7, 1996: part II). On the other hand, the latter refers to a situation in which agrarian transition takes place from 'below', that is, from the peasantry, when either a landlord class is absent or when the power of the landowners is weak, being combined with a high level of peasant differentiation i.e. a high level of divergence and hierarchical organisation of peasants. Byres holds that peasant differentiation accelerates commodity production in agriculture, which enables rich peasants to transform themselves into capitalist farmers as a driving-force of capitalist transition (Byres 1991: 27–34, 1996: part III).

Byres's categorisation of two paths to capitalist transition has merit in providing a referential guide to assessing the distinctive features of primitive accumulation in other social formations. However, he also tends to take primitive accumulation as a process compartmentalised along the lines of the boundaries of the nation. As shall be shown below, the case of Korea's agrarian relations shows highly complex characteristics that Byres's nationally focussed and schematic framework is unable to grasp. Analysis of the agrarian relations in colonial Korea shows that while peasant differentiation accelerated, it was accompanied by the consolidation of the tenant structure and the overall impoverishment of the rural economy, resulting in the exodus of the rural population. Furthermore, the land reform enacted after national independence from Japan turned most peasants and landless farmers into self-cultivators, thereby reversing the trend of peasant differentiation and simultaneously undermining the position and power of the landlords, the majority of whom failed to make the transformation into capitalists (Hong S-C 2013: 26; see below). In other words, agrarian relations in postcolonial Korea were characterised by a high level of differentiation among landlords and the homogenisation of the peasants as self-cultivators. Capitalists emerged neither from the landlords nor from the peasants: they were created by the Korean state in the process of 'forced capital accumulation' under the auspices of an external power, namely the US occupation authority. These peculiar attributes of class relations can only be comprehended when the changes in agrarian relations in Korea are analysed within the context of Japanese colonialism and US occupation, both of which intervened in class struggle as powerful class forces.

Colonial modernity vs. indigenous capitalist development

The question of the genesis of capitalism in the specific case of Korea has also been intensively debated and highly contentious as it touches on the relation between Japanese colonialism and the 'successful' capitalist development of Korea in the post-Second World War period. One of the key debates around this subject has taken place around the thesis of 'colonial modernity', the proposition that the origins of the successful industrialisation of Korea (and Taiwan) after the Second World War were laid during the Japanese colonial period.

Referring to the case of Korea, Carter Eckert, one of the key advocates of the colonial modernity thesis, proposes the view that 'the roots of the vibrant and internationally recognized capitalism of South Korea today might in some way be traceable to Japan' (Eckert 2014: 2). Eckert grounds this argument on the fact that the Korean capitalist class emerged and was cultivated under the influence of Japan: the Korean capitalists originated from the land-owning class, who had accumulated capital from success in commercialised rice farming since the signing of the Kanghwa Treaty with Japan in 1876 and subsequently from manufacturing in the textile industry during Japanese colonialism. Particularly, Korean capitalists could grow and benefit from the business opportunities rendered open to them by Japanese imperialist expansion to Asia (e.g. Manchuria), a notable example being *Kyongbang* (first Korean-owned large-scale enterprise), established by the *Kochang* Kims, a family of the prominent landed class (Eckert 2014: 254). From this, Eckert (2014: 56) emphasises the continuities between the landlord class and the industrial capitalists: the forming and nurturing of Korean capitalists under Japanese rule served as 'a training ground and crucible' for what subsequently became the successful business conglomerates, the *chaebol*. According to Eckert, these economic opportunities were not limited to the privileged few. As he puts it, 'the door … was never completely closed to the native [Korean] population, even at some of the higher levels, and positions in the Japanese corporate or bureaucratic world … attract[ing] many of the educated Korean elite' (Eckert 1996: 24).

Similarly, Atul Kohli, another key proponent of the 'colonial modernity' thesis, contends that the original impetus for capitalist growth did not generate endogenously within Korea but was implanted during the period of Japanese colonialism. He holds that the rapid industrialisation of Korea after the Second World War, under the guidance of the Korean developmental state, owed a great deal to the Japanese colonial legacy, whereby industrial infrastructure was constructed and modern institutions, particularly efficient state bureaucracy, were established (Kohli 2004: 27–61). Although Kohli acknowledges that 'rapid decolonization in Korea created considerable economic chaos and decline', and 'the Korea War wreaked havoc on Korean industry', he argues that its fast recovery 'underlines how much Koreans had learned during the colonial phases about running modern industry' (Kohli1997: 884). On the basis of this reasoning, Kohli (1997: 884) argues that 'unique colonial developments paved Korea's foundation for subsequent economic dynamism'. The colonial modernity thesis is closely related to what others refer to as 'Japanese colonial exceptionalism', the view that the 'stellar performance of these economies [Taiwan and South Korea] since 1960 must be due, in part at least, to the Japanese legacy' (Booth and Deng 2017: 62). According to this view, Japanese colonialism is distinguished from other European colonizers in that 'the best colonial master of all time has been Japan, for no ex-colonies have done so well as South Korea and Taiwan' (Landes 1999: 437).

Many Korean scholars have critically responded to the 'colonial modernity' thesis on the basis that it overestimates the significance of the Japanese colonial legacy in the capitalist development of Korea. If the (Western) authors who advocate 'colonial modernity' emphasise the link between Japanese colonialism and the 'successful' and rapid development of Korea, the Korean critics try to dissociate the two. These scholars tend to stress the immense damage that Japanese colonialism inflicted on Korea: a vast amount of national wealth (gold) was taken out of the country, the national economic structure became distorted as it was mainly made to serve the interests of Japanese imperialism and a majority of ordinary Koreans suffered discrimination and exploitation (see Lee B-C 2011; Yi M-Y 1997). These critics characterise the industrialisation that took place in colonial Korea as 'limited', 'temporary', 'distorted' or 'improper', an argument that is often termed 'the theory of enclave development' (Park S-W 1999: 138). The Korean scholars are particularly critical of the 'reactionary' political implication that the 'colonial modernity' thesis entails: the thesis of 'colonial modernity' implicitly or explicitly supports the view held by Japanese colonialists themselves that the drive for capitalist development did not emerge endogenously in Korea, an idea referred to as 'stagnation theory', and that Japan 'helped' Korea transform into a modern (capitalist) society.[1]

While both of these accounts regarding the significance of colonial industrialisation in determining and contributing to Korea's subsequent rapid economic growth in the post-Second World War period make some valid points, they also have crucial limitations. As opposed to the nationalistic accounts held by some Korean scholars, the 'colonial modernity' thesis seems to escape from the problem of nationally centred approaches. Nevertheless, apart from the fact that the advocates of the 'colonial modernity' thesis pay scant attention to class conflicts (e.g. the Korean War) that eliminated the remnants of pre-modern rural relations *after* Japanese colonialism, they narrow the drive of modernisation (capitalist development) to Japanese colonialism. While the impulse to modernise arrived in Korea in the form of external pressures just as capitalist modernity originated from the West, the desire to 'catch-up' was a *universal* dynamic generated by capitalist modernity itself that gave rise to the particular form and content of interstate competition, on the one hand, and aspirations for social reforms (social levelling and nationalism), on the other.

As shall be seen, the peasant revolts and *Tonghak* ('Eastern-learning') movements of the late nineteenth century in Korea were influenced by Western science, philosophy and religion (Christianity), commonly referred to as 'Western-learning'. These were the expressions of modern and universal aspirations to build a society without hereditary hierarchies and a modern political authority (the state) allegedly able to withstand external encroachment: namely a nation-state. Korean elites and intellectuals in this period also pondered how to embrace and apply Western modernisation to Korea, and reformers within the Yi state and the Great Han Empire strove to achieve modernisation from above, albeit only with partial success (see Hwang K-M 2004, 2007; Kim S-Y 2012; Kim S-J 2001; Kim S-B 2012).

Therefore, it would be facile to conclude, as Kohli does against the Korean (nationalist) historians, that it is counterfactual to argue that a capitalist dynamic would have emerged endogenously without Japanese intervention and colonialism (see Kohli 1997: 885–6). In fact, it is equally impossible to prove that capitalist development in Korea would *not* have occurred without Japanese colonialism. Methodologically speaking, counterfactual argumentation is a relevant way of testing any claim of causality in historical analysis: when the 'colonial modernity' theorists argue that there is a relation of causality between Japanese colonisation and Korean modernisation, they must allow the thought-play of the counterfactual argument to test whether other causalities might have been at work. The evaluation of this problem depends on the theoretical framework of the argument: given, as I have developed in Part II of this book, that the 'catch-up' drive was internal to the capitalist world-system, causality comes first of all from the totality, the 'world system' itself. Within this framework, there were various attempts to overcome 'backwardness' in Korea at various levels of social actors, and likewise, the colonisation of Korea by Japan and Japanese colonial policies were made possible and shaped by various other factors within and outside Korea (see below), all of which are moulded by the overarching dynamic of the global capitalist system.[2]

On the other hand, Korean scholars' argument that the seeds of capitalist development were indigenously growing are also crucially limited. Above all, in critiquing the 'stagnation theory' implicit in the 'colonial modernity' thesis, they tend to underestimate or neglect the class content of the pre-modern Yi state that existed prior to Japanese colonisation. In other words, they seem to assume that the capitalist transition could have taken place gradually, had it not been for external intervention, primarily by the benevolence of the Yi Dynasty and reformist elites (e.g. Kang M-K 2000; Shin Y-O 1998, 2000). However, this view is based on the unrealistic assumption that the hegemony of the landed class and the aristocrats of the Yi Dynasty could have been broken without involving a revolutionary level of class conflict or war. As shall be discussed, the entire politics of the Yi Dynasty was characterised by the tension between the king who sought to strengthen his power and the *yang-ban* class (the landed aristocrats) who sought to undermine it.

Moreover, when the Yi state encountered the demand for social reform from below, as expressed in the Peasant War in 1894, it called on Qing Chinese troops to crush the rebellious peasants, which opened the door for further Japanese intervention. It was the Yi state that chose foreign intervention over catering to demands for social reform. The Korean scholars' nationalistic accounts, by prioritising the conflict between the nation and imperial powers, fail to notice that the Yi Dynasty failed to establish not only a formally independent sovereign nation-state amid intensifying rivalry between neighbouring imperialist powers but a new form of class domination that would have been able to *continue* class rule but in the *new form* that befits the arrival of capitalist modernity. As Marx put it, the

> starting-point of the development that gave rise to the wage-labourer as well as to the capitalist, was the servitude of the labourer. The advance consisted in a change of form of this servitude, in the transformation of feudal exploitation into capitalist exploitation.
>
> (Marx 1967: 669)

Having contextualised the question of the origins of capitalist development and the formation of the modern Korean state with reference to key approaches to capitalist transition that either prioritise class struggle at the national level or frame the history of modern Korea on the basis of the national-external (imperialism) binary, in what follows, I will assess the formation of the modern Korean state as a process that is inherently global. I will show that the particular attributes of the modern Korean state are products of its integration into the capitalist-world economy at a certain point in world time and at a specific location in the hierarchical capitalist world-system, which not only interacted with but mediated the content of class and social struggles.

Disintegration of the old order and integration into the capitalist world-economy

The Yi (Chosŭn) Dynasty that governed the Korean peninsula for 500 years (1392–1910) until Japanese annexation was 'an agrarian bureaucratic dynasty' (Cumings 1981: 8), a 'highly centralised agrarian-bureaucratic kingdom' (Wade 1983: 13), where 75 per cent of peasants rented all or part of their land. The class structure under the Yi dynasty was underpinned by the presence of the powerful landlord class, called *yang-ban*, whose social and political power was based both on 'access to hereditary land wealth' and 'on a close identification with the centralized bureaucracy' (Kohli 1999: 98; see also Amsden 1989: 29–31; Sorensen 1999: 293). While the Yi Dynasty was characterised by the highly centralised political power around the king, the latter was in permanent struggle with the *yang-ban*, who possessed great intellectual, social and political power, to the extent that some argue that 'the ostensibly centralized and autocratic structure was merely a façade that obscured the reality of aristocratic power' (Palais 1975: 2). The aristocracy and the state were in competition for available surplus resources, with the latter often losing out, while the Yi state had only weak and tenuous links to the peripheral parts of the country (Cumings 1981: 10, 40; Palais 1975: 8). Eckert (2014: 69) even notes that 'the Korean monarch was at best only another aristocrat, slightly more exalted, but essentially a *primus inter pares* figure'.[3]

If the Yi state and the *yang-ban* class maintained a symbiotic relation through a fine power balance for five centuries, the Yi Dynasty increasingly faced immense economic and political challenges at various levels, particularly from the nineteenth century onwards. The Yi state was put under intensifying pressure by foreign powers (e.g. America and France) to open itself to international trade but was able to fend them off relatively successfully and maintain an isolationist policy until the mid-nineteenth century. However, after the defeat in the Kangwha Island Incident, a clash with Japan in 1875, the Yi state eventually gave in to the demands of Japan and opened its ports to international commerce in 1876 by concluding the Kanghwa (Island) Treaty with Japan, which was soon followed by similar treaties with other foreign powers.

The Kanghwa Treaty signalled Korea's integration into the capitalist world-economy, but it was an unequal treaty that encroached on the Yi state's political authority over the territory of Korea. It granted the Japanese freedom to do business in Korea without government interference or any restrictions, in addition to the right of extraterritoriality (Eckert 2014: 9–10; Kim Y-H et al. 2000: 32–3). The Yi state was neither prepared nor equipped to introduce modern policy measures to manage and protect domestic industries and markets. While international commerce and commodity production had expanded since the signing of the Treaty, the increase in the importation of cheap manufacture goods (e.g. cotton products) from

Japan adversely affected Korean producers and merchants (Cumings 1997: 116; Eckert 2014: 11–2; Kim Y-H et al. 2000: 38–9). Agrarian relations also underwent significant changes. As rice exportation increased, rice production became increasingly commercialised. This expedited peasant differentiation, i.e. the creation and consolidation of hierarchies among peasants, but strengthened the tenant structure at the same time, as land ownership became concentrated in the hands of a few large-scale enterprise landlords, while self-cultivating farmers became tenant farmers or agricultural labourers, which contributed to the general deterioration of the living conditions of the rural population (Kim Y-H et al. 2000: 71–6).

The polarisation of land ownership and the collapse of subsistence farming were amongst the immediate causes of the Peasant War of 1894 and the *Tonghak* ('Eastern-learning') movement.[4] However, the plight of the peasants was one of the defining features of late Chosŭn, and peasant revolts took place sporadically in the early 1910s and intensified toward the mid-to-late nineteenth century (see Oh G-B 2002: 264–5). This in part reflected the growing power of the *yang-ban* class *vis-à-vis* the monarch: the power of the *yang-ban*, particularly some influential clans (e.g. the Kim clan of Andong), became strengthened against the king, which resulted in the expansion of land under their possession and diminished tax revenues for the Yi state. Peasants suffered from rampant corruption and the abuse of power by the *yang-ban* and local officials, on the one hand, and a high level of tax and duties, on the other, as the state attempted to compensate for the loss of state revenues caused by the increase in *yang-ban* land ownership that was exempted from taxation (Kim D-T 2001; Palais 1975: 16–8). The demands the peasant army put forward to the Yi state included elements of radical social reform, such as 'the removal of *yang ban* oppression, the burning of slave registers, an end to the social hierarchy and a general redistribution of the land' as well as anti-imperialist (anti-Japanese) inclinations (Cumings 1997: 118; Wang H-J 2014: 151–5). To the extent that the Peasant War and *Tonghak* movement called for social levelling and political autonomy from foreign intervention, they signified, though nascent in their form, the rise of aspirations from below to build a modern society based on nationalism and a modern form of polity, that is, a nation-state based on equality of citizenship (Hwang K-M 2007: 334)

However, the construction of a modern society that is socially equal and politically independent enough to withstand foreign intervention, desired and envisioned by the peasant army and the *Tonghak* movement, did not materialise. Threatened by the victory of the peasants over the state's forces in the first Peasant War, the Yi state sought an agreement with the peasant army by promising to accommodate their demands while at the same time calling on Qing Chinese troops to repress them (see below). When an agreement was reached, the peasant army took control of local administrations and implemented reform programmes at the local level, while the Yi state set up a special council to carry out social reforms at the government level, referred to as *Kabo* Reform or the Reform of 1894. The most significant *Kabo* Reform was the abolition of slavery and hereditary class distinctions, and the emancipation of the most despised groups, such as 'the *paekchŏng* [butchers] that occupied the lowest rung' in Chosŭn society (Kim J-S 1999: 313; see also Cumings 1997: 120). However, while the Yi state led by reformers was ready to implement moderate tax reforms, due to the fact that the state was still the largest landlord (possessing 'royal places lands' and 'public office lands'), it was reluctant to reform the existing landlord-tenant structure, a subject that was highly contested between the state and the peasants (Chang D-O 2009: 74; Wang H-J 2014: 158–60). In addition, even if the Yi state might have had the will to implement tax reforms, it did not possess adequate resources and administrative capacities to carry out a thorough cadastral survey, a prerequisite to establishing a modern and rational fiscal system (Wang H-J 2014: 158–60; see also Lee Y-H 2017).

Though significant in undertaking modernisation from above and leaving the legacy for subsequent modernisation reform, the limited extent of *Kabo* Reform cannot be explained solely by the class content of the Yi state: namely that the state elites' intention was ultimately to preserve their class rule or confine the aspirations of social change from below to a level that did not fundamentally challenge the existing order (see Kim S-J 2001: 221, 234). Equally importantly, the Yi state was not able to defend its political autonomy against foreign intervention in a situation in which Chosŭn Korea was increasingly becoming a territory that neighbouring imperialist powers were competing to subjugate. To make the situation more complex and chaotic, different political factions within the Yi state allied with different imperialist countries as leverage to enhance their respective positions in their hegemony struggle. A bitter intra-elite struggle between the father of king *Kojong* (*Hŭngsŏn Taewongun*) and queen *Min*, on the one hand, and the struggle between royalists, Confucian conservatives and moderate and radical modernising reformers, on the other, were intertwined with the escalating rivalry between Qing China, Japan and Russia over Chosŭn Korea in the late nineteenth century.

To illustrate this point, the Kangwha Treaty coincided with the fall of *Hŭngsŏn Taewongun,* the representative of a conservative isolationist sect, the ascendancy of queen Min and the relative rise of reformers within the Yi state, which led Japan to augment her influence over Korea. However, the *Imo* Mutiny that was begun in 1882 by disaffected soldiers against the delayed payment and poor quality of wages (in the form of rice) developed into a full-blown intra-state elite and interstate competition, which changed the balance of power domestically and regionally. Utilising the *Imo* Mutiny's anti-Japanese and anti-government reform sentiments, *Hŭngsŏn Taewongun* tried to return to power but was stopped by the intervention of Qing Chinese troops called on by queen Min, which resulted in placing Korea under stronger Qing China influence. After the repression of the *Imo* Munity, early modernisation reforms were rolled back under the pro-Qing Chinese government dominated by queen Min and her clan – Japan's intensifying imperialist ambition over Korea on the back of reformers within the state led her to reverse her initial favouritism towards Japan. Subsequently, the *Kapsin* Coup, led by radical modernisers supported by Japan, broke out in 1884 but was defeated again by the intervention of Qing Chinese troops.

The situation turned around a decade later. When the first Peasant War broke out in 1894, the Yi government called on Qing Chinese troops, but Japan, afraid of losing its influence over Korea *vis-à-vis* Qing China, also sent troops. Militarily strengthened for the last decade, Japan refused to follow king *Kojong*'s demand to remove her troops when an agreement with the peasant army was made (see above). Instead, Japanese troops occupied the royal palace and intervened in government affairs. This brought about the heightened presence of the Japanese in Chosŭn, the fall of queen Min and the empowerment of the reformers within the Yi state. This underscores not only that elite-level struggle in the late nineteenth century was intermingled with the imperialist rivalry but that the modernisers had a weak connection to the general population, so they could only ascend to power by relying on Japan's imperialist ambition (Kim S-J 2001: 221).

The competition between Japan and Qing China over Chosŭn finally came to an end with the victory of Japan in the First Sino-Japanese War in 1894. When the second Peasant War broke out in late 1894 as the government failed to deliver its earlier promises in addition to the fact that the government was not able to fend off heightening Japanese intervention, the Yi state brutally crushed the peasant army, with the help of Japanese troops equipped with advanced modern weaponry. The repression of the peasants was also aided by an army (*minbogun*) organised by the Confucian ruling elites (Wang H-J 2014: 162). This unveils the class content of the Yi state and the ruling class: the Yi state's primary concern was defending its old form of class domination; the pro-Japanese reformers and the pro-Qing conservatives, the two main elite groups that had been in bitter hegemony struggles for decades, were unified when they were challenged by class forces from below.

The changing alignments of the different political fractions and their vicissitudes in accordance with the struggle between imperialist powers continued until the fall of the Yi Dynasty itself. After the First Sino-Japanese War, Russia replaced Qing China as the major rival of Japan. After the fall of Qing China, the Yi government sought to establish ties with Russia in order to eschew the dominance of Japan. Japan, however, attempted to tighten her grip on Korea, going as far as to assassinate queen Min, the most prominent anti-Japanese figure within the Yi government, in 1895. This not only ignited outrage among other foreign powers but flared up anti-Japanese sentiment amongst Koreans. Nationwide protests against the Japanese erupted, and king *Kojong* fled to the Russian legation in 1896, which consequently allowed Russia to augment its influence on Korea. When king *Kojong* returned to the palace a year later, in 1897, in an attempt to establish a sovereign modern state, amidst a relatively stable power balance between imperialist states in Europe and Asia, he declared the founding of the Korean Empire (Great Han Empire).

Now Emperor, *Kojong* implemented various modernisation measures: he endeavoured to strengthen the authority of the monarch (Wang H-J 2010) while simultaneously modernising tax systems to make them suitable for a capitalist market economy by carrying out cadastral surveys (Lee Y-H 2017). However, the Korean Empire's modernisation reform from above failed to come to fruition partly because of the contradictory and limited nature of the reforms (see Wang H-J 2010). More crucially, Japan emerged as the dominant regional power in East Asia by defeating Russia in the Russo-Japanese War in 1905. Consequently, the Korean Empire's manoeuvre to transform itself into a modern sovereign state by playing one imperialist power out against another became less relevant. Korea became a protectorate of Japan in 1905 and was formally annexed in 1910.

Korea's integration into the capitalist world-economy and the dissolution of the Yi Dynasty discussed thus far highlights the invalidity of the antithetical juxtaposition of the national and the global. First, these were processes in which intensive social and class struggles were enmeshed with interstate and imperialist struggles to the extent that 'domestic' struggles were inseparable from 'external' struggles. Second, the desire to construct a modern society by abolishing hereditary hierarchies and to build a modern state equal to other sovereign states in the interstate system was formed in the process of Korea's integration into the capitalist world-economy and of experiencing intensifying foreign intervention. Third, as much as the Yi state, aristocrat bureaucrats and peasants, the imperialist foreign powers were themselves active class forces, inseparable from and heavily involved in 'domestic' social and class struggles. As seen in the case of the Japanese forces' brutal repression of the Peasant War of 1894, and as shall be shown below, 'foreign' powers always acted with clear class orientations, leaving important repercussions on 'domestic' class relations.

Primitive accumulation under the Japanese colonial state

After Korea became a formal colony of Japan in 1910, its modernisation came to be led by the colonial state, the Government-General of Korea, headed by a Japanese army or naval general under the auspices of the prime minister of Japan. In this section, I will trace what amounts to the first stage of primitive accumulation in Korea, a process of laying down the conditions for capitalist relations of production.

Perpetuating the landlord-tenant structure in the 1910s and the 1920s

Driven to manage colonial Korea more effectively and to facilitate the economic activities of the Japanese in Korea, the Japanese colonial state implemented various modernisation measures: modern financial institutions, such as the central bank and commercial banks, were set up, and a centralised fiscal system was implemented (Lee S-S and Jeong B-O 2000: 87–94). However, one of the most notable modernisation measures that the Japanese colonial state undertook was a cadastral survey. The survey was a success not least because it dramatically increased the fiscal base of the colonial state (Lee S-S and Jeong B-O 2000: 96).[5] Its utmost significance lies in its establishing modern land ownership based on the Japanese Civil Code (Lee Y-H 2017: 178): land became commodified on the basis of establishing the exclusive rights of private ownership. The establishment of private ownership was a process of re-categorising land ownership into state-owned and private-owned while removing 'royal land' ownership (Lee Y-H 2017: 172–3). For instance, multi-layered (feudal) land ownership was removed by denying the rights of intermediary landowners, e.g. the palace land agents, *de facto* landlords who managed the royal farms and paid low rents to the palace. The Japanese colonial state integrated all royal land into state-land, thereby bringing these lands under its control (Lee Y-H 2017: 173).

Another significant outcome of the cadastral survey was that farmers were deprived of the inherited land ownership and life-long tenant rights of cultivation which had been guaranteed during the Yi Dynasty (Chang D-O 2009: 75; Park N-J 2006: 288). This was caused in part by the fact that while the Korean landlords and the new colonial administrations were able to establish and secure their land ownerships, small farmers were often dispossessed of their land entitlements due to the ignorance of the new laws or deliberate misinformation (Cumings 1981: 42). Through the survey, the Japanese landlords and the colonial state came to own more than 10 per cent of the total arable land in colonial Korea by 'nationalising' royal land as well as undeclared and hitherto communal land. This process of establishing private land ownership, helped by the cadastral survey, amounts to a form of primitive accumulation to the extent that it was simultaneously a process of eliminating intermediary tenant agents and farmers of the means of subsistence, on the one hand, and of denying their customary rights to the use of communal lands and forests, on the other (Cumings 1981: 42; Lee S-S and Jeong B-O 2000: 96; Lee Y-H 2017: 173).

Primitive accumulation associated with the cadastral survey, which brought about the detachment of direct producers from the (communal) land and the privatisation and commodification of the land, however, did not significantly affect the material interests of traditional (large) landowners. While land acquisition by the Japanese increased, poor peasant owners or owner-tenants were the main losers as the land acquired by Japanese landlords had originally been part of the public or royal domain (Eckert 2014: 16). Even though Korean landlords became tax-payers under Japanese colonial rule as the rights of prerogative tax exemption attached to hereditary privileges were abolished, the large-scale landowners benefited from various kinds of direct and indirect support provided by the colonial state, such as preferential tax tariff and subsidised loans, particularly with the launch of the 'Campaign to Increase Rice Production' in 1920 (Lee S-S and Jeong B-O 2000: 97–9; see below). They also profited from the high price of rice until 1925, particularly between 1914 and 1920, when the price in Japan tripled due to the economic boom associated with the First World War (Eckert 2014: 17; Lee S-S and Jeong B-O 2000: 98; see below).

The defining characteristic of Japanese colonial policy in the 1910s and 1920s was thus to maintain the traditional landlord-tenant structure, thereby protecting the interest of the Korean (large-scale) landlord class. The colonial state purposely safeguarded the economic interests of the Korean landlord class and their traditional status as a means to consolidate its colonial rule, particularly in the countryside (Shin G-W and Han D-H 1999: 73). During the first half of the period of Japanese colonial rule, Korea was a simple agricultural colony and a market for Japanese manufactured products. Reflecting this, Japan-Korea trade shows a typical metropole-colony trading pattern, in which Korea was the prime provider of rice (grain) and raw materials, and an importer of Japanese industrial products, mainly cotton products, which amounted to 93 per cent of the total imports in 1919 (Kim Y-H et al. 2000: 39). Concomitantly, only those industries that were directly related to agriculture (e.g. railroads and rice mills) developed or were allowed to develop in colonial Korea (Eckert 1996: 4, 2014: 40–1).

The Japanese colonial policy against Korea in the 1910s and 1920s was largely conditioned by Japan's changing place in the world-system and the concomitantly intensifying class and social struggles in Japan. First, Japan experienced an unprecedented economic boom during the First World War thanks to the absence of competition from Western industrial powers in Asian markets. It transformed itself from a debtor into a creditor country and became a major industrialised country (Eckert 1996: 5). However, the economic boom was accompanied by and caused intensive social and class conflicts in Japan. While Japanese landlords, merchants and industrialists benefited from high rice prices during the War, low wages caused by inflation and high rice prices triggered 'a nationwide explosion of discontent among the Japanese urban and rural poor that became collectively known as the "Rice Riots"' in 1918 (Eckert 2014: 38). In addition, labour struggles intensified with 'a massive outbreak of strikes and the widespread formation of assertive labour unions' in the 1920s (Garon 1989: 2, as cited in Chang D-O 2009: 76; see also Byres 1991: 51). Japanese interest in the extraction of cheap rice from Korea (and Taiwan) became a matter of urgency to install domestic peace, which induced the Japanese colonial state to launch the Campaign to Increase Rice Production in colonial Korea in 1920.

The 'Campaign to Increase Rice Production' was primarily a response by the Japanese government to domestic social and class conflicts, but it affected class relations in Korea to a great extent. The Campaign helped the traditional Korean landlords to continue to preserve and even augment their economic power by strengthening the landlord-tenant structures in colonial Korea. At the same time it signified important changes in the nature of the landlord class and in overall agrarian class relations beneath the apparent continuation of the traditional rural relations. The Campaign accelerated the commodification of rice and intensive rice production, and with them the concentration of land ownership, which was already very high even before the launch of the Campaign. By the time the cadastral survey was completed in 1918, 3 per cent of rural landlord households possessed 50 per cent of the total arable land (Lee S-S and Jeong B-O 2000: 111). Some commercially successful large-scale landowners were transformed into entrepreneur landlords and, to a limited degree, into industrial capitalists who invested in the non-agricultural sector (Eckert 2014: 40; Lee S-S and Jeong B-O 2000: 112–3). In this process, small-scale landowners and subsistence farmers were hit adversely. Even if the production and export of rice increased, the consumption of rice by average Korean farmers decreased, and many suffered extreme poverty caused by the shortage of rice (Lee S-S and Jeong B-O 2000: 126). Booth and Deng (2017: 90) note that although 'rice yields per hectare were higher in … Korea than in Southeast Asia, per capita availability of rice was lower', and the fall in rice consumption per capita in Korea was continuous from 1915 to 1919. As shall be seen below, the living conditions of tenant farmers would continue to deteriorate in accordance with an agrarian depression from the mid-1920s onwards.

While there were signs indicating the rise of industrial, non-agricultural entrepreneurs amongst Koreans in the early colonial period, overall industrial development in this period was small in scale and limited in scope. In fact, the economic boom in Japan, in association with the First World War and the subsequent overaccumulation problems caused by lax lending policy and over-investment during the boom, increasingly led Japanese capital to see the Japanese colonies as new venues for investment. This new appetite to expand to colonial Korea resulted in the abolition of Company Law in 1920, a licensing system that controlled and limited the establishment of business entities in Korea (see below). However, it did not translate into an immediate and meaningful industrial development in Korea as the Japanese colonial state's policy was still defined by 'agriculture first' (Eckert 2014: 49), and Japanese capital's interests had more to do with preventing the rise of competitors from the colonies. Accordingly, the colonial state controlled and restrained industrial capitalist development by Koreans, and at best Korean capitalists were allowed to operate at the margins (Lee S-S and Jeong B-O 2000: 102). Nevertheless, under the surface of the preservation of the old landlord-tenant relations and the limited degree of industrial development in Korea in the first half of the colonial period, various forces were in operation, both at global and domestic levels, pushing Japan to change the course of its colonial policy in a way that facilitated industrialisation in colonial Korea.

Rural stabilisation and decline of the landlords in the 1930s

Towards the 1930s and 1940s, the Japanese colonial policy on Korea decisively shifted from one that was centred on the extraction of rice and raw materials to one initiating industrialisation at the expense of the Korean landowning class. The main drivers of this shift were the changing needs of Japanese capital and the concomitant change in Japan's place in the capitalist world-system, which interplayed with class and social struggles both in Korea and Japan.

After the economic boom associated with the First World War ended, Japan faced a recession and financial crises in 1923 and 1927, followed by the global crisis of 1929 (Chang D-O 2009: 76; Eckert 1996: 6–7). While Japanese capitalists managed to persuade the Government-General of Korea to abolish the Company Law in 1920 so that they became relatively free to invest in colonial Korea (see above), it became imperative for them to find venues for their surplus capital to overcome the problem of overaccumulation. If Japanese capital's need to invest overseas was one of the main causes for Japan's thirst for imperialist expansion to North China and the Russian Far East, with the establishment of Manchukuo in 1932, some degree of industrialisation in colonial Korea was considered necessary as Korea was seen by the Japanese colonialists as the base for their advance into the North East (Booth and Dent 2017: 74; Eckert 2014: 45).

In addition to the relative ascent of Japan in the world-system and the overaccumulation of Japanese capital, the pursuit of industrialisation in colonial Korea from the 1930s onwards was also driven by social and class struggles in Korea. One of the key incidents was a massive, nationwide anti-Japanese nationalist demonstration: the March First Movement of 1919. The extent and scale of the movement – one million out of a 16 million strong population participated – shocked Japan and induced it to alter its mode of colonial governance from outright repression to a more moderate kind, which is often referred to as the Cultural Rule policy (Lee S-S and Jeong B-O 2000: 118; Shin G-W and Han D-Y 1999: 73). The March First Movement and the subsequent relative easing of Japanese repression from the 1920s helped the formation of various political groups, both in urban and in rural areas. Particularly, social and class conflicts intensified in the rural areas by the deteriorating living conditions of most of the population. The Great Depression, followed by the global crisis of 1929, resulted in a fall in the price of rice and its excess supply in Japan, which was worsened by the Campaign to Increase Rice Production pursued in the previous decade. While the Campaign was abandoned in 1934, the Korean landlords tried to compensate for falling profits by squeezing tenant farmers, which triggered large-scale peasant revolts. Furthermore, the influence of socialism grew during this period, and some peasant sects (e.g. red peasant unions) and political groups became increasingly radicalised and organised (Lee S-S and Jeong B-O 2000: 134–5; Moon Y-J and Song K-J 2000: 146–8; Park S-W 1999: 133; Shin G-W and Han D-Y 1999: 78–9; see also Kim J-S 1999).

Against this backdrop, newly created by the interactions between the interstate rivalry within the heightening contradictions of the capitalist world-economy and class and social struggles in metropolitan Japan and colonial Korea, the Japanese colonial state pursued a rural stabilisation policy, on the one hand, and industrialisation in Korea, on the other. The Rural Revitalisation Campaign in 1932, introduced as part of the rural stabilisation policy, included programmes to alleviate the economic hardship of tenant farmers by offering loans and debt relief, and helping them to own land (Shin G-W and Han D-H 1999: 84–6). It also established a formal and administrative channel through which tenant farmers could redress grievances and tenancy disputes could be resolved as well as a law that put a restraint on the discretionary power of the landlords over the tenancy rents and terms (Moon Y-J and Song K-J 2000: 147–8). In addition, the Campaign encompassed 'spiritual education' at the village level, designed to make the rural population better conform to Japanese colonial rule, assigning local leadership roles to the educated local youth rather than to the landlords (Shin G-W and Han D-H 1999: 86–7).

This series of interventions in the rural relations by the colonial state brought about moderate improvement for the tenant farmers. However, more crucially, it signalled and brought about the conditions for important changes in the relation between state and society. Above all, it strengthened the authority of the colonial state in administrating and policing landlord-tenant relations at the expense of the Korean landowning class. While, until the 1920s, the colonial state had intervened in rural relations only indirectly by utilising the existing landlord-tenant structure, through the new rural policy in the 1930s, it was able to relate directly to the peasants, bypassing the landlord class. In fact, as long as rural exploitation took place through the medium of the traditional landowning class in the earlier phase of colonial rule, the landlords were the direct target of peasant revolts, and their social power was challenged from within. The replacement of the landlord class by the educated local youth as local leaders in the Rural Revitalisation Campaign also suggests that the Korean landlords as the means of safeguarding rural order outlived their usefulness from the perspective of the Japanese colonial state.

The social and economic power of the landlord class continued to be undermined, even when, in conjunction with the Second Sino-Japanese War in 1937 and a famine in Korea in 1939, rice production became a matter of urgency again. As a wartime economy set in, the colonial state tightened its grip on rural production relations, which undermined the position of landlords further. For instance, the landowners, who were either insolvent or had difficulties in management entrusted their lands to land management companies (e.g. Chosŭn Land Trust Company) and were paid a share of profits according to the latter's performance. The size of these lands and the periods for which they were entrusted to these companies increased, especially after the Second Sino-Japanese War. Furthermore, the landlords were prohibited from arbitrarily raising the tenancy rent and from receiving rent in kind (rice) directly from tenants: the government bought rice from the tenants at a fixed price (*kongchul*), and the landlords received a cash income from the rice management companies (Moon Y-J and Song K-J 2000: 156–7). The colonial state even ordered the lands owned by (unproductive) absentee landlords to be managed by agricultural and industrial associations to increase productivity (Hong S-C 2013: 29). Through this series of measures undertaken in the second half of the period of Japanese colonial rule, the landlord class continued to decline and would never recover their social and political power. By the time, soon after national independence, that land reform was implemented, they hardly constituted a meaningful, let alone a dominant, social class (see below).

War-led colonial industrialisation in the 1940s

In parallel with the restructuring of rural production and social relations, the promotion of industrialisation in colonial Korea constituted another pillar of Japanese colonial policy in the second half of its rule. Once industrialisation in Korea was perceived as necessary for Japanese capital's expansion to the Asian continent and to mitigate the agrarian crisis both in metropolitan Japan and in colonial Korea, the Government-General of Korea attempted to attract Japanese capital to Korea by providing a favourable investment environment: it offered projective tariffs, subsidies and other inducements (Eckert 1996: 11), and it exempted Japanese capital from anti-cartel and minimum labour protection laws, which were in operation in the metropole (Eckert 1996: 7–8; Moon Y-J and Song K-J 2000: 163). Reflecting in part that the economic development of Korea as an economic link to Manchuria was inextricably intertwined with Japanese military goals, i.e. the defence against the Soviet Union and China, it was not only led by army officers but pursued in a military fashion (Eckert 1996: 11, 2014: 69–72; Lee B-C 2011: 367–8).

Especially since the start of the Second Sino-Japanese War, industrial production in Korea was organised to meet the needs of the Japanese war effort. The colonial state exercised extreme social and production control in every sphere of economic and social life, from production processes and financial flows to labour allocation: investment in the heavy industry was prioritised; financial flows into non-military production were prohibited or subject to permission by state authority; stringent control on imports and exports was enforced and consumption goods were rationed; skilled-labourers were allocated to military-related production; the free movement of labourers from one sector to another was restricted; and surplus labour and women were mobilised as a workforce for industrial production and sex slavery.

With the help of this top-down mobilisation of natural and human resources by the militarised colonial state, the scale of industrialisation in colonial Korea towards the end of the 1930s was large, and the pace was rapid. The extent of industrialisation in this period can be illustrated by the following statistics: total industrial production amounted to around 200 million Yen in 1921 but rocketed to around 1 billion Yen in 1937 and exceeded 2 billion Yen by 1943 (Eckert 1996: 13). Heavy and chemical industry grew rapidly from 1937 and overtook light industry, constituting more than half of the total industrial production. During the period of 1931–43, the ratio of the light industry (food processing, textile) decreased from 62 per cent to 37 per cent, while that of the heavy and chemical industry increased from 24 per cent to 51 per cent (Moon Y-J and Song K-J 2000: 171). Accordingly, from 1933 to 1942, 'the number of factory workers increased 3.9 times, miners 4.0 times, and construction workers a remarkable 8.7 times' (Park S-W 1999: 139). The number of industrial workers increased from 384,951 in 1932 to 1,321,713 in 1943 (Cumings 1997: 170). The total number of the industrial working class in late 1944 was reported to be over two million (KFTU 1979: 224, cited from Chang D-O 2009: 77). Although half of these workers were informal workers, such as day labourers, 'the number of factory, mining, and construction workers who are generally considered as the full-time, regular, core group of industrial workers ... constituted more than half the group by 1945' (Park S-W 1999: 139). This rapid rise of the number of industrial workers meant the dislocation of a large part of the population. While a large pool of floating labour that existed as a result of the agrarian crisis in the 1920s became factory workers, the new industrial sector employment facilitated a massive scale of out-migration from the rural areas, from 60,000 men during 1930–35 to 220,000 during 1935–45, half of whom were absorbed within Korea, while the other half went to Manchuria and Japan (Park S-W 1999: 139).

These figures are indicative of the fact that Korea underwent social upheaval and transformation on an unprecedented scale. Furthermore, they show that industrial development in colonial Korea was part and parcel of a global process from its inception, to which class conflict was also inherent. Industrialisation in colonial Korea was simultaneously linked to capitalist accumulation in Japan and her changing place in the capitalist word-system. Furthermore, the 'external' power that drove primitive accumulation in Korea, Japan, was herself undergoing state-led 'catch-up' industrialisation under the pressure of European imperialist powers (Cumings 1984: 8–9).[6] The shift in Japanese colonial policy from intercepting to favouring industrialisation in colonial Korea was first induced by her imperialist expansion to Manchuria amid escalating interstate rivalry, which, in turn, changed Korea's place in the world-system: Korea moved up in the hierarchy and occupied an intermediary position between Japan and Manchuria with the establishment of Manchukuo in 1932. As Cumings (1984: 13) aptly put it,

> Korea's ... periphery was Manchuria, where it sent workers, merchants, soldiers, and bureaucrats who occupied a middle position between Japanese overlords and Chinese peasants; as Korean rice was shipped to Japan, millet was imported from Manchuria to feed Korean peasants in a classic core-semiperiphery-periphery relationship.

As much as industrialisation in colonial Korea reflected the world-system compulsion for Japan to 'catch-up' with and defend itself against the West, it was reinforced by social and class struggles in colonial Korea. In the face of massive anti-imperialist struggles (e.g. the March First Movement) and the politicisation and radicalisation of the peasant movements, industrialisation was demanded not only by the necessity arising from imperialist interstate rivalry but to restore stability in rural areas by absorbing the surplus rural population caused by the agrarian crisis of the 1920s. This suggests that the two pillars of the Japanese colonial policy of the 1930s and the 1940s against Korea, the rural stabilisation policy and industrialisation, were inextricably related. More tellingly, however, it reveals the class content of the Japanese colonial state as a capitalist state. In addition to providing the tenant farmers with debt relief and financial assistance in an attempt to incorporate them into the colonial system of governance, the colonial state tolerated and even encouraged the activities of (moderate) liberal political groups while repressing more radical ones with socialist or communist orientations (see Kim J-S 1999: 330–3; Park W-S 1999: 153–6). Similarly, while supporting the upper echelons of the Korean enterprises to expand and grow by granting privileged access to bank loans and to foreign markets (Manchuria), the Japanese colonial state was on the side of the Korean enterprises by crushing labour strikes and unions. In other words, the Japanese colonial state was not simply a foreign state that exploited Korea as a country subordinated to Japan but a *capitalist state* that supported the exploitation of labour by capital at home and in the colonies. While the peculiar attributes of industrial development in colonial Korea were shaped and conditioned by its place within the hierarchical capitalist world-systematic dynamic and its interaction with class and social struggles both in Japan and in Korea, industrialisation in colonial Korea was first and foremost *capitalist* development, to which class and social struggles were intrinsic.

The intensive industrialisation pursued since the mid-1930s was abruptly halted with the defeat of Japan in the Second World War in August 1945, whereupon Korea became 'nationally liberated' from Japan. Even if the conditions of capitalist transition were laid and matured to some extent during Japanese colonialism, the reproduction of capitalist social relations was still not assured, not least because there still existed feudal relations, and a sovereign nation-state was yet to be established in the postcolonial context. Equally importantly, there was an explosion of social and political activism that called for a mode of development other than capitalism (see below). The total elimination of pre-modern social relations represented by the landlord-tenant agrarian structure and the formation of a nation-state setting the stage for 'catch-up' development would require another round of primitive accumulation.

Primitive accumulation under the US army occupation

This section assesses what amounts to the second stage of primitive accumulation that took place in postcolonial Korea under the US military army occupation by assessing two instances: land reform and the disposal of Japanese-held properties. Particularly, the land reform has often been seen as positively correlated to post-Second World War 'successful' capitalist development in Korea (see Hong S-C 2013; Jeon Y-D and Kim Y-Y 2000; You J-S 2017). Similarly, land reform in Korea (as well as in Japan and Taiwan) has been identified as a key factor that explains the divergent development outcomes between East Asia and Latin America: successful land reform in East Asia eliminated the power of the landlord class, who could have put up serious opposition to industrialisation (see Evans 1987: 215; Jang S-H 2000: 150; Jenkins 1991: 206–7; Jeong J-S 2000: 39; Kong J-O 2000 55). Basing my argument on rich research done on land reform in postcolonial Korea, I will bring to the fore how its implementation, timing and actual content resulted from intensive class struggle, which not only domestic social forces but also those that are usually seen as 'external' and 'foreign' forces actively participated in.

Land reform as class struggle and the US as a class force

After colonial rule ended with the defeat of Japan in the Second World War, the southern part of Korea ('Korea', hereafter) below the 38th parallel was occupied by the American military government, while the northern part was occupied by the Soviet Union. Postcolonial Korea saw the proliferation of political groups and intensifying ideological struggles between capitalism, socialism and communism. According to a survey conducted by the US occupation army in 1946, 77 per cent of Korean respondents (out of 8,453) said '"yes" in support of socialism and communism' (Jeon Y-D and Kim Y-Y 2000: 257). To the extent that those who prospered under Japanese colonial rule were (large-scale) landlords and capitalists who collaborated with Japan, their possessions and landholdings were in danger of being confiscated, and even their physical survival was in question as they were often subject to physical assaults. Especially peasants were politicised and organised as a powerful social force: the National Farmers Alliance was formed in December 8, 1945 and co-operated with other radical social forces, including the *Chosŭn* Communist Party (Jeong J-S 2000: 24; Jeong T-H 2000: 218; see Park N-J 2006: 289). Against this backdrop, the land question, the highly unequal landlord-tenant structure, emerged as one of the most pressing issues to be resolved in the politically volatile context, especially when North Korea implemented a land reform in March 1946 on a scale unprecedented in other postcolonial countries: all lands from Japanese and Korean landlords were confiscated without compensation and distributed to farmers for free (Jeong J-S 2000: 28; Jeong T-H 2000: 230; Kim I 2016: 125; You S-J 2017: 544). In the face of immense pressure coming from below and the radical land reform carried out in the North in a way that denied private land ownership, it was believed by most, including the ruling elites and the landlord class, that land reform in the South was unavoidable (Hong S-C 2013: 24; Jeong J-S 2000: 25–6).

Although the political elites commonly acknowledged the pressure to implement a land reform as a matter of fact, the content and scale of land reform remained contentious. For instance, it was intensely debated whether small- and medium-scale or large-scale landholdings should be subject to land reform and whether the lands owned by Koreans or only those owned by collaborators of Japanese colonists should be repossessed by the government for redistribution. On the one hand, *Hanmingdang*, the Korea Democratic Party (KDP), which represented the interests of the landlords, tacitly agreed to land reform but envisioned one that would assist the landlords in transforming themselves into capitalists through the provision of proper compensation (Jang S-H 1994: 99). On the other hand, the *Chosŭn* Communist Party initially held the view that only large-scale landholdings and the lands owned by the Japanese and Korean collaborators should be repossessed for non-compensated land redistribution (Jeong T-H 2000: 229). Nationalist and centre-left political groups shared this view, hoping to broaden their political base by embracing national capitalists and small-scale Korean landholders. However, in light of the land reform in the North, the *Chosŭn* Communist Party changed its stance and argued for a reform plan similar to what had been implemented in North Korea. Furthermore, political parties went through a series of re-alignments with regard to land reform. More than 100 members of the KDP, mainly nationalists and left-leaning members, defected owing to disagreement over the content of land reform. Those supporting a more radical version of land reform within the centre-left and nationalist parties, such as *Chosŭn Sinmindang* (Chosŭn New People's Party) and *Chosŭn Inmindang* (Chosŭn People's Party), defected and formed the *Nam Chosŭn* (South Chosŭn) Labour Party in November 1946 (Jeong T-H 2000: 231–2).

Amongst the various land reform plans that were on the table (see Yang D-A 2008: 47), one of the most conservative versions, offering compensation to the landlords and requiring the tenants to purchase lands, was eventually legislated in February 1950. The law stipulated that the government would purchase land from landlords in excess of three *Chŏngbo* and sell it to tenant and landless farmers (Hong S-C 2013: 24).[7] The price of the land was decided at 150 per cent of the annual yield, and the tenants (purchasers) were expected to pay 30 per cent of annual yields in kind (rice) for the following five years (Jeong T-H 2000: 236; You J-S 2017: 545), while landlords were to be given bonds first and paid in cash in instalments of 30 per cent annually for five years (Hong S-C 2013: 24). Even this conservative reform was implemented only after the US occupation authority kick-started land reform by redistributing formerly Japanese-held land at its disposal in March 1948. The proportion of the lands the US distributed only amounted to 18.7 per cent of the total land targeted (Kim I 2016: 125), but it set a precedent for the terms of land reform and had the effect of pressing the Korean government to implement land reform without further delay.

The US initiation of a moderate form of land reform was above all driven to ensure that 'the South [was] buffered from socialism and communism' (Jeon Y-D and Kim Y-Y 2000: 257). While the US judged that moderate land reform was necessary to 'suffocate the Communists' appeal in the rural areas' by allowing the peasants to have a sense of land ownership (Kim I 2016: 121), it feared that the implementation of land reform would continue to be delayed due to the opposition of the conservative wing of the political elites, particularly after the elections to constitute the new South Korean government in May 1948, after which the US occupation army was scheduled to withdraw (Kim I 2016: 124). As the left-wing movements from below became relatively dormant after a successful crackdown on communist-inspired general strikes and peasant uprisings, particularly the October Uprising of 1946 under the US occupation army, the conservative political elites gradually gained power *vis-à-vis* the liberals, resulting in the delay of the implementation of land reform (Kim I 2016: 118–20). Furthermore, the US's initiation of the land reform was also in part explained by its intention to undermine the Korean landlord class, given the huge agricultural surplus production at home (see Shin Y-O 2001). In fact, US surplus agricultural products were provided to Korea as a form of aid beyond the level required for domestic consumption after the Korean War, which contributed to the destruction of the Korean agricultural industry (Jeong J-S 2000: 27, 38–9; Jeong T-H 2000: 234; Shin Y-O 2000: 286; see below).

In addition to the pressure to implement a land reform coming from the US, the newly formed Korean government itself increasingly came to see the political benefits of land reform. The first Korean government, led by Syngman Rhee, that came to power in August 1948 after elections held only in the South had a weak popular base. While Rhee was supported by the US, nationalist leaders and left-wing social forces had opposed the formation of the South Korean government in defence of a unified Korea, and the left-wing social forces organised mass rallies to boycott the elections (Hong Y-P 2000: 24; Jeong J-S 2000: 29–30; see also Jeong H-K 1996). The elections to form the first government of South Korea took place amid intensive struggles between the political elites and various groups in society, creating a situation similar to a civil war (Yang D-M 2008: 57–64). In this context, land reform was seen to enhance the legitimacy of the new government and weaken the opposition (You J-S 2017: 545). Moreover, as the land reform was enacted only a few months before the outbreak of the Korean War, it became irreversible. In addition to the necessity to mobilise the rural population for the War, the areas that had been occupied by the North Korean army during the War underwent a land reform equivalent to that in the North (Jeong J-S 2000: 31–4).

Even though only a moderate version of land reform was eventually enforced, its significance in changing class relations and their political implications cannot be overemphasised. One of the immediate outcomes was the drastic increase in the number of self-cultivators (i.e. small freeholders): the 'proportion of self-cultivated farmland ... increased sharply from around 35 per cent at the end of 1945 to 96 per cent in 1951' (Hong S-C 2013: 24; see also Shin Y-O 2000: 258). The proposition of tenant households decreased from 48.9 per cent in 1945 to 21 per cent in 1949 and 6.7 per cent in 1960 (Jeong J-S 2000: 36). Beyond these quantitative changes, the land reform produced fundamental societal change: the dissolution of the landlord-tenant system and of the landlords as a dominant class.

Hyperinflation caused by the Korean War diminished the monetary value of the payments made to the landlords. Payment for the purchased lands was not made as planned due to the poor living conditions of farmers following the Korean War. The rate of payment made in 1950–54 for the distributed land repossessed by the state from the Japanese was 61.9 per cent, and for private land it was only 28 per cent (Jeong J-S 2000: 37). The compensation that most landlords received was too small to allow them to become commercial and industrial capitalists (Hong S-C 2013: 27). Consequently, only a small minority of large-scale landlords were able to make the transition, some of whom went on to develop into *chaebols*, family-run monopoly conglomerates (see below and Chapter 8). In this respect, Korea's path to capitalist transition is characterised by differentiation among landlords and homogenisation of the tenants as self-cultivators.

The land reform turned most tenant and landless farmers into small-scale self-cultivators and thus had an equalising effect, particularly with the collapse of the landlord class (You J-S 2017: 545–6). Nevertheless, many farmers' living conditions did not greatly improve. After the Korean War, 78.6 per cent of the self-cultivating farmers owned no more than 1 *Chŏngbo,* which could hardly meet their needs in terms of self-consumption (Korea Agricultural Economy Institute 1989: 1041). Furthermore, the rural population was burdened with heavy taxes during and after the War. Illustratively, if the tax burden imposed on farmers in kind (rice) at 15 per cent of their annual yields was added to the 30 per cent of annual yields to be paid for the purchase of the land under the land reform, farmers were levied 45 per cent of their annual production as tax (Jeong J-S 2000: 37–8). Lee D-K (1987: 172–4) estimates that the 'Provisional Land Acquisition Tax', one of the taxes levied on farmers during the Korean War, amounted to 70–90 per cent of total fiscal revenues.

In addition, the importation of US surplus agricultural products adversely affected the rural economy further. The amount of US food aid exceeded what was needed for consumption in 1953 and 1954, which pushed the price of grain down relative to other consumption goods, resulting in the deterioration of the living conditions of a large section of the rural population (Lee D-K 1987: 181–2). This led many farmers either to return to tenant farming or to abandon the land (Jeong J-S 2000: 39; Lee D-K 1987: 217; Shin Y-O 2000: 258–9). Although the land reform law prohibited the disposal of the land distributed before the compensation was fully made, a large amount of land was resold, particularly after 1954. According to a study conducted on a few sample villages in the Kyŏnggi, Chungch'ŏng and Kyŏngsang provinces between 1950 and 1975, 58 per cent of distributed land was resold in the case of land less than 0.3 *Chŏngbo* and 32 per cent in the case of land sized between 0.3 and 0.5 *Chŏngbo*, respectively (Shin Y-O 2000: 291). A large pool of surplus labour in the rural economy was created as a consequence, which was ready to be absorbed into the urban areas once industrialisation began.

The trajectory of Korean land reform implemented after national independence shows how intensely various political groups contested its timing and content, and how much it was conditioned by intensive class and social struggles. Not only did the various classes and groups of Korean society play their parts, but the US occupation authority itself intervened in the process as an effective class force by contributing greatly to determining the content of land reform in the context of a highly volatile period, which eventually lead to the Korean (Civil) War, an intensive class war itself. Moreover, the land reform laid one of most important conditions for capitalist production relations. It contributed to dissolving the pre-modern social and class relations based on the landlord-tenant structure, turning most farmers into self-cultivators and producing an impoverished rural surplus population detached from, or only tenuously attached to, land. Furthermore, as intended by the US and the Korean government, the land reform helped turn the rural population into supporters of the authoritarian ruling party, which helped stabilise the political environment (Jeon Y-D and Kim Y-Y 2000: 266; You J-S 2017: 548). In Hong's words, '[m]any farmers in the 1950s possessed a sense of being petit bourgeois with their lands, along with having strong anti-communist and anti-landlord sentiments' (Hong S-C 2013: 39). However, even if the landlords as a powerful social force disappeared, and stability in the rural economy was restored, the capitalist class was yet to be born with the help of the state through the process of privatising what hitherto had been public assets, another instance of primitive accumulation.

The formation of the capitalists and 'forced accumulation'

If the land reform dissolved the landlord class, the capitalist class surfaced as a new dominant class through the process of the privatisation of properties repossessed from the former Japanese colonialists. As much as the land reform resulted from intensive class and social struggles, the privatisation of repossessed assets was highly contested. Its specific outcome was circumscribed by class struggles, in which the US occupation army played a crucial role. This process determined, to a large extent, the particular relations between the state and capital, and thereby the trajectory of capitalist development in Korea itself.

When Japanese colonial rule ended in 1945, all properties, including factories, industrial plants, shares and lands owned by the Japanese, were repossessed and managed by the US military government of Korea. As of 1948, Japanese-held firms and plants accounted for 80 per cent of total industrial production (Chung J-A 2008: 92). It was widely believed across political lines that large-scale industrial plants and industries (e.g. transport, communication, finance) and those relating to energy generation should be manged publicly (Chung J-A 2008: 92; Jeong T-H 2000: 197–8; Kong J-O 2000: 61–2). In the first constitution of the Republic of Korea, established in July 1948, it was stated that many of the repossessed properties, in particular, large-scale corporations, factories and banks would be run publicly, i.e. nationalised.[8] In spite of this broad consensus in the early post-independence period, these assets were primarily sold to private agents. Given that the repossessed properties from the former colonialists had been disposed of in various ways,[9] the privatising or selling of the majority of them to private agents, which laid the ground for the rise of monopoly conglomerates (the *chaebol*) in the case of Korea, was not pre-determined as necessary or inevitable. This change of course can be explained by the defeat of the left in the class struggle, into which the US intervened as an effective class force.

When the US military government of Korea put all Japanese-held public and private properties under its management, it acted with a clear class orientation. It made it clear that until a democratic (pro-capitalist) government was in place in Korea, the US would not give up its rights to manage the properties repossessed from the Japanese colonialists. Even after the US handed over the right to manage the properties to Koreans in 1947, it still held the power to make the final decision on who was given control of them (Jeong T-H 2000: 209–41). For instance, the US rejected self-management by labourers and employees, which had been practiced, though marginally, immediately after national independence, and adopted a system in which the managers of the properties were appointed by the US occupation authority itself. These managers consisted of those who had previously worked as managers or shareholders, those who were entrusted by the Japanese or Japanese collaborators in the colonial period and those who had personal connections with the US occupation authority (Jeong T-H 2000: 241). These initial groups of managers were the nuclei of the future networks of core capitalists as they became the owners of the properties later, after they were given the privileged status of priority buyers. Although the scale and value of the properties sold under the US occupation army were small, only amounting 0.85 per cent of the total estimated value of the repossessed properties (Jeong T-H 2000: 244), it influenced greatly the ways in which the remaining properties were disposed of subsequently under the Korean government. Under the US occupation authority and the Korean government three quarters of the corporations repossessed from Japan were sold to their managers (Jeong T-H 2000: 243; Shin Y-O 2000: 263).

The priority buyers benefited from extremely favourable terms of purchase. They purchased the factory plants and properties at below market prices with down-payments of only 20 per cent of the value, with the remaining 80 per cent being paid in instalments over the following ten years at an annual interest rate of 7 per cent. Given the hyperinflation of the time, this meant that the production facilities and properties were virtually given away for free (Jeong T-H 2000: 246; Kong J-O 2000: 69; Shin Y-O 2000: 261). As the repossessed properties were sold at a reduced concessional price, the larger the properties, the bigger the benefits accrued to buyers. Buyers of large companies particularly enjoyed special terms of purchase, being granted the ability to make the payment over an extended 15-year period (Kong J-O 2000: 80; Shin Y-O 2000: 264–5).

The capitalists emerged newly in this context, neither from the landlord class nor through business establishments. The *chaebol*, family-run business conglomerates emerged first in this process in an embryonic form. Amongst the top *chaebol* founders in the 1950s, 10 out of 23 grew to become *chaebol* by purchasing repossessed firms. Others did so either by taking over properties from others or buying up state-owned corporations built by US aid (Kong J-O 2000: 87–90; see Chapter 8).[10] In this respect, there is a disjuncture between the traditional landlord class and the new capitalist class. While a few large landlords made the successful transformation into capitalists, most were largely excluded from the process of privatisation (Kong J-O 2000: 80; see also Suh J-J 1988a). Of the top 1.4 per cent of the landlords who sold 20 *Chŏngbo* and above, only 5 per cent purchased Japanese-held firms (Shin Y-O 2000: 260).[11]

The privatisation of repossessed properties constitutes the Korean version of primitive accumulation: the capitalist class formation took place in the process of transferring public assets into private hands (echoing the enclosures described by Marx in *Capital*), with the active facilitation of the process by the state in favour of the rising new capitalist class. It brought about a new trajectory of class relations in which capitalists were favoured at the expense of the landlord class and the rural population at large. While the capitalist transition described by Marx with reference to the case of England was characterised by the rise of commercial and capitalist farmers in agriculture, whose dominance forced the state to act to their advantage, what is distinctive about this process in Korea is that the capitalist class itself was given birth to by the state. Puzzlingly, the Korean state operated on behalf of the future dominant class, which was not yet existent, let alone predominant at that point.

This puzzle can be resolved only when considering the imperialist or 'external' force at play in the process of primitive accumulation in Korea, whereby capitalist social relations were to be created 'politically' by the state in the form of 'forced accumulation'. The Korean state acted as the 'vehicle of the capitalist mode of production' under 'world-market compulsion'. To restate this point in von Braunmühl's words, 'class relations and the relations of the state apparatus to society bear in a specific manner the imprint of that country's position on the world market' (1978: 171). However, as a country of the world-economic periphery, its sovereign autonomy was restrained under the heavy influence of the 'external' power (the US). As much as a moderate form of land reform was a strategic act initiated by the US occupation authority with a view to making the appeal of communism ineffectual in the rural areas, the precedent of the privatisation of the Japanese-held industrial facilities and firms was set by the US authority in a way that ensured the prevalence of private acquisition over public ownership or self-management by workers. This suggests that the US was not merely an 'external' power but a powerful class force that influenced and even determined the rise of a new power balance between classes, on the one hand, and state-society relations, on the other.

Following the successful crackdown on the left-wing (peasant) movements (e.g. the October Uprising in 1946) by the US occupation authority and subsequently by the Korean government, the Korean War (1950–53) had the effect of further weakening left-wing and communist forces. During the Korean War, an ideological battle took place as a matter of survival. The Rhee government legislated for a National Security Law in 1948 as a means to oppress political opponents and carried out a massive 'cleansing' of communists during and after the Korean War (see Kim S-O 2013).[12] For fear of being executed, many communists and influential left-wing intellectuals who were lucky enough to survive fled to the North. This in part contributed to the perpetuation of anti-communist conservatism and the dormancy of the left-wing social and labour forces in Korea for decades to come. Anti-communism became a *de facto* national ideology (see Hong Y-P 2000: 38–9). The prevalence of anti-communist ideology also explains the 1954 amendments to the clauses on the privatisation of properties repossessed from the Japanese colonialists in the Korean constitution, in which the elements of nationalisation and labour's participation in management became reduced, while those safeguarding private ownership and individual freedom were expanded (Jeong T-H 2000: 246; Kong J-O 2000: 66–8; Shin Y-O 2000: 293, 2008: 162; Yang W-J 2005: 124): any form of property management by collective means was condemned as communism. This was a remarkable turnaround from the situation immediately after national independence when socialism and communism were favoured over capitalism by most Koreans (see above).

In the same process, the Korean state fortified its military strengths and political legitimacy as the defender of national security. In the 1950s, together with Taiwan, Korea had one of 'the highest military/civilian ratios in the world' (Cumings 1984: 26), with the armed forces expanding from 100,000 to 600,000 during the Korean War (Hong Y-P 2000: 153). A new modern state surfaced in Korea, one that exerted disproportionate dominance over society, in which the social-economic power of the landlord class was dismantled, the capitalist class was still in the process of formation and anti-government and left-wing social forces were effectively destroyed. This state-society and state-capital relation rendered 'development from above' or 'state-led development' highly probable, though, as shall be seen in the next chapter, the dominance of the state over society in and of itself did not guarantee 'successful' and 'rapid' industrialisation.

Conclusion

In this chapter, I have traced the origins of the modern Korean state by examining primitive accumulation processes before and after de-colonisation from Japan in 1945, and how in this process the modern Korean state arose as an element intrinsic to the process of its integration into the world capitalist-economy and the formation of capitalist production and social relations. I have highlighted the fact that capitalist development in Korea was a global process from its inception, to which intense class struggles and conflicts were intrinsic, and how a state-dominated society emerged over the course of intensive class struggles, of which not only domestic but foreign (imperialist) forces were an integral part.

I have shown that nationally focussed approaches to primitive accumulation or capitalist transition (e.g. Brenner and Byres) are limited in capturing the complex trajectory of capitalist development, particularly in the context of the world-economic periphery. Moreover, I have shown that Japanese colonial experiences alone cannot explain the specific attributes of the formation of the Korean modern state and capitalist development in Korea as suggested by the 'colonial modernity' thesis (e.g. Eckert and Kohli). The pressure to integrate into the capitalist world-economy and the desire to modernise ('catch-up') were a *universal* dynamic generated by capitalist modernity itself that gave rise to the particular form and content of interstate competition, on the one hand, and aspirations for social reforms (social levelling and nationalism), on the other. Furthermore, while it is indisputable that Japanese colonialism contributed to laying the conditions for capitalist development in Korea, it required another round of primitive accumulation and intensive social and class struggles, including the land reform, the Korean War and the disposal of the Japanese-held properties that took place *after* Japanese colonial rule.

At the same time, I have offered an analysis alternative to the claim of nationalist Korean scholars that the drive for capitalist development could have sprung endogenously and could have been more 'balanced', had it not been for the intervention by 'external' powers. Apart from the fact that there is no such thing as a 'balanced' capitalist transition, as the latter denotes by definition a violent process that creates the conditions for the capitalist form of class domination, such counterfactual speculation would need to abstract entirely from modern Korean history. I have highlighted that the 'external' powers were in fact not 'external' insofar as they acted very much as class forces *within* the 'domestic' context and were aligned with existing and emergent class forces in Korea, which reflects the fact that their interventions were to an extent invited and desired by certain strata or fractions of classes in Korea. Equally, the Japanese colonial state and the US occupation authority were not simply alien foreign powers but acted with a clear class orientation as *capitalist*, thereby supporting the exploitation of labour by capital at home and in the (former) colonies.

Notes

1 Eckert noted in his preface to the 2014 edition of his *Offspring of Empire* (first published in 1991) that he did not anticipate that his book would provoke highly politicised responses both from Korean academics and from Japanese apologists for colonialism. For instance, some Korean historians criticised him for whitewashing Japanese colonial rule in Korea, while the title of his book was rendered *The Japanese Empire's Gift of the Gods* in its Japanese translation (2014: xviii).
2 Kohli has not only been criticised by nationalist Korean scholars. For instance, Booth and Deng (2017) argue that Japanese colonial policies and the economic performance of Japanese colonies were not dissimilar to those of other colonial powers and their colonies. Some researchers, while recognising the limitations of some Korean historians' 'nationalistic' accounts of Japanese colonialism, argue that what happened after Japanese colonialism was more important than or at least equally important as what happened during Japanese colonialism in determining the development trajectory of Korea (see Shin and Robinson 1999; Park S-W 1999).
3 To some, the strength of the bureaucrats, as opposed to that of the king, was a factor that contributed to the longevity of the Yi Dynasty (see Park N-J 2006: 280).
4 It is not uncommon to conflate *Tonghak*, a semi-religious, anti-imperialist and pro-modernisation reformist movement with the Peasant War of 1894, as seen in Cumings (1997: 115–20). According to this view, *Tonghak* provided the peasants with spiritual as well as organisational leadership. This view has been challenged, particularly by North Korean scholars, who argue that the Peasant War of 1894 was independent of *Tonghak* influence. According to them, while there was an overlap, the history of *Tonghak* was too short to penetrate into the lives of peasants, and the class bases of the two movements were different: while the leadership of *Tonghak* consisted of old aristocrats, the Peasant War army was primarily led by peasants with a more radical vision for social change (see Oh G-B 2002 [1959]). For differences in the reception of the history of *Tonghak* and the Peasant War by Korean scholars see Wang H-J (2015). For a general critique of Cuming's assessment of modern Korean history, see Sonn H-C (1989b).
5 Hwang K-M (2004: 367) notes that more households were registered in the Household Registration surveys carried out under the Japanese Protectorate in 1909 than under the Korean Han Empire in 1896. He suggests that this is not because of national population increases but because of the better surveying process of the Japanese system.
6 Park N-J (2006: 242–3) explains the strong anti-Japanese sentiment among many Koreans today, in comparison to other postcolonial countries, from the fact the Korea was colonised relatively late in world time by a country that itself had entered imperialist interstate rivalry at a late stage, compared to the European powers. Consequently, by the time Korea was colonised, nationalism was already developed and embedded in Korean society. In this context, Japan was seen as more a *national competitor* than a mere foreign (dynastic) power.
7 One *Chŏngbo* equals 9,917.4 m^2 - 9,917.4 m^2.
8 It was stipulated that the 'main national resources shall be nationalised (Clause 85), public corporations of transportation, communication and finance shall be managed by the state or public authorities (Clause 87), and foreign trade shall be under control of the state (Clause 87)' (Jeong T-H 2000: 200).
9 The Korean government took over properties and assets held by the former Japanese colonialists because Japan was defeated in the Second World War. By contrast, when India and the Philippines gained national independence, assets held by the former colonialists, Britain and the US, respectively, were neither

repossessed nor nationalised. Furthermore, the ways in which Japanese-held properties were disposed of differed amongst the former Japanese colonies. For instance, in the case of Taiwan, the properties repossessed from Japanese colonialists were managed and controlled as national or public assets (Kong J-O 2000: 61).

10 The consolidation of *the chaebol* with the help of US aid will be discussed in Chapter 8.

11 As discussed above, Eckert (2014: 254) emphasises the continuities between the landlord class and the industrial capitalists. However, the Korean landlords who managed to transform themselves into capitalists were small in number and were able to do so only by becoming the managers of the Japanese-held properties or receiving some form of US aid *after* national independence. The *Kochang* Kims were no exception in this regard (see Chapter 8).

12 The massacre of the *Podoyŏnmaeng* members by the Rhee government after the outbreak of the Korean War is one of the incidents that contributed to solidifying the fear of communism. The *Podoyŏnmaeng* was formed by the Rhee government in 1949, consisting of 30,000 communist affiliates, for the purpose of converting these affiliates into supporters of the South Korean regime. In order to prevent them from cooperating with the communist North during the Korean War, the Rhee government carried out a massacre of the members, killing more than 3,000 in Ch'ungbuk province alone (Jeong J-S 2000: 41–2; Kang J-M 2004a: 86–9). According to Seo J-S (2011: 28–30), the scale of the massacres committed by the Rhee government was larger than those committed by the Japanese colonialists.

8 The global and social origins of the Korean developmental state

While the modern-state dominating society emerged through the land reform and the Korean War, this did not immediately give rise to what is referred to as the developmental state, the state that was autonomous domestically and externally, and thereby able to deliver successful *national* development. The Rhee Syngman government that was established in 1948 as the first government of the Republic of Korea shared some of what are often seen as the key characteristics of the developmental state: it was autocratic, it oppressed political opponents under the pretext of national security and it pursued state-led economic development in the name of achieving a 'nationally independent economy'. However, rapid industrialisation took place only under the subsequent Park Chung Hee government (1961–79), as a result of which it was given the epithet of 'developmental state'. In this chapter, I contextualise the transition from a mere autocratic government to the developmental state within the changes in the economic and geopolitical positioning of Korea in the world-system, the changes in the US aid policy towards Korea and a concomitant shift in the predominant mode of capital accumulation from commercial to industrial, on the one hand, and a new class power balance ushered in by social forces from below (i.e. the April Uprising of 1960), on the other. I demonstrate historically that the Korean state was given a chance to become 'developmental' when the world-systematic imperative to 'catch up' met favourable geopolitical conditions for rapid growth, i.e. the Cold War in the face of regime competition with the North and pressure from below to live up to the (nationalist) revolutionary sprit of the April Uprising. After assessing the global and social origins of the Korean developmental state, I analyse the statist concept of the developmental state from the perspective of a critique of the 'fetishism of national development' set out in Chapter 6.

Dialectics of world-system constraints and the April Uprising of 1960

Since Korea integrated into the capitalist world economy in the late nineteenth century, the conditions for capitalist development were laid during and after Japanese colonialism through processes such as the privatisation of land by cadastral surveys, industrialisation to meet Japanese imperialist expansion, land reform during the Korean War and privatisation of Japanese-held properties after independence, amounting to a form of 'primitive accumulation' (see Chapter 7). A highly militarised modern state emerged out of these processes.

The first government of the Republic of Korea, led by Rhee Syngman, formerly a US-based national independence activist who was ideologically committed to the 'free market', pursued or intended to pursue a mode of economic development that can be characterised as nationalist and highly interventionist. In spite of the apparent similarities between the orientations of the Rhee government and those of the subsequent Park government, rapid economic growth and industrialisation occurred only during the latter period. In tracing the global and social origins of the developmental state, in this section, I will first assess the Rhee government in terms of how it related to the US and Japan on the one hand, and to newly emerging Korean capital (the *chaebol*) on the other, and how it was eventually brought down, due to mounting internal and external pressure and contradictions, by social forces from below in 1960 (the April Uprising). The specific contradictions of the Rhee government and the manner in which it fell were to condition the rise and key characteristics of the subsequent Park government, the epitome of the 'developmental state'.

Post-Korean War security relations with the US and Japan

After the Korean War (1950–53), security and economic reconstruction were arguably the two most urgent issues for the Korean government to deal with. However, the US and Korean governments had different visions about these issues, which increasingly became the main source of conflict between them. While US military commitment to Korea became heightened after the Korean War and provided it with a large amount of aid on this basis,[1] 'American interests in South Korea lay in "peacefully" ensuring the status quo and in maintaining US prestige as a leader of the Western World in the Cold War' (Hong Y-P 2000: 38). To the extent that the US perceived Korea as no more than a strategic location to prevent the spread of communism in East Asia, at least in the early years of the Eisenhower administration (1953–61), economic development in Korea was not considered seriously (Kong J-O 2000: 72; Shin Y-O 2000: 266). For example, the guiding rules for the disbursement of the 'Counterpart Fund' (*Taechungjagŭm*) set by the US-Korea Combined Economic Board stated that it should prioritise supporting the military activities of United Nations forces in Korea.[2] Between 1954 and 1963, 48 per cent of the 'Counterpart Fund' was spent on defence (Jeong T-H 2000: 204; Kong J-O 2000: 72–3; Shin Y-O 2000: 267).

The country's heavy dependence on US aid and the fact that a large proportion of it was spent on defence were indicative of the contradictory nature of the Rhee government and the fundamental barriers to its pursuit of economic development. Although the need for post-Korean War economic reconstruction was paramount, the Rhee government prioritised security and military expansion not only to accommodate the US military interests in Korea but also to enhance its legitimacy in domestic politics. Immediately after the Korean War, the Rhee government enjoyed a relatively high level of mass popularity due to its opposition to the armistice with North Korea (Hong Y-P 2000: 2). It advocated military invasion of the North to 'unify the Korean nation' even before the Korean War, which was halted only by US disapproval (see Cha S-C 2005; Chang J-K 2002). Most Koreans opposed the armistice as they saw it as a step towards dividing the country permanently. In this context, Rhee's exhortation to 'March North and Unify Korea' was received positively amongst the Korean population. Furthermore, his hostile position towards the North provided him with a strong bargaining chip in attaining concessions from the US that tried to contain his attempt to 'march North', including the mutual defence treaty concluded in 1953 (Kim I-Y 2000: 238–48; Lee 2000: 87).[3] In an attempt to take full advantage of this situation, the Rhee government strove to position Korea as a key anti-communist frontier country in East Asia and tried to receive as much aid from the US as possible (Kim I-Y 2000: 245; Park T-G 2010: 111; see also Jeong I-Y 1989). The US military interest in Korea and the Rhee government's need to consolidate its domestic power base allowed both parties, at least tacitly, to share an interest in the expansion of military forces in Korea, at least until the early 1950s.

Even if the US and the Rhee government found common ground in the area of security in the name of safeguarding the 'free world' against communism, their divergence in the issues of economic development became increasingly apparent and unbridgeable. Although the latter declared that it was committed to the 'free market', as opposed to a 'controlled economy', due to the immature state of capital accumulation and the intellectual influence of the German historical school on the policy makers of that generation, an economic development plan that the Rhee government proposed to the Combined Economic Board in 1954 entailed strong elements of state interventionism (Chung J-A 2008: 97–101). The plan aimed to lay the conditions for a 'nationally independent economy', referring to a situation in which Korea could sustain itself by participating in international trade and maintain a stable balance of trade (Chung J-A 2008: 98). It envisioned the strategy of Import Substitution Industrialisation (ISI), particularly of capital goods and state-led, large-scale infrastructure and heavy industry development (Chung J-A 2008: 100; Shin Y-O 2000: 267). According to the new economic development plan drafted in the latter period of the 1950s under the partial approval of the US, the state *de facto* took the role of capital in the sectors that private businesses were unable to invest in (see Chung J-A 2009: 373–81).

The US opposed Rhee's initial proposal mainly because it was at odds with its own blueprint. The Eisenhower administration that came to office in 1953 with the pledge to cut the federal deficit introduced the New Look policy of nuclear deterrence in an attempt to reduce funding for expensive military divisions overseas (Shin W-H 2004: 39). The US desired Japan-centred regional post-War reconstruction, whereby Korea was meant to use US dollars to buy up industrial goods from Japan (Cumings 1984: 17–8; Kim I-Y 2000: 258; Shin Y-O 2000: 267–8). The US saw this as a cost-effective way of supporting the post-War economic reconstruction of Japan and Korea (and Taiwan) at the same time and therefore opposed the development of heavy industry in Korea (Chung J-A 2008: 102–3; Kim I-Y 2000: 258). US government officials also shared the view that massive aid provided to Korea thus far had not brought about positive development outcomes (Park T-G 2010: 112). The 'Kennedy administration [during the first few months] called Korea "the sick man of Asia" ... lacking "the sense of national self-responsibility without which growth and development is impossible"' (Brazinsky 2005: 87).

Above all, the US design of Japan-centred post-War economic reconstruction required diplomatic normalisation between Korea and Japan, which the Rhee government fiercely opposed. The reasons for this can be seen at several levels. First, given the depth of anti-Japanese sentiment shared by most Koreans, the Rhee government could not pursue normalisation, at least not openly. Ironically, the fact that the ruling Liberal Party consisted of a large number of former collaborators forced the government to resort to anti-Japanese nationalism to cover this up and enhance the government's political legitimacy (Jeong K-M 1991: 213; Seo J-S 1995a: 41–2). Second, as the Rhee government's bargaining position *vis-à-vis* the US was weakened after the armistice with North Korea was signed, it needed to utilise an anti-Japanese stance to gain concessions from the US (Kim I-Y 2000: 237; Shin W-H 2004: 50). In fact, the Rhee government agreed to normalise diplomatic relations with Japan towards the 1950s in return for US approval, albeit partially, of its economic development plan (see below). Third, the Rhee government saw Japan-centred economic reconstruction as the revival of Japanese colonialism, which would deepen the Korean economy's dependency on Japan (Chung J-A 2009: 358). Rhee warned the US repeatedly that Japan-centred post-War construction in the region would enrage the populations of the former Japanese colonies at large, which, in turn, would undermine the US's position as the leader of the 'free world' in opposition to the Soviet Union (Park T-G 2010: 113–4; Shin W-H 2004: 45–9; see also Brazinsky 2005: 85).

The Rhee government initially tried to put into practice its economic development plan against US opposition. However, it met serious barriers, mainly due to limited investment resources. In the fiscal year of 1957, taxation amounted only to 27 per cent of the total fiscal revenue, while aid and deficit financing contributed to 53 per cent and 13 per cent, respectively

(Shin Y-O 2000: 298). The Rhee government was only able to fund infrastructure development either through US aid (the Counterpart Fund) or deficit financing, i.e. issuing bonds. The Counterpart Fund was the main source for governmental investment and lending, amounting to 69 per cent of the total between 1953 and 1960 (Shin Y-O 2000: 272). To make the situation worse, the disagreement between the Rhee government and the US only delayed the arrival of US aid and the implementation of US military and economic assistance (Chung J-A 2008: 102; Hong Y-P 2000: 149). This proved that insofar as post-War reconstruction was highly dependent on US aid, without securing an alternative source of capital investment, a development plan disapproved and unsupported by the US proved to be unsustainable. Consequently, the mode and degree of economic development pursued by the Rhee government was in the end confined within the limits set by the US.

Aid-dependent capital accumulation and the formation of the chaebol

Restrained by the heavy dependence on US aid, large-scale infrastructure development (e.g. roads, ports, transport, energy) and investment in the heavy and chemical industry, as initially envisioned in the Rhee government's economic development plan, turned out to be only marginal in the 1950s. A great proportion of aid-financed import consisted of consumption rather than capital goods: capital goods accounted for a very small share of total imports, 3.4 per cent in 1953 and 11.7 per cent in 1960 (Amsden 1989: 45). The ISI strategy was restricted mainly to processing a narrow range of consumption goods. In accordance with the US prioritisation of stabilisation over development, e.g. tight money, devaluation and a balanced budget (Amsden 1989: 44), the kinds of aid goods the US preferred to provide Korea with were those that did not require (large) new investments and those for which there was a high level of domestic demand. The items that met these criteria were cotton, wheat and sugar, dubbed the 'three white items'. During 1954 –60, manufacturing amounted to from 13.5 to 19.4 per cent of GNP, of which the production of capital goods accounted for from 19.7 to 21.7 per cent. The average annual growth rate of consumption goods exceeded 20 per cent, while that of capital goods was 8.6 per cent (Shin Y-O 2000: 279). While industrial development in the 1950s was not unimpressive, it diverged from the Rhee government's initial proposal and expectations.

Although industrial development in Korea in the 1950s was limited in degree and scope, it consolidated Korean capital in the form of the *chaebol*, i.e. a monopoly conglomerate structure. While the capitalist class was given birth to by the state that privatised Japanese-held properties to a selected number of individuals (see Chapter 7), it became consolidated in the *chaebol* form under the Rhee government in the process of US aid being allocated and disposed of. The Rhee government's favouritism of large-scale companies over small- and medium-sized ones reflected, in part, Rhee's long-held belief that the concentration of national capital or merging of small companies into large ones would be advantageous in competing with Japanese capital (Chung J-A 2008: 104). It is also attributable to the sense of urgency of development shared amongst policy and academic elites. As evidenced in the series of meetings and dialogues held between policy makers and academics in drafting a new development plan in the late 1950s, they consented, though after intense debates, that productivity enhancement nurturing large-scale capital was the most viable and effective path to post-War reconstruction (see Chang J-A 2009: 365–81).

There were two important ways in which the Rhee government helped the newly emerging capitalists to grow into *chaebol*. First, in selecting the beneficiaries and recipients of foreign aid, the Rhee government prioritised those who already possessed production or processing facilities. In particular, key materials, such as cotton, wheat and sugar, were sold exclusively to the owners of production facilities rather than through open bidding competition (Shin Y-O 2000: 276). For instance, the government sold the 'three white items' to the respective cartel-like associations at a bargain price. Each cartel then sold them to their own member companies according to the size of the respective members' processing and production facilities. In this process, small- and medium-sized firms were marginalised (Chung J-A 2008: 104). Having access to or being granted the right to purchase aid goods itself amounted to an exclusive privilege, as simply placing them in the market guaranteed a huge profit, given the serious shortage of goods after the Korean War. The buyers of aid goods also reaped a large profit from the difference between the official and the real exchange rates: the aid goods were sold at the former rate, which was half of the latter (Chung J-A 2008: 104; Kong J-O 2000: 76; Shin Y-O 2000: 295–6).[4]

Second, if the allocation of aid goods to a small number of cartels directly supported the already well-organised large-scale companies, the Rhee government also indirectly helped them by providing them with loans and cheap credit. A portion of the Counterpart Fund was channelled mainly through the Korea Industrial Bank to capitalists as a form of government lending. The Rhee government adopted a lending policy whereby lending was offered to a few selected industries at the lowest interest rate (Kong J-O 2000: 79). As the official interest rate of the banks did not reach even the level of inflation, being able to borrow money from them alone allowed lenders to reap a high level of profits. It is estimated that the annual average interest rate of private lending in the mid-1950s was 48 per cent, while the highest interest rate of commercial banks was 18.25 per cent (Kong J-O 2000: 78; Shin Y-O 2000: 277). The interest rate of the Korean Industrial Bank was even lower than that of commercial banks. Additionally, an even lower interest rate was applied to lending associated with purchasing aid goods, and the larger the scale of lending and the longer the lending periods were, the more favourable terms were applied.

Now if these measures implemented by the Rhee government to support and nurture large-scale capitalists are seen in connection with the privatisation of the Japanese-held properties immediately after national independence, the origins of the *chaebol* become more clearly discernible. The Korean capitalist class first emerged by purchasing state-vested properties seized from the Japanese at a bargain price as the former managers of the properties and/or through personal connections with the US occupation army (see Chapter 7). They then grew larger by being granted the exclusive right to acquire foreign aid, purchasing aid goods, often with money borrowed from the banks at much lower than market interest rates. Large-scale businesses benefited most: the possession of production facilities itself placed them in a privileged position to access foreign aid, and for this very reason they were allowed to borrow bank loans under the most favourable terms.

The modality of state-capital relations in the 1950s

The specific ways in which the Korean capitalist class emerged and consolidated in a monopoly structure underline the particular modality of state-capital relations in the 1950s. As much as the capitalist class was given birth to by the state, its survival and expansion remained dependent on the latter: acquisition of raw materials and bank credit were channelled and allocated by the state. However, even if capitalists surfaced as the new dominant class in the absence of serious challengers, neither from the landlord class nor from labourers and peasants, their reproduction was not secure. Given the embryonic state of the capitalist class, as well as the immature level of capitalist social and production relations, the reproduction of capital and its extended accumulation were mediated by direct state intervention.

Another key characteristic of capital accumulation in the 1950s was that it was led by the textile and food industries, primarily thanks to exclusive access to foreign aid and the monopolisation of distribution (Lee J-H 1991: 163). A handful of large-scale cotton and food industries formed cartels and prevented market entry of new businesses. These corporate behaviours, which some might consider illegal, were encouraged by the Rhee government. As much as the state guaranteed commercial profits, capitalists actively sought to form personal connections and cooperated with state elites. One illustration would be that it was an unwritten rule that the capitalists who were granted the right to buy aid goods or bank loans from the Korean Industrial Bank gave back 10–15 per cent of the rebate to the ruling party officials (Chung J-A 2008: 104).

To the extent that capital accumulation in the 1950s resulted mainly from monopolised access to foreign aid and bank loans, which were preferentially given to a select few capitalists by state officials, state-capital relations in this period were direct and immediate. The state and capital were linked through personal connections and favouritism; state and capital appeared to be linked *personally*. The state appeared to serve, or indeed did serve, the interests of a few capitalist *individuals* at the expense of others and the general population at large. The capitalist state in this context served the interests of a certain fraction of capitalists rather than the dynamic process and social relation of capital as a whole, in a form wherein the state detaches itself from immediate class interests to better exercise plan rationality for capitalist development, appearing to stand over and against any particular social classes or groups.

In this respect, while the *content* of the state under the Rhee government was capitalist, its *form* was not capitalist in the full sense of the (ideal-typical) concept of the capitalist state. In other words, the state in this period was capitalist in its *content*, serving the interests of the capitalist class rather than those of other classes, but the *form* it assumed still bore traces of the pre-capitalist state in the sense that it appeared to serve the dominant class, or even favoured individuals from that class, *directly* rather than as a mediating political form detached from direct surplus extraction and class exploitation. The essence of the capitalist state is embodied not merely in the fact that it serves the interests of the ruling class (capitalists in capitalism) but in its distance from the economic sphere, giving rise to the fetishised notion that the state is a class-neutral, impartial, benign third party that stands outside and beyond the capitalist relations between formally equal citizens who are exchangers of equivalent quantities of value (see Chapter 6). As a postcolonial country in the context of 'catch-up' development whereby the foundations of capital accumulation were laid *politically* by the state, notwithstanding that the state lacked autonomy from the US, it dominated the domestic capitalists. Consequently, the state's intervention in the economy was direct, and the state officials' personal ties with the capitalists *as individuals* were of supreme importance: the separation between the state and the economy, and the differentiation between state elites and capitalists were not yet actualised. This particular modality of state-capital relations in the 1950s conditioned the specific manner in which economic and political crises manifested themselves towards the end of the 1950s.

Economic and political crises, and the fall of the Rhee government

If capital accumulation in the 1950s was maintained by a fine balance between the US's geopolitical interest in Korea and the Rhee government's manoeuvre to position Korea as a frontier of anti-communism, from the mid-1950s onwards, this arrangement started to break down. One of the new developments in geopolitics in the mid-1950s was the relative easing of the tension between the US and the Soviet Union, which moved toward peaceful coexistence (détente) (Hong Y-P 2000: 39; Shin W-H 2004: 38; Yang W-J 2005: 128). While it is debatable how real this change was, at least there were no military conflicts in East Asia until the Vietnam War.

Moreover, in the face of the competition between the Soviet Union and China to augment their influence over the Third World by sponsoring socialist revolutions and development, the Eisenhower administration came to recognise the importance of Third World development not only for the successful post-War reconstruction of the First World but to be able to defend 'the West' ideologically against the Soviet camp. In 1953, China and the Soviet Union agreed to provide North Korea with 320 million US dollars and 250 million US dollars, respectively, in the following two to four years (Lee 2000: 90). The Soviet Union, China and North Korea also showed remarkably rapid industrialisation, which positioned them as models for other developing countries (Kim I-Y 2000: 260). In particular, North Korea recorded an impressive average growth rate of 20 per cent in the 1950s (Park T-G 2010: 109). In this context, long-term economic development, as opposed to the short-term provision of aid, surfaced as an alternative policy, an approach which the Kennedy administration later labelled as 'aid to end aid' or 'helping people to help themselves' (Brazinsky 2005: 85). This new approach was also seen to help the US to reduce military expenditure (Lee J-H 1991: 159; Seo J-S 1995b: 161; Shin W-H 2004: 39; Shin Y-O 2000: 294–7). Against this backdrop, the US approved some degree of industrialisation in Korea in return for the Rhee government's consent to normalise diplomatic relations with Japan (Shin W-H 2004: 55; see above). Referring to this process, some noted that the dominant mode of competition between capitalism and socialism shifted from the sphere of the military to that of the economic (Shin W-H 2004: 39–40).

These new developments in international politics and the US government's imperatives to reduce the federal deficit translated into a new governing strategy in Korea. A new aid plan proposed by the Combined Economic Board in 1958 encouraged investment in exportation, the construction of key industries that could aid manufacturing and productivity enhancement in Korea. In achieving these ends, diversification of financial sources was recommended, whereby investment funds were procured not only from US aid but also from foreign governments and private loans. Accordingly, the US started to reduce aid in 1957 and pressed the Korean government to switch from aid to loans to allow importation of Japanese capital and to stabilise the monetary and fiscal systems (Shin Y-O 2000: 293–9; Sonn H-C 1991b: 163). However, this only reaffirmed that the Rhee government's anti-Japanese stance and economic development plan through deficit financing were irreconcilable with the US's intentions. Furthermore, as the Kim Il-Sung regime of North Korea gradually began to increase its peace offensive, capitalising on the easing international tension, the Rhee government's rationale for 'March North and Unify Korea' became increasingly untenable (Hong Y-P 2000: 151).

Coinciding with the reduction in US aid in the late 1950s,[5] the Korean economy plunged into a serious slump (Yang W-J 2005: 124–5). For instance, in 1958, of 2,757 factories randomly surveyed, only 35.4 per cent were in full operation (Sonn H-C 1991: 162). The growth rate of the textile industry, the backbone of the economic growth of the 1950s apart from food processing, marked minus 7.5 per cent, and the overall growth rate fell to 0.8 per cent in 1961 (Korea Industry Bank 1962: 17, as cited in Lee J-H 1991: 159). While some noted correctly that the economic slump was worsened by the fact that 'the [Rhee] regime did not introduce any substantial change in the way it managed the economy, except for efforts to stall any reduction in foreign aid' (Yang W-J 2005: 125), it was more a reflection of the specific nature of capitalist accumulation in the late 1950s.

As capitalists' profits were more or less guaranteed by the state as long as they maintained close personal ties with state elites, capitalists concentrated on securing more foreign aid. Capital in this period was monopolistic and at the same time commercial rather than industrial (Lee J-H 1991: 163). As foreign aid was given in proportion to the size and the scale of the production facilities of firms, in order to acquire more aid, inter-firm competition took place around the increase in production facilities (Shin Y-O 2000: 282–3; Sonn H-C 1991: 162). The underdevelopment of the internal market relative to the scale of production facilities was worsened through the extension of the latter, exacerbating overproduction (Sonn H-C 1991: 162). A large segment of the population was in poverty, and the rural population in particular suffered harsh living conditions (see Chapter 7). It was estimated that in 1960 the number of the unemployed in the rural population reached two million, and the total number of the unemployed amounted to 4.5 million, that is, 45 per cent of the total economically active population (Shin Y-O 2000: 285).

The economic crisis finally transformed into and merged with a full-blown political crisis. The Rhee government's increasingly autocratic rule fuelled discontent among the population as well as state elites, including the military. For instance, anticipating that president Rhee stood little chance of being re-elected for a second-term by the National Assembly under the existing constitution in 1952, he proposed an amendment bill to introduce direct presidential elections: as he enjoyed, though briefly, a relatively high level of mass popularity during the Korean War (see above), he thought that he would have a higher chance of being re-elected by direct elections. When his proposal was rejected by an overwhelming majority of 143 to 19 in the National Assembly, he mobilised youth corps and the local parliaments to stage demonstrations against it, declared martial law and had 183 members of the National Assembly detained by military police. While the proposal was passed eventually, as a result of which Rhee was re-elected president by direct elections, this incident had the effect of destroying his popularity, even amongst (conservative) political elites (Ra J-Y 1992: 301–3).[6]

Subsequently, Rhee amended the constitution in 1954 to allow himself to stay in power for life. While he was elected president in 1956, the election results confirmed growing popular discontent with his regime. In 1956 he won only 56 per cent of the popular vote, compared to 73 per cent in the 1952 election. The vice-president (Chang Myeon) was elected from the opposition *Minju* (Democratic) Party, and the ruling Liberal party lost five seats in the 1958 National Assembly election (Kim Q-Y 1996: 1186). Threatened by the rising popularity of the liberal opposition party as well as the *Chinbo* (Progressive) Party, in 1958, the government 'forcefully enacted the new National Security Law which was said to be a "hunting licence" to punish any opposition to the regime on the pretext of "treason"' (Hong Y-P 2000: 147). Anxious to win the presidential elections scheduled in 1960, the government pressured the Supreme Court to sentence to death the main political contender from the *Chinbo* Party, Cho Pong-Am, for espionage; as a result, he was executed before the elections. This series of measures to suppress the opposition further de-legitimised the Rhee regime. Finally, angered by the flagrant election-rigging around the victory of the pro-Rhee candidate in the election held in March 19, 1960, student-led anti-government protests broke out in April 1960, soon to be joined and supported by intellectuals and other social groups, which became known as the April Uprising. In the face of escalating pressure from below, President Rhee stepped down and sought exile in Hawaii, whereupon the First Republic came to an end.

A challenge to the personalised state-capital relations

To the extent that immediate and personal connections between state elites and capitalists prevailed under the Rhee government, once the legitimacy of this government was challenged, the practices of Korean capitalists, particularly the accumulation of wealth by the *chaebol,* came to be seen as unlawful. The social forces of the April Uprising of 1960 demanded that capitalists be prosecuted and their properties be confiscated. However, even if the April Uprising brought to the fore the problem of corruption caused by personal ties between state elites and capitalists, it fell short of directly addressing the problems of capitalism and class contradictions as such. The forces of the April Uprising questioned the manner in which capitalists were connected to state elites, and the illegitimate and unlawful ways of accumulating wealth, but did not challenge capitalists as the class of labour exploitation and surplus extraction.

Some note that the April Uprising 'was revolutionary in that it changed in a sudden and violent way the rules, procedures, norms and principles of the regime, but ... fell short of revolution' as the protests did not go on to form a new government (Kim Q-Y 1996: 1190). Others find the causes of the failure of the April Uprising to go beyond the ousting of the Rhee government to the immature level of capitalist development itself, resulting in the low level of class consciousness among workers and the virtual absence of organised left-wing social forces (Cho H-Y 2002: 311; Shin Y-O 2000: 303). The social forces of the April Uprising primarily aimed to sever the personal relations between state elites and capitalists. This suggests that the particular modality of the state-capital relations of the 1950s, characterised by close personal ties between state and capital, conditioned the ways in which social discontent was expressed.

The April Uprising of 1960 was nevertheless significant in fashioning the subsequent economic and political development. Its 'incomplete revolution' gave way to a military coup led by Park Chung-Hee and constrained how the Park government related to capitalists and society at large to attain political legitimacy. This became one of the factors that conditioned the rise of the so-called developmental state.

From the autocratic to the developmental state

The ending of the Rhee regime did not give rise to the 'developmental state' automatically and immediately, though. The following section traces, first, how the development trajectory under Park and the characteristics of the developmental state were moulded through the interplay between the imperative to 'catch up' – generated by the capitalist world-system, geopolitics and demands from social forces from below; second, how Park's *aspirations* for rapid industrial development became a reality only under the historically specific geopolitical conditions of the Cold War; and third, how and why the developmental state, its global and social origins notwithstanding, *appears* to be autonomous internally and externally, and thus attains the appearance of being the main agent of *national* development.

Internal and external constraints on **chaebol** *reform*

Following the end of the First Republic, Chang Myeon, the former vice president, formed the Second Republic as democratically elected Prime Minister under the new system of a parliamentary democracy, which had been newly adopted in response to the Rhee government's abuse of presidential power.

The Chang government pursued economic and political reform amid social and economic turmoil. Complementary to Rhee's economic development plan (see above), the Chang government planned to implement a five-year economic development plan, which entailed a strong element of state-led initiatives and was intended to correct the imbalance between different sectors of industries by widening the remit of the ISI to the heavy industries (Seo J-S 1995b: 159; Shin Y-O 2000: 305–6). It also initiated *chaebol* reform. While the Chang government did not pursue a radical overhaul of the *chaebol* structure, it regularised the exchange rate and banned the *chaebol's* monopolisation of access to foreign aid and monopolisation of market distribution channels. In addition, it sought to normalise diplomatic relations with Japan (Kong J-O 2000: 92; Shin Y-O 2000: 306).

Before any of these reform initiatives could be put to the test, the Chang government was overthrown by a military coup led by Major General Park Chung-Hee and his young army colonels on May 16, 1961. Yet the Chang government's reform initiatives showed that any government that came to power after the April Uprising had to deal with the economic crisis associated with and in part caused by the new US aid policy, on the one hand, and the April Uprising's demands for *chaebol* reform, on the other. The Park government faced these challenges even more acutely as it had come to power through a military coup: it understood it was imperative to showcase rapid and visible economic development as a way to justify its regime (Branzinsky 2005: 84).

However, the Park government found that the task of delivering rapid economic growth and meeting the demands of the April Uprising, particularly *chaebol* reform, was not easily reconcilable. First, the US objected to the 'excessive' punishment of the *chaebol* founders and expressed its concerns that the anti-*chaebol* impulse could develop into the repossession of their properties, i.e. the violation of private property, a trajectory recently seen in the aftermath of the Cuban revolution of 1959 (Kong J-O 2000: 91–2). The US stressed that the April Uprising was an 'anti-dictatorship' movement rather than a 'socialist revolution' (Kang J-M 2004b: 62–3). Especially because the US was reluctant to acknowledge the military junta as a legitimate political force that could govern Korea, Park could not afford to go against the US.

In fact, Park had a politically ambivalent past. While he was trained in the Changchun Military Academy of the Manchukuo Imperial Army and subsequently held the rank of second lieutenant during the Japanese colonial period, he had also allegedly been affiliated after national independence with a communist group, of which his brother was a key figure (see Podoler 2016: 288). The US took 'a strategy of wait-and-see rather than veto the coup if he accommodated the superpower's vital interests, including an unambiguous anticommunism' (Han Y-S 2011: 36). In an effort to prove to the US its commitment to anti-communism, within less than two months of the military coup, on July 4, 1961, on US Independence Day, the military junta declared an anti-communism law and arrested communist associates (Jeong K-M 1991: 219; Kang J-M 2004b: 322–3; Sonn H-C 1991: 167–8). Finally, the Kennedy administration (January 1961-November 1963) officially approved Park on July 29, 1961 (Jeong K-M 1991: 220). Subsequently, under US pressure he formed the Democratic Republican Party and ran for the presidential elections in 1963, during which he was elected.[7]

Second, Park found the pursuit of radical *chaebol* reform counterproductive to his own political interests. Immediately after the coup, he made some hawkish gestures against capitalists who were politically connected to the previous government, charging and imprisoning them for the unlawful accumulation of wealth and capital. However, with the perceived urgency of economic development he came to soften his initial anti-*chaebol* stance, increasingly seeing the *chaebol* as a group to be utilised in achieving his political and economic goals. The Park government set 'saving Korea from poverty and misery' as one of the top policy priorities and sought to overcome its lack of democratic legitimacy by showcasing rapid economic development. In fact, one of the main causes of the US's reservations about Park's economic development plans was that the latter pursued unrealistic, ostentatious and expensive show-case projects (Brazinsky 2005: 109). Furthermore, Park saw the utility of the *chaebol* in the context of the urgency to drive rapid economic development in competition with the North. North Korea had shown highly successful and rapid post-War industrialisation. As of 1965, when the Park government launched its first Five-Year economic development plan, Gross National Product (GNP) per capita in the South was only 60 per cent of that in the North. Steel and electricity production capacity in the South was 20 and 30 per cent of that in the North, respectively (Kim H-K 1999: 23–4; see also Hahn B-H 1980: 1087–8; Park T-G 2010: 109).

Against this backdrop, Park's early plan to confiscate the shares from the *chaebol* softened; in the end it was legislated that the *chaebol* would build the factory and production plants necessary for national reconstruction and hand over their shares to the government (Kong J-O 2000: 94). Those who had imprisoned earlier were released on this condition and charged only a penalty fine, merely 5 per cent of what they had initially been obliged to reimburse (Sonn H-C 1991: 169; see also Chibber 1999: 325). In this process, the *chaebol* were invited by the government to be the main participants in the construction of Ulsan industrial city, whereby their position became consolidated (Kong J-O 2000: 94–5). This is a remarkable turnaround: the *chaebol* had been challenged by the social forces from below to the point of dismantlement but were revived by the military government, which desperately needed to showcase rapid development for its political legitimacy, especially due to the systemic competition with North Korea, and had to seek the approval of the US, which opposed radical *chaebol* reform.

From ISI to ELI and the dual characteristics of state autonomy

In pursuing 'rapid' and 'visible' development, the Park government was pressed by the US to modify its initial economic development plan in the same manner that it was forced to withdraw its original plan to reform the *chaebol*. Reminiscent of the motto of the North Korean regime, the Park government initially intended to implement a nationalistic development plan centred on import-substituting industrialisation (ISI) strategy with the declared aim to build a nationally 'self-reliant' economy (Brazinsky 2005: 90; Sonn H-C 1991: 167, 2006: 141–4). Similar to the governments of Rhee and Chang (see above), Park's initial development plan prioritised investment in heavy industry in an attempt to widen the range of import-substituting products. The plan also envisioned that export would be restricted to primary commodities, and investment resources would be procured not through loans but from domestic savings, the mobilisation of idle capital and capital repossessed from the *chaebol*. In addition, the plan entailed strong elements of state interventionism or 'guided capitalism', whereby the government directly participates in managing the economy and provides guidance to basic industries, particularly through the nationalisation of financial institutions (Kim H-A and Sorensen 2011: 5–6; Lee B-C 2011: 375–6; Sonn H-C 1991: 167).

As in the case of the Rhee government, the US frustrated Park's ISI-oriented strategy. It denied economic aid asked for by the Park government, reduced the promised aid and questioned the relevance of heavy industrialisation in Korea (Payer 1975: 156–7). Park's original plan for heavy industry-based development was 'considered dangerous and unrealistic' by US officials (Brazinsky 2005: 92) and deemed to breach the principle of comparative advantage (Sonn H-C 2006: 144). Consequently, in the economic development plan that was subsequently implemented as a condition for receiving US aid the earlier initiative of heavy industry development was dropped. Instead the role of private capital rather than governmental investment was emphasised, and industrialisation for export, reliant on foreign loans, and the liberalisation of foreign capital investment were envisioned (Mason et al. 1980: 47; Sonn H-C 1991: 168). Accordingly, Korea's development strategy from the 1960s turned out to be export-led industrialisation (ELI), chiefly specialising in consumer and light industries. In this respect, the pursuit of ELI only became Park's strategy once ISI was not a viable option (see Haggard 1990). The incomplete *chaebol* reform and the change in the content of development strategy under US pressure highlight the fact that the policy autonomy of the Park government was first and foremost constrained by the position of Korea in the world market as a postcolonial late-developing country, on the one hand, and its role as a subordinate anti-communist ally of the US, on the other.

Although the content of Park's initial development plan proved to have been naïvely based on ignorance of the historical and international conditions of the Third World and was altered in the face of US objections (Sonn H-C 1991: 167), the Park government managed to nationalise financial institutions and thereby came to have a grip on the financial system. This was rendered possible largely by a new class power balance brought about by the April Uprising. Having seized state power after the Rhee government was toppled by social forces from below, the military junta was forced to accommodate the nationalistic aspirations it had unleashed. Park used nationalistic rhetoric to legitimise his coup and claimed to inherit and uphold the revolutionary spirit of the April Uprising. Under circumstances in which capitalists were threatened with prosecution for their unlawful accumulation of capital, and in which they were nurtured by direct state protection, they could not oppose the nationalisation of the financial institutions. The defensive position of the capitalists at the time is illustrated by an episode after the fall of the Rhee government when a group of capitalists were forced to march through the streets carrying sandwich signs that read, 'I was a parasite on the people' (Cumings 1984: 26). Against this backdrop, the military government was able to take control of commercial banks, and with the amendment of the Korean Bank Act in 1962, it transferred the right to draft and implement financial policy from the Korean Central Bank to the government.

Furthermore, with the establishment of the Bank for Small- and Medium-Sized Industries in 1961, the Park government instituted a financial system in which lending took the form of policy loans and was decided on the basis of the commands of the government according to development plans (Lee J-H 1991: 160). It also set up the Economic Planning Board (EPB), which took over the entire budgeting function from a previous ministry (Cumings 1984: 29) and became the main agent of negotiating and allocating foreign loans. The firm hold of the domestic financial system gave the government a material power with which it was able to direct and guide industrialisation in the 1960s and 1970s, one of the key characteristics of what is defined as 'the developmental state' (see Chapter 1). This highlights the fact that what allowed the Park government to possess the power to 'direct' and 'discipline' the capitalists was a particular class power balance ushered in by the social movements from below: the government's apparent autonomy over the capitalists was a reflection of, rather than immunity from, class relations.

In this manner, the development strategy shaped and implemented by the Park regime, or what are seen as the key characteristics of the developmental state, can be contextualised in relation to the position of Korea in the world market and inter-state system, on the one hand, and class power relations that emerged out of the particular state-capital and state-society relations under the Rhee government, on the other. Though it came into power amid the 'revolutionary' situation opened up by the April Uprising, in which a significant reform of the *chaebol* could have been carried out, the policy autonomy of the Park government was restrained from implementing its original development plans and *chaebol* reform. Consequently, the initial development plan based on ISI strategy had to be replaced by ELI, while the monopoly structure of the *chaebol* not only remained untouched but was strengthened. On the other hand, within these world-systematic limitations, the April Uprising that had brought down the Rhee government by releasing anti-US and anti-*chaebol* sentiments allowed the Park regime to nationalise financial institutions and thereby possess the material power with which to direct and control financial resources.

Towards the capitalist form of the state

The shift in development strategy from ISI to ELI and the state's control of the financial system induced changes in the ways in which the government intervened in the economy and the primary mode of capitalist accumulation. As economic development was financed by foreign borrowing rather than foreign aid and geared towards the production of light and consumer goods in order to pay off loans and purchase capital goods, exportation became more and more important. Accordingly, the Park government carried out fiscal and financial reforms in a way that stimulated export (Lee J-H 1991: 160). Amongst others, the Park government directed the *chaebol* to engage in industrial production by eliminating opportunities accruing from purely commercial activities that had prevailed during the Rhee period. It normalised the exchange rate in 1964 and adapted a uniform exchange rate regime in 1965. As is well documented by the theorists of the developmental state and institutionalists, the Park government decided which industries and firms to promote; directed the capitalists accordingly; and rewarded them, depending on their performance: firms exporting manufacturing goods were exempted from paying taxes on their imports of raw materials and offered low interest rates on bank loans (see Chapters 1 and 2; Brazinsky 2002: 100; Chang H-J 1993; Woo J-E 1991). Subsequently, the Park government promoted and initiated the structural transformation of capital, such as industrial restructuring and upgrading in times of economic crises and overproduction, a notable example being a switch from light to heavy industrialisation in the early 1970s (Woo J-E 1991: ch. 5; see Chapter 9).

The development trajectory of the Park regime, whose shape resulted from changes in US aid policy and a concomitant shift in the predominant mode of capital accumulation from commercial to industrial, meant a transformation in state-capital and state-society relations at large. At this juncture, the differences between the Rhee and Park governments became more clearly discernible. The two governments, on the surface, shared many common features: they were autocratic, oppressed political opponents under the pretext of national security and pursued state-led economic development in the name of achieving a 'nationally independent economy'. However, they differed in the ways in which they intervened in the economy and related to society. Some note that while the Rhee government exercised, as a means of social control, an unmediated and crude mode of physical force, the Park government possessed a more systematic and penetrative capacity (see Sonn H-C 1993: 40). For instance, the Korean Central Intelligence Agency (KCIA), an 'arm of the executive [under the Park government] ... penetrated nearly every arena of Korean life, with agents in factories, central and local government offices, and university classrooms' (Cumings 1984: 29).

This penetrative capacity of the state can be analysed in relation to the heightened capacity and necessity to impose discipline over the entire society for capital accumulation. If the oppression of the Rhee government was geared towards implanting and establishing capitalist social relations in the process of primitive accumulation by repressing social dissent and political opponents, the coercion of the Park government was more geared toward the extraction of absolute surplus value. Expressed bluntly, if the Rhee government's autocracy served the *political* purpose of laying the conditions for capitalist development, the Park regime's oppression had a more *economic* function. To the extent that industrial production took over commercial activities as the dominant mode of capital accumulation, the Park government intervened in accumulation processes to ensure the appropriation of absolute surplus value, i.e. low wages and long working hours, by imposing discipline at the societal level: it deployed an extremely oppressive labour regime, militarising the entire society for the goal of industrialisation, outlawing labour unionism and brutally crushing labour strikes and social dissent. If state-capital relations under the Rhee government assumed immediate personal relations by favouring a fraction of individual capitalists over others and guaranteeing the former commercial profits, the Park government managed to create the impression that economic development was not a matter of privileging a few capitalists but of enhancing the industrial capacity of 'the nation'.

In this respect, US pressure and the April Uprising ushered in *truly* capitalist state-capital relations. Although close personal relations between state elites and capitalists, particularly the *chaebol*, continued to exist, the state appeared to be autonomous from any immediate class interests by being able to transform its class content as a capitalist state into the relation between the state and (national) citizens. The developmental state's apparently high degree of state autonomy is indicative of the fact that it was *properly* capitalist in the sense that it could appear to serve the interest of capital *in general* as opposed to that of *fractions or individuals* of the capitalist class. Expressed differently, the high level of state autonomy points not to the fact that it is neutral and autonomous from class interests but to the fact that the detachment of the state itself from the immediate (fractions) of class interests is the very essence of the capitalist state.

The developmental state as a capitalist state in 'catch-up' development

While the Park regime signified a move towards attaining the general characteristics of the relations between the capitalist state and the dominant class of capitalists, its apparently high level of policy autonomy needs further explanation: the statist concept of the developmental state, characterised by its capacity to 'govern the market' and 'discipline' capitalists, cannot be explained fully by this general level of state-capital relations (see Chapter 6).

State interventionism under the Park government to initiate economic development was far-reaching and extensive. As is amply documented by the developmental state literature, the state and the state-owned banks not only channelled foreign loans to capitalists but also helped the latter to access foreign borrowing by guaranteeing loan repayment (see Chapter 1; Lee J-H 1991: 166). Moreover, due to the low quality of products and lack of marketing skills, in spite of the advantage of very low wages, the profitability of the *chaebol* or Korean exporters in general in the world market was not guaranteed. In order to compensate for their low level of competitiveness, the state allowed them to monopolise the internal market and introduced the dual pricing system in which the domestic prices of the *chaebol* products were higher than those on the world market (Amsden 1989: 144–5; Chibber 1999: 330; Shin Y-O 2000: 307): low profit margins of the *chaebol* in the world market were compensated for by higher domestic prices.

The Park regime's all-out endeavours to facilitate rapid industrialisation, in addition to its famous industrial planning and upgrading (Chang H-J 1993; Woo J-E 1991) and state-initiated rural modernisation campaign, *Saemaŏl Undong* (Douglass 1983; Wade 1983), can be further illustrated by the following examples. It posited achieving high economic growth rates through an increase in export as the *de facto* 'national religion'. It set targets for the volume of export and the rate of economic growth to be met. The government controlled what would be imported, placed high tariffs on the importation of (luxury) consumer goods and created a milieu in which public purchases of foreign consumer goods were condemned as anti-national. The list goes on. The Park government did not shy away from intervening in the realm of 'the private', going as far as setting an appropriate length of hair for men and of skirts for women: the police could enforce a hair-cut on the spot and arrested women wearing skirts shorter than the 'desirable' length. Before the diplomatic normalisation with Japan in 1965, in order to secure foreign bank loans, the Park government had foreign currency earnings by Koreans who had migrated to West Germany to work as nurses and minders forcibly saved in a German bank for three years and used them as a collateral for commercial loans (Kang J-M 2004c: 256–7). It also banned overseas travel on the pretext of minimising the outflow of foreign currency and promoted prostitution (sex tourism) for foreign visitors as a means to earn foreign currency (Kang J-M 2002b: 56–69).

To be sure, as noted above, the highly penetrative state interventionism seen in the Park government can in part be explained by its willingness to undertake whatever was necessary to promote *visible* and *rapid* development as a way to enhance its political legitimacy, especially under the pretext of national security against the (perceived) threat from North Korea. However, it is better understood as a response to the structure-like constraints of the capitalist world-system, which operated as an obstacle to development in the world-economic periphery. The early stage of industrialisation in the world-economic periphery took place at a low level of technology and productivity, which necessitated large-scale foreign borrowing, typically requiring state guarantees of repayment. Similarly, capitalist development in 1960s Korea reliant on low-level technology meant specialisation in producing low-end manufacturing goods, which presupposed low wage levels and long working hours, to which an oppressive mode of labour discipline is intrinsic. This suggests that the positioning of Korea and its timing of development in the hierarchical capitalist world-system to a large extent conditions, if not determines, the characteristics of the state and the intensity of labour exploitation. As seen in the Rhee and Chang governments in Korea, despite their ideological commitments to the 'free market' their economic plans incorporated a great extent of state interventionism in an attempt to overcome 'backwardness'. In short, insofar as successful 'catch-up' development presupposes and requires the imposition of harsh working conditions on and super-exploitation of labour, the modern state is likely to be assigned the role of initiating capitalist development from above as it possesses the right to mobilise physical force and violence.

Seen in this way, the apparently high level of state autonomy and heavy state interventionism seen in the Park government point to the fact that the developmental state is not only a capitalist state but a particular kind of capitalist state that practiced capitalist plan rationality in a social formation where capitalist social and production relations were immature: the Korean state was forced to eliminate societal barriers to capital accumulation under conditions of a low level of development of capitalist social and production relations. The Park government, highly militarised and in control of the financial system, acted and 'actually appeared' as the embodiment of capitalist plan rationality and carried out this function in the form of pursuing *national* development. In this respect, the fact that the Park government attempted to mobilise the population for the goal of 'national development' and imposed strict social and work discipline is not merely accidental, nor can it be reduced to national distinctiveness or the lack of democratic culture. These characteristics are integral to and given by the oppressive and exploitative nature of capitalism and the hierarchical capitalist world-system itself. This suggests that while the imperative to 'catch up' is generated by the uneven and hierarchical capitalist world-system, the state that pursues 'catch-up' development in the Third World is highly likely, albeit not bound, to be authoritarian.

From developmental aspirations to realisation

While the late development context is likely to give rise to a type of state that aspires to and is obsessed with 'catching up', of which the developmental state is an ideal representation, the aspirations in and of themselves do not automatically promise their actual realisation. As seen above, the Park government implemented various, at times extraordinary, measures to achieve rapid economic development. However, economic growth only started to take off after the mid-1960s, when Japanese investment and loans were secured, and Korea started to receive the declining labour-intensive and pollutant industries from Japan.

Upon the conclusion of the normalisation treaty with Japan in 1965 amidst popular dissent, the Korean government was able to facilitate the influx of Japanese capital investments that were in search of a new venue, with fewer regulations on environmental and labour protection. As some noted, 'there existed a harmony of interest between the Korean government and Japanese industries that were finding it difficult to expand … within Japan' (Hahn B-H 1980: 1090). The Park government created 'free export zones' where 100 per cent foreign-owned factories could export their products free of tax and where Korean workers' right to strike was denied. The total Japanese direct capital investment in Korea over the 1965–75 period amounted to 1 billion US dollars, which accounted for 60 per cent of cumulative foreign investment in Korean industry. The number of Japanese ventures (978 factories) was larger than that of any other non-Korean investor. In addition, Japan provided more than 1.5 billion US dollars to Korea in the same period in the form of gratis aid, credits and loans (Hahn B-H 1980: 1090–1; see also Brazinsky 2005: 108).[8]

The Korean economic 'miracle' finally occurred in the context of an economic boom associated with the Vietnam War and the opening of the US market for Korean exports, which was *exceptionally* granted in return for Korea's participation in the Vietnam War (Cumings 1984: 33–4; Jeong S-J 2000: 113–24). Amidst international and domestic criticism, the Park government sent troops to Vietnam as an anti-communist US ally for a fraction of what American soldiers were paid for risking their lives (Kang J-M 2004d: 50–7; Shin Y-O 2002: 66–7). Apart from the fact that Korea was the only US ally in Asia that volunteered to send troops to Vietnam, the fact that Park's offer to send troops was accepted by the US amounted to a 'privilege' – Rhee's earlier offers of sending troops to Indochina, Indonesia and Laos, made in the 1950s, had all been rejected by the US (Park T-G 2010: 116–7). In return for the Korean troops' participation in the Vietnam War, private companies of Korea (and Taiwan), many of whom became prevalent *chaebol* subsequently (e.g. Hyundai), were given unique opportunities to upgrade their technological knowhow and accumulate capital through various forms of assistance and procurement contracts which were denied to other countries, such as the Philippines (Glassman 2016; Glassman and Choi 2014). In short, 'the Vietnam War eventually became an economic bonanza for South Korea that greatly accelerated the country's economic development' (Brazinsky 2005: 109). In the first four years of its involvement in the War (1965–68), Korea earned 402 million US dollars through exports to Vietnam, sales to the US military and other arrangements.

The fact that the Korean industrial take-off was fuelled by extensive investment and advancement of loans by Japanese capital, followed by the Vietnam War, suggests that the aspiration to 'catch up' is a universal tendency generated by the uneven and hierarchical dynamic of global capitalism itself, whereas its successful *realisation* must be facilitated by historically specific international and domestic conditions.

First, the rapid industrialisation under the Park regime was made possible by the US-dominated geopolitical conditions of the Cold War. Korea's rapid industrialisation was owed much to the fact that it was favoured over other (developing) countries in terms of its preferential access to the US consumer market and was *chosen* over others as the re-location site of declining Japanese industries within the international geo-political context of the Cold War.

Second, the rapid economic growth led by the 'autonomous' Korean state was possible under a particular class power balance. As discussed in Chapter 7 and above, the modern Korean state emerged from the demobilisation and destruction of the left-wing and radical social forces from below. In addition, there was no class or social group strong enough to challenge the state. Militant and organised labour activism was still lacking, the landlord class had been destroyed and the capitalists failed to act as a powerful class force. Although the capitalists' position was strengthened at the economic level, they still lacked 'social legitimacy': demands for the reform and dismantlement of the *chaebol* would remain one of the recurrent demands made by the social forces of democratisation in subsequent decades (see Chapters 9 and Conclusion). To the extent that prominent Korean capitalists, and particularly the *chaebol*, originated and grew as collaborators of Japanese colonialists and subsequently of politically corrupt governments, they were politically suspect and mostly unable to challenge the state overtly.

While this particular class power balance was an outcome of a series of intensive class and social struggles, these particular characteristics of state-capital relations and of the *chaebol* themselves were conditioned, to a great extent, by the context of 'catch-up' development, where the capitalist social relations had to be created hastily from external power and from above: namely by 'forced accumulation'. Given that the creation of the capitalist class itself was mediated by the direct intervention of the state due to the imperative to impose capitalist social relations and that its continued viability as capital was heavily dependent on state sponsorship, the apparently dominant position of the state over capital was also given by Korea's position in the world market. This suggests that the origins and the characteristics of the developmental state can be fully grasped neither as a matter of institutional innovations nor as a product of class and social struggles at the national level.

A critique of the fetishism of national development

Having assessed the characteristics of the developmental state as products of the interaction between the world-systematic imperative to 'catch up', the historically specific geopolitical conditions and a particular class power balance, one of the core statist propositions that the developmental state was autonomous from social groups domestically and independent from the global economy, and thus *national* in orientation is a false or fetishised notion. As the case of Korea illustrates, insofar as the success of 'catch-up' capitalist development requires, as one of many other conditions, an enormous mobilisation of resources, both human and natural, typically coordinated by the authoritarian state from above, development in backward economies is expressed as *national* development, a process of enriching national productivity and industrial power. To put this simply, *national* development is the way in which capitalist class contradictions are expressed in a fetishised form, a tendency that becomes stronger when 'backwardness' is to be overcome from above, i.e. when the state plays the role of exerting capitalist plan rationality (see Chapter 6).

The class content of the developmental state can now be analysed as follows. First, the notion that the developmental state was nationally autonomous amounts to a fetish to the extent that it conceals the global and social origins within which it emerged: while the characteristics of the developmental state merely reflect the 'backwardness' within the hierarchical world-system, and the imperative to 'catch up' was given by the hieratical and uneven dynamic of the capitalist world economy, the 'catch-up' drive appears to emanate from the orientation of state elites or the nature of the state itself.

Second, it is a fetish because it obscures the fact that *national* development as promoted by the developmental state was a process deepening the 'dependent' characteristics of the Korean economy. In fact, the more the Park government strove to achieve a self-reliant national economy, the more it relied on foreign capital and export: the dependence on foreign loans and on US markets has been a notable feature of the Korean economy (Hart-Landsberg 2004; Jeong S-J 1993, 2004).[9] The heavy dependence on foreign borrowing and the US consumer market made Korea one of the most highly indebted countries and rendered its economy particularly vulnerable to changes in global demand and the cycles of the world market, which often led to overproduction problems (see Cumings 1984: 35–7; see below and Chapter 9). Whenever overproduction problems loomed, they were overcome by state-initiated industrial restructuring and upgrading, which resulted in further capital concentration and the incurrence of more foreign debt. Illustratively, Korea's new industrial plans, e.g. a strategic investment in heavy and chemical industry in the early 1970s, was also a reaction to the deteriorating profitability of light manufacturing sectors and was made possible by special loans offered by Japan (see Hahn B-H 1980: 1091; see Chapter 9). The dependency of Korean development on the US and Japan is also reflected in its trade patterns. Except for a brief period in the late 1980s, Korea ran trade and current account deficits for the entire four decades prior to the Asian financial crisis of 1997–98. Contrary to Park's claim to empower 'national' industrial power, the deficits largely reflected Korea's heavy reliance on imported technologies and intermediate goods, mainly from Japan (Hart-Landsberg and Burkett 2001: 413; see also Bello and Rosenfeld 1990: 114).

Third, the notion that the developmental state was autonomous from the global and thus served the national interest is a fetish in the sense that it conceals the state's capital serving functions. What *national* development actually meant was protecting the national bourgeoisie from competition from more advanced bourgeoisies and granting the former the freedom to exploit domestic labour, usually through absolute value extraction or an extremely oppressive mode of labour control.[10] The class content of the developmental state or its capital serving function can also be exemplified by the fact that it was sustained by incessant class struggle from above, i.e. the imposition of coercive measures on social dissent. Contrary to the portrayal of the Park government by the theorists of the developmental state as having a high degree of popular support and legitimacy (see Part I), during the Park regime period, Martial Law was enacted three times, lasting 31 months; the additional Garrison Act was activated three times for 5 months. Various emergency measures were also enacted for another 69 months. These 'abnormal' periods of emergency status of 105 months in total amount to half the time in which Park was in power (Jeong H-K 1998: 90). What the critique of the concept of the developmental state from the perspective of the critique of the fetishism of national development suggests is that successful and rapid industrialisation in the world-economic periphery is, in essence, an intensive and brutal form of capital exploitation that serves the capitalists and elites of the countries in the low end of the world-system, while it expresses itself as successful 'catch-up' national development.

Undeniably, under the Park government, rapid economic growth occurred – an average GDP growth in 1966–70 was 10.6 per cent, followed by 7.4 per cent and 7.2 per cent in 1971–75 and 1976–80, respectively (Kim H-A and Sorensen 2011: 4). The more industrialisation accelerated, the more class struggle and industrial disputes intensified. Coinciding with an economic crisis towards the end of the 1970s, i.e. overproduction caused by the decrease in international demand, large-scale labour strikes and demonstration movements exploded, which led to divisions among the ruling elites and eventually the assassination of Park. As shall be discussed in the following chapter, this, in turn, formed the background in which General Chun Doo-Hwan staged a military coup, which gave a particular content and meaning to the process of democratisation and economic liberalisation, thereby conditioning the ways in which the 'developmental state' was transformed.

Conclusion

In this chapter, I have aimed to provide a theoretically informed historical analysis of the origins of the Korean developmental state and its class form and content as the capitalist state on the one hand and a particular type of state that emerged in 'catch-up' conditions on the other. First, I have contextualised the rise of the developmental state within its place in the world-system and its relation to the US and Japan, on the one hand, and in terms of class relations, on the other. In so doing, I have also tried to offer a comparative analysis of the characteristics of the Park government, seen as the heyday of the developmental state, and the Rhee regime that preceded it in terms of the respective governments' places in the world market and the modalities of class relations.

In the modern uneven and hierarchical capitalist world-system, where capitalist contradictions and dynamics are expressed as competition between nation-states, the state is likely to be given the role of overcoming the 'backwardness' of capitalist social and production relations, and 'catch-up' development takes the form of delivering national development and enhancing the industrial power of the national economy. From this I argued that the notion of national development led by the autonomous state is a fetishistic notion not only because capitalist development was integral to global relations and it was heavily dependent on foreign capital and technology but also because it erases the material and social foundations from which the autonomous form of the state arises as if it emerged within the nature of the state itself.

The critique of the developmental state that I have presented here, however, does not suggest that national development is merely illusionary. To the extent that Marx's critique of commodity fetishism intends to explain the form through which social relations in capitalism actually *do* exist, a critique of the fetishism of national development is not meant to argue that the notion of national development is an illusion. Rather, it is to reveal that national development is the way in which capitalist class contradictions will necessarily appear especially when capitalist development is initiated from above in the condition of 'catch-up' development.

This view allows for the characteristics of the Korean developmental state to be analysed not merely as emanating from capitalist development at a general level or from national distinctiveness but from the timing of development and the positioning of a particular economy in the world-system. Above all, this understanding elucidates that what are generally taken to be *national* characteristics are in fact contradictions and limits associated with 'catch-up' capitalist development, which presupposes the world-system or the world market as the totality of capitalist social relations (see Chapter 6). On the one hand, this reading challenges the view that 'catch-up' development in the world-economic periphery can be achieved by implementation of the 'correct' policy at the national level. On the other hand, it calls into question the notion that the *national* is an alternative or antithesis to the *global*: national development is the *form* that both expresses and veils the *essence* of capitalism as a system of *global* class exploitation.

Notes

1 The total of nearly six billion US dollars that Korea received in the form of US economic grants and loans in 1948–1978 compares with a total for all of Africa of 6.89 billion and for all of Latin America of 14.8 billion (CIA Handbook 1979, as cited in Cumings 1984: 24; see also Jeong S-J (2000: 112–3).

2 According to the US-Korea Treaty on Aid, concluded in 1948, the majority of the goods, machinery, materials and others provided to Korea in the form of US aid were resold in Korea, and the proceeds were deposited into the 'Counterpart Fund Account' at the Bank of Korea. After the Korean War, the US-Korea Combined Economic Board was set up to facilitate the use of US aid.

3 The evaluation of the Rhee government by Korean academics and the general population had been broadly negative, at least until the 1990s. As shall be seen below, Rhee Syngman amended the constitution in 1954 and rigged the election results in 1960 to stay in power permanently. He is also remembered for having introduced the notorious National Security Law. However, his legacy has been

revisited and exalted by the 'New Conservatives' since the 2000s. Particularly, his ability to attain concessions from and make deals with the US, e.g. the mutual defence treaty, was considered his important contribution to enhancing the security of Korea. For debates on the legacy of Rhee Syngman see Kim S-O (2013); Macrae (2016); Seo J-S (2011).

4 While the US pressed the Korean government to devalue its currency to reduce the costs of the US troops in Korea, the Rhee government favoured keeping the value of the Korean currency appreciated in the hopes of maximising the acquisition of US dollars. Moreover, the Korean economy in the 1950s benefited from the overvaluation of the currency as it cheapened the import price of capital and intermediary goods under the ISI oriented strategy (Kong J-O 2000: 76–7; Shin Y-O 2000: 275).

5 US aid to Korea decreased from 38,300 million US dollars in 1957 to 32,100 million in 1958 and 2,200 million in 1959 (Sonn H-C 1991: 162).

6 The discontent against Rhee amongst political elites was evidenced in their attempts to plot a military coup. In fact, Park Chung-Hee was considered one of the key military members to lead a coup. The subversion of the Rhee regime was only frustrated by the disapproval of the US, though it was close to the point of consenting to it (see Ra J-Y 1992).

7 After the military coup, Park Chung-Hee took over government business but did not form a formal government until the election of 1963. Between 1961 and 1963, he was the chairman of the Supreme Council for National Reconstruction.

8 Brazinsky notes that the US ironically allowed the Korean government to gain greater leverage against the US in pursuing an economic policy of investing in cement and fertilizer plants, which Japanese capital was interested in, although the US generally opposed Korea's investment in heavy and chemical industries. This happened in the context of the US being a major driving force behind the diplomatic normalisation between Korea and Japan (Brazinsky 2005: 108–9).

9 Characterising Korean capitalist development as *dependent* development does not necessarily mean that the Korean economy was prevented from growing or suffered from underdevelopment, as some extreme versions of dependency theory suggest (see Brewer 1980; Krishnan 1982; Sunoo 1978). Dependent development here points to specific contradictions emanating from 'late' development, which typically requires heavy dependence on foreign capital and technology, and thereby generates distinctive economic and social dynamics.

10 There are numerous data available that indicate the poor working conditions of Korean workers in the rapid industrialisation period. To cite a few, the annual paid holiday in Korea was 10.3 days in 1989 in comparison to 15.3 days in Japan in 1978 and 10.3 days in Taiwan in 1987. Most Koreans worked more than 5 days a week: only 1 per cent of Korean workers worked 5 days a week, as opposed to 29.5 per cent of Japanese. As of 1989, the total annual working hours in Korea were 2,590 in comparison to 2,522 in Japan, 2,214 in Singapore and 2,423 in Taiwan. This is in sharp contrast to France's 1,683, Germany's 1,598 and the US's 1,948. The rate of work-related deaths was 0.18 per cent in Korea and 0.13 per cent in Taiwan in 1989, which are 7–9 times those of Sweden and the US (Shin K-Y 1999: 48).

9 The dialectic of political and economic liberalisation, and the transition of the Korean developmental state

In this chapter, I assess the transformation of the developmental state by examining the dissolution of the Park government with reference to democratisation and economic liberalisation. Aiming to offer an alternative historical analysis of the transformation of the developmental state beyond the statist framework, I first assess the process of democratisation as constituting a part of class and social struggles whose content and mode of expression were conditioned by the capitalist social form and the position of Korea in the world-system. I ask why democratisation in Korea in the 1980s was expressed as a call for attaining political and labour rights against the authoritarian state, why the outcome of democratisation lacked socio-economic substance beyond formal and procedural democracy in spite of its militant mode of struggle, and how and why democratisation accelerated economic liberalisation and contributed to and coincided with the financial crisis of 1997/98. I argue that the legacy of the developmental state, a product and expression of the contradictions of 'catch-up' (late) capitalist development, and the marginalisation of the left in the struggle for democracy largely account for this outcome. The emergence of right-wing liberal elites as the dominant political force from the democratisation and labour struggles (the 'Great Workers' Struggle') gave a particular meaning to democracy and had the effect of accelerating economic liberalisation: democracy meant ending military dictatorship and rationalising the relation between state and capital, which in effect resulted in liberalising the economy when the authoritarian character of the interventionist developmental state (the Park government) was challenged. In the second section, I assess how economic liberalisation accelerated by democratisation subsequently translated in Korea into the 'Asian financial crisis' of 1997/98, when the crisis-ridden dynamics of global capitalism met with the specific contradictions of Korean capitalist development. I discuss what the rise of the new state-capital and state-society relations brought about by the dialectic of democratisation and economic liberalisation can tell us about the transformation of the developmental state.

Democratisation as class struggle and the developmental state in transition

As discussed in Part I, the concept of the developmental state is underpinned by the juxtaposition of the state and the market, and the national and the global as antagonistic categories. To the extent that this statist framework remains unquestioned, the transformation of the developmental state is perceived as a process in which either the state shows resilience against either capitalist domestic society or the global economy, or the latter encroaches onto the supposed autonomy of the (not anymore 'developmental') state. Otherwise, as seen in the debate on the 'hybridity' of the developmental state, the question of its transformation is framed in terms of how much and to what extent the Korean state entails elements of both developmentalism (state-centrism) and neoliberalism (market-centrism). An effect of assessing the transformation of the developmental state in this manner is the perpetuating of the statist concept, reducing the question of the transformation of the developmental state to a matter of the conciliations between the state and the market, on the one hand, and the national and the global, on the other. In the statist framework, the essence of the developmental state as a *capitalist* state and its class form and content remain secondary or invisible.

In an attempt to assess the transformation of the developmental state beyond the statist framework, in this chapter, I contextualise it within the process of democratisation and economic liberalisation. I base my analysis on the following two propositions. First, I appraise democratisation as social and class struggles: the content of democracy, i.e. what constitutes democracy and the extent of its realisation are determined by a class power balance emerging out of class struggle. However, the aspirations for and content of democracy are conditioned by the capitalist social form and the place of Korea in the world-system, although the outcomes are not predetermined.

Class conflict in capitalism is structured by and embedded within the social forms of the commodity and capital; class antagonism is inherent in a society constituted by the commodity as a totalising and totalised form (see Chapter 6). However, the mode in which class conflict expresses itself is also given by the capitalist social form: to the extent that individuals exist in capitalism as legal subjects equal to other owners of commodities, class conflict between capital and labour is likely to be expressed as aspirations for equality and claims on a 'fair share' of the surplus value (e.g. equal pay beyond differential social categories, demands for higher wages and shorter working hours) (Pashukanis 1989; see Chapter 6). Furthermore, world-systematic factors, the location of an economy in the hierarchical capitalist world-economy and the timing of development in world time also condition the ways in which class conflict is expressed. To the extent that the 'catch-up' development context gives rise to and indeed necessitates an authoritarian state that is able to forcefully impose capitalist social relations from above, a process that is inherently violent, social struggle is likely to be expressed in the form of challenges to an authoritarian state, e.g. demands for freedom of expression and political rights.

Second, while democratisation constitutes a form of class struggle, not only domestic but also 'external' or 'foreign' forces took part in the process as class forces. As much as the US occupation army influenced to a great degree the forming and sustaining of the autocratic Rhee regime and the Park government after the Korean War (see Chapters 7 and 8), the US reacted with a clear class orientation to the military coup led by Park and subsequently Chun Doo-Hwan, and to the *Kwangju Uprising* (see below). It supported military regimes willing and able to consolidate and restore capitalist order in the context of the rise of (seemingly) anti-capitalist revolutions elsewhere, namely Cuba, in the case of Park's coup, and Iran, in the case of Chun's coup (see below). This suggests that what appear as *external* forces need to be seen as dynamic and active class forces within what appear as 'domestic' struggles.

In what follows, I will analyse democratisation from the late 1970s through to the 1990s in Korea and highlight how rapid and successful capitalist development was also the process of embedding and augmenting capitalist contradictions and class antagonism. I will trace how the Park government came to an end as a result of the deepening contradictions of capitalist development expressed as a political and economic crisis, and how these set the stage for another military coup and provided a further impetus for social struggles for democracy.

The economic crisis of the late 1970s and the dissolution of the Park regime

Park Chung-Hee was in power for 18 years after his military coup in May 1961, until he was assassinated by one of his closest confidants in October 1979. His power appeared to be unassailable, especially after the amendment of the constitution in 1972, referred to as *Yushin* (October Restoration), which allowed him to remain in power permanently (see Kim B-K 2011). After narrowly winning the presidential elections in 1971 against opposition leader Kim Dae-Jung, Park committed what amounted to a coup against himself by abolishing democratic procedures, e.g. direct presidential elections that existed at least formally. Under the *Yushin* constitution, in December 1972, Park Chung-Hee was elected unanimously to a new six-year term as president, with no debate permitted, by the National Conference of Unification, the institution that was headed by Park himself and whose members consisted of his supporters (Kang J-M 2002a: 222–4; Oberdorfer 1997: 45).

While rapid industrialisation occurred in the 1960s and 1970s under the Park government, it was simultaneously the process of laying the ground for intensive social and class struggle. The Park government's foreign loan dependent, export-led development led to falling profits in the light manufacturing sector, high inflation and an increasing number of insolvent companies towards the end of the 1960s (Park S-H 2013: 90). Together with the extant harsh labour conditions, capital's attempt to overcome these barriers to accumulation by either cutting wages or reducing the operation of factories fuelled labour and social discontent from the late 1960s onwards. One key instance was the self-immolation of garment factory worker Jeon Tae-Il in 1970 (Park S-H 2013: 90–1). Park's narrow victory in the presidential elections in 1971 was also a sign of increasing public discontent. Furthermore, even in the face of North Korea's attempts to assassinate Park in the mid-1960, the US (the Johnson Administration) was reluctant to retaliate and instead sought a diplomatic solution (Kwon 2017: 189). Subsequently, the Nixon Administration, promoting an East-West détente, forged ahead with plans to withdraw troops from Korea (Kwon 2017: 193; Park S-H 2013: 91). Amidst these multiple political and economic crises, in 1973, the Park government launched the Heavy and Chemical Industrialisation Plan (HCIP). While its pursuit of the HCIP was in part initiated to nationalise the mass production of weapons and modernise the Korean army in the face of diminishing US willingness to support Korea against the North (see Kwon 2017), it was also an attempt to overcome the deepening economic and political crises.

However, the HCIP intensified the impending economic crisis. Coinciding with the decrease in international demand triggered by the second oil shock in the late 1970s, the heavy and chemical industries on which investment of foreign loans was concentrated faced problems of overproduction and overcapacity (Sonn H-C 2004: 299). To the extent that the Korean economy was heavily dependent on the importation of oil, the second oil shock affected it adversely. By the end of the 1970s, the level of plant operation in *Changwon* Industrial Complex, a cluster of heavy and chemical industries, was merely 30 per cent, and plant closures increased by 40–130 per cent compared to previous years (Sonn H-C 2004: 299). As of 1979, trade deficit reached 4.1 billion US dollars, the worst figure in this decade (Kang J-M 2002c: 305).

The Park government tried to resolve the problems of overcapacity and ill-coordinated investment by devising a stabilisation measure. However, apart from the complexity resulting from the sheer scale of overproduction, in the face of the resistance of the *chaebol* the government primarily placed the cost of stabilisation on small- and medium-scale capitalists, workers and farmers, for instance through high taxation, redundancies and wage cuts (Kang J-M 2002c: 257; Park S-H 2013: 91). In Pusan, tax revenues hiked 32 per cent between 1978 and 1979. As of 1978, the proportion of workers that earned a lower income than the minimum subsistence level reached 64.9 per cent. This turned hitherto government supporters into an anti-government force (Sonn H-C 2004: 299). The rising discontent of the general public against the Park government was confirmed in the general elections held in 1978. The opposition New Democratic Party won more votes than the ruling Democratic Republican Party, despite the latter's fraudulent activities to earn votes (Sonn H-C 2004: 299).

Amid the deepening economic crisis, the light industry was adversely affected. The bank loans made to the garment sector decreased by half in the period of 1975–77 (Choi I-C 1991: 71–2; Kang J-M 2002c: 260–1). Concomitantly, labour struggles intensified. Even under Park's harsh oppression of labour activism, the number of labour disputes soared from 754 in 1976 to 1,064 in 1977, 1,206 in 1978 and 1,697 in 1979 (Sonn H-C 2004: 299). The more Park tried to repress social dissent indiscriminately through violent means, the more the diverse social forces became unified under the banner of the anti-dictatorship, anti-government democratisation movement. Illustratively, a labour strike by female workers of the YH trading company in 1979, which took place against the fraudulent closure of the factory, received support from the opposition party, the New Democratic Party (Kang J-M 2002c: 231). The unlawful deprivation of the National Assembly membership of Kim Young-Sam, the leader of the New Democratic Party, triggered a large-scale demonstration in October 1979 in the areas of Pusan and Masan, which developed into what was later known as the *Puma* Struggle. The extreme mode of Park's repression of social dissent also prevented democratisation forces from seeking moderate or mid-way compromises and pushed them to a militant mode of struggle (Cho H-Y 1994, 2002; Lee K-I 2006; Sonn H-C 2004).

The escalating confrontation between the Park government and anti-government social forces split the elites into soft- and hardliners over how to respond to the *Puma* Struggle. Park was killed in this conflict by a softliner, Kim Jae-Gyu, the director of the Korean Central Intelligence Agency (KCIA).[1] Kim was engaged in a power struggle with Cha Ji-Chul, the Chief of Presidential Security, who pushed for a hardline solution, proposing, for instance, that tanks be deployed against the YH strikers and New Democratic Party members, believing that killing a couple hundred would quieten the *Puma* Struggle (Kang J-M 2002c: 259). While superficially the Park regime was brought to an end by the competition between state elites, it was ended by an economic and political crisis that was an expression of the intrinsic contradictions associated with the state-led development trajectory of the Park government, together with the social and labour forces of democratisation that were also a product of rapid industrialisation. It was not accidental that the demonstrations against the government in the late 1970s took place in Pusan and Masan, where the light industries were concentrated, and that labour forces also joined anti-government movements.

Another military government and the Kwangju uprising

The end of the Park regime did not bring about a democratic government, though. Immediately after Park's death, prime minister Choi Gyu-Hwa assumed the role of acting president and was elected president under the *Yushin* constitution in December 6, 1979. Even before the formal inauguration of the new president, scheduled on December 21, another military coup was on the way. *Hana-hoe* (One-Group), a club of military personnel formed by graduates of the Korean Military Academy, who occupied core positions in the military, organised a multi-staged coup.[2] The leader of the group, General Chun Doo-Hwan, led an organisation established to investigate Park's assassination. He first seized control of the military in December 12, 1979 by arresting Army Chief of Staff Jeong Seung-Hwa, who had been in charge of national security under Martial Law since Park's death. Chun then moved to seize state executive power, taking a key position as acting director of the KCIA on April 14, 1980. In addition to these visible moves, the junta also imposed censorship on the media and lobbied US officials and foreign (financial) companies to get support and approval for the coup (Kang J-M 2003a: 52–3).

In the meantime, the opposition parties were divided along the lines of support for two leaders: Kim Young-Sam and Kim Dae-Jung. Formerly allies in anti-*Yushin* movements, they were separated and did not take any serious action against the coup. Kim Young-Sam misread the situation entirely and was optimistic about his own prospects for becoming president after future elections,[3] and Kim Dae-Jung, though concerned about Chun's moves, refused to join Kim Young-Sam's New Democratic Party: the two Kims were more preoccupied with increasing their respective power bases for a presidential election that they believed was soon to be held (Kang J-M 2003a: 73–4). With the new military junta having succeeded in taking control of the military and the KCIA, a situation was created in which any kind of social unrest would lead to military intervention (Cho H-Y 1994: 259). Subsequent student demonstrations against Chun provided the needed excuse for the junta to extend Martial Law to the national level, which meant activating a direct command structure between the president and the chief of the army. This allowed the military junta to deploy the army when it saw this to be necessary, a situation that eventually occurred in Kwangju on May 18, 1980.

Since the death of Park, anti-*Yushin* demonstrations had spread across the country, starting with student demonstrations in Seoul. Particularly in May 1980, nationwide student demonstrations demanded the withdrawal of Martial Law, which allowed the presence of the military in the government. Under the pretext of an alleged threat from North Korea, the military junta started to arrest demonstrators and leaders of opposition groups, including Kim Dae-Jung, for allegedly allying with the North. After extending Martial Law to the national level on May 17, 1980, special army troops were sent to the Southern city of Kwangju on May 18. Brutal violence and indiscriminate mass killing of demonstrators and civilians ensued. Students and Kwangju citizens fought against the troops but were eventually defeated with an approximate death toll between 800 and 2,000.[4] Soon after the successful oppression of Kwangju, Chun was elected president under the *Yushin* charter by the National Conference of Unification, on August 27, 1980, with 2,524 approvals out of 2,525 voting members.

The place of the Kwangju Uprising in the democratisation process

The Kwangju Uprising left an important imprint on the future democratisation movement of Korea. First, as Chun rose to power by brutally repressing Kwangju citizens and demonstrators, his government was founded on fragile political legitimacy (Cho H-Y 1984: 259). His 'immoral' path to power mobilised and unified a broad array of social classes and groups, from opposition parties, labour unionists, students, farmers, members of the middle class and intellectuals to religious associations in anti-government movements.[5] The Kwangju Uprising provided the frame of reference for democratisation movements and fuelled the pan-national struggle for democracy in the 1980s, which culminated in the 'June Resistance' of 1987 (see below).

Second, the Kwangju Uprising also called into question the role of the US in Korea. Evidence suggests that the US supported, if not opted for, the military junta's deploying army troops to Kwangju (Lee S-S 1996: 111–35; Oberdorfer 1997: 130).[6] Even before full Martial Law was declared, the Korean military, as required, notified the US Army command of its intention to remove two units of the ROK (Republic of Korea, i.e. South Korea) Infantry Division from operational control by the Combined Forces Command, which directed the US-ROK defence against North Korea. In the second week of the conflict, the senior US commander in Korea, General John Wickham, approved the redeployment of the Twentieth Division to Kwangju, with the agreement of US Ambassador Gleysteen after consulting with Washington (Oberdorfer 1997: 129–30). In addition to backing Chun's deployment of the army, the US supported Chun's military coup financially. Two weeks after the Kwangju Uprising, the US Export-Import Bank finalised terms under which to extend more than 600 million US dollars' worth of import credits to Chun. The 'heads of Chase Manhattan Bank and First National Bank also travelled to South Korea to pledge their financial support. Not long after, the Japanese government extended a massive loan of 4 billion US dollars under exceptionally generous terms' (Hart-Landsberg 2004: 200–1).

There were various factors at play that led the US to back Chun's coup, from its ultimate foreign policy priority of maintaining Korea as an anti-communist frontier in Asia to the hegemonic rise of militarists against liberals within the US political elite towards the end of the 1970s (Halliday 1986: 214–7; Lee S-S 1996: 86–97). Most of all, though, the Korean political upheaval coincided with the Iranian Revolution of 1979, which turned a hitherto pro-US state that was geopolitically important for the US into an anti-US regime. This made the US political elites highly sensitive to the mounting social unrest in Korea, a country seen as equally geopolitically significant in the Asian-Pacific region. US ambivalence at the beginning and eventual support for Chun were motivated by the desire not to create 'another Iran' (Lee S-S 1996: 95–6; Oberdorfer 1997: 123). To the extent that implicit or explicit US support contributed to the success of Chun's military coup, the US was co-responsible for determining the content and meaning of democracy in Korea. As shall be discussed below US involvement in the Kwangju massacre, at least indirectly reinforced the anti-imperialist and anti-US stance of the democratisation movements (see below).

Third, the experience of violent oppression brought about particular patterns of political behaviour among the Kwangju population, which characterises modern Korean politics itself. Kwangju, Korea's fifth-largest city by population, situated in the southwest of Korea, had been relatively backward and rural. The Park regime had deliberately discriminated against it and the surrounding Chŏlla province in terms of industrial investment. Most major industrial cities were located in the southeast (e.g. Taegu, Pusan and Masan), which is also where most of the Korean ruling elites, with the exception of Kim Dae-Jung, are from.[7] The disparity or antagonism between Kwangju and the rest of the country created a phenomenon called 'regionalism' (*Chiiyŏkjuŭi*). Although regionalism came to dominate Korean politics, it was a relatively new phenomenon that became prevalent only under the Park government (Park H-J and Jeong K-Y 1989: 224). The Park government and its associated elites devised an anti-Kwangju sentiment as a means to secure their popular bases in their home regions, fashioning the notion of a supposed unity amongst those who come from Taegu and Kyŏngbuk (North Kyŏngsang) provinces, particularly by projecting the idea that Kwangju was inhabited by communists. The 'red' image of Kwangju was also exploited by the military political elites to isolate Kim Dae-Jung from other social groups. The socio-economic and political status of Kwangju in part explains why the massacre, with which Chun completed his coup, took place there rather than elsewhere (Sonn H-C 2004: 359–63).

The fact that the violent oppression of Kwangju took place in isolation from other parts of the country without being reported by any national media, combined with the widely held assumption that Kwangju was targeted in line with the arrest of Kim Dae-Jung, helped strengthen a sense of anger and alienation amongst Kwangju citizens.[8] This translated into unconditional support for Kim Dae-Jung and his party. Kim Dae-Jung was later sentenced to death on trumped-up sedition charges, accused of having manipulated the Kwangju Uprising in cooperation with North Korea. The Kwangju people internalised Kim's oppression by Chun as much as their own (Choi J-J 1993: 35–6; Sonn H-C 2004: 577–605). While the strong sense of unity among the Kwangju people was a product of the military governments, it fed into strengthening regionalism, which affected democratisation both negatively and positively.

On the one hand, regionalism has been recurrently utilised by political elites as a means to secure their power by confining election agendas to regional issues: political parties framed their political agendas on the basis of their respective regional affinities rather than on class lines or policy differentials (see Lee Y 2015a: 198). On the other hand, the all-out support for the opposition party by Kwangju citizens led to the defeat of the ruling party in the general elections in 1985 and 1988, which contributed to inducing a constitutional reform process by forcing the ruling party to make concessions (see below). In this way, the Kwangju Uprising marks one of the most significant conjunctures in the Korean democratisation process, having provided impetus and aspirations for democratisation movements in the 1980s and the 1990s.

Democratisation from below and the 6/29 Declaration

While the Chun government oppressed political and labour activism as much as the previous Park government, it differentiated itself from the latter by permitting some level of cultural freedom. In January 1982, it abolished the curfew that had been in place since September 1945 and allowed 'freedom of hair-style'. Stringent censorship was still imposed on the expression of socio-political issues in films, TV dramas and literature, but sexual expressions, consumption and sports were permitted. It was under the Chun government that professional baseball leagues were created in 1982. The government also made much propagandistic use of the fact that national unity and social order were necessary conditions for the successful hosting of the Asian Games in 1986 and the Olympic Games in 1988 as a means to control social discontent. On this ground, the Chun government was often referred to as 'the Republic of Sports' (Kang J-M 2003b, 2003c).

Along similar lines, from 1983 onwards, with the exception of some important figures, including Kim Dae-Jung and Kim Young-Sam, the Chun government released political activists and demonstrators who had been imprisoned or under house arrest. The new military government tried to prevent the radicalisation of social movements by allowing some degree of political and cultural freedom (Cho H-Y 1994: 261). However, Chun's relatively softened approach to social dissent did not stop a broad spectrum of social forces from joining anti-government democratisation movements.

On the third anniversary of the Kwangju Uprising, Kim Young-Sam, who was held under house arrest, went on 23 days of hunger strike, demanding democratic reform. Kim Dae-Jung, who narrowly escaped the death penalty by seeking exile in the US after being charged in association with the Kwangju Uprising, announced his support for Kim Young-Sam. The two Kims made a joint declaration for democratisation, recognising that they bore responsibility for the Kwangju massacre as they had failed to act against Chun's coup. This led to the formation of a pan-national democratisation alliance and the opposition New Korea Democratic Party in January 1985. The New Korea Democratic Party, of which Kim Dae-Jung and Kim Young-Sam held joint leadership, emerged as the largest opposition party in the general elections held in February 1985 (Kang J-M 2003a: 224). Its successful performance in the general elections gave further momentum to unify the social forces in the struggle for democracy, including those hitherto separated, such as the 'People's Democracy' tendency and the 'National Unification' tendency, forming the United *Minjung* Movement for Democracy and Unification (UMDU).[9]

In parallel with the increasing unity among political organisations under the banner of democratisation, anti-government movements became increasingly radicalised, embracing the agenda of 'anti-US imperialism' and 'labour emancipation'. Two radical student groups emerged in 1986: the Struggle Committee for Anti-Imperialism and the National Democratic Struggle Committee for Anti-Fascism (Hart-Landsberg 1989: 64). Anti-military government movements were also increasingly synchronised with anti-US and labour movements. Students attacked the US embassy in Pusan in 1982 and occupied the US Cultural Centre in Seoul in 1985. A strike that started at *Daewoo* Apparel in 1985 developed into a solidarity strike whereby other workers and unions operating in the same *Kuro* industrial complex joined forces (Kang K-M 2003b: 283–91). At the height of the tension between the government and social forces of democratisation, the death of a university student, Park Jong-Chul, by torture provided a crucial impetus for the explosion of a pan-national anti-government movement, which led to what has become known as the June Resistance. On June 10, 1987, demonstrations took place across the country, with a total of 500,000 people joining 514 different anti-government gatherings and peaked on 26 June, when the number of people who joined demonstrations across the country reached 1.8 million. It was estimated that 2,145 demonstrations took place and the police fired 350,000 canisters of tear gas between June 10 and June 27 (Kang J-M 2003c: 170). The social forces of democratisation, consisting of the opposition parties, labour unions and students, were united in demanding constitutional reform that would allow direct presidential elections.

In the face of mounting social unrest, Chun initially considered deploying the army against the demonstrators, as in Kwangju. However, he was in the end restrained from doing so. First, anti-government demonstrations in the June Resistance were taking place nationwide and were comprehensive in terms of class composition, with strong white-collar and middle-class support to the extent that this was labelled 'the Rebellion by the Middle Class' (Kang J-M 2003c: 159–60). Second, given that the Korean public perceived the US as responsible for the Kwangju massacre, the US expressed its reservations about Chun deploying the army to suppress the demonstrations (Kang J-M 2003c: 167; Oberdorfer 1997: 167–72). Third, in the face of the Olympic Games scheduled to take place in 1988, Chun was also warned by the International Olympic Committee that if social unrest continued in Seoul, Korea's hosting would be cancelled and the games might be moved elsewhere (Oberdorfer 1997: 164).

Under immense pressure from various directions, the Chun government finally gave in to the demand of the democratisation forces. On June 29, 1987, Roh Tae-Woo, the presidential candidate of the ruling party, declared the adoption of direct universal suffrage in the upcoming presidential elections, an event that came to be known as the 6/29 Declaration. It also included the prospect of an open campaign without threats of repression; amnesties for political prisoners, including Kim Dae-Jung; guarantees of basic rights; and revision or abolishment of the press law (Cumings 1999a: 34). The 6/29 Declaration highlights that although there were various factors at play, the democratisation forces from below were ultimately decisive in pressing the Chun government to accept constitutional reform. The persistent and unified voice from below made it clear to state elites and others, including the US, that the tide of democratisation was irreversible.

Democratisation as class struggle

Soon after the 6/29 Declaration, however, cleavages along different class lines surfaced between liberals (liberal party elites) and more radical social forces, including labour unions.[10] The June Resistance transformed into a large-scale labour struggle in July and August, which developed into what is known as 'the Great Workers' Struggle'. During these two months, more than 3,000 labour disputes occurred, accompanied by rapid labour unionisation. The number of unions increased from 2,658 to 7,883, and the number of union members increased from 1,036,000 to 1,932,000 between 1986 and 1989 (Koo H 2001: 231). Labour movements began to be highly organised and militant from the mid-1980s onwards. The explosion of combative labour strikes and unionisation were in part explained by the shift in the locus of labour movements from the light industry of female workers to the heavy industry of male workers in accordance with the development of heavy and chemical industries (Lim H-B 1994: 289).

The increasing labour unionisation was also helped by an alliance between students and workers, called *Nohakyŏndae*, in which students entered factories as workers and were involved in the establishment of labour unions with more radical agendas. The number of university students who became factory workers during the first half of the 1980s reached 3,000 to 4,000 in the area of Seoul alone (Kang J-M 2003b: 179–84). The increasingly organised labour movement opposed the pro-capital, state-controlled Korean Federation of Trade Unions (KFTU), and the aspirations of Korean workers for a democratic union led to the foundation of an alternative nationwide union, the Korean Confederation of Trade Unions (KCTU) (see Chang D-O 2009: chs. 7–9; Ogle 1990). Concomitantly, radical intellectuals became more visible (Lee K-I 2007: 120–1). They founded alternative journals and fought against the anti-communist and right-wing ideologies that had long governed Korean society. In line with the strong forces of democratisation from below unleashed in the June Resistance, labour and radical social forces took constitutional reform as a step towards further social changes.

In contrast to the labour movements and radical social forces, opposition party leaders Kim Young-Sam and Kim Dae-Jung tried to limit the democratic aspirations to institutional and constitutional reform. Distancing themselves from radical social forces and ignoring the plea for unity by various social and political groups, Kim Young-Sam and Kim Dae-Jung finally ran for the presidential elections separately: the New Korean Democratic Party was split into the Reunification Democratic Party and the Peace Democratic Party, with one of the two Kims leading each one. This meant that they went back on what they had declared previously (see Kang J-M 2003c: 224–9). The division between the two Kims in fact contributed to dividing left-wing social forces: in the election, one tendency was 'supporting Kim Dae-Jung; another trying to force one of two Kims to withdraw; and a third supporting an independent people's candidate' (Hart-Landsberg 1989: 67; see Park H-J and Jeong K-Y 1989: 233–4). Thanks to the split between the two candidates, the candidate from the ruling party, Roh Tae-Woo, an accomplice of Chun in the Kwangju massacre, was elected.

While the 6/29 Declaration symbolised the advancement of democracy to the extent that it secured direct presidential elections, it also exposed the divide between political and social groups along class positions as well as their divergence in political objectives. On the one hand, it separated opposition party elites from left-wing social forces of democratisation, hitherto allied under anti-government movements. On the other hand, it unified the softliners of the ruling military elites, led by Roh Tae-Woo, and right-wing liberal elites, represented by Kim Young-Sam (Lim H-B 1994: 290). Kim Young-Sam can be referred to as a right-wing liberal, and Kim Dae-Jung as a left-wing liberal. While both were liberals to the extent that they supported liberal democracy and the market economy, Kim Dae-Jung, in addition to holding a reconciliatory stance toward North Korea, based his popularity on the less privileged, particularly the population in the Kwangju region, and small- and medium-sized firms rather than the *chaebol*. The union between the softliners of the ruling military elites and right-wing liberal elites was cemented in 1990 through a three-party merger, that is, the formation of the Democratic Liberty Party. The two respective parties of Roh Tae-Woo and Kim Young-Sam, and the New Democratic Republican Party of Kim Jong-Pil, a key figure representing the traditional military elites as a collaborator in Park Chung Hee's coup in 1961, took part in the merger. While the military elites could, through the three-party merger, extend their hold on power by embracing right-wing liberals, the latter emerged soon as the dominant political force, with Kim Young-Sam being nominated as the presidential candidate for the new party and elected president in 1992.

While right-wing liberals emerged as the dominant political force, progressives and left-wing social groups were ineffective in counteracting the liberal agenda. Under the extreme mode of labour oppression under military rule and the anti-communist ideology that had governed every aspect of Korean life since the Korean War, labour lacked unionisation until the mid-1980s. Although it became increasingly unionised and its mode of struggle became more militant, the left-wing groups did not develop into a leading social force strong or radical enough to enforce a version of democracy alternative to the liberal form (Kim S-K 2007: 84, 89–90). Their militant mode of struggle notwithstanding, labour movements called for nothing more radical than labour rights within capitalism (Lee K-I 2006: 193–4; see also Cho H-Y 2004). While these were indisputably of crucial importance, labour movements and left-wing social forces were on the defensive against the liberals and confined their immediate goals to actualising the norms and rights of liberal and political democracy, including labour rights. Even after the 6/29 Declaration, labour rights, e.g. the right to collective actions by public sector workers, were still denied and the National Security Law, the notorious anti-communist law, remained intact.[11]

This outcome must be accounted for in relation to the capitalist development trajectory of Korea, as shaped and conditioned by its place in the world market. The super-oppressive form of the Korean state arose in the context of 'catch-up' capitalist development, which intrinsically necessitated or presupposed an overt mode of social discipline (see Chapters 6 and 8). Democratisation struggles had to fight against highly authoritarian military governments, which conditioned their mode of struggle and its contents: under the condition of the authoritarian state imposing an extreme mode of social control, social movements are likely to manifest themselves foremost as demands for political freedom or a challenge to the authoritarian character of the state. This not only suggests that the aspirations for democracy are internal to capitalist development and given by the capitalist social form; it also means that Korea's place in the world-system and the timing of her development mediate the ways in which class and social struggles are expressed and limit these social groups' political agendas.

In summary, what can be derived from an assessment of democratisation in Korea in the 1970s and 1980s is that democratisation constituted a form of social and class struggle, conditioned by the capitalist social form and the location of Korea in the world market, though its precise content and level of actualisation were determined by a class power balance emerging from the struggle. It also underscores that not only domestic but external forces took part in democratisation. As much as Japanese colonialism and US occupation authority contributed, as powerful class forces in themselves, to bringing about particular class configurations and the formation of the super-oppressive modern Korean state, the US reacted with a clear class orientation to the military coups led by Park and Chun, and to the mass democratisation movements in Korea. In this respect, the *external* forces were not merely external but acted as dynamic class forces on the domestic stage.

The dialectic of democratisation and the financial crisis of 1997/98

The election of Kim Young-Sam as president in 1992 brought to power the first civilian government since 1960. While formal democracy made progress, it became a force to facilitate economic (financial) liberalisation, which had the effect of intensifying the magnitude of the economic crisis that eventuated in the Asian financial crisis of 1997/98. In this section, I will trace how democracy whose content was limited to attaining formal political rights came to condition the content and pace of subsequent political reform and economic liberalisation. I will then assess the causes and implications of the Asian financial crisis by examining how the liberalisation of the financial markets that intensified in the 1970s in the West interacted with the particular trajectory of Korean capitalism, on the one hand, and new class configurations that emerged after democratisation and labour movements in the 1980s and the 1990s, on the other.

The rise of civilian democratic government and political and economic reform

Although Kim Young-Sam became president by allying with the military ruling elites, as a former leader of anti-military civil movements, he attempted to differentiate himself from the previous military governments by implementing a series of ambitious political and economic reforms. First, the Kim government tried to eliminate military influence on the government by expelling *Hana-hoe* members. It strengthened the moral code of conduct for high-ranking government officials by obliging them to disclose the assets and properties under their possession, and prosecuting those who had attained them illegally (Sonn H-C 2004: 456). It also brought the two previous presidents, Chun and Roh, to court on charges of corruption and treason in relation to masterminding the Kwangju massacre. Chun was sentenced to death and Roh to life in prison, although they were later pardoned with the inauguration of Kim Dae-Jung as president in 1998.

Second, the Kim government pursued economic reform under the New Economic Policy (NEP). It tried to tackle the problem of corruption, particularly the 'close relationship' between state elites and businesses by enhancing financial transparency. It banned the holding of financial accounts under a false name and political donations from non-transparent sources (Sonn H-C 2004: 456). In addition, the Kim government introduced measures to put a limit on the tendency of ever-increasing capital concentration.[12] It placed a ceiling on the percentage of the shares of other firms that a *chaebol* can acquire *vis-à-vis* its total assets (25 per cent) and restricted inter-subsidiary loan guarantees and other internal deals. Along the same lines, it strengthened the status of the Fair Trade Commission while downgrading that of the Economic Planning Board (EPB) to a vice-ministerial level administration under the Ministry of Finance (Lee Y-H et al. 2002: 206). Cumings once described the EPB as 'the Korean locus of administrative guidance' (1998: 54). Woo-Cumings even took it as the symbol of the developmental state itself, as an institution that drafted and implemented industrial development plans (see Woo-Cumings 1997, 1999b). These reforms indicate the diminishing importance of industrial policy and the government's role in financial intermediation.

These political and economic reforms were implemented in parallel with economic liberalisation. From 1994 onwards the Kim Young-Sam government initiated bold economic liberalisation in the name of *sekyehwa* or 'globalisation' (Lee K-K 2005: 329; Lee Y-H et al. 2002: 210). The government announced its intention to depart from the old development model characterised by heavy state interventionism in the economy. In this context, 'globalisation' was understood to make the Korean economy run according to free-market rules, business autonomy and competition. As an initiative to liberalise the economy, the government actively sought to join the Organisation for Economic Co-operation and Development (OECD), considered as the club of the most industrialised and advanced countries – it even appreciated the Korean currency, the *won*, to inflate GDP per capita in an effort to meet OECD membership requirements, as a result of which Korea became a member in 1996.

Another significant move made by the Kim government was the facilitating of the liberalisation of the financial market. It relaxed rules on foreign and off-shore borrowing (Lee K-K 2005: 332). After liberalising the short-term lending rates of banks and non-bank financial institutions (NBFIs) by 1993, it deregulated all lending rates of financial institutions and rates on long-term deposits in the following year, and all remaining interest rates by 1997 (Lee K-K 2005: 329; Woo-Cumings 1997: 85). Additionally, the Kim government relaxed regulations on banking and non-banking financial businesses and allowed second-tier financial institutions such as insurance companies to engage in NBFIs, resulting in 30 investment firms' switching to merchant banks between 1994 and 1996 (Lee K-K 2005: 329). Under the same liberalisation motif, the Kim government opened the stock market to foreign investors in 1992 and loosened the rules on short-term borrowing by domestic firms and financial institutions from 1993 onwards (Lee K-K 2005: 330).

The dialectic of global capitalism and class struggle

The liberalisation of the financial market under the Kim Young-Sam government before the Asian financial crisis in 1997/98 has been well researched and documented by neoclassical economists (Balino and Ubide 1999; Krueger and Yoo 2002; Krugman 2000) as well as by institutionalists and Keynesian economists (Chang H-J 1998; Chang H-J et al. 1998; Chang H-J and Yoo C-G 1999; Choi D-Y and Lee Y-H 2002; Crotty 2000, 2002; Lee K-K 2005; Stiglitz 2000; Wade 1998a, 1998b; Woo-Cumings 1997, 1999b). Most commentators agree that the opening of the financial markets and the liberalisation of the capital accounts contributed to the Asian financial crisis of 1997/98 that wreaked havoc on the Korean economy. From this, it is often concluded, at least by implication, that proper regulatory and supervisory institutions, or indeed the continued existence of the developmental state itself, could have avoided the crisis, while only neoclassical economists suggest that not having the developmental state in the first place could have done so (see Part I). While these assessments offer important insights and entail some valid points, they tend to base their analyses on the assumption that financial liberalisation can be looked at in isolation from capitalist (class) contradictions emanating from real accumulation processes, whether it is seen to be caused by 'external' pressure or by the (non-) existence of the developmental state. What has to be explained is why financial liberalisation took place in such an intensive form at that particular time, and how and why it developed into an economic crisis at an historically unprecedented level.

Periodic crises and overaccumulation, and alternating booms and recessions, are intrinsic to the dynamics of capitalism (Clarke 1994; Harvey 1982: chs. 7, 10; Itoh and Lapavitsas 1999: ch. 6; Marx 1976: part 2). The Korean economy has experienced a series of cycles of expansion and contraction over the course of rapid development in the pre-crisis decades (Kim S-H and Cho B-H 1999: 216). At the general level, therefore, the financial crisis of 1997/98 was first an expression of the general contradictions of capitalism, in which the expanded production and credit in the expansionary phase met the barriers of accumulation and realisation in the down-phase, manifested through over-accumulation (overcapacity), problems that needed to be redressed through a crisis, i.e. the devaluation of capital. However, heavy foreign (short-term) borrowing in the 1990s by the *chaebol* added to the effects of the increasing contradictions of the global economy, and these interacted in turn with contradictions specific to the Korean capitalist development, expressed as and augmented by new class constellations.

On the one hand, coinciding with the end of the long post-War boom, there has been increasing mobility of capital and deepening integration of global financial markets.[13] The renewed globalising financial markets, coupled with the breakdown of the Bretton Woods system in the early 1970s, increased the volatility of the financial markets on a global scale as well as the pressure for financial liberalisation and deregulation of the financial markets in the developing countries (Gowan 1999, 2002; Harvey 2003; Panitch and Gindin 2005; Rude 2005; Wood 2003). While the Western and Japanese economies were in stagnation, Asia (minus Japan) emerged as the only rapidly growing region in the 1980s, with the effect that foreign investment and capital flowed into the region in a feverish fashion. Foreign banks were more than willing to lend (short-term) credit to Korean banks and firms. Japanese credit agencies continued to give Korea their highest rating until mid-1997. '[A]ccording to the Bank of International Settlement, bank lending to East Asia rose to a record peak of $14.1 billion in the third quarter of 1997' (Hale 1998: 5–7, as cited in Cumings 1998: 52). International inter-bank lending to Korea soared, accelerating from an annual growth rate of about 15 billion US dollars in 1994 to about 25 billion US dollars in 1995/96 and 108.5 billion US dollars at the end of 1996 (BIS 1997).

On the other hand, the needs of Korean capital to liberalise the financial markets had been concomitantly heightening since the 1980s. First, there was a major change taking place in US-Japan-Korea trade relations, which had hitherto been one of the important conditions that allowed the rapid economic growth of Korea in the context of the Cold War (Hart-Landsberg 2004: 201; see Chapter 8). With the re-emergence of Japan and Germany as industrial powers relative to the US, a by-product of the US-led post-Second World War reconstruction alignment itself (Armstrong et al. 1991: part I; Block 1977: chs. 3–5), protectionism resurfaced in the US, particularly in the face of its mounting trade deficit with Japan. The Plaza Accord that resulted from US pressure to appreciate the Japanese *yen* against the US dollar in 1985 brought about a situation in which the trade deficit of the US with Japan levelled off, but that with Korea increased: Korean exports to the US surged as a result of the enhanced competitiveness of Korean exports due to the relative devaluation of the Korean *won* against the Japanese *yen*. Consequently, on the one hand, Korea faced heightening pressure from the US to open its markets to US imports and intensifying protectionist retaliation by the US (Shin K-Y 1999: 55).[14] On the other hand, Japan, losing market shares to Korea, banned the export of 200 ultra-modern technologies to Korea between 1990 and 1995 so that 'Japanese firms will have exploited much of the market potential of the technology' (Bello 1992: 88). Korea's trade balance with the US turned from surplus to deficit from 1991 and carried on until 1996, while its trade deficit with Japan was persistent and even rising throughout the 1980s and 1990s (Jeong S-J 2005: 133). 'Export growth fell from 36.2 per cent in 1987, to 28.4 per cent in 1988, 5.7 per cent in 1989, and 3 per cent in 1990' (Hart-Landsberg 2004: 203). In addition, the rise of Southeast Asian economies placed another strain on Korean exporters by causing intensive competition over the world-market share of the same line of products (Hart-Landsberg 2004: 206–8; see also Hart-Landsberg and Burkett 2006; Kim S-J 2005: 13; Kim Y-C 1998: 1146; Shin K-Y 1999: ch. 2).

Second, heightening democratisation and increasing labour unionisation and militancy in the 1980s, especially in line with the Great Workers' Struggle, placed another strain on Korean capital (see Kim Y-C 1998: 1146). To the extent that the profitability of Korean capital was sustained largely by low wages and long working hours, Korean capital became vulnerable to the enhancement of labour working conditions. The explosion of labour movements in the 1980s brought about a rise in real wages and a reduction in labour time and in the rate of exploitation, at least in the sectors where labour unionism was strong, i.e. heavy and motor industries. For instance, 'Korean wages were the lowest among the Asian NICs until 1988 … [but] Korean wages rose above Hong Kong's in 1989, Taiwan's in 1990, and Singapore's in 1991. During the period of 1991–94, Korean workers enjoyed the highest manufacturing wages in Asia except for Japan' (Kim Y-C 1998: 1147). Labour union density increased from 12.3 per cent in 1986 to 18.6 per cent in 1989 (Lee Y 2015b: 185–6). Similarly, average weekly labour hours in the manufacturing industry started to decrease from 1987, the year of the Great Workers' Struggle, onwards, from 54.7 hours in 1986 to 52.6 hours in 1988, 49.8 in 1990 and 49.2 in 1995 (Jeong S-J 2005: 134, 148–9).

Concomitantly, the rate of exploitation reduced from 431 per cent in 1984 to 354 per cent in 1989.[15] The shortage of labour (decrease in unemployment) also helped strengthen the bargaining position of labour *vis-à-vis* capital: the unemployment rate continuously decreased from 5.2 per cent in 1980 to 4 per cent in 1985, 3.8 per cent in 1986 and 3.1 per cent in 1987 (Jeong S-J 2005: 134, 149). These figures underline the fact that it had become difficult for the previous modes of labour discipline and super-exploitation to be imposed on the Korean workers. As a study shows, the drastic increase in Foreign Direct Investment (FDI) by Korean capital in Southeast Asia (ASEAN) between 1986 and 1995 was mainly driven by the goal of obtaining cheap labour (Lee Y 2015b: 450; Shin K-Y 1999: 102–3). Illustratively, while the rate of profit fell in the manufacturing sector from the 1970s onwards, for instance, from 16 per cent in the 1970s to 12 per cent in the 1980s, the rate of profit declined sharply for the ten years leading up to the financial crisis, sliding from 16.3 per cent in 1986 to 6.7 per cent in 1996 (Jeong S-J 2005: 16–8).

If the hasty financial liberalisation and deregulation pursued by the Kim Young-Sam government is contextualised within the contradictory dynamics of capitalism, which gave rise to and at the same time was magnified by social and class struggles, it can be seen foremost as an expression of the thrust of Korean capital to overcome barriers to accumulation. In the face of deteriorating profitability and escalating labour militancy from the mid-1980s onwards, liberalised access to foreign borrowing and credit became a matter of urgency for Korean capital to deter a crisis. However, if it was logical from the perspective of capital for it to resort to borrowing and credit in times of economic downturn, the exposure of the *chaebol* to foreign debt reached unsustainable levels towards the mid-1990s, which became a prelude to the financial crisis of 1997/98. Korean capital faced barriers to accumulation as soon as the factors that had sustained its rapid economic growth, such as US-Japanese favouritism and a super-repressive labour regime, started to break down. In this way, the specific characteristics of *Korean* capitalist development augmented the scale at which the *general* capitalist crisis unfolded.

Once located within the new global economic conditions, as well as a changed social context brought about by democratisation and labour movements, the financial crisis of 1997/98 was one in which the crisis-prone general tendency of capitalism became manifest in a specific way, mediated by Korea's development trajectory, which has been shaped and conditioned by its location in and timing of development in the context of the capitalist world-system. The particular state-bank-*chaebol* relations that characterised the developmental state magnified the intensity of the crisis when they met the dynamics of material social and class forces at various levels, from global and regional to domestic.

Seen in this way, the causes of the financial crisis of 1997/98 and the scale at which it unfolded cannot be explained solely by the pressure of the US and neoliberal institutions, i.e. the IMF and the OECD, to liberalise the financial markets, as if they were disturbing, from outside, an otherwise well-functioning 'national' economy. Nor was the crisis a self-contained process, taking place in isolation from the dynamics of material and social forces, as if finance were separable from production or reducible to a matter of 'policy mistakes', as institutionalists and critics of financial imperialism seem to suggest (see Chapters 2 and 3).

The democratic transition and the developmental state in transition

In the dramatic unfolding of the political and economic crises in late 1997, the Korean state was neither an innocent victim of a global economy nor immune from class contradictions. If financial liberalisation was in part an expression of Korean capital's attempt to overcome deteriorating profitability, the increasing difficulty in imposing a super-exploitative mode of labour discipline was translated into pressure on the government to attack labour by legislating an anti-labour law. The Kim Young-Sam government set up the Labour-Management Relations Reform Committee in May 1996 under the pretext of 'updating' the labour market in accordance with the new democratic era, and tried to legalise flexible layoffs and strengthen legal requirements for strike actions. When the government's initiative for the labour market flexibilisation met strong objections from the labour unions and a lukewarm reception by the opposition parties, it railroaded a labour market reform bill through the National Assembly. In the early morning on December 26, 1996, a day after Christmas, the Kim government passed a labour market reform bill in the presence of only the delegates of the ruling party, without giving notice to the opposition parties. The legislation was completed within seven minutes (see Kim Y-C 1998).

The way in which Kim legislated the anti-labour law not only tarnished his credentials as a former civil activist for democracy; more importantly, the new bill stipulated that the Korean Federation of Trade Unions (KFTU), a state-controlled trade union, was to be the only officially approved labour organisation for three more years. Furthermore, the new bill legalised flexible layoffs, though these were conditional upon corporate emergency, and flexible forms of employment such as temporary agency (dispatch) workers. It also allowed firms to replace strikers with scabs and adopted the principle of 'no wage for strikers' (The *Kyunghyang Shinmun* December 27, 1996; Cumings 1998: 54; Kim Y-C 1998: 1149; Lee Y 2015a: 187). While Kim's anti-labour legislation was immediately met with international criticism and a massive nationwide general strike, the revised laws that were later finalised jointly by the government and opposition parties 'preserved the basic outlines of their controversial predecessors with only a few concessions made' (Kim Y-C 1998: 1156). This reveals the class content of the democratic government – it turned against labour in favour of capital rather blatantly in times when the latter met serious barriers of accumulation. The unconcealed pursuit of anti-labour legislation by the Kim government confirmed the essence of the Korean state as a capitalist state with a clear class orientation.

However, it was not only the Kim Young-Sam government that sought to make the labour market more flexible. Opposition parties, including the National Congress for New Politics led by Kim Dae-Jung, were ambivalent about the labour reform bill until the general strike erupted (Kim Y-C 1998: 1150, 1153–4). It was in fact under the subsequent Kim Dae-Jung government that the labour market was to be further liberalised through the implementation of flexible layoffs with immediate effect (see Conclusion). This underscores the fact that the ultimate objective of the democratic governments lay in their servicing the interests of capital.

On the other hand, economic liberalisation by the Kim government signalled changes in how the Korean state related to capital and society. A peculiar aspect of Kim's liberalisation initiative lay in the fact that it was pursued in the name of democracy. Under circumstances in which the state exercised tight control at the level of economic development, democratisation meant the process of not only removing the authoritarian traits of the state but also withdrawing its interventionist role in the economy: a situation was created in which the civilian government that came into power via democratisation forces from below was empowered to pursue radical economic liberalisation. The tendency of democratisation to facilitate economic liberalisation was also solidified owing to the hitherto close relationship between state elites and capitalist individuals, which had long been criticised as cronyism by radicals and liberals alike (see Chapter 8). While *chaebol* reform failed to alter heightening capital concentration,[16] in the Korean context, democratisation meant regulating the *chaebol* through market rules rather than via state discretion. In this respect, political and economic liberalisation, as introduced by the Kim government, signified an attempt to form 'objective' and 'impartial' relations between state and capital, namely regulation *through the market*, as opposed to 'subjective' and 'personalised' relations, namely through direct state intervention.

Arguably the process to 'rationalise' the state-capital relation had already begun under the previous governments. In fact, the economic liberalisation of the Kim government was the acceleration of what had been initiated by the Chun and Roh governments. For instance, the Chun government liberalised financial markets to a significant degree in an attempt to give the *chaebol* more freedom to raise and borrow capital. At the same time, it made an attempt to form a new kind of relationship with the *chaebol* by regulating them through rules and regulations, and even by employing seemingly anti-*chaebol* (anti-trust) measures, as well as applying the Fair Trade Act more stringently and introducing policies for smaller-scale businesses (Choi I-C 1991).

Democratisation powered and accelerated this process and was to accelerate it even further under the subsequent left-wing liberal governments under Kim Dae-Jung and Roh Moo-Hyun: the more democracy advanced with left-wing liberal governments in power, the more economic liberalisation was accelerated in the name of rationalising the state-capital relation. This tendency in turn strengthened the fetishistic appearance of the Korean state, as if it had suddenly and deliberately shifted its policy orientation from the national to the global and from the state to the market, (see Chapter 3).

Conclusion

The aim of this chapter has been to assess the transformation of the Korean developmental state beyond the statist framework by contextualising it within the dual process of political and economic liberalisation. I have assessed democratisation as a constituting part of class struggles, by which the content of democracy and the extent of its actualisation were determined, and in which the internal and external forces were intertwined. Framing the question of democratisation in this way, I have tried to shed light on why the content of democracy in Korea barely fulfilled the criteria of formal and procedural democracy as prescribed by the ascendancy of liberals over radical social forces, on the one hand and how much the US was an active class force co-responsible for this outcome on the other.

I have also contextualised the specific contents and meanings of democracy in Korea in relation to the capitalist social form and its place in the world market as a 'catch-up' development country. The aspirations for democracy that are primarily geared towards improving political and labour equal rights are given by the capitalist social form, e.g. the apparent equality between exchanges of values, on the one hand, and by the authoritarian government that emerged to 'catch-up' in the hierarchical world-system, on the other. Given the heavy involvement of the state in economic development and the extreme level of social mobilisation for the goal of 'catch-up' development, democratisation was expressed as a challenge to the authoritarian state, reducing state interventionism and rationalising state-capital relations. I have further shown how this particular meaning and content of democracy, in turn, accelerated economic liberalisation under the Kim Young-Sam government, which became a prelude to the financial crisis of 1997/98 once it met the crisis-ridden global capitalist dynamic and intensifying class antagonism created by rapid industrialisation itself.

By placing the causes and intensity of political and economic liberalisation in the interaction of the new global capitalist dynamic and the state-capital-labour relations shaped and underpinned by the developmental state itself, I have offered an analysis alternative to those of the theorists of the developmental state and institutionalists that posit democratisation and labour movements as forces that affect and disintegrate the developmental state externally. I have also tried to overcome the statist accounts enforced by the institutionalists, critics of financial imperialism and recent debates that postulate financial liberalisation and the financial crisis of 1997/98 in terms of the encroachment of the market over the state, of 'the external' over 'the internal' and of 'financial' over 'industrial' interests, i.e. the encroachment of one term of a conceptual dichotomy over the other.

From the dialectic of political and economic liberalisation, I have finally drawn out the implications in relation to the transformation of the Korean developmental state. On the one hand, while democratisation transformed a military dictatorship into a democratically elected civilian government, the class content of the state was expressed in its attack on labour, particularly through the legislation of labour market flexibilisation. On the other hand, while economic liberalisation was primarily an attempt to liberate capital from barriers to accumulation in new economic and social conditions, it signalled a step towards 'objective' and 'depersonalised' state-capital and state-capital-labour relations. The role of democratisation as a force to accelerate economic liberalisation and to depersonalise state-capital and state-society relations was further consolidated in the process of post-crisis reform under the left-wing liberal governments led by Kim Dae-Jung and Roh Moo-Hyun.

Notes

1 The KCIA, established in 1961 with help by the American CIA, symbolised the Park government itself, controlling every arena of Korean life as 'the supreme state agency' (Cumings 1989: 10). Oberdorfer (1997: 15) noted that 'by the early 1970s, the director of the KCIA was more powerful and more feared at home than the prime minister or any other governmental figure except the president himself'.

2 Chun was inaugurated as president on September 1, 1980, after the launch of the coup (the arrest of the head of the Army) on December 12, 1979. This is the slowest coup that has ever taken place anywhere in the world (Kang J-M 2003a: 235).

3 In an interview with journalists, Kim Young-Sam expressed an optimistic view about the prospects of democracy rather than worry about Chun taking a key position in the KCIA and control of the military at the same time. He even expressed his support of Chun on the basis that the junta could restore social order (Kang J-M 2003a: 71–2).

4 On May 30, 1980, the government released an official death toll of 170, of which 144 were civilians, 22 were soldiers and 4 were policemen. Under pressure from the opposition party in 1985, the government released the new figure of 191. This figure is still well below the estimates made unofficially by civil organisations based on witnesses and local-level investigations.

5 For the role of Christians in the democratisation movement in the 1970s and 1980s, see Cumings (1991a: 33) and Lee K-I (2006: 191–2).

6 More evidence of US involvement in Kwangju was revealed later, with US state documents being made available to the public as well as by a special investigation

committee on the Kwangju massacre in the National Assembly in 1989. For a detailed analysis of US relations with Chun and the US reaction to Kwangju based on US state documents declassified in 1996, see Lee S-S (1996).

7 From 1966 to 1982, more than 40 per cent of total investment was made in South and North Kyŏngsang provinces, while 7.3 per cent was made in Kwangju and Chŏlla province. As of 1982, South and North Kyŏngsang provinces amounted to 43.5 per cent of the total capital stock, while Kwangju (Chŏlla province) made up 7.3 per cent (Park H-J and Jeong K-Y 1989: 224).

8 For photographs and oral historiography of the Kwangju massacre, see 'May 18th History Compilation Committee of Kwangju City' (2013) and the film The Taxi Driver, released in 2017.

9 While there is no agreed-upon definition of the term *minjung*, it broadly refers to the social forces that opposed the authoritarian governments and the ruling class. In terms of its composition, it embraces the working class, peasants, urban poor, middle class and petite-bourgeoisies (Sonn H-C 2004: 550). Koo (1993a: 17) offers a different definition. According to him, *minjung* consists of those who were made peripheral to, or alienated from, the political process because of direct and indirect restrictions placed on their political participation by the authoritarian regimes. Koo also emphasises that *minjung* is not a fixed socio-political entity but embodies a dynamic, liberating subjectivity that arises from a history of oppression. For a collection of various essays on Korean minjung movements, see Wells (1995).

10 Some argue that tensions between liberals and radicals were apparent even before the 6/29 Declaration: for instance, in the clash between radicals and liberals in the Incheon Rally in 1986, which revealed their class differences and social orientations (Hart-Landsberg 1989: 65–6; Kang J-M 2003c: 26–30; Lee K-I 2007: 119).

11 For divergent traditions of democracy that emphasise 'socio-economic equality' vis-à-vis 'individual liberty from state interference' and 'political democracy', see Held (1997). For a radical interpretation of democracy as a route to socialism see Wood (1995). For assessments of a limited kind of democracy in Korea, see Kim S-K (1989, 1991, 1999).

12 Measured by the value of products, the ratio of the top 30 firms contributing to GNP increased from 36.6 per cent in 1980 to 38.8 per cent in 1991, 39.6 per cent in 1994 and 40 per cent in 1997 (Lee Y-H et al. 2002: 208: see also Cumings 1999a: 38; Woo-Cumings 1999b: 121).

13 For Marxist discussions of the structural crisis in the Western countries in the 1970s as an outcome of the falling rate of profits, see Shaikh (1979, 1980), Shaikh and Tonak (1994), Moseley (1991), and Duménil and Levy (1993). For Marxist literature on how the structural crisis is related to financial liberalisation, see Itoh and Lapavitsas (1999), Fine et al. (1999), Duménil and Levy (2004). For mainstream or liberal approaches to a move from financial repression during the post-Second World War period to liberalisation from the 1970s onwards, see Helleiner (1994) and Eichengreen (1996).

14 For instance, 'the share of exports subject to import restrictions in industrialised countries had already increased from 32.3 per cent in 1981 to 42.9 per cent of Korea's total exports in 1982, and the number of Korean cases brought under antidumping and countervailing charges jumped from 13 in 1981 to 23 in 1983 and 31 in 1984' (Woo-Cumings 1997: 75). For examples of US protectionist retaliation, see Wood-Cumings (1997: 75–6).

15 The rate of exploitation (calculated as rate of surplus value = [(value added-wages)/wages] × 100) in the manufacturing sector was more than 400 per cent in the 1970s–80s. This rate is nearly twice as high as those of the US and India (Jeong S-J 2005: 130–1).

16 The Kim Young-Sam government's initial reform initiatives gradually lost their early enthusiasm. A measure to enhance financial transparency, *Kŭmyungsilmyŏngje*, which was arguably most welcomed by the Korean public and considered a sign of economic democratisation, was amended twice to make it less stringent. Kim also gradually took on a reconciliatory approach to the former military ruling elites (Kim Y-S 1993).

Conclusion

Democratisation, fetishisation and the transformation of the developmental state

The political economy of Korea after the financial crisis 1997/98 has not been short of political drama. In the midst of the crisis, a left-liberal government led by Kim Dae-Jung came to power, followed by another one under Roh Moon-Hyun. While the rise of these left-liberal governments meant progress in democracy at the formal and procedural level, the tendency of democratisation to accelerate economic liberalisation became more prominent. Deepening economic and social polarisation under the left-liberal governments that came to power on the backs of democratisation movements from below, in turn, contributed to increasingly widespread disillusionment with democracy and to the election of the right-wing conservative Lee Myung-Bak and Park Geun-Hye governments. In the face of the heightening economic polarisation under Lee and Park, public anger eventually developed into the mass candle-light demonstrations against the Park government in 2016, which led to the impeachment of the government and ushered in another left-liberal government led by Moon Jae-In in 2017. In this concluding chapter, I will draw out some of the implications of the transformation of the developmental state by tracing the rise of the left-liberal government in 1997, its fall in 2007 and its re-emergence in 2017.

'Democratising' and 'rationalising' state-capital relations

One of most significant changes that the financial crisis of 1997/98 made possible was the advancement of democracy at the political level, with the left-liberal Kim Dae-Jung elected president in December 1997. The significance of Kim's election lies not only in the fact that it was the first government led by an opposition party; more significantly, as he had failed on three previous attempts to be elected president, partly owing to his 'red' image, having been suspected of sympathies for North Korea, his victory in the presidential election in 1997 marked a step towards a more open and ideologically diverse party-political landscape beyond anti-communism.

Elected in the midst of economic and political turmoil, the Kim Dae-Jung government launched an encompassing and extensive reform programme in a variety of areas, from monetary, fiscal, financial, corporate and labour to social welfare policies. The government dubbed its commitment to carrying out thorough reform 'the second nation-building' (see Seo J-M and Kim H-J 2013: 168–70). It envisioned, as the core aspects of post-crisis reform, reducing state interventionism, strengthening market autonomy, i.e. more economic and financial liberalisation, and deregulation, on the one hand, and 'rationalising' or 'de-personalising' state-capital relations, on the other. In his inauguration speech, Kim Dae-Jung pledged to have 'democracy and market economy harmonize and develop in tandem … there [would be] no collusion between government and business circles'. He argued that 'this kind of misfortune [the financial crisis of 1997/98] would not have happened if leaders who led the nation's politics, economy and finance did not … rely on a government-controlled economy' (Kim D-J 1998). Kim understood the autonomous market as antithetical to direct state intervention as in the old developmental state model: the more the state intervenes in the economy and social affairs, the more it hinders the efficient operation of the market and nurtures corruption (see Kim D-J 1985). The Kim government's tendency to associate 'rationalising' state-capital relations with 'democratisation' and its eventual *realisation* can be explained by several factors.

Throughout the history of Korean capitalism, the Korean public and (left) liberals alike have shown strong antipathy towards the *chaebol* as much as towards the authoritarian and military governments. Much more than being merely accused of being capitalist, i.e. existing by exploiting labour, the *chaebol* were publicly resented and criticised for being 'immoral' and 'illegitimate' in how they went about their businesses (see Choi I-C 2000; Lee J-H 1991; Soh B-H 1997). As discussed in Chapters 7 and 8, from their origins, Korean capitalists could exist as capitalists only by collaborating with the Japanese colonial power and subsequently under the state's favouritism and protection. Particularly the *chaebol* grew into monopoly conglomerates by being given the exclusive right to purchase Japanese-held properties after national independence from Japan and to monopolise foreign aid after the Korean War. Owing to the blatant state favouritism that individual capitalists had enjoyed, these capitalists were also seen as part of the illegitimate state when the Rhee government was ousted by student movements (the April Uprising) in 1960. The strength of public resentment helped Park Chung-Hee, who came to power in 1961, to nationalise banks and control the financial system: the general public and demonstrators perceived the capitalists as 'parasitic' rather than as 'productive' elements of the 'national' economy (see Chapter 8).

Public antipathy towards the *chaebol* did not recede during the periods of the military governments of Park and Chun. When the Park government failed to fulfil its initial pledge to dismantle the monopolistic structure of the *chaebol* in the face of US objections and its own interests, the *chaebol* not only survived dissolution but were offered fresh ways to accumulate by the new military government. The Park government utilised its control of the financial system and the defensive position of the capitalists as means to consolidate and justify Park's 'illegitimate' seizure of state power by achieving rapid and visible development. While the Park government was able to direct and herd capitalists as a collective towards export-led industrial production using financial incentives according to its industrialisation plan, military governments and the *chaebol* were mutually dependent on each other through the exchanges of various forms of state favouritism and bribery.[1] Either actively or tacitly, the *chaebol* cooperated with the Park and Chun governments by financing their political and election campaigns. Furthermore, the *chaebol* benefited from an extreme mode of labour discipline ensured by the authoritarian military governments and relied on state violence in crushing labour unionism and activism. While the *chaebol* formed the Federation of Korean Industry in 1962 to represent their class interests and strove to spread free-market ideology against the state's direct intervention in the economy, no *chaebol* ever allied with social groups to oppose military government.[2] They not only existed antithetically to the working population or *minjung* but were perceived widely by Koreans as the main culprits causing the ills of Korean capitalism.

This legacy of strong public resentment towards the *chaebol* interplayed with new domestic and global forces unleashed by the financial crisis of 1997/98. As it became undeniable that the closely tied and corrupt state-bank-*chaebol* nexus had contributed to the unprecedented scale of the financial crisis, various political and social groups called into question the alleged specific institutional features of Korean capitalism. While a wide range of *chaebol* reforms were being discussed, from restructuring to dismantlement (Jeong S-J 2005: 158–66; see Jeong S-J and Shin J-Y 1999), the arrival of the left-liberal government gave a determinate and narrower meaning to *chaebol* reform. Kim Dae-Jung himself was a victim of the military governments as well as a fierce critic of 'crony' state-*chaebol* relations. The dominant view amongst left-liberals was that the crisis was caused primarily by the 'abnormalities' of Korean capitalism, that is, the particular state-*chaebol* relations shaped under the military government or the 'cronyism' of the 'developmental state'. A consensus formed between left-liberals and democratisation social forces that the heavy borrowing and reckless expansion of businesses by the *chaebol* were a manifestation of a lack of democracy and transparency. In this context, subjecting capital or the *chaebol* to the market logic and taking the state's hands off the market became priorities of post-crisis reform, presented as measures for 'democratising' state-capital relations.[3]

This particular reading of the ills of Korean capitalism and the motif of 'rationalising' state-market relations were also commensurate with what the International Monetary Fund (IMF) demanded. In granting rescue loans to the Korean government to bail out the debt-ridden economy, the IMF demanded, as conditionality, that rationalisation measures be implemented. These involved restructuring and eliminating non-performing banks and bad loans; expansion of commercialisation (marketisation) in the banking business; developing the capital market; and liberalisation of the securities markets, including their opening to foreigners and allowing foreign investment in the domestic financial sector (Bank of Korea 1999; Kim S-J 2005; Lim S-H 2000). In association with corporate (*chaebol*) reform, it also required the Korean government 'to eliminate intersubsidiary loan guarantees, lower debt-to-equity ratios, and to improve transparency' (Cumings 1998: 63). In other words, the agenda of the IMF was, to a large extent, in tune with that of the Kim Dae-Jung government and left liberals in general. The commensurability between Kim's position and that of the IMF is further evidenced by the fact that US officials praised Kim as the man who transcended the divide between Asian and Western values (Lee 2000: 100). Cumings even called him 'the IMF's man in Seoul' (1998: 60).

Seen in this way, the direction, content and intensity of post-crisis reform were determined by the interplay between the rise of the left-liberal government led by Kim Dae-Jung, a particular trajectory of state-capital relations that represented the 'developmental state' itself, and the specific post-crisis context in which Korea had to accommodate the demands of the IMF. In a situation in which the left-liberals became a hegemonic force at the specific historical conjuncture of the aftermath of the financial crisis, the primary goal of post-crisis reform was limited to the rationalisation or 'normalisation' of state-capital relations. Put differently, the content and scale of post-crisis reform were *neither* driven by external imposition alone, e.g. by the IMF, *nor* the result of the state losing its supposed policy autonomy over the class of capitalists. Misinterpreting the contents and processes of post-crisis reform in either of these ways results from a conceptual framework that counterposes the internal and the external, and the national and the global, as categories antagonistic to each other.

The class content and form of the democratic state

The limitations of the conceptual framework that posits the national and the global as antithetical can be further demonstrated by bringing to the fore the class content of the Kim government or the capital-serving function of post-crisis reform. As has been demonstrated by authors from various intellectual and political positions, the Kim government actively pursued radical restructuring programmes in the financial (banking) sector and the corporate sector (see Baliño and Ubide 1999; Cho B-H 2004; Cumings 1999b; Kim K-W 2002; Kim S-J and Jang S-H 2003; Lee B-C 2005; Lee Y-H 2001, 2002; Pirie 2008). On the one hand, the government proactively carried out banking and corporate reforms by inducing, coaxing and forcing dissolution, merger and acquisition of banks, financial institutions and the *chaebol* in trouble. For instance, it implemented 'the big deal', whereby the top five *chaebol* were forced to swap each of their subsidiaries so that they would specialise in core businesses. On the other hand, the government 'de-politicised' the financial sector so that the latter attained a greater degree of autonomy from the government in lending decisions.

When the Kim government's post-crisis reform is assessed under the framework of the conceptual dichotomies of the state-market and the internal-external, it appears to be contradictory in terms of what it claimed to achieve and the manner in which it acted: while the Korean state claimed to become less interventionist, it still performed the role of providing plan rationality in economic management. In fact, for some, the manner in which the banking reform and the 'big deal' were implemented, and the kinds of policies devised for small venture companies are reminiscent of the highly interventionist 'developmental state' (Choi I-C 1991; Kim K-W 2002; Lee Y-H 2001, 2002, 2006; Mosley 2005; Weiss 2005). To others, the state's refraining from financial allocation attests to the decline or dismantlement of the Korean developmental state or a shift to a regulatory (neoliberal) state (Jayasuriya 2005; Pirie 2005, 2008) – although commentators differ over whether these changes were rational (Matthew 1998; Pirie 2005, 2008) or policy failures (Chang H-J 1998; Chang H-J and Yoo C-G 1999; Weiss 2005) (see Chapters 2 and 3).

However, the tension between heavy state intervention and market-orientated reform appears to be puzzling insofar as state and market are assumed to play a zero-sum game, that is, one loses its power inevitably over the other, and different types of states are categorised primarily by the extent to which they intervene in and control the market, and how much the state orientation shifts from the national to the global. An alternative perspective that can resolve the apparent contradictions between the post-crisis Korean state's enforcement of post-crisis reform in the 'developmental state style' and its claim to establish a market-regulated economy brings the question of the *capitalist* state to the fore, analysing it in terms of its class content (its capital-serving function) and form.

The Kim government's post-crisis financial and corporate reforms were tightly intertwined with the liberalisation of the financial markets that were opened to foreign capital. Since the financial crisis of 1997/98, the foreign share of ownership of major listed companies and financial institutions has dramatically increased (see Kim S-J 2005). The foreign investors' share in the stock market also soared after the financial crisis. The share of foreign investors *vis-à-vis* the total share prices in the stock market was on the rise under the Kim Young-Sam government's 'globalisation' policy initiative: for instance, from 7.7 per cent in 1993 to 14.5 per cent in 1997. After the financial crisis, it increased to 21.9 per cent in 1999, 31.1 per cent in 2000 and 36.6 per cent in 2001 (Kim S-J and Jang S-H 2003: 83). Within two years of the inauguration of the Kim Dae-Jung government, four major commercial banks became foreign owned and seven securities companies and three life insurance companies became owned by foreign capital (Sonn H-C 2004: 534). As of August 2004, of the total eight commercial banks, four were more than 50 per cent foreign-held, and three of these had a foreign institution as the largest shareholder, which put 62.5 per cent of the banks under foreign management (Cho B-H 2004: 14). The ratio of foreign shareholding of prominent firms amounted to, as of November 2002, 80.5 per cent of SK Telecom, 54.7

per cent of *Samsung* Electronics, 60.8 per cent of *Pohang* Iron and Steel Company (POSCO) and 48.6 per cent of *Hyundai* Motors (Kim S-J and Jang S-H 2003: 83).

The heightened foreign investment in the stock market and ownership of banks and firms have not endangered the predominance of the *chaebol* in the Korean economy. The state's official endorsement of the stock market as the main mechanism for capital to be raised further benefits the *chaebol* because only highly recognisable firms, mostly the *chaebol*, are able to raise capital through the stock market. Investments, whether from domestic or foreign investors, were concentrated on these firms, which has the effect of enriching the *chaebol*. Illustratively, the proportion of the top 10 *chaebol*'s share value in the stock market against the total of all listed firms increased from 45.1 per cent in 1999 to 52 per cent in 2002. Within the general trend of heightening capital concentration, with the collapse of many prominent *chaebol* firms during the financial crisis of 1997/98, capital concentration *among* the *chaebol* also became apparent, with *Samsung* emerging as predominant. As of 2002, the value-added production by *Samsung* amounted to 28.9 per cent of that contributed by the top 30 *chaebol* firms (Kim K-W 2002: 47). The share value of *Samsung* alone *vis-à-vis* the total share of listed firms in the stock market rose from 12.6 per cent in 1995 to 25 per cent in 2002 (Kim K-W 2002: 47). The trend of capital concentration has been strengthened continuously since – the asset value of the top 10 *chaebol* increased from 48 per cent of GDP in 2003 to 84 per cent in 2012 (Lee Y 2015a: 195). The share of asset value of the top 5 *chaebol vis-à-vis* GDP increased from 57 per cent in 2012 to 60 per cent in 2015 (Kim T-K 2017: 57).

The fact that post-crisis reform involved the radical opening of the financial markets to foreign investors stirred nationalist sentiment amongst some Koreans and led many left-leaning (including Marxist) scholars to address the transfer of domestic value to the external forces (the US), which some define as the imperialist characteristics of finance-dominated contemporary capitalism (see Chapter 3). While there is some truth to this, those who perceive 'external' forces as driving post-crisis reform and being responsible for the negative aspects of post-crisis reform, e.g. an increase in the volatility of the financial market and a decrease in productive investment, implicitly prioritise the antagonism between the internal and the external over that of capital and labour. However, as seen above, a view that opposes the interests of the external (i.e. global capital) and the internal (i.e. the nation) cannot fully account for the persistent dominance of 'domestic' capital, the *chaebol*. Moreover, such a view is flawed in that it tends to downplay the fact that domestic and industrial capital *pushed for* financial liberalisation as much as financial and foreign capital did before the crisis (see Chapter 9). While the financial market has become more volatile, and stock market prices have become increasingly dependent on the movements of large institutional investors (Choi Y-C 2007; Kim S-H and Choi B-H 1999), a study of investor behaviour in the financial markets showed that domestic institutional investors have proven to be more short-term oriented than foreign investors: there is no evidence that domestic investors are more productive and more concerned with long-term industrial investment (Kim S-J 2005: 24–5).

To the extent that financial and banking reform presupposed and was accompanied by labour market reform (see below), the 'external' forces of global capital constitute a dynamic element of the overall constellation of class and social struggle rather than a structure superimposed upon, or a force antithetical to, the national, the domestic or the internal. No less than domestic and industrial capital, foreign and financial capital that took over domestic firms and banks had a major stake in flexibilising the labour market. Contrary to its rhetorical opposition to state interventionism, the IMF 'tolerated' a massive amount of public funds being spent on re-capitalising (and nationalising) banks and firms in bankruptcy before they were sold to foreign capital or taken over by other firms. The existence of a hierarchy amongst portions of capital in terms of nationality and scale notwithstanding, *capital as a universal social form* – irrespective of its particular forms of appearance as foreign, domestic, financial or industrial – is bound by its *constitutive* interest to subordinate and exploit labour, and impose or restore labour discipline.

Seen in this way, the transformation of the Korean developmental state cannot be comprehended by the statist conception that opposes the categories of state-market, internal-external and industrial-financial interests to each other. The existence of the Korean state is an expression of class domination within the capitalist world-system before it is developmental, neoliberal or regulatory. The Korean state is capitalist not because it represents 'national' or 'domestic' capital but because it ensures capital interest in general by *transcending* and synthesising the partially differential interests of 'global', 'domestic', 'financial' and 'industrial' capital. The very interests of capital-in-general are represented and ensured by the state.

While it is important to recognise the continued capital-serving function (the class content) of the Kim Dae-Jung government as a capitalist state, it is equally crucial to recognise changes in the way in which the Korean state relates to capital and society at large. Even if the post-crisis reform did not alter but rather strengthened the predominant position of the *chaebol*, it had the effect of rationalising their corporate practices by reducing their levels of debt (leverage ratio). In the case of the electronics and manufacturing sectors, the average ratio of debt was reduced to 114 per cent and 104 per cent in 2004, respectively, from 424.6 per cent and 396.3 per cent in 1997 (Bank of Korea, as cited in Kim C-K 2006: 14). This level of corporate debt was lower than what had been asked for by the IMF (200 per cent), and this trend has stabilised.

The decreasing ratio of debt servicing by the *chaebol* produced the tendency of industrial capital to become more *independent* of rather than subordinated to financial capital. This trend should, of course, be understood in relative terms, given that Korean non-financial firms had been highly indebted throughout the post-Korean War development period: the drain of profits from the industrial sector to the financial sector had been a defining feature of the Korean economy during the high-growth period (Jeong S-J 2004: 170). In this respect, contrary to what is understood as a key characteristic of contemporary capitalism, sometimes defined as 'financialisation', that is, the flow of value from the industrial to the financial sector (Arrighi 1994; Cho B-Y 2007; Crotty 2000; Duménil and Levy 2004; Krippner 2005; Lee K-K 2005), in the context of Korea, due to its legacy of a development model based on a high level of debt, the reverse is taking place, with a lowering level of servicing debt and interest. This declining dependency of industrial capital on financial capital suggests the rise of new state-capital relations in which, at an immediate level, industrial capital has become freer from direct state discretion, which had been exercised primarily through the control of the domestic financial system.

Together with the *chaebol's* diminishing reliance on the state's financial intermediation, post-crisis reform that prioritised 'democratising' state-capital relations has contributed to making the state appear to lose its power against the latter. To the degree that financial liberalisation and post-crisis reform were geared towards and succeeded in rationalising corporate practices, they facilitated the tendency to transform the role of the state into one akin to an objective and neutral party, assuming more 'normal' characteristics as a capitalist state: the state appears to be further detached from the 'economic' sphere, and class domination is assured more by economic than by extra-economic means, such as direct state oppression. Seen from a critique of state fetishism and the national development fetish, as set out in Chapter 6, this does not point to the loss of state autonomy *vis-à-vis* the market and the global economy but to the 'normalisation' of state-society relations or the consolidation of state fetishism.

Democratisation and 'insecure society'

As much as the Kim government's financial and corporate reforms unveiled its capitalist nature, its labour market reform confirmed this characterisation. In fact, labour market reform had been one of the most contentious issues since the previous government. When the Kim Young-Sam government's controversial railroading of a bill on legalising flexible layoffs and subcontracting instantly provoked a nationwide general strike (see Chapter 9), it was withheld and revised to the effect that the enforcement of flexible layoffs was meant to be delayed for two years and permitted only under corporate emergency. However, as soon as the Kim Dae-Jung government came into power, it legislated for new labour laws that would allow the *immediate* implementation of flexible layoffs with practically no restrictions (see Kim Y-C 1998: 1157). Prior to this legal change, although workers were under a repressive labour regime, layoffs had required court approval and supervision (see Doucette and Kang 2018: 205).

The enormity of the social and economic repercussions of the new labour laws cannot be overemphasised. Under the Kim Dae-Jung government, Korea became the country with the highest proportion of irregular workers in the Organisation for Economic Co-operation and Development (OECD) (Martin and Torres 2001: 6, as cited in Chang D-O and Chae J-H 2004: 436). More fundamentally, a large proportion of insecure employment has become a defining and permanent feature of the Korean labour market in the post-crisis era. The ratio of irregular workers ('fixed-term employment' and 'part-time employment', taken together) was one of the highest by international standards, standing at 51.9 per cent as opposed to 45 per cent in the Netherlands, 28.4 per cent in the UK and 16.1 per cent in the US as of 2012 (Lee Y 2015a: 190).[4] As of 2017, Korea's share (20.6 per cent) of 'temporary employment' was among the highest in the OECD, well above the G7 average (8.1 per cent) and the OECD average (11.2 per cent).

The upsurge of irregular employment meant the rise of a precarious, 'insecure society' characterised by deteriorating living conditions of the lower strata of the population and deepening economic and societal polarisation. Wage income disparities between the bottom 90 and the top 10 per cent increasingly widened to 5.2 times in 2001, 5.5 times in 2002 and 5.6 times in 2003, which was even higher than those in the US at 4.3 times (Kim Y-S 2004: 16; see also Hwang S-O 2009; Kim C-K 2006: 18).[5] Irregular contract workers received only half of what regular contract workers did for the same kind of labour: an average ratio of the monthly income of irregular workers *vis-à-vis* that of regular ones stood at 52.7 per cent in 2002, even decreasing to 51 per cent in 2003 (Kim Y-S 2004: 16; see Lee Y 2015b: 452). The ratio of workers with low-paid employment, i.e. earning less than two-thirds of the average income, increased from 22.9 per cent in 2001 to 25.9 per cent in 2005. This was the highest level within the OECD, even higher than that of the US at 18.1 per cent (Lee B-C 2005: 56). This trend not only continued but worsened over the following decade (see Jang G-Y 2013). Furthermore, Korea has been among the lowest spending countries in terms of social or welfare spending. Even as of 2016, it was still the country with the lowest social spending amongst the OECD members, spending 10.4 per cent of its GDP, a figure lower than that of Chile at 11.2 per cent and that of Turkey at 13.5 per cent.

An increase in the number of irregular workers to above 50 per cent of the total labour force has in effect changed the mode and content of labour struggles and the general position of labour in Korean society (see Jeong S-J 2003; Lee J-S 2002; Lim H-C and Jang J-H 2006). As there is a slim chance for a regular worker made redundant to be reemployed as a regular worker, the labour union movements led by regular workers have increasingly prioritised maintaining their continuous employment as regular workers, whereas irregular workers have struggled to attain the status of regular workers (Lee Y 2015b: 453; see also Kim W 2005). The sharpening division within the labour market along the lines of regular versus irregular workers has made it difficult to form a broad labour movement, which has fundamentally weakened the (bargaining) position of labour in general (Chun 2009: 544; Lee Y 2015b: 455).

The tendency for democratisation to proceed in parallel with deepening economic polarisation and a weakening of the position of labour was strengthened under another left-liberal government: that of Roh Moon-Hyun (2003–07). Roh was from a much humbler background than Kim Dae-Jung and indeed most other politicians: he was from a poor peasant family, did not have university education and was a self-taught human rights lawyer and democratisation activist. Roh's election itself can be seen as significant for democracy to the extent that a person from such a modest background could rise to the presidency. However, the Roh government proved to be similar to the previous Kim Dae-Jung government in pursuing labour market reform along neoliberal lines. Tellingly, Roh himself described his own government as 'left-wing neoliberal' (*Nodongja Chŏnsŏn* 2017: 12). Reneging on his promise to serve 'ordinary' Koreans and carry out democratic reforms, he did not fulfil his pledge to abolish the National Security Law, even when his party, the *Uri* Party, which he established when, soon after his election, he defected from the New Millennium Democratic Party, became the majority ruling party. The Roh government then gradually shifted its priority from 'democratic reform' to 'reviving the economy' (Kang S-D 2009). It consented to the US's request to send troops to Iraq in spite of strong public opposition, claiming that it was a 'strategic choice in the national interest'. It also drove economic liberalisation under the motto of 'making Korea the Financial Hub of North East Asia' and actively sought to conclude Free Trade Agreements (FTAs) with the US and various other countries (Choi H-I 2007; Kim Y-H and Jeong J-H 2006; Seo J-M and Kim H-J 2013: 171–3).

More significantly, the Roh government made the labour market even *more* flexible. Overturning his initial vow to put a stop to the abuse of irregular contracts, Roh legislated new labour laws that *extended* flexible employment. Under the laws legislated in November 2006, the categories of jobs in which 'dispatch/subcontracting' employment would be permitted were expanded, and the time limit on the use of such employment was lengthened (Korea Human Rights 2012; Sonn H-C 2006: 346–7). While the new laws included a clause obliging the conversion of irregular to regular contracts after two years of employment, namely the Irregular Employment Protection Act, they had the effect of consolidating the legal base of irregular contracts and the 'dispatch/subcontracting' form of employment. As one commentator put it, 'the Irregular Employment Protection Act was … legal pathways for illegal employer practices' (Chun 2009: 544). Moreover, the Roh government did not refrain itself from exercising state violence when it saw this to be necessary. It responded to labour strikes by relying on hard-line measures, particularly against those operating outside the legal limit – the institutionalisation and legalisation of labour management provided the state with a better justification to intervene and break up *illegal* activities. The Roh government deployed riot police to break up labour protests led by female irregular workers, as seen in the Korea Train Express (KTX) Crew Workers' struggle in 2006/07 and E-Land Trade Union's occupation movement in 2007/08 (see Chun 2009).

The fact that economic and social polarisation deepened under the left-liberal governments created the paradox that Koreans live in the most economically unequal society under the most democratic governments. This contradictory dynamic had the effect of undermining democracy itself by nurturing the ground for the rise of right-wing conservative governments.[6] Koreans' support for democracy decreased, while the prioritisation of economic growth over democracy increased (Kalinowski 2008: 458): a survey revealed that the ratio of Koreans who think 'democracy is always preferable' dropped from 69 per cent in 1997 to 49 per cent in 2001/02, whereas those who think 'authoritarianism is sometimes preferable' increased from 20 per cent to 33 per cent in the same period (Korea Barometer Survey 2004). This signalled that Koreans were becoming increasingly susceptible to nostalgia for past military regimes, particularly that of Park Chung-Hee, who had been presented by the conservative media as a figure who saved the country from poverty and achieved rapid industrialisation. In fact, Korean scholars attentive to the rapid social polarisation under the left-liberal governments warned that this would lead to a nostalgia for the Park dictatorship, often described as 'fascism' (see Baek N-C 2005; Kim S-H and Park S-H 2005; Lee K-I 1997, 1998, 2001; Sonn 2006: 350). The resurgence of nostalgia for Park was manifest in the election of the right-wing conservative governments of Lee Myung-Bak in 2008 and Park Geun-Hye, the eldest daughter of Park Chung Hee, in 2012.

The election of right-wing conservative governments with a strong heritage from the Park Chung-Hee dictatorship can be explained on several levels. First, even if democratisation allowed former anti-military dissidents to be elected, including Kim Young-Sam, Kim Dae-Jung and Roh Moo-Hyun, these presidents were 'progressive' only to the degree that they challenged military rule and dictatorship. Once military rule ended, and at least formal and procedural democracy was in place, they became part of a force that prevented democracy from advancing in a more progressive direction. In retrospect, Korean liberal elites only allied with mass democratisation movements to secure their ascension to power and bitterly competed with each other for personal gain at the expense of larger social goals, which in the end contributed to debasing the achievements hard earned by democratisation and labour struggles from below (see Chapter 9 and above). In this respect, Korean liberal elites are co-responsible for fostering the cynicism and disillusionment with democracy that enabled the election of the right-wing governments.

On the other hand, the limitations of the governments led by the liberal elites need to be addressed beyond personal and moral grounds. The fact that they were considered 'progressive', even though they were merely supporters of a market economy and liberal democracy, can also be explained by the fact that Korean society had long been denied a minimum level of civil rights under ultra-oppressive military regimes. Under such circumstances, social movements are likely to take the form of a challenge to the authoritarian state with an agenda centred on calling for civil and political rights (see Chapter 6). In this respect, the 'catch-up' conditions can even determine what counts as 'progressive' at any particular historical juncture. In other words, if the authoritarian developmental state bears the imprint of Korea's position in the world market, enforcing the capitalist plan rationality through overt social control and violence, Korea's positioning in the world market also mediated how class and social struggles manifested themselves, and defined the limits of the agendas these forces could embrace. To the extent that the actions of the liberals are a product of the historical dynamic of global capitalism, their limitations are also inherent to the capitalist world-system itself.

Finally, the rise of the conservative governments was also related to the fact that the financial crisis of 1997/98 was overcome at the expense of the working population and the poor in a more intensive mode than it was in developed countries. The costs of economic crises in contemporary 'democratic' capitalist societies are socialised through the mobilisation of and injection of public money into the financial system by the governments. However, the financial crisis in Korea was overcome by imposing austerity measures from without (as an IMF conditionality) as opposed to policies that could have improved liquidity, e.g. quantitative easing, as usually devised for developed countries, notably the US, which reduce in relative terms the adverse impacts on working people.[7] This also points to the fact that the positioning of the Korean economy in the hierarchical world-system conditions the ways in which crises are managed and, to a great degree, determines the intensity and impacts of crises on the general public and the lower strata of the population.

Combined with a minimum level of social welfare and increasing casualisation of the labour market, in the context of Korea, austerity measures, such as the imposition of stringent capital adequacy ratio rules on banks, contracted the economy and augmented the severity of the adverse impacts of the crisis on working people and the poor. The hardship that Koreans had to bear thus resulted in part from the position of the Korean economy in the capitalist world-system, which, in turn, limited the liberal governments' room for policy manoeuvre and the possibilities to expand democratisation beyond the formal and procedural levels. In this respect, the meaning of democracy cannot be solely determined at the domestic level of social and class struggle: world-systematic factors and the need for 'catch-up' development condition the social and economic substance of democracy and its resilience.

The right-wing governments and the arrival of 'Hell-Chosŏn'

While the failure of democratisation to further socio-economic equality allowed the rise of the right-wing governments, economic and social polarisation deepened even further under the Lee and Park governments. The Lee government pursued what were deemed 'pro-market' policies, such as the large-scale privatisation of the public sector, from electricity, water and railways to education, and at the same time what appeared to be 'developmental' policies, such as a large-scale, government-led infrastructure project. In addition to actively pursuing trade and financial liberalisation (e.g. a Free Trade Agreement with the US), it relaxed the rules on industrial capital's (the *chaebol's*) ownership of commercial banks. Whilst reducing corporate tax, it adopted 'flexible working hours', i.e. allowed employers to change and decide flexibly the working hours of employees (see Cho W-K 2008; Goldner 2008; Kalinowski 2007, 2008; Kalinowski and Cho 2008; Kim T-K 2008; Korea Human Rights April 5, 2012; Park J-S 2008; Roh J-K 2009).

While pursuing pro-rich and pro-*chaebol* policies, the Lee government resorted to authoritarian methods in handling social and labour movements. It denied the public servants' union (Korea Government Employees Union) the status of a legal entity, on the basis of which unionists who were either openly critical of the government or engaged in collective action were prosecuted. It also coercively broke up the candle-light demonstrations in 2008 (Koh B-K 2008), the Korean Rail strike in 2009 (Chang H-C 2010) and the *Ssangyong* Motors strike in 2009, which took place against massive layoffs (Goldner 2009). The Lee government deployed more than 3,000 policemen to repress the *Ssangyong* Motors strike case, which ended with the imprisonment of 22 leading union members.

Similarly, Park abandoned her election campaign pledge of 'economic democratisation' as well as her promise to carry out a parliamentary investigation of the *Ssangyong* Motors strike case (Lee Y 2015b: 457). The Park government implemented labour policies aimed at making the labour market more flexible and competitive, including a peak salary system whereby the highest wage level is capped, after which wage decreases in return for continued employment, and the extension of the competitive performance-based salary system to the public sector (Jung H-J 2018). The government even filed a petition with the Constitutional Court in November 2013 to have a small left-wing party, the United Progressive Party (UPP), disbanded on the grounds that it was unconstitutional, even though political parties representing the interests of labour and distributive justice issues had long been absent or very weak in Korean politics (see Sung D-H 2016). The UPP was accused of having violated the National Security Law and was dissolved by order of the Constitutional Court a year later (Doucette and Koo 2016: 200; Lee Y 2015b 454).

The Lee and Park governments cannot be equated with the former military governments in their social and labour management as they avoided indiscriminate outright repression and resorted to democratic values to justify their courses of action, at least superficially, such as the rule of law (see Doucette and Koo 2016: 204). However, under these governments, the authoritarian features of government were strengthened, and at the same time economic polarisation reached the point of endangering the reproduction of the capitalist social relation itself. Numerous signs of social disintegration surfaced.

Korea was infamously the country with the highest rate of suicide amongst OECD members from 2003 to 2015: it fell to second place in 2016 only because the state with the highest suicide rate in the world, Lithuania, joined the club. If 'economic downturn and weakening social integration' can account for the high rate of suicide, as the OECD put it, post-crisis Korea is characterised by a heightening of the economic hardship of working people and an increase in social polarisation. Similarly, starting from a phrase invented in the late 2000s, '800,000 won (800 USD) Generation', which referenced the average monthly income of irregular workers in their 20s (Ooh S-H and K-I Park 2008), other new phrases that express the hardship of the youth have proliferated since. For instance, '*Sam-Po* (three give-up) generation' denotes the youth who have given up 'dating, marriage and children', and '*Oh-Po* (five give-up) generation' denotes those who have given up 'friendship and home ownership' in addition to the other three give-ups. Above all, the term that encapsulates a sense of deep social despair is 'hell-Chosŏn' (see Park N-J 2014, 2016). It refers to the notion that Korean society turned into a hell. It is notable that present Korean society is equated with that under the pre-modern Chosŏn Dynasty, where social mobility was blocked. Heightening precarity of living conditions, particularly amongst youth, is reflected in a low birth rate: the birth rate of Korea has been one of the lowest in the world for the last decade and was the lowest in the OECD in 2015.

Amidst the signs of social disintegration, public discontent was eventually expressed against the Park government in late 2016, initially triggered by a seemingly 'apolitical' probe into a group of people who allegedly conducted illegal gambling. This gradually turned into a serious corruption scandal between the *chaebol* and high-level state officials, with the revelation that the closest confidants of President Park had been involved. In addition, it was exposed that President Park had been under the influence of a shaman woman called Choi Soon-Sil, who was at the centre of the corruption scandal. Candle-light anti-government demonstrations re-emerged and developed into a nationwide mass movement that called for the impeachment of President Park. On December 3, 2016, 2.32 million people joined anti-government demonstrations nationwide (*The Korea Herald* December 11, 2016). In the face of anti-government demonstrations widely joined by trade unions, various civil society groups, ordinary citizens and (junior) students, the National Assembly was forced to propose and pass the bill for the impeachment of President Park on December 9, 2016. The Constitutional Court unanimously ruled in favour of Park's impeachment in March 2017. After the fall of the Park government, presidential elections soon followed on May 9, 2017. Moon Jae-In, from the opposition Democratic (*Minju*) Party, was elected president (see Dudden 2017; Han H-K 2017).

Democratisation and state fetishism

Although the candle-light demonstrations fell short of forming an alternative political force from below and only allowed a conventional liberal party to be elected, they were still significant for advancing democracy. Above all, the fall of the Park government due to mass movements from below has contributed to weakening the legacy and the myth built around former President Park Chung-Hee that was the hallmark of an ultra-conservative right-wing sect, which had long exerted strong influence on Korean politics. After the demise of the Park Geun-Hye government, her party, *Saenuri*, split into two, with 30 defectors setting up a new party claiming to represent 'proper' conservatism. These two conservative parties, the right-wing and left-wing liberal parties as well as a small left-wing labour party (the Justice Party) took part in the presidential election. If the previous elections had primarily been framed in terms of competition between democratisation *vis-à-vis* anti-democratisation (military) forces, this time the election was framed in terms of competition between conservatives, moderates and progressives (*Nodongja Chŏnsŏn* 2017: 10). This change is highly significant as it meant that Korean party politics had made an important step towards 'normal' multiparty competition along different political lines and policy differentials rather than along regional affiliations, one of the defining features of Korean politics since the Park Chung Hee government (see Chapter 9).

Moreover, the fall of the Park government due to the candle-light demonstrations pressured the Moon government to adopt what a commentator labelled 'social liberalism' by addressing economic polarisation as a key issue to be dealt with and emphasising the 'social' aspects of the market (Kim H-I 2017: 34). Coming to power through the explosive discontent expressed against the Park government, Moon pledged to pursue 'development led by income growth', aiming to alleviate the problem of social disintegration caused by the casualisation of the labour market. The new government claimed to build a 'democracy centred on citizens rather than the state' and named 'justice' as the core principle that would guide its policies. It promised to prioritise the resolution of economic and social polarisation, and place citizens' rights before business interests or interests of the state (The Moon Jae-In Government 2017: 8–9). Notable moves the Moon government undertook along these lines included raising the minimum wage, converting irregular contracts into regular ones in the public sector and initiating public sector-led job creation (Jung H-J 2018: 12–4; Lee J-S 2018; *Nodongja Chŏnsŏn* 2017: 14–5). The Moon government abolished the performance-based salary system in the public sector introduced by Park, which had been a source of tension between the Korea Government Employees Union and the government. It also launched ambitious anti-corruption reforms, particularly targeting the Prosecution Office, which had been the locus of political power and abuse. It filled the cabinet with former democratisation activists, many of whom had a history of imprisonment (like President Moon himself), and appointed left-leaning reformists to key government positions.

Nevertheless, the rise of the left-liberal government does not alter the fundamental fact that it remains capitalist. The class content of the left-liberal government is found most obviously in the fact that it pursues a *functioning* capitalist economy. The kind of society that the Democratic Party envisions as desirable is a 'human-centred democratic market economy whereby the rights of citizens are protected, social discrimination and inequality are reduced, and capital and labour coexist' (The Democratic Party Manifesto). Although the Moon government puts emphasis on the 'social' aspects of the market, its embrace of the 'social' is, first of all, meant to make the market function well. As a reflection of this, it takes the view that the predominance of the *chaebol* in the Korean economy, particularly their abusive relations with smaller companies (subcontractors or suppliers), can be resolved by strengthening the fairness of the market and through the principle of comparative advantage: the former specialise in the global markets, while the latter focus on innovation (The Moon Jae-In Government 2017: 19).

Apart from the fact that the left-liberal government is, in the context of the capitalist mode of production, inevitably a capitalist government, its limits in realising even its moderate reform plans have quickly become evident. The Moon government has softened its *chaebol* reform plan, aimed at ensuring 'fairness' in the market: the chairperson of the Fair Trade Commission, formerly known to be a fierce critic of the *chaebol*, stated that 'we would implement a sustainable reform through close dialogue with enterprises (the *chaebol*)' (see Kim H-I 2017: 41). The government also legislated what could be seen as straightforwardly free-market and pro-rich policies in July 2018 under the pretext of reviving the market and entrepreneurship. The new laws stipulated the gradual reduction of income tax, corporate tax and VAT until 2023; the real estate tax for resident houses was to be raised, whilst the same tax for the land owned by the *chaebol* was to be frozen. The government passed a law significantly relaxing the restrictions on industrial capital's ownership of financial firms in the area of internet banking in October 2018, which Moon's Democratic Party, as opposition, had fiercely opposed when it was proposed by the Park government (see *Pressian* August 7, 2018; *Ohmynews* October 16, 2018).

While more complete evaluations of the Moon governments will be produced in the years to come, the Moon government has thus far shown a pattern typical of all Korean liberal governments: it gestured towards *chaebol* reform in the name of democratisation at the beginning but soon softened its approach and attempted to solve what are described as economic problems by relying on and supporting the *chaebol*. Another common feature of the left-liberal governments has also been in evidence: forming an alliance with democratisation social forces, including labour against authoritarian governments, then turning against labour once in power. It is true that the Moon government tried to fulfil its promise to implement the conversion of irregular contracts to regular ones in the public sector. However, the conversion scheme was modest in scale and primarily involved the extension of irregular contracts without improving wages and other welfare conditions, in addition to causing a great deal of confusion and antagonism among workers (Jung H-J 2018: 17–8): the labour unions diverged over whether all irregular workers should be converted unconditionally to regular employees or go through a new round of recruitment competition; some existing regular workers opposed the unconditional conversion of irregular workers to regular ones on the basis this would breach the principle of meritocracy. In addition, while the minimum wage increased in 2017, new labour laws that have the effect of cancelling out the rise were passed in May 2018. The new laws stipulated that a bonus and welfare subsidies (e.g. meals and transport fares) would be included in the minimum wage, and that the employers would be permitted to change and apply related rules without an agreement with workers.

Now, the implications of the re-emergence of the left-liberal government can be formulated in relation to the class content and form of the Korean state. The Moon government clearly showed itself to be a capital-serving force. If the previous left-liberal governments led by Kim and Roh were the active agents of implementing neoliberal reforms in an attempt to remove barriers to capital accumulation by 'rationalising' corporate practices and attacking labour in the name of democratisation, the Moon government carries out the mission to safeguard capitalist social reproduction by mitigating the adverse social impacts of the very same neoliberal reforms that the left-liberals had been actively pursuing. Put differently, the Kim and Roh governments utilised the economic crisis to attack labour in the name of socialising the costs of the Asian financial crisis, while the Moon government exploits the candle-light demonstration movements as an opportunity to mitigate the contradictions of capitalism in a situation in which the reproduction of capitalist social relations increasingly meets its own limits.

It is beyond dispute that democratisation in Korea has been a progressive force as an expression of mass aspirations for a freer and more equal society. At the same time, it has been a force that served capital by providing the channels through which the contradictions of capitalism and class antagonism, particularly those accelerated after the financial crisis of 1997/98, are diluted. These dual aspects of democratisation are inherent in the capitalist social form, but their specific actualisation is associated with 'catch-up' development: class antagonism and the demand for equality as one of its forms of expression are given in the capitalist value form as such, but the particular conditions of 'catch-up' development magnified the intensity of the financial crisis and its adverse impact on the general population and the working class. These effects, in turn, rendered democracy vulnerable to being reversed and lacking socio-economic substance beyond political and legal rights.

At the same time, democratisation movements from the 1960s to the 2016 candle-light demonstrations cumulatively contributed to eliminating the authoritarian façade of the state. They have changed the mode of existence of the capitalist state and the ways in which the capitalist class contradiction expresses itself. They have helped to transform the form of appearance of the Korean state into an objective and neutral instance, in its *form* more in keeping with the 'normal' (ideal-typical) relation between the state and capital, although this tendency was somewhat interrupted under the right-wing Lee and Park governments. In brief, democratisation allows the Korean state to increasingly assume the form that is in keeping with this 'normality' of state and society as fetish-forms of the capitalist mode of production. In this respect, democratisation is simultaneously a process of consolidating state fetishism.

Notes

1 On the scale of corruption and the amount of bribery by the *chaebol* to the military governments, see Kang (2002). The trials of Chun and Roh revealed that big business groups had supplied more than 1.5 billion US dollars to Chun and Roh in the 1980s (Cumings 1999a: 35).

2 The fact that military governments and *chaebol* mutually supported each other does not mean that there were no conflicts between them and within segments of the ruling class. For a study of the struggle for hegemony between the state and the capitalist class from the 1960s to the 1980s, see Suh J-J (1989, 1990). For a study of the political and social networks, including personal ties via marriages between state elites and the families of the *chaebol*, see Suh J-J (1988b).

3 The most commonly articulated form of criticism of *Samsung* is confined to its illegal, immoral, undemocratic and antiquated (family-run and top-down management) characteristics. See, for instance, Pressian (2008). For a liberal critique of *chaebols'* internal structures, see Kim K-W (2002).

4 Different definitions of 'irregular workers' affect the statistics. For instance, the Korean government excludes long-term temporary workers and seasonal workers, while Lee Y (2015a: 190) calculates the number of 'irregular workers' as the sum of those in fixed-term employment and part-time employment.

5 For a study of the most prominent mode of wealth disparities in Korea that is associated with landownership rather than income differentials, see Sonn N-K (2008). For a general structure of class inequality in Korea, see Shin K-Y (2004).

6 I assessed this contradictory dynamic in depth elsewhere within the framework of the dialectic of democratisation and de-democratisation (see Song H-Y 2013a).

7 For the differences between developed and developing countries concerning the ways in which financial crises are managed, and the disproportionately adverse impacts on the working population and the poor in the developing countries, see Rude (2005).

Bibliography

Abrams, P. (1982) *Historical Sociology*. Ithaca, NY: Cornell University Press.

Adams, J., Clemens, E. S. and Orloff, A. S. (eds). (2005) *Remaking Modernity: Politics, History, and Sociology*. Durham, NC: Duke University Press.

Amin, S. (1976) *Unequal Development*. New York: Monthly Review Press.

Amin, S. (1978) 'Unequal Development: An Essay on the Social Formations of Peripheral Capitalism', *Science and Society* 42(2): 219–22.

Amin, S. (2013) 'China 2013', *Monthly Review* 60(4). https://monthlyreview.org/2013/03/01/china-2013/ (accessed November 19, 2014).

Amsden, A. (1979) 'Taiwan's Economic History: A Case of Etatisme and a Challenge to Dependency Theory', *Modern China* 5(3): 341–80.

Amsden, A. (1985) 'Taiwan's State and Economic Development', in P. B. Evans, D. Rueschemeyer and T. Skocpol (eds) *Bringing the State Back In*, pp. 78–106. Cambridge: Cambridge University Press.

Amsden, A. (1989) *Asia's Next Giant: South Korea and Late Industrialization*. New York: Oxford University Press.

Amsden, A. (1990) 'Third World Industrialization: "Global Fordism" or a New Model?', *New Left Review* 182: 5–31.

Amsden, A. (1994) 'Why Isn't the Whole World Experimenting with the East Asia Model to Develop? Review of the East Asian Miracle', *World Development* 22(4): 627–33.

Amsden, A. (1997) 'Editorial: Bringing Production Back In – Understanding Government's Economic Role in Late Industrialization', *World Development* 25(4): 469–80.

Amsden, A. (2001) *The Rise of 'the Rest': Challenges to the West from Late-Industrializing Economies*. Oxford: Oxford University Press.

Amsden, A. (2007) *Escape from Empire: The Developing World's Journey through Heaven and Hell*. Cambridge, MA and London: MIT Press.

Anderson, P. (1974) *Lineages of the Absolute State*. London: New Left Books.

Andreoni, A. and Chang, H-J. (2017) 'Bringing Production and Employment Back into Development: Alice Amsden's Legacy for a New Developmentalist Agenda', Special Issue *Cambridge Journal of Regions, Economy and Society* 10(1): 173–87.

Armstrong, P., Glyn, A. and Harrison, A. (1991) *Capitalism since 1945*. Oxford: Blackwell.

Arrighi, G. (1990) 'The Developmentalist Illusion: A Reconceptualization of the Semiperiphery', in G. W. Martin (ed) *Semiperipheral States in the World-Economy*, pp. 11–42. New York: Greenwood Press.

Arrighi, G. (1994) *The Long Twentieth Century: Money, Power, and the Origins of Our Times*. London: Verso.

Arrighi, G. (2007) *Adam Smith in Beijing*. London: Verso.

Arrighi, G. and Drangel, J. (1996) 'The Stratification of the World-Economy: An Exploration of the Semiperipheral Zone', *Review* (Summer): 9–74.

Arrighi, G., Silver, B. J. and Brewer B. D. (2003) 'Industrial Convergence, Globalization, and the Persistence of the North–South Divide', *Studies in Comparative International Development* 38(1): 3–31.

Arthur, C. J. (1989) 'Editor's Introduction', in E. B. Pashukanis. *Law and Marxism: A General Theory*, pp. 9–35. Worcester: Pluto Press.

Baek, Nak-Cheong. (2005) 'Pak Chŏng-hŭi rŭl ŏttŏt'ge saenggak halkka' ('How to Think of Park Chung-Hee?'), *Ch'angjak kwa Pip'yŏng* (*Creations and Criticism*) 128: 289–97.

Balassa, B. (1980) 'The Process of Industrial Development and Alternative Development Strategies', *Princeton University, Essays in International Finance* (No. 141): 1–44.

Balassa, B. (1988) 'The Lessons of East Asian Development: An Overview', *Economic Development and Cultural Change* 36(3): S273–90.

Balibar, E. (1991) 'Preface', in E. Balibar and I. Wallerstein. *Race, Nation, Class: Ambiguous Identities*, pp. 1–14. London and New York: Verso.

Baliño, T. J. and Ubide, A. (1999) 'The Korean Financial Crisis of 1997 – A Strategy of Financial Sector Reform', *Monetary and Exchange Affairs Department, IMF Working Paper* (No. 99/28): 1–66.

Bank of Korea. (1999) *Sinhŭng sijangguk ŭi ŭnhaeng kucho chojŏng hyŏnhwang* (*Restructuring of the Banking Sector in Emerging Markets*). Seoul: Bank of Korea.

Barker, C. (1978) 'A Note on the Theory of Capitalist States', *Capital and Class* 4(1): 118–26.

Barrow, C. W. (1993) *Critical Theories of the State: Marxist, Neo-Marxist, Post-Marxist*. Madison: University of Wisconsin Press.

Barrow, C. W. (2005) 'The Return of the State: Globalization, State Theory, and the New Imperialism', *New Political Science* 27(2): 123–45.

Beeson, M. (2009) 'Developmental States in East Asia: A Comparison of the Japanese and Chinese Experience', *Asian Perspective* 33(2): 5–39.

Beeson, M. and Islam, I. (2005) 'Neo-Liberalism and East Asia: Resisting the Washington Consensus', *Journal of Development Studies* 41(2): 197–219.

Bello, W. (1992) *People and Power in the Pacific: The Struggle for the Post-Cold War Order*. London: Pluto Press.

Bello, W. (1998) 'The End of the Asian Miracle'. www.tni.org/en/article/the-end-of-the-asian-miracle (accessed June 22, 2019).

Bello, W. and Cunningham, S. (1994) 'Trade Warfare and Regional Integration in the Pacific: The USA, Japan and the Asian NICs', *Third World Quarterly* 15(3): 445–58.

Bello, W. and Rosenfeld, S. (1990) *Dragons in Distress: Asia's Miracle Economies in Crisis*. San Francisco: Institute for Food and Development Policy.

Bergesen, A. (1984) 'The Critique of World-System Theory: Class Relations or Division of Labor?', *Sociological Theory* 2: 365–72.

Bergeson, A. (2015) 'World-System Theory after André Gunder Frank', Review Symposium on André Guner Frank's ReOrienting the 19th Century, *Journal of World-Systems Research* 21(1): 147–61. http://jwsr.pitt.edu/ojs/index.php/jwsr/issue/view/61 (accessed June 15, 2015).

Berman, M. (1982) *All That Is Solid Melts into Air.* New York: Penguin Books.
Bhagwati, J. (1978) 'Foreign Trade Regimes: Overall Conclusions', in National Bureau of Economic Research, *Anatomy and Consequences of Exchange Control Regimes*, pp. 205–18. www.nber.org/chapters/c1025.pdf (accessed November 15, 2017).
Bhagwati, J. (1988) 'Export-Promoting Trade Strategy: Issues and Evidence', *World Bank Research Observer* 3(1): 27–57.
Bieler, A., Bonefeld, W., Burham, P. and Morton, A. D. (2006) *Global Restructuring, State, Capital & Labour: Contesting Neo-Gramscian Perspective.* Basingstoke: Palgrave Macmillan.
Bieler, A. and Morton, D. A. (2003) 'Globalisation, the State and Class Struggle: A 'Critical Economy' Engagement with Open Marxism', *British Journal of Politics and International Relations* 5(4): 467–99.
Bank for International Settlements (BIS) (1997). 67th Annual Report. www.bis.org/publ/ar67f01.pdf (accessed September 9, 2019).
Black, T. and Black, S. (1999) 'The Korean Financial Crisis: Causes, Effects and Solutions', *Policy* (Autumn): 42–47.
Blanke, B., Jürgens, U. and Kastendiek, H. (1978) 'On the Current Marxist Discussion on the Analysis of Form and Function of the Bourgeois State: Reflections on the Relationship of Politics to Economics', in J. Holloway and S. Picciotto (eds) *State and Capital: A Marxist Debate*, pp. 108–47. London: Edward Arnold.
Block, F. (1977) *The Origins of International Economic Disorder: A Study of US International Monetary Policy from World War II to the Present.* Berkeley: University of California Press.
Bonefed, W. (1987) 'Reformulation of State Theory', *Capital and Class* 33(1): 96–127.
Bonefeld, W. (1992) 'Social Constitution and the Form of the Capitalist State', in W. Bonefeld, R. Gunn and K. Psychopedis (eds) *Open Marxism*, vol. 1, pp. 93–132. London: Pluto Press.
Bonefeld, W. (2000) 'The Spectre of Globalisation: On the Form and Content of the World Market', in W. Bonefeld and K. Psychopedis (eds) *The Politics of Change: Globalisation, Ideology, and Critique*, pp. 31–68. Basingstoke and New York: Palgrave.
Bonefeld, W. (2004a) 'Critical Economy' and Social Constitution: A Reply to Bieler and Morton', *British Journal of Politics and International Relations* 6(2): 231–37.
Bonefeld, W. (2004b) 'On Postone's Courageous but Unsuccessful Attempt to Banish the Class Antagonism from the Critique of Political Economy', *Historical Materialism* 12(3): 103–24.
Bonefeld, W. (2006) 'Social Constitution and the Spectre of Globalisation', in A. Bieler, W. Bonefeld, P. Burham and A. D. Morton (eds) *Global Restructuring, State, Capital & Labour: Contesting Neo-Gramscian Perspective*, pp. 45–67. Basingstoke: Palgrave Macmillan.
Bonefeld, W. (2008) 'Global Capital, National State, and the International', *Critique* 36(1): 63–72.
Bonefeld, W., Brown, A. and Burnham, P. (1995) *A Major Crisis? The Politics of Economic Crisis in the 1990s.* Aldershot: Dartmouth.
Bonefeld, W., Gunn, G. and Psychopedis, K. (1992) 'Introduction', in W. Bonefeld, R. Gunn and K. Psychopedis (eds) *Open Marxism*, vol. 1, pp. ix–xx. London: Pluto Press.
Bonefeld, W. and Holloway, J. (eds). (1995) *Global Capital, National States and the Politics of Money.* London: Macmillan.

Booth, A. and Deng, K. (2017) Japanese Colonialism in Comparative Perspective, *Journal of World History* 28(1): 61–98.

Brazinsky, G. (2005) 'From Pupil to Model: South Korea and American Development Policy during the Early Park Chung Hee Era', *Diplomatic History* 29(1): 83–115.

Brenner, R. (1977) 'The Origins of Capitalist Development: A Critique of Neo-Smithian Marxism', *New Left Review* 104: 25–92.

Brenner, R. (1998) 'The Economics of Global Turbulence', Special Issue *New Left Review* 229.

Brewer, A. (1980) *Marxist Theories of Imperialism*. London: Routledge.

Bruff, I. (2009) 'The Totalisation of Human Social Practice: Open Marxists and Capitalist Social Relations, Foucauldians and Power Relations', *The British Journal of Politics and International Relations* 11(2): 332–51.

Burkett, P. and Hart-Landsberg, M. (1996) 'The Use and Abuse of Japan as a Progressive Model', *Socialist Register* 32: 62–92.

Burnham, P. (1991) 'Neo-Gramscian Hegemony and the International Order', *Capital and Class* 15(3): 73–92.

Burnham, P. (1994) 'Open Marxism and Vulgar International Political Economy', *Review of International Political Economy* 1(2): 221–31.

Burnham, P. (1997) 'Globalisation: States, Markets and Class Relations', *Historical Materialism* 1(1): 150–60.

Burnham, P. (2001) 'Marx, International Political Economy and Globalisation', *Capital and Class* 25(3): 103–12.

Byres, T. (1991) 'The Agrarian Question and Differing Forms of Capitalist Agrarian Transition: An Essay with Reference to Asia', in J. Breman and S. Mundle (eds) *Rural Transformation in Asia*, pp. 3–76. Oxford: Oxford University Press.

Byres, T. (1996) *Capitalism from Above and Capitalism from Below: An Essay on Comparative Political Economy*. London: Macmillan Press.

Calhoun, C. (1996) 'The Rise and Domestication of Historical Sociology', in T. J. McDonald (ed) *The Historic Turn in the Human Sciences*, pp. 305–36. Ann Arbor, MI: The University of Michigan Press.

Cammack, P. (1989) 'Review Article: Brining the State Back In?', *British Journal of Political Science* 19(2): 261–90.

Cammack, P. (2003) 'The Governance of Global Capitalism', *Historical Materialism* 11(2): 37–59.

Cammack. P. (2007) 'Class Politics, Competitiveness and the Developmental State', *Manchester Metropolitan University, Papers in the Politics of Global Competitiveness* (No. 4): 1–16.

Cathie, J. (1997) 'Financial Contagion in East Asia and the Origins of the Economic and Financial Crisis in Korea', *Asia Pacific Business Review* 4(2/3): 18–28.

Cha, Sang-Chul. (2005) 'Ijenhawŏ, Yi Sŭng-man, kŭrigo 1950-yŏndae ŭi hanmi kwange' ('Eisenhower, Rhee Syngman, and Korea-US Relations in the 1950s'), *Mikuksa Yŏn'gu* (*Korean Journal of American History*) 13: 121–67.

Chang, Dae-Oup. (2001) 'Bringing Class Struggle Back into the Economic Crisis: Development of the Crisis in Class Struggle in Korea', *Historical Materialism* 8(1): 185–213.

Chang, Dae-Oup. (2009) *Capitalist Development in Korea: Labour, Capital and the Myth of the Developmental State*. London: Routledge.

Chang, Dae-Oup. and Chae, Jun-Ho. (2004) 'The Transformation of Korean Labour Relations Since 1997', *Journal of Contemporary Asia* 34(4): 427–48.

Chang, Ha-Joon. (1993) 'The Political Economy of Industrial Policy in Korea', *Cambridge Journal of Economics* 17(2): 131–57.

Chang, Ha-Joon. (1994) 'State, Institutions and Structural Change', *Structural Change and Economic Dynamics* 5(2): 293–313.

Chang, Ha-Joon. (1997) 'Critical Survey: Economics and Politics of Regulation', *Cambridge Journal of Economics* 21(6): 703–28.

Chang, Ha-Joon. (1998) 'Korea: The Misunderstood Crisis', *World Development* 26(8): 1555–61.

Chang, Ha-Joon. (1999) 'Industrial Policy and East Asia – The Miracle, the Crisis, and the Future', paper presented at the World Bank Workshop on *Re-thinking East Asian Miracle*, pp. 1–45. San Francisco, CA (February 16–17).

Chang, Ha-Joon. (2000) 'An Institutionalist Perspective on the Role of the State: Towards an Institutionalist Political Economy', in L. Burlamaqui, A. C. Castro and H-J Chang (eds) *Institutions and the Role of the State*, pp. 3–26. Cheltenham: Edward Elgar.

Chang, Ha-Joon. (2002a) 'Breaking the Mould: An Institutionalist Political Economy Alternative to the Neo-liberal Theory of the Market and the State', *Cambridge Journal of Economics* 26(5): 539–59.

Chang, Ha-Joon. (2002b) *Kicking Away the Ladder: Development Strategy in Historical Perspective*. London: Anthem Press.

Chang, Ha-Joon. (2003) *Globalization, Economic Development and the Role of the State*. London: Zed Books.

Chang, Hae-Chul. (2010) 'Yi Myŏng-bak chŏngbu e matsŏn ch'ŏldo nodongjadŭl ŭi t'ujaeng' ('Railway Labour's Struggle against the Lee Myeong-Bak Government'), *Chŏngse wa Nodong* (*Situations and Labour*) 57: 19–27.

Chang, H-J., Park, H-J. and Yoo, C-G. (1998) 'Interpreting the Korean Crisis: Financial Liberalization, Industrial Policy and Corporate Governance', *Cambridge Journal of Economics* 22(6): 735–46.

Chang, H-J. and Yoo, C-G. (1999) 'The Triumph of the Rentiers? The 1997 Korean Crisis in a Historical Perspective', *New School for Social Research, Center for Economic Policy Analysis Working Paper* (No. 12): 1–36.

Chang, Jun-Kab. (2002) 'Han'guk chŏngjaeng chikhu miguk ŭi hanbando chŏngch'aek (1953–54)' ('American Policy toward Korea, 1953–54'), *Mikuksa Yŏn'gu* (*Korean Journal of American History*) 15: 133–55.

Chase-Dunn, C. (1981) 'Interstate System and Capitalist World-Economy: One Logic or Two?', in W. L. Hollist and J. N. Rosenau (eds) *World System Structure: Continuity and Change*, pp. 30–53. Beverly Hills, CA: Sage.

Chibber, V. (1999) 'Building a Developmental State: The Korean Case Reconsidered', *Politics and Society* 7(3): 309–45.

Chibber, V. (2002) 'Bureaucratic Rationality and the Developmental State', *American Journal of Sociology* 107(4): 951–89.

Chibber, V. (2003) *Locked in Place: State-Building and Late Industrialization in India*. Princeton, NJ: Princeton University Press.

Chibber, V. (2005) 'Reviving the Developmental State? The Myth of the "National Bourgeoisie"', *Socialist Register* 41: 144–65.

Cho, Bok-Hyun. (2004) 'Oewhanwigi ihu kŭmyung chedo ŭi pyŏnhwa wa kyŏngjejŏk hyokwa' ('Changes in Financial Institutions and Effects on the Economy after the Financial Crisis'), paper presented at the Conference *Han'guk Sahoe Kyŏngje*

Hakhoe (*Korea Society Economy Conference*), pp. 1–29. Seoul: Kookmin University (November 6).

Cho, Bok-Hyun. (2007) 'Kŭmyung chudo ch'ukjŏkch'eje ŭi hyŏngsŏng kwa kŭmyung chabon ŭi chibae' ('The Formation of Finance-led Accumulation and the Rule by Finance Capital'), in Hyeong-Ki Kim et al. (eds) *Hyŏndae chabonjuŭi punsŏk* (*An Analysis of Contemporary Capitalism*), pp. 381–428. Seoul: Hanul.

Cho, Hee-Yeon. (1994) 'Han'guk esŏ ŭi minjujuŭi ŭi ihaeng e kwanhan chŏngch'i sahoehakjŏk yŏn'gu: kukka, chŏngch'i sahoe, simin sahoe pyŏnhwa e taehayŏ' ('A Political Sociological Study of Democratisation in Korea: Division of the State, Political Society and Civil Society'), *Tonghyang kwa Chŏnmang* (*Current and Prospect*) 121: 245–98.

Cho, Hee-Yeon. (2002) '"Paljŏn kukka" ŭi pyŏnhwa wa kukka – simin sahoe, sahoe undong ŭi pyŏnwha' ('Changes in the 'Developmental State': Changes in Civil Society and Social Movements'), *Sahoe wa Chŏlhak* (*Society and Philosophy*) 4: 293–351.

Cho, Hee-Yeon. (2004) 'Pangong kyuyul sahoe wa nodonja kyekŭp ŭi kusŏngjŏk ch'ulhyŏn' ('Anti-Communist Society and the Emergence of the Working Class'), *Tangdae Pip'yŏng* (*Current Review*) 26: 195–213.

Cho, Hee-Yeon. (2005a) 'Pak Chŏng-hŭi ch'eje ŭi pokhapsŏng kwa mosunsŏng' ('The Complexities and Contradictions of the Park Chung-Hee Regime'), *Yŏksa Pip'yŏng* (*Critical Review of History*) 70: 387–426.

Cho, Hee-Yeon. (2005b) 'Pak Chŏng-hŭi sidae chaepyŏngga nonŭi ŭi insinronjŏk sŏnggyŏk kwa chaengjŏmdŭl' ('A Study on the Epistemological Characters and Issues in the Recent Debate on the Re-evaluation of the Park Chung-Hee Era'), *Kyŏngje wa Sahoe* (*Economy and Society*) 67: 298–365.

Cho, Myong-Rae. (2008) 'Taeunha wa sin(jayujuŭi) kaebal kukka ŭi pongyŏkhwa' ('The Grand Waterway Project and the Full-Fledged Manifestation of Neoliberal Developmentalism'), *Whankyŏng kwa Saengmyŏng* (*Environment and Life*) 56: 63–82.

Cho, Won-Kwang. (2008) 'Yuyŏnhwa ch'eje ŭi pŭroletariatŭ, pijŏnggyujik' ('Proletarians in the Flexible Labour Regime, Irregular Workers'), *alteRevolution* 2: 156–79.

Cho, Young-Chul. (2007) 'Oewhanwigi ihu han'guk kyŏngje kujo ŭi pyŏnhwa' ('The Structural Transformation of the Korean Economy since the Financial Crisis'), *Tonghyang kwa Chŏnmang* (*Current and Prospect*) 69: 147–76.

Choi, Doo-Yull. and Lee, Yeon-Ho. (2002) 'Kŭmyung kamdok kwa oehwan wigi: chonghap kŭmyung hoesa e taehan chaedojŏk chŏpkŭn' ('Financial Supervision and the Financial Crisis: An Institutional Approach to Korea' Merchant Banking Corporations'), *Han'guk Kyŏngje Yŏn'gu* (*Journal of Korean Economic Studies*) 8: 171–208.

Choi, Hyeong-Ick. (2007) 'Hanmi FTA, kongwhaguk minjujuŭi ŭi wigi' ('Korea-US FTA, Republican Democracy at Risk'), *Chinbo P'yŏnron* (*Progressive Review*) 28: 225–39.

Choi, In-Chul. (1991) '1980-yŏndae pusilgiŏp chŏngri kwajŏng e kwanhan yŏn'gu' ('A Study on the Restructuring of Non-Performing Firms in the 1980s'), *Sahoe Kyŏngje Pyŏngron* (*Society Economy Review*) 3: 65–118.

Choi, In-Chul. (2000) 'Han'guk ŭi ŭnhaeng chungsim kŭmyung chedo wa kiŏp chibae kujo' ('Korea's Bank-based Financial System and Corporate Structure'), *Tonghyang kwa Chŏngmang* (*Current and Prospect*) 46: 201–7.

Choi, Jang-Jip. (1993) 'Political Cleavages in South Korea', in H. Koo (ed) *State and Society in Contemporary Korea*, pp. 13–50. Ithaca, NY: Cornell University Press.

Chu, Yin-wah. (2009) 'Eclipse or Reconfigured? South Korea's Developmental State and Challenges of the Global Knowledge Economy', *Economy and Society* 38(2): 278–303.

Chun, J. J. (2009) 'Legal Liminality: The Gender and Labour Politics of Organising South Korea's Irregular Workforce', *Third World Quarterly* 30(3): 535–50.

Chung, Jin-A. (2008) 'Yi Sŭng-man chŏngkwŏn ŭi charip kyŏngjeron, kŭ chihyang kwa hyŏnsil' ('The Economic Independence Plan and Policy of the Rhee Syngman Government: The Chasm between Intention and Reality'), *Yŏksa Pip'yŏng (Critical Review of History)* 83: 89–116.

Chung, Jin-A. (2009) 'Yi Sŭngman chŏngkwŏngi kyŏngje kaebal 3-kaenyŏn kaehoek ŭi naeyong kwa sŏnggyŏk' ('Rhee Syngman Government's Three-year Economic Development Plan'), *Han'kukhak Yŏn'gu (Journal of Korean Studies)* 31: 353–86.

Clarke, S. (1977) 'Marxism, Sociology and Poulantzas's Theory of the State', *Capital and Class* 1(2): 1–33.

Clarke, S. (1988) *Keynesianism, Monetarism and the Crisis of the State*. Cambridge: Edward Elgar.

Clarke, S. (1991) 'The State Debate', in S. Clarke (ed) *The State Debate*, pp. 1–69. London: Macmillan.

Clarke, S. (1992) 'The Global Accumulation of Capital and the Periodisation of the Capitalist State Form', in W. Bonefeld, R. Gunn and K. Psychopedis (eds) *Open Marxism*, vol. 1, pp. 133–50. London: Pluto Press.

Clarke, S. (1994) *Marx's Theory of Crisis*. London: Macmillan.

Cox, R. W. (1996) *Approaches to World Order*. Cambridge: Cambridge University Press.

Crotty, J. (2000) 'Trading State-Led Prosperity for Market-Led Stagnation: From the Golden Age to Global Neoliberalism', *University of Massachusetts Amherst, Political Economy Research Institute*. 1–36.

Crotty, J. (2002) 'The Effects of Increased Product Market Competition and Changes in Financial Markets on the Performance of Nonfinancial Corporations in the Neoliberal Era', *University of Massachusetts Amherst, Political Economy Research Institute Working Paper* (No. 44): 1–41.

Cumings, B. (1981) *The Origins of the Korean War*. Princeton, NJ: Princeton University Press.

Cumings, B. (1984) 'The Origins and Development of the Northeast Asian Political Economy: Industrial Sectors, Product Cycles, and Political Consequences', *International Organization* 38(1): 1–40.

Cumings, B. (1989) 'The Abortive Abertura: South Korea in the Light of Latin American Experience', *New Left Review* 173: 5–32.

Cumings, B. (1997) *Korea's Place in the Sun: A Modern History*. New York: Norton.

Cumings, B. (1998) 'The Korean Crisis and the End of "Late" Development', *New Left Review* 231: 43–72.

Cumings, B. (1999a) 'The Asian Crisis, Democracy, the End of "Late" Development', in T. J. Pempel (ed) *The Politics of Asian Economic Crisis*, pp. 17–44. Ithaca, NY: Cornell University Press.

Cumings, B. (1999b) 'Webs with No Spiders, Spiders with No Webs: The Genealogy of the Developmental State', in M. Woo-Cumings (ed) *The Developmental State*, pp. 61–92. Ithaca, NY and London: Cornell University Press.

The Democratic Party of Korea, Manifesto. http://theminjoo.kr/platform.do#n; http://bomiscoming.tistory.com/24 (accessed October 30, 2017).

Deyo, F. C. (1987) 'State and Labor: Modes of Political Exclusion in East Asian Development', in F. C. Deyo (ed) *The Political Economy of the New Asian Industrialism*, pp. 182–202. Ithaca, NY: Cornell University Press.

Dikötter, F. (ed). (1997) *The Construction of Racial Identities in China and Japan.* London: Hurst & Company.

Doucette, J. and Kang, S. (2018) 'Legal Geographies of Labour and Postdemocracy: Reinforcing Non-standard Work in South Korea', *Transactions of the Institute of British Geographers* 43(2): 200–14.

Doucette, J. and Koo, S-W. (2016) 'Pursuing Post-Democratisation: The Resilience of Politics by Public Security in Contemporary South Korea', *Journal of Contemporary Asia* 46(2): 198–221.

Douglass, M. (1983) 'The Korean Saemaul Undong: Accelerated Rural Development in An Open Economy', in M. A. Lea and D. P. Chaudhri (eds) *Rural Development and the State*, pp. 186–213. London: Methuen & Co. Ltd.

Dudden, A. (2017) 'Revolution by Candlelight: How South Koreans Toppled a Government', *Dissent* (Fall). www.dissentmagazine.org/article/revolution-by-candlelight-how-south-koreans-toppled-a-government (accessed April 15, 2019).

Duménil, G. and Levy, D. (1993) *The Economics of the Profit Rate: Competition, Crises, and Historical Tendencies.* Aldershot, Hants, England: Edward Elgar.

Duménil, G. and Levy, D. (2004) *Capital Resurgent: Roots of the Neoliberal Revolution.* Cambridge, MA: Harvard University Press.

Eckert, C. J. (1996) 'Total War, Industrialization, and Social Change in Late Colonial Korea', in P. Duus, R. H. Myers and M. R. Peattie (eds) *The Japanese Wartime Empire 1931–1945*, pp. 3–39. Princeton, NJ: Princeton University Press.

Eckert, C. J. (2014) *Offspring of Empire: The Koch'ang and the Colonial Origins of Korean Capitalism, 1987–1945.* Seattle: University of Washington Press.

Eichengreen, B. (1996) *Globalizing Capital: A History of the International Monetary System.* Princeton, NJ: Princeton University Press.

Emmanuel. A. (1972) *Unequal Exchange: A Study of the Imperialism of Trade.* New York and London: NLB.

Engels, F. (1850) *Peasant War in Germany.* www.marxists.org/archive/marx/works/1850/peasant-war-germany/index.htm (accessed March 5, 2017).

Escobar, A. (1995) *Encountering Development: The Making and Unmaking of the Third World.* Princeton, NJ: Princeton University Press.

Evans, P. B. (1987) 'Class, State and Dependence in East Asia: Lessons for Latin Americanists', F. Deyo (ed) *The Political Economy of the New Asian Industrialism*, pp. 203–26. Ithaca, NY: Cornell University Press.

Evans, P. B. (1989) 'Predatory, Developmental and Other Apparatuses: A Comparative Political Economy Perspective on the Third World State', *Sociological Forum* 4(4): 561–87.

Evans, P. B. (1995) *Embedded Autonomy.* Princeton, NJ: Princeton University Press.

Evans, P. B. (1997) 'The Eclipse of the State? Reflections on Stateness in an Era of Globalization', *World Politics* 50(1): 62–87.

Evans, P. B. (2008a) 'In Search of the 21st Century Developmental State', *University of Sussex, Centre for Global Political Economy Working Paper* (No. 4): 1–22.

Evans, P. B. (2008b) 'Is an Alternative Globalisation Possible', *Politics and Society* 36(2): 271–305.

Evans, P. B., Rueschemeyer, D. and Skocpol, T. (1985) 'On the Road toward a More Adequate Understanding of the State', in P. B. Evans, D. Rueschemeyer and T. Skocpol (eds) *Bringing the State Back In*, pp. 347–66. Cambridge: Cambridge University Press.

Evans, T. (2004) 'Marxism and Post-Keynesian Theories of Finance and Business Cycle', *Capital and Class* 28(2): 47–100.

Fei, J. C. (1983) 'Evolution of Growth Policies of NICs in a Historical and Typological Perspective', paper presented at the Conference on *Patterns of Growth and Structural Change in Asia's NICs and Near-INCs in the Context of Economic Interdependence*. Honolulu: University of Hawaii (April 3–8).

Fine, B. (2001) 'Neither the Washington nor the Post-Washington Consensus', in B. Fine, C. Lapavitsas and J. Pincus (eds) *Development Policy in the 21st Century: Beyond the Post-Washington Consensus*, pp. 1–27. New York: Routledge.

Fine, B. (2006a) 'The New Development Economics', in K. S. Jomo and B. Fine (eds) *The New Development Economics: After the Washington Consensus*, pp. 1–20. London: Zed Books.

Fine, B. (2006b) 'The Developmental State and the Political Economy of Development', in K. S. Komo and B. Fine (eds) *The New Development Economics: After the Washington Consensus*, pp. 101–22. London: Zed Books.

Fine. B. (2013) 'Beyond the Developmental State: An Introduction', in B. Fine, J. Saraswati and D. Tavasci (eds) *Beyond the Developmental State*, pp. 1–32. London: Pluto.

Fine, B., Lapavitsas, C. and Milonakis, D. (1999) 'Addressing the World Economy: Two Steps Back', *Capital and Class* 23(1): 47–90.

Fine, B., Lapavitsas, C. and Pincus, J. (eds). (2001) *Development Policy in the 21st Century: Beyond the Post-Washington Consensus*. New York: Routledge.

Fine, B. and Saad-Filho, A. (2004) (4th ed.) *Marx's Capital*. London: Pluto Press.

Fine, R. (2002) *Democracy and The Rule of Law: Marx's Critique of the Legal Form*. Caldwell: Blackburn Press.

Fischer, A. M. (2015) 'The End of Peripheries? On the Enduring Relevance of Structuralism for Understanding Contemporary Global Development', *Development and Change* 46(4): 700–32.

Fischer, A. M. (2018) 'Debt and Development in Historical Perspective: The External Constraints of Late Industrialisation Revisited through South Korea and Brazil', *The World Economy* 41(12): 3359–78.

Frank, A. G. (1979) *Dependent Accumulation and Underdevelopment*. New York: Monthly Review Press.

Furman, J. and Stiglitz, J. (1998) 'Economic Crises: Evidence and Insights from East Asia', *Brookings Papers on Economic Activity* 2: 1–115.

Gereffi, G. and Fonda, S. (1992) 'Regional Paths of Development', *Annual Review of Sociology* 18: 419–48.

Gereffi, G. and Wyman, D. (eds). (1990) *Manufacturing Miracles: Paths of Industrialisation in Latin America and East Asia*. Princeton, NJ: Princeton University Press.

Gerschenkron, A. (1962) *Economic Backwardness in Historical Perspective*. Cambridge, MA: Harvard University Press.

Gerstenberger, H. (1978) 'Class Conflict, Competition and State Formation', in J. Holloway and S. Picciotto (eds) *State and Capital: A Marxist Debate*, pp. 148–59. London: Edward Arnold.

Gerstenberger, H. (1992) 'The Bourgeois State Form Revisited', in W. Bonefeld, R. Gunn and K. Psychopedis (eds) *Open Marxism*, vol. 1, pp. 151–76. London: Pluto Press.

Giddens, A. (1979) *Central Problems in Social Theory*. London: Macmillan.

Gills, B. and Rocamora, J. (1992) 'Low Intensity Democracy', *Third World Quarterly* 13(3): 501–23.

Gills, B., Rocamora, J. and Wilson, R. (1993) *Low Intensity Democracy: Political Power in the New World Order*. London: Pluto Press.

Gills, S. (1999) 'The Geopolitics of the Asian Crisis', *Monthly Review* 50(10): 1–10.

Glassman, J. (2015) 'Emerging Asias: Transnational Forces, Developmental States, and "Asian Values"', *The Professional Geographer* 68(2): 322–9.

Glassman, J. and Choi, Y-J. (2014) 'The *Chaebol* and the US Military-Industrial Complex: Cold War Geopolitical Economy and South Korean Industrialization', *Environment and Planning A* 46(5): 1160–80.

Goldner, L. (2008) 'The Korean Working Class: From Mass Strike to Casualization and Retreat, 1987–2008'. https://libcom.org/history/korean-working-class-mass-strike-casualization-retreat-1987-20071 (accessed September 08, 2019).

Goldner, L. (2009) 'Ssangyong Motors Strike in South Korea Ends in Defeat and Heavy Repression'. https://libcom.org/news/ssangyong-motors-strike-south-korea-ends-defeat-heavy-repression-17082009 (accessed September 08, 2019).

Gowan, P. (1999) *Global Gamble: Washington's Faustian Bid for World Dominance*. London and New York: Verso.

Gowan, P. (2004) 'Triumphing to International Disaster: The Impasse of American Grand Strategy', *Critical Asian Studies* 36(1): 3–36.

Haggard, S. (1990) *Pathways from the Periphery: Politics of Growth in the Newly Industrializing Countries*. Ithaca, NY and London: Cornell University Press.

Haggard, S., Kang, D. and Moon, C-I. (1997) 'Japanese Colonialism and Korean Development: A Critique', *World Development* 25(6): 867–81.

Haggard, S. and Zheng, Y. (2013) 'Institutional Innovation and Investment in Taiwan: The Micro-foundations of the Developmental State', *Business and Politics* 15(4): 435–66.

Hahn, Bae-ho. (1980) 'Korea-Japan Relations in the 1970s', *Asian Survey* 20(11): 1087–97.

Halliday, F. (1986) (2nd ed.) *The Makings of the Second Cold War*. London: Verso.

Han, Hong-Koo. (2017) 'Ch'otpul kwa kwangjang ŭi han'guk hyŏndaesa' ('The Korean History of Candle-Light Demonstrations'), *Ch'angjak kwa Pip'yŏng* (*Creations and Criticism*) 45(1): 301–28.

Han, Yong-Sup. (2011) 'The May Sixteenth Military Coup', in B-K Kim and E. F. Vogel (eds) *The Park Chung Hee Era: Transformation of South Korea*, pp. 35–57. Cambridge, MA: Harvard University Press.

Hardy, J. (2013) 'New Divisions of Labour in the Global Economy', *International Socialism* 137. http://isj.org.uk/new-divisions-of-labour-in-the-global-economy/ (accessed November 15, 2017).

Harriss, J., Hunter, J. and Lewis, C. (eds). (1995) *The New Institutional Economics and Third World Development*. London: Routledge.

Hart-Landsberg, M. (1989) 'South Korea: Looking at the Left', *Monthly Review* 41(3): 56–70.

Hart-Landsberg, M. (1993) *Rush to Development: Economic Change and Political Struggle in South Korea*. New York: Month Review Press.

Hart-Landsberg, M. (2004) 'International Conditions and South Korean Capital Accumulation, 1987–2003', paper presented on *World Economy in the 21st Century: Marxist Perspectives*, pp. 196–228. Jinju (South Korea): Institute for Social Sciences, Gyeongsang National University (May 21–22).

Hart-Landsberg, M. and Burkett, P. (2000) *Development, Crisis and Struggle: Learning from Japan and East Asia*. New York: St. Martin's Press.

Hart-Landsberg, M. and Burkett, P. (2001) 'Economic Crisis and Restructuring in South Korea: Beyond the Free Market-Statist Debate', *Critical Asian Studies* 33(3): 403–30.

Hart-Landsberg, M. and Burkett, P. (2006) 'China and the Dynamics of Transnational Accumulation: Causes and Consequences of Global Restructuring', *Historical Materialism* 14(3): 3–43.

Harvey, D. (1982) *The Limits to Capital*. Oxford: Basil Blackwell.

Harvey, D. (2003) *The New Imperialism*. Oxford: Oxford University Press.

Harvey, D. (2005) *A Brief History of Neoliberalism*. Oxford: Oxford University Press.

Hayashi, S. (2010) 'The Developmental State in the Era of Globalization', *The Pacific Review* 23(1): 45–69.

Held, D. (1987) *Models of Democracy*. Cambridge: Blackwell.

Held, D. and McGrew, A. (eds). (2000) *The Global Transformations Reader: An Introduction to the Globalization Debate*. Malden, MA: Polity Press.

Helleiner, E. (1994) *Status and the Reemergence of Global Finance: From Bretton Woods to the 1990s*. Ithaca, NY: Cornell University Press.

Hewitt, T. Johnson, H. and Wield, D. (eds). (1992) *Industrialization and Development*. Oxford: Oxford University Press.

Hilferding. R. (2007 [1910]) *Finance Capital: A Study of the Latest Phrase of Capitalist Development*. Abingdon: Routledge.

Holloway, J. (1988) 'The Great Bear, Post-Fordism and Class Struggle: A Comment on Bonefeld and Jessop', *Capital and Class* 36(1): 93–104.

Holloway, J. (1994) 'Global Capital and the National State', *Capital and Class* 18(1): 23–49.

Holloway, J. and Picciotto, S. (1977) 'Capital, Crisis and the State', *Capital and Class* 1(2): 76–101.

Holloway, J. and Picciotto, S. (eds). (1978) *State and Capital: A Marxist Debate*. London: Edward Arnold.

Holloway, J. and Picciotto, S. (1978) 'Introduction: Toward a Materialist Theory of the State', in J. Holloway and S. Picciotto (eds) *State and Capital: A Marxist Debate*, pp. 1–31. London: Edward Arnold.

Hong, Sung-Chan. (2013) 'Land Reform and Large Landlords in South Korea's Modernization Project', *Seoul Journal of Korean Studies* 26(1): 23–45.

Hong, Yong-Pyo. (2000) *State Security and Regime Security: President Syngman Rhee and the Insecurity Dilemma in South Korea, 1953–60*. London: Macmillan.

Hong, Yoon-Kee. (2003) 'Minjuwha sidae ŭi "Park Chŏng-hŭi": Pak Chŏng-hŭi singyŏkwha tamron kwa ilsangjŏk p'asijŭm tamron e taehan pip'anjŏk koch'al' ('Park Chung-Hee in the Era of Democracy: A Critical Appraisal of Mystification and Fascism Discourses on Park Chung-Hee'), in Byeong-Cheon Lee (ed) *Kaebal Tokjae wa Pak Chŏng-hŭi Sidae* (*Developmental Dictatorship and the Park Chung-Hee Era*), pp. 365–98. Paju: Ch'angbi.

Hundt, D. (2014) 'Economic Crisis in Korea and the Degraded Developmental State', *Australian Journal of International Affairs* 68(5): 499–514.

Hundt, D. (2015) 'Neoliberalism, the Developmental State and Civil Society in Korea', *Asian Studies Reviews* 39(3): 466–82.

Hung, Ho-fung. (2008) 'Agricultural Revolution and Elite Reproduction in Qing China: The Transition to Capitalism Debate Revisited', *American Sociological Review* 73: 569–88.

Hwang, Kyung-Moon. (2004) 'Citizenship, Social Equality and Government Reform: Changes in the Household Registration System in Korea, 1894–1910', *Modern Asian Studies* 38(2): 355–87.

Hwang, Kyung-Moon. (2007) 'Nation, State and the Modern Transformation of Korea Social Structure in the Early Twentieth Century', *History Compass* 5(2): 330–46.

Hwang, Seon-Oong. (2009) 'Pijŏnggyujik koyong ŭi whakdae, sodŭkbunbae, kyŏngje sŏngjang' ('The Expansion of Irregular Employment, Income Distribution and Economic Growth'), *Tonghyang kwa Chŏnmang* (*Current and Prospect*) 77: 169–201.

Itoh, M. and Lapavitsas, C. (1999) *Political Economy of Money and Finance*. Basingstoke: Palgrave Macmillan.

Jang, Gui-Yeon. (2013) 'Sinjayujuŭi sidae han'guk ŭi kyegŭp kujo' ('The Class Structure of Korea in the Neoliberal Age'), *Marxism 21* 10(3): 12–40.

Jang, Sang-Hwan. (1994) *Nongji kaehyŏk* (*The Land Reform*). Seoul: Hangilsa.

Jang, Sang-Hwan. (2000) 'Han'guk chŏnjaeng kwa han'guk chabonjuŭi – kukka poanpŏp che'je ŭi sŏngrip kwa mollak' ('The Korean War and Korean Capitalism: From the Birth to the End of the National Security Law Regime'), in Institute for Social Science, Gyŏngsang National University (eds) *Han'guk chŏnjaeng kwa Han'guk chabonjuŭi* (*The Korean War and Korean Capitalism*), pp. 130–80. Seoul: Hanul.

Jayasuriya, K. (2000) 'Authoritarian Liberalism, Governance and the Emergence of the Regulatory State in Post-Crisis East Asia', in R. Robinson, M. Beeson, K. Jayasuriya and H-R Kim (eds) *Politics and Market in the Wake of the Asian Crisis*, pp. 315–30. London: Routledge.

Jayasuriya, K. (2001) 'Globalisation and the Changing Architecture of the State: The Regulatory State and the Politics of Negative Co-ordination', *Journal of European Public Policy* 8(1): 101–23.

Jayasuriya, K. (2005) 'Beyond Institutional Fetishism: From Developmental to the Regulatory State', *New Political Economy* 10(3): 381–87.

Jayasuriya, K. and Rosser, A. (2001) 'Economic Orthodoxy and the East Asian Crisis', *Third World Quarterly* 22(3): 381–96.

Jenkins, R. (1991) 'A Political Economy of Industrialization: A Comparison of Latin American and East Asian Industrializing Countries', *Development and Change* 22(2): 197–231.

Jenkins, R. (1994) 'Capitalist Development in the NICs', in L. Sklair (ed) *Capitalism and Development*, pp. 72–86. London: Routledge.

Jeon, Yoong-Deok. and Kim, Young-Yung. (2000) 'Land Reform, Income Redistribution, and Agricultural Production in Korea', *Economic Development & Cultural Change* 48(2): 253–68.

Jeong, Hae-Koo. (1996) 'Pundan kwa Yi Sŭng-man: 1945–1948' ('The Division of Korea and Rhee Syngman': 1845–1948'), *Yŏksa Pip'yŏng* (*Critical Review of History*) 34: 252–88.

Jeong, Hae-Koo. (1998) 'Pak Chŏng-hŭi sindŭrom ŭi yangsang kwa sŏnggyŏk' ('The Trends and Characteristics of the Park Chun-Hee Syndrome'), *Pak Chŏng-hŭi rŭl Nŏmŏsŏ* (*Beyond Park Chung-Hee*). Seoul: Purŭnsup.

Jeong, Il-Yong. (1989) 'Pangong tokjae chŏngkwŏn ŭl kiun mikuk ŭi kyŏngje wonjo' ('US Aid Responsible for Anti-Communist Dictatorship'), *Yŏksa Pip'yŏng* (*Critical Review of History*) 9: 187–92.

Jeong, Jin-Sang. (2000) 'Han'guk chŏnjaeng kwa chŏn kŭndaejŏk kyegŭp kwange ŭi haech'e' ('The Korean War and the Dissolution of Pre-Modern Class Relations'), in Institute for Social Science, Gyeongsang National University (eds) *Han'guk chŏnjaeng kwa Han'guk chabonjuŭi* (*The Korean War and Korean Capitalism*), pp. 11–58. Seoul: Hanul.

Jeong, Kyeong-Mo. (1991) 'Pak Chŏng-hŭi, kwŏnlyŏk pusang esŏ pigŭkjŏk chongmal kkaji' ('Park Jung-Hee: From the Rise to Power to the Tragic End'), *Yeoksa Pipyŏng* (*Critical Review of History*) 15: 212–48.

Jeong, Seong-Jin. (1993) 'Han'guk chabonjuŭi wa kyŏngjejŏk chongsokjŏk chŏnmang' ('Korean Capitalism and Prospects for Economic Dependency'), *Sahoe Pip'ŏng* (*Society Review*) 9: 429–53.

Jeong, Seong-Jin. (2000) 'Han'guk chŏnjaeng kwa yŏnggu kunbi kyŏngjeang' ('The Korean War and Permanent Military Competition'), in Institute for Social Science, Gyeongsang National University (eds) *Han'guk chŏnjaeng kwa Han'guk chabonjuŭi* (*The Korean War and Korean Capitalism*), pp. 100–28. Seoul: Hanul.

Jeong, Seong-Jin. (2003) 'Sinjayujuŭijŏk segewha wa nosa kwange pyŏnwha ŭi kukche pikyo' ('Neoliberal Globalisation and an International Comparative Study on Changes in Capital-Labour Relations'), in Institute for Social Science, Gyeongsang National University (eds) *Sinjayujuŭijŏk kujo chojŏng kwa nodong munje 1997–2001* (*Neoliberal Restructuring and Labour*), pp. 15–52. Seoul: Hanul.

Jeong, Seong-Jin. (2004) 'Trend of Capital Accumulation in Korea after 1997 Crisis', paper presented on *World Economy in the 21st Century: Marxist Perspectives*, pp. 162–96. Jinju (South Korea): Institute for Social Sciences, Gyeongsang National University (May 21–22).

Jeong, Seong-Jin. (2005) *Marx wa han'guk kyŏngje* (*Marx and the Korean Economy*). Seoul: Ch'aekkalp'i.

Jeong, Seong-Jin. (2009) 'Korean Developmental State from Dirigisme to Neoliberalism', *Historical Materialism* 17(3): 244–57.

Jeong, Seong-Jin. and Shin, Jo-Young. (1999) 'Debates on the Current Economic Crisis within the Korean Left', *Rethinking Marxism* 11(2): 85–97.

Jeong, Tae-Heon. (2000) '8·15 wa Han'guk chabonjuŭi chongsokjŏk chaep'yŏn' ('8·15 National Independence and the Dependent Reorganisation of Korean Capitalism'), in Man-Kil Kang (ed) *Han'guk chabonjuŭi yŏksa* (*A History of Korean Capitalism*), pp. 193–248. Seoul: Yŏksa Pip'ŏngsa.

Jessop, B. (1990) *State Theory: Putting the Capitalist State in its Place*. Oxford: Blackwell.

Ji, Joo-Hyoung. (2009) 'Han'guk kukka hyŏngtae wa kwonlyŏk haengsa pangsik ŭi chŏngwhan – kwŏnwijuŭi kaebal kukka esŏ sinjayujuŭi kukka kwŏnlyŏk ŭro' ('The Transformation of State Form and the Mode of Power Exercise in Korea – from the Authoritarian Developmental State to Neoliberal State'), *Han'kuk Chŏngch'i Hakhoebo* (*Korean Political Science Review*) 43(4): 175–203.

Ji, Joo-Hyoung. (2013) 'Han'guk ŭi kukka paljŏn' – kaebaljuŭi esŏ sinjayujuŭi ro' ('The Development of the Korean State – from Developmental to Neoliberal'), *Han'kuk Sahoehakhoe* (*Korean Sociological Association*): 203–11.

Johnson, C. (1982) *MITI and the Japanese Miracle: The Growth of Industrial Policy 1925–1975*. Stanford, CA: Stanford University Press.

Johnson, C. (1987) 'Political Institutions and Economic Performance: The Government-Business Relationship in Japan, South Korea, and Taiwan', in F. Deyo (ed) *The Political Economy of the New Asian Industrialism*, pp. 136–64. Ithaca, NY: Cornell University Press.

Johnson, C. (1995) *Japan: Who Governs: The Rise of the Developmental State*. New York and London: Norton.

Johnson, C. (1998) 'Economic Crisis in East Asia: The Clash of Capitalisms', *Cambridge Journal of Economics* 22(6): 653–61.

Johnson, C. (1999) 'The Developmental State: Odyssey of a Concept', in M. Woo-Cumings (ed) *The Developmental State*, pp. 32–60. Ithaca, NY and London: Cornell University Press.

Johnson, C. (2004) *The Sorrows of Empire: Militarism, Secrecy, and the End of the Republic*. New York: Metropolitan Books.

Jones, G. S. (1976) 'From Historical Sociology to Theoretical History', *British Journal of Sociology* 27(3): 295–305.

Jung, Heung-Jun. (2018) 'Koyong nodong chŏngch'aek ŭi chŏnwhangi, 2017-yŏn nosa kwangwe p'yŏngga wa 2018-yŏn chŏnmang' ('Employment Policy in Transition, An Appraisal of Industrial Relations in 2017 and A Prospect for Industrial Relations in 2018'), *Korea Labour Institute, Monthly Labour Review* (Jan.): 7–26.

Kalinowski, T. (2007) 'Democracy, Economic Crisis and Market Oriented Reforms', *Comparative Sociology* 6(3): 344–73.

Kalinowski, T. (2008) 'Korea's Recovery since the 1997/98 Financial Crisis: The Last Stage of the Developmental State', *New Political Economy* 13(4): 447–62.

Kalinowski, T. (2015) 'Crisis Management and the Diversity of Capitalism: Fiscal Stimulus Packages and the East Asian (Neo-) Developmental State', *Economy and Society* 44(2): 244–70.

Kalinowski, T. and Cho, H-Y. (2009) 'The Political Economy of Financial Liberalisation in South Korea', *Asian Survey* 49(2): 221–42.

Kang, D. C. (2002) 'Bad Loans to Good Friends: Money Politics and the Developmental State in South Korea', *International Organization* 56(1): 177–207.

Kang, Joon-Man. (2002a) *Han'guk hyŏndaesa sanch'aek 1970-yŏndae I* (*Korean Modern History in the 1970s I*). Seoul: Inmul kwa Sasang.

Kang, Joon-Man. (2002b) *Han'guk hyŏndaesa sanch'aek 1970-yŏndae. II* (*Korean Modern History in the 1970s II*). Seoul: Inmul kwa Sasang.

Kang, Joon-Man. (2002c) *Han'guk hyŏndaesa sanch'aek 1970-yŏndae. III* (*Korean Modern History in the 1970s III*). Seoul: Inmul kwa Sasang.

Kang, Joon-Man. (2003a) *Han'guk hyŏndaesa sanch'aek 1980-yŏndae. I* (*Korean Modern History in the 1980s I*). Seoul: Inmul kwa Sasang.

Kang, Joon-Man. (2003b) *Han'guk hyŏndaesa sanch'aek 1980-yŏndae. II* (*Korean Modern History in the 1980s II*). Seoul: Inmul kwa Sasang.

Kang, Joon-Man. (2003c) *Han'guk hyŏndaesa sanch'aek 1980-yŏndae. III* (*Korean Modern History in the 1980s III*). Seoul: Inmul kwa Sasang.

Kang, Joon-Man. (2004a) *Han'guk hyŏndaesa sanch'aek 1950-yŏndae. I* (*Korean Modern History in the 1950s I*). Seoul: Inmul kwa Sasang.

Kang, Joon-Man. (2004b) *Han'guk hyŏndaesa sanch'aek 1960-yŏndae. I* (*Korean Modern History in the 1960s I*). Seoul: Inmul kwa Sasang.

Kang, Joon-Man. (2004c) *Han'guk hyŏndaesa sanch'aek 1960-yŏndae. II* (*Korean Modern History in the 1960s II*). Seoul: Inmul kwa Sasang.

Kang, Joon-Man. (2004d) *Han'guk hyŏndaesa sanch'aek 1960-yŏndae. III* (*Korean Modern History in the 1960s III*). Seoul: Inmul kwa Sasang.

Kang, Man-Kil. (2000) 'Han'guk chabonjuŭi ŭi yŏksa rŭl ŏttŏk'e ihae hal kŏsinga' ('How Can We Understand Korean Capitalism?'), in Man-Kil Kang (ed) *Han'guk chabonjuŭiŭi Yŏksa* (*A History of Korean Capitalism*), pp. 11–27. Seoul: Yŏksa Pip'ŏgsa.

Kang, Soo-Dol. (2009) '"Ch'amyŏ chŏngbu" ŭi kyŏngjejuŭi pip'an kwa taean kyŏngje ŭi chŏnmang' ('A Critique of Economism of the 'Participatory Government' and Prospect for an Alternative Economy'), *Munhak kwa Kwahak* (*Literature and Science*) 43: 91–117.

Khan, M. H. (1996) 'A Typology of Corruption in Developing Countries', *IDS Bulletin* 27(2): 12–21.

Khan, M. H. (2000) 'Rent-Seeking as a Process', in M. H. Khan and K. S. Jomo (eds) *Rents, Rent-Seeking and Economic Development: Theory and Evidence in Asia*, pp. 70–144. Cambridge: Cambridge University Press.

Khan, M. H. (2005) 'Markets, States and Democracy: Patron-Client Networks and the Case for Democracy in Developing Countries', *Democratization* 12(5): 705–25.

Kim, Byung-Kook. (2011) 'Introduction: The Case for Political History', in B-K Kim and E. F. Vogel (eds) *The Park Chung Hee Era: Transformation of South Korea*, pp. 1–31. Cambridge, MA: Harvard University Press.

Kim, Chang-Kun. (2006) '1997-yŏn kyŏngjewigi ihu ŭi han'guk chabonjuŭi ŭi ch'ukjŏk kujo ŭi pyŏnwha' ('The Changes in the Accumulation Structure of Korean Capitalism since the Economic Crisis of 1997'), *Chinbo P'yŏngnon* (*Progressive Review*) 27: 1–22.

Kim, Dae-Jung. (1985) *Mass-Participatory Economy: A Democratic Alternative for Korea*. Lanham, MD: University Press of America.

Kim, Dae-Jung. (1998) 'Kim Dae Jung's Inauguration Speech: South Korean Report'. http://news.bbc.co.uk/2/hi/world/monitoring/59967.stm (accessed May 15, 2009).

Kim, Dong-Taek. (2001) '19-segimal kŭndae kukka kŏnsŏl kwajŏng esŏ natanan chŏngch'ijŏk kyunyŏl' ('Political Cleavages in the Process of Modern State Building in late 19th Century Korea'), *Han'guk Chŏngch'i Hakhoebo* (*Korean Political Science Review*) 34(4): 41–55.

Kim, Hae-In. (2017) 'Munjaein chŏngkwŏn ŭi sŏnggyŏk kwa nodongja kyegŭp ŭi kwaje' ('The Nature of the Moon Jae-In Government and the Task of the Working Class'), *Chŏngse wa Nodong* (*Situations and Labour*) 136: 32–57.

Kim, Hong-Ki. (1999) *Yŏngyok ŭi han'guk kyŏngje* (*The Ups and Downs of the Korean Economy*). Seoul: Maeil Kyŏngje Sinmunsa.

Kim, Hyung-A. and Sorensen, W. C. (eds). (2011) *Reassessing the Park Chung Hee era, 1961–1979: Development, Political Thought, Democracy and Cultural Influence*. Seattle: University of Washington Press.

Kim, Il-Young. (2000) 'Li Sŭng-man chŏngbu esŏ ŭi oegyo chŏngch'aek kwa kungnae chŏngch'i – pukjin·panil chŏngch'aek kwa kungnae chŏngch'i wa ŭi yŏn'ge' ('The Linkage Between Foreign Policy and Domestic Politics in Rhee Syngman Government'), *Kukje Chŏngch'i Nonchong* (*Korea Journal of International Studies*) 39(3): 243–62.

Kim, Inhae. (2016) 'Land Reform in South Korea under the U.S. Military Occupation, 1945–1948', *Journal of Cold War Studies* 18(2): 97–129.

Kim, Joong-Seop. (1999) 'In Search of Human Rights: The Paekchŏng Movement in Colonial Korea', in Gi-Wook Shin and Michael Robinson (eds) *Colonial Modernity in Korea*, pp. 311–35. Cambridge, MA: Harvard University Press.

Kim, Ki-Won. (2002) *Chaebol kaehyŏk ŭn kkŭnanŭnga?* (*Is Chaebol Reform Over?*). Seoul: Hanul.

Kim, Quee-Young. (1996) 'From Protest to Change of Regime: The 4–19 Revolt and the Fall of the Rhee Regime in South Korea', *Social Forces* 74(4): 1179–208.

Kim, Sang-Jo. (2005) 'Kyŏngje wigi ihu han'guk ŭi chaebŏl kyehyŏk ŭi hyŏnhwang kwa kwaje' ('Changes in Corporate Governance and Financial System in Korea after the 1997 Crisis'), *The Journal of Asiatic Studies* 48(3): 7–42.

Kim, Sang-Oong. (2013) 'Kongan chŏngch'i ŭi wŏnjo Yi Sŭng-man' ('The Origins of Anti-Communist Security Politics, Rhee Syngman'), *Naeil ŭl yŏnŭn yŏksa* (*History Opening Tomorrow*) 53: 36–51.

Kim, Se-Kyun. (1989) '"Chayuminjujŭi" hŏul 40-yŏn' ('40 Years of 'Liberal Democracy' Fallacies'), *Yŏksa Pip'yŏng* (*Critical Review of History*) 8: 14–30.

Kim, Se-Kyun. (1991) 'Han'guk esŏ ŭi minjujuŭi nonŭi e taehan pip'anjŏk kŏmt'o' ('A Critical Appraisal of Debates on Democracy in Korea'), *Sahoe Pip'ŏng* (*Society Review*) 6: 305–25.

Kim, Se-Kyun. (1999) 'Han'gukjŏk minjujuŭi' ('Korean Democracy'), *Yŏksa Pip'ŏng* (*Critical Review of History*) 47: 290–8.

Kim, Se-Kyun. (2007) 'Sinjayujuŭi kyŏngch'al kukka wa han'guk minjujuŭi' ('The Neoliberal Police State and Democracy in Korea'), *Marxism 21* 4(2): 82–100.

Kim, Seok-Jun. and Jang, Sang-Hwan. (2003) 'Sinjayujuŭi kujo chojŏng kwa chabonjuŭi mosun ŭi simhwa' ('Neoliberal Restructuring and Deepening Contradictions of Capitalism'), in Institute for Social Science, Gyeongsang National University (eds) *Sinjayujuŭijŏk kujo chojŏng kwa nodong munje: 1997–2001* (*Neoliberal Restructuring and Labour Issues in Korea 1997–2001*), pp. 53–113. Seoul: Hanul.

Kim, Sin-Jae. (2001) 'Kabo kaehyŏkki ŭi kukka hyŏngtae kaehyŏk' ('A Reform of Nation Form in Kabo Reform Period'), *Kyŏngju Sahak* (*Kyoung-Ju Historical Society*) 21: 253–78.

Kim, So-Young. (2012) 'Hanmal chisikindŭl ŭi iphŏnlon kwa kŭndae kukka kŏnsŏl' ('Korean Intellectuals' Discourse on Establishing a Constitution and Nation at the Turn of the Century'), *Han'gukhak Yŏn'gu* (*Korean Studies*) 43: 339–74.

Kim, Soo-Haeng. and Cho, Bok-Hyeon. (1999) 'Han'guk ŭi kyŏngje kongwhang kwa asia model' ('Korea Economic Crisis and Asian Model'), *Sahoe Kyŏngje P'yŏngnon* (*Society Economy Review*) 13: 209–37.

Kim, Soo-Haeng. and Park, Shung-Ho. (2005) '"Pak Chŏng-hŭi ch'eje" ŭi kyŏngjejŏk sŏnggwa e kwanhan pip'anjŏk p'yŏngga' ('A Critical Appraisal of the Economic Achievements of the "Park Chung-Hee Regime"'), *Marxism 21* 2(2): 120–62.

Kim, Sung-Bae. (2012) 'Han'guk kŭndae kukka kaenyŏm hyŏngsŏngsa yŏn'gu – kaewhagi rŭl chungsim ŭro' ('A Study of the Formation of the Concept of the Modern State in Korea'), *Kukje Chŏngch'i Nonchong* (*Korea Journal of International Studies*) 52(2): 7–35.

Kim, Tae-Keon. (2008) 'Yi Myŏng-bak chŏngkwŏn ha ŭi nodong undong ŭi kwaje' ('The Direction of Labour Movements under the Lee Myong-Bak Government'), *Chinbo P'yŏngnon* (*Progressive Review*) 36: 144–59.

Kim, Tae-Kyun. (2017) 'Cheobŏl t'ujaeng ŭl ŏttŏke pol kŏsinga'?' ('How to Appraise Struggle against the Chaebol?'), *Left Daegu* 13: 52–78.

Kim, Won. (2005) 'Sinjayujuŭi ha esŏ nodong chohap ŭi kyunyŏl kujo wa pyŏnhwa' ('The Changes of Cleavage Structure of Labour Union in the Period of Globalisation'), *Asea Yŏn'gu* (*Journal of Asiatic Studies*) 48(3): 75–105.

Kim, Yang-Hee. and Jeong, Joon-Ho. (2006) 'Han'guk ŭi FTA chŏngch'aek ŭi pipanjŏk kŏmt'o wa taean' ('A Critical Appraisal of FTA Policy in Korea and Alternatives'), *Tonghyan kwa Chŏnmang* (*Current and Prospect*) 67: 205–36.

Kim, Yong Cheol. (1998) 'Industrial Reform and Labor Backlash in South Korea: Genesis, Escalation, and Termination of the 1997 General Strike', *Asian Survey* 38(12): 1142–60.

Kim, Yoo-Seon. (2004) *Nodong sijang yuyŏnhwa wa pijŏngkyujik koyong* (*Labour Market Flexibility and the Rise in Irregular Employment*). Seoul: Korea Labour & Society Institute.

Kim, Young-Soo. (1993) '12·12, 5·18 ŭi chinsang kyumyŏng kwa kimyŏngsam chŏngbu' ('The Investigation of 12/12 [Chun's Military Coup] and 5/18 [Gwangju Uprising] and the Kim Young-Sam Government'), *Chŏngse Yŏn'gu* (*Current Research*) 46: 37–45.

Kim, Yun-Hee., Park, Eun-Suk., Lee Heon-Ju. and Hah Won-Ho. (2000) 'Sege chabonjuŭi ch'eje ro ŭi pyŏnip kwa kungmin kyŏngje hyŏngsŏng ŭi choajŏl' ('Integration into Global Capitalism and the Failure of the Formation of the National Economy'), in Man-Kil Kang (ed) *Han'guk chabonjuŭi ŭi Yŏksa* (*A History of Korean Capitalism*), pp. 29–81. Seoul: Yŏksa Pip'yŏngsa.

Knuttila, K. M. and Kubik, W. (2001) *State Theories: Classical, Global & Feminist Perspectives*. London: Zed.

Koh, Beong-Kwon. (2008) 'Hyŏkmyŏng ape sŏ ŭi mŏmutgŏrim: 2008-yŏn ch'otpulsiwi ŭi palbal kwa chŏngae' ('Hesitation in the Face of the Revolution: The Beginning and Development of the Candle Strike of 2008'), *alteRevolution* 2: 242–71.

Kohli, A. (1997) 'Japanese Colonialism and Korean Development: A Reply', *World Development* 25(6): 883–8.

Kohli, A. (1999) 'Where Do High-Growth Political Economies Come From? The Japanese Lineage of Korea's "Developmental State"', in M. Woo-Cumings (ed) *The Developmental State*, pp. 93–126. Ithaca, NY and London: Cornell University Press.

Kohli, A. (2004) 'The Colonial Origins of a Modern Political Economy: The Japanese Lineage of Korea's Cohesive-Capitalist State', in A. Kolhi (ed), *State-Directed Development: Public Power and Industrialization in the Global Periphery*, pp. 27–60. Cambridge: Cambridge University Press.

Kong, Jae-Ook. (2000) 'Han'guk chŏnjaeng kwa chabŏl ŭi hyŏngsŏng' ('The Korean War and the Formation of the *Chaebol*'), in Institute for Social Science, Gyeongsang National University (eds) *Han'guk chŏnjaeng kwa Han'guk chabonjuŭi* (*The Korean War and Korean Capitalism*), pp. 59–99. Seoul: Hanul.

Koo, Hagen. (1987) 'The Interplay of State, Social Class and World System in East Asian Development', in D. C. Frederic (ed) *The Political Economy of the New Asian Industrialism*, pp. 165–81. Ithaca, NY: Cornell University Press.

Koo, Hagen. (1993a) 'Introduction: Beyond State-Market Relations', in H. Koo (ed) *State and Society in Contemporary Korea*, pp. 1–11. Ithaca, NY: Cornell University Press.

Koo, Hagen. (1993b) 'The State, Minjung, and the Working Class in South Korea', in H. Koo (ed) *State and Society in Contemporary Korea*, pp. 131–62. Ithaca, NY: Cornell University Press.

Koo, Hagen. (2001) *Korean workers; the Culture and Politics of Class Formation.* Ithaca, NY: Cornell University Press.

Korea Agricultural Economy Institute. (1989) *Nongji kaehyŏksa yŏn'gu* (*A Study on Land Reform History*). Seoul: Han'guk nongch'on kyŏngje yŏn'guwŏn.

Korea Barometer Survey. (2004) www.koreabarometer.org/Database.htm (accessed May 15, 2010).

Korea Human Rights. (April 5, 2012) www.khnews.com/home/bbs/view.php?id=newest&no=2648(accessed October 30, 2018).

Krippner, G. (2005) 'The Financialization of the American Economy', *Socio-Economic Review* 3(2): 173–208.

Krishnan, R, R. (1982) 'The South Korean "Miracle": Sell-Out to Japan, U.S.', *Social Scientist* 10(3): 25–37.

Krueger, A. and Yoo, J. (2002) 'Falling Profitability, Higher Borrowing Costs, and Chaebol Finances during the Korean Crisis', in D. T. Coe and S-J. Kim (eds) *The Korean Crisis and Recovery*, pp. 157–98, Washington, DC: International Monetary Fund; Korea Institute for International Economic Policy.

Kruger, A. O. (1978) 'Liberalization Attempts and Consequences', pp. 245–76. *National Bureau of Economic Research Books.*

Kruger, A. O. (1980) 'Trade Policy as an Input to Development', *American Economic Review* 70(2): 288–92.

Krugman, P. (2000) *The Return of Depression Economics.* New York: Norton & Company.

Kwon, J. (1994) 'The East Asia Challenge to Neoclassical Orthodoxy', *World Development* 22(4): 635–44.

Kwon, P. B. (2017) 'Beyond Patron and Client: Historicizing the Dialectics of US-ROK Relations amid Park Chung Hee's Independent Defence Industry Development in South Korea, 1968–1979', *Seoul Journal of Korea Studies* 30(2): 185–216.

Laclau, E. (1975) 'The Specificity of the Political: The Poulantzas and Miliband Debate', *Economy and Society* 4(1): 87–111.

Lal, T. (1983) *The Poverty of Development Economics.* London: Institute of Economic Affairs.

Landes, D. S. (1999) *The Wealth and Poverty of Nations: Why Some Are So Rich and Some So Poor.* New York: W.W. Norton.

Lee, Byeong-Cheon. (2003a) 'Kaebal kukkaron tik'o nŏmŏsŏgi' ('Beyond Developmental State Theories'), *Kyŏngje wa Sahoe* (*Economy and Society*) 57: 99–124.

Lee, Byeon-Cheon. (eds). (2003b) *Kaebal tokjae wa Pak Chŏng-hŭi sidae* (*Developmental Dictatorship and the Park Chung-Hee Era*). Paju: Ch'angbi.

Lee, Byeon-Cheon. (2005) 'Chayuhwa, yangŭkhwa sidae wa much'aekim chabonjuŭi' ('Irresponsible Capitalism in the Era of Liberalisation and Polarisation: An Alternative of Social Integrative Civic Economy'), *The Journal of Asiatic Studies* 48(3): 43–71.

Lee, Byeong-Cheon. (2011) 'Kwŏnwijuŭijŏk kŭndaehwa ŭi yŏksajŏk kiwŏn – sikminji kiwŏnlon ŭi pip'anjŏk kŏmt'o' ('The Historical Origins of Authoritarian Modernisation in Korea: A Critical Appraisal of Colonial Modernity'), *Yŏksa Pip'yŏng* (*Critical Review of History*) 97: 349–96.

Lee, Dae-Kun. (1987) *Han'guk chŏnjaeng kwa 1950-yŏndae ŭi chabon ch'ukjŏk* (*The Korean War and Capital Accumulation in the 1950s*). Seoul: Kkach'i.

Lee, H. Chung, Lee, Keun. and Lee, Kangkook. (2002) '*Chaebol*, Financial Liberalization, and Economic Crisis: Transformation of Quasi-Internal Organization in Korea', *Asian Economic Journal* 16(1): 17–35.

Lee, Jae-Hee. (1991) '5·16 kunsa chŏngbu ŭi kyŏngje kaebal ŭi sŏngkyŏk' ('The Nature of Economic Development by the 5·16 [Park's Coup] Military Government'), *Yŏksa Pip'ŏng* (*Critical Review of History*) 14: 158–68.

Lee, Jong-Sun. (2002) 'Han'guk sinjayujuŭijŏk kujo kaehyŏk kwa nodong sijang pyŏnhwa – yuyŏnhwa ŭi p'aerŏdoksŭ' ('The Neoliberal Economic Restructuring and the Change of the Labour Market in South Korea: Paradox of Flexibilisation'), *Han'guk Sahoehak* (*Korean Journal of Sociology*) 36(3): 25–45.

Lee, Jong-Sun. (2018) 'Tasi yŏllin kaehyŏk ŭi ch'ang, Mun Jae-in chŏngbu ŭi nodong chŏngch'aek p'yŏngga' ('Reopening the Windows of Reform: Evaluation of the Moon Jae-In Government's Labour Policy'), *Nonong Yŏn'gu* (*Journal of Labour Studies*) 36: 143–85.

Lee, Kang-Kook. (2005) *Davos, Porto Alegre, and Seoul*. Seoul: Humanitas.

Lee, Kwang-Il. (1997) 'Chŏngdang chŏngch'i ŭi hyŏnjae wa minju chŏngchi ŭi kwaje' ('Present Party Politics and Democratic Politics'), *Kidokgyo Sasang* (*Christian Thought*) 41(12): 18–27.

Lee, Kwang-Il. (1998) 'Pak Chŏng-hŭi chŏngkwon e kwanhan yŏn'gu hyŏnhwang kwa kwaje' ('Current Research of the Park Chung-Hee Regime and Future Research Agenda'), *Yŏksa wa Hyŏnsil* (*History and Present*) 29: 275–96.

Lee, Kwang-Il. (2001) 'Minjuwha ihaeng, 80-yŏndae "kŭpjin undong" ŭi wishang kŭrigo hegemony' ('Democratisation, the Status and Hegemony of 'Progressive Social Movements'), *Chinbo P'yŏngnon* (*Progressive Review*) 9: 263–96.

Lee, Kwang-Il. (2006) 'Haebang 60-yŏn, han'guk sahoe esŏ nodong kwa minjujuŭi' ('The 60th Anniversary of National Independence, Labour and Democracy in Korea'), *Simin kwa Sahoe* (*Citizen and Society*) 8: 182–202.

Lee, Kwang-Il. (2007) '"Minjuhwa" chŏnhu ideologi tokjŏm kwa pyŏnhyŏng' ('Monopolisation and Transformation of Ideology before and after "Democratisation"'), *Marxism 21* 4(2): 101–39.

Lee, S. H. (2000) 'Negotiating the Cold War: The United States and the Two Koreas', *The Journal of American-East Asian Relations* 9(1/2): 85–105.

Lee, Sam-Seong. (1996) 'Gwangju haksal, miguk·singunbu ŭi hyŏpjo wa kongmo' ('The Gwangju Massacre, US-Chun Military Junta Complicity'), *Yŏksa Pip'yŏng* (*Critical Review of History*) 36: 79–139.

Lee, Song-Soon. and Jeong, Byeong-Ook. (2000) 'Sikminji chabonjuŭi ŭi hyŏngsŏng kwa paljŏn' ('The Formation and Development of Colonial Capitalism'), in Man-Kil Kang (ed) *Han'guk chabonjuŭi ŭi Yŏksa* (*A History of Korean Capitalism*), pp. 83–140. Seoul: Yŏksa Pip'yŏngsa.

Lee Yeon-Ho. (2000) 'The Failure of the Weak State in Economic Liberalization: Liberalization, Democratization and the Financial Crisis in South Korea', *The Pacific Review* 13(1): 115–31.

Lee, Yeon-Ho. (2001) 'DJ kyehyŏk ŭi sinjayujuŭijŏk hangye' ('Limits of Kim Dae-Jung's Neoliberal Reforms'), *Sasang* (*Thought*) 49: 103–23.

Lee, Yeon-Ho. (2002) 'Han'guk ŭi kŭmyung kujo kaehyŏk kwa kyuje kukka ŭi tŭngjang e kwanhan nonjaeng' ('Financial System Restructuring and the Debate on the Rise of the Regulatory State'), *Han'guk Sahoehak* (*Korean Journal of Sociology*) 36(4): 59–88.

Lee, Yeon-Ho. (2006) 'Han'guk esŏ minjujuŭi simhwa ka chojŏng kukka ŭi pyŏnghwa e mich'in yŏnghyang' ('Democratic Deepening and Its Impact on the Changes in the Nature of the Regulatory State: the Korean Case'), *Sinasia* (*New Asia*) 13(2): 26–54.

Lee, Yeon-Ho., Lim, Yoo-Jin. and Chung, Suk-Kyu. (2002) 'Han'guk esŏ kyuje kukka ŭi tŭngjang kwa chŏngbu-kiŏp kwangye' ('The Rise of the Regulatory

State and Government-Business Relations in South Korea'), *Han'guk Chŏngchi Hakhoebo* (*Korean Political Science Review*) 36(3): 199–222.

Lee, Yoonkyung. (2015a) 'Labor after Neoliberalism: The Birth of the Insecure Class in South Korea', *Globalizations* 12(2): 184–202.

Lee, Yoonkyung. (2015b) 'Sky Protest: New Forms of Labour Resistance in Neo-Liberal Korea', *Journal of Contemporary Asia* 45(3): 443–64.

Lee, Young-ho. (2017) 'Land Reform and Colonial Land Legislation in Korea, 1894–1910', in Sui-Wai Cheung (ed) *Colonial Administration and Land Reform in East Asia*, pp. 166–80. Abingdon: Routledge.

Leftwich, A. (1995) 'Bringing Politics Back In: Towards a Model of the Developmental State', *The Journal of Development Studies* 31(3): 400–27.

Leftwich, A. (2005) 'Politics in Command: Development Studies and the Recovery of Social Science', *New Political Economy* 10(4): 573–607.

Leftwich, A. (2010) 'Beyond Institutions: Rethinking the Role of Leaders, Elites and Coalitions in the Institutional Formation of Developmental States and Strategies', *Forum for Development Studies* 37(1): 93–111.

Lenin, V. (1907) *The Agrarian Programme of Social-Democracy in the First Russian Revolution, 1905–1907.* www.marxists.org/archive/lenin/works/1907/agrprogr/ (accessed March 15, 2018).

Lenin, V. (1990 [1918]) *State and Revolution.* New York: International Publishers.

Lenin, V. (2010 [1916]) *Imperialism: The Highest Stage of Capitalism.* London: Penguin Classics.

Lie, J. (2001) *Multi-Ethnic Japan.* Cambridge, MA: Harvard University Press.

Lim, Hyeok-Baek. (1994) *Sijang, kukka, minjujuŭi* (*The Market, The State, and Democracy*). Seoul: Nanam.

Lim, Hyun-Chin. and Jang, Jin-Ho. (2006) 'Neo-Liberalism in Post-Crisis South Korea: Social Conditions and Outcomes', *Journal of Contemporary Asia* 36(4): 442–63.

Lim, Ji-Hyeon. (2000) 'Minjung, hisaengja inga kongbŏmja inga: p'asijŭm ŭi chinjijŏn kwa hapŭi tokjae' ('Minjung [people], Victims or Accomplices? Fascism and Consensus-Based Dictatorship'), *Tangdae Pip'yŏng* (*Current Review*) 12: 24–45.

Lim, Sung-Hack. (2000) 'Han'guk ŭi ŭnhaeng maegak kwa kŭmyung kaehyŏk' ('Sale of Korean Banks and Financial Reform'), *Kukje Chŏngch'i Nonchong* (*Korea Journal of International Studies*) 40(4): 485–509.

Lin, J. Y. (2017) 'Alice H. Amsden's Contributions to Development Economics', Special Issue *Cambridge Journal of Regions, Economy and Society* 10(1): 77–81.

Lipietz, A. (1971) *Mirages and Miracles: The Crises of Global Fordism.* London: Verso.

List, F. (2005 [1841]) *National System of Political Economy.* New York: Cosimo Classics.

Macrae, K. (2016) 'Post-Cold War Conservative Reappraisals of Syngman Rhee: Neoliberalism and the New Right', *Seoul Journal of Korean Studies* 29(2): 327–59.

Martin, G. W. (1990) 'Introduction: The Challenge of the Semiperiphery', in W. G. Martin (ed) *Semiperipheral States in the World-Economy*, pp. 3–10. New York: Greenwood Press.

Marx, K. (1845) Draft of an Article on Friedrich List's Book: Das Nationale System der Politischen Oekonomie. www.marxists.org/archive/marx/works/1845/03/list.htm (accessed March 10, 2010).

Marx, K. (1850) *The Class Struggles in France, 1848–1850*. www.marxists.org/archive/marx/works/1850/class-struggles-france/index.htm (accessed March 10, 2010).

Marx, K. (1852) *The Eighteenth Brumaire of Louis Bonaparte*. www.marxists.org/archive/marx/works/download/pdf/18th-Brumaire.pdf (accessed March 10, 2010).

Marx, K. (1967[1867; 1887]) *Capital: A Critical Analysis of Capitalist Production*, vol. 1. London: Lawrence & Wishart.

Marx, K. (1976[1867; 1887]) *Capital: A Critique of Political Economy*, vol. 1. London: Penguin Books.

Marx, K. (1956[1894]) *Capital: A Critique of Political Economy*, vol. 2. London: Lawrence & Wishart.

Marx, K. (1959[1894]) *Capital: A Critique of Political Economy*, vol. 3. London: Lawrence & Wishart.

Marx, K. (1973 [1939–41]) *Grundrisse*. London: Penguin Books.

Marx, K. and Engels, F. (1985 [1848]) *The Communist Manifesto*. London: Penguin Books.

Mason, E. S., Kim, M-J. and Perkins, D. H. (1980) *The Economic and Social Modernization of the Republic of Korea*. Cambridge, MA: Harvard University Press.

Mathews, J. A. (1998) 'Fashioning a New Korean Model Out of the Crisis: The Rebuilding of Institutional Capabilities', *Cambridge Journal of Economics* 22(6): 747–59.

May 18th History Compilation Committee of Kwangju City. (2013) *The May 18 Gwangju Democratic Uprising*. Gwangju. https://libcom.org/files/May-18-Gwangju-uprising.pdf (accessed September 9, 2019).

McGowan, P. (1981) 'Imperialism in World-System Perspective', in W. L. Hollist and J. N. Rosenau (eds) *World System Structure: Continuity and Change*, pp. 54–79. Beverly Hills, CA: Sage.

McLeod, R. and Garnaut, R. (eds). (1998) *East Asia in Crisis: From Being a Miracle to Needing One?* London: Routledge.

Migdal, J. (1994) *State in Society: Studying How States and Societies Transform and Constitute One Another*. Cambridge and New York: Cambridge University Press.

Miliband, R. (1965) 'Marx and the State', *Socialist Register* 2: 278–96.

Miliband, R. (1969) *The State in Capitalist Society*. Quarter Books: London.

Miliband, R. (1970) 'The Capitalist State: Reply to Nicos Poulantzas', *New Left Review* 59: 53–60.

Miliband, R. (1973) Poulantzas and the Capitalist State, *New Left Review* 82: 83–92.

Miliband, R. (1977) *Marxism and Politics*. Oxford: Oxford University Press.

Miliband, R. (1983) 'State Power and Class Interests', *New Left Review* 138: 37–68.

Moon, Don. and Chung, Jin-Young. (2014), '"Paljŏn kukka" model esŏ "sinjayujuŭi model" ro – "han'guk paljŏn model" nonjaeng e taehan pip'anjŏk p'yŏngga' ('From a "Developmental State Model" to a "Neo-Liberal Model": A Critical Review of the Debate on the "Developmental State"'), *Atae Yŏn'gu* (*Journal of Asia-Pacific Studies*) 21(2): 129–64.

Moon Jae-In Cheŏngbu (Government). (2017) *Kukjŏng Unyŏng 5-kyenyŏn Kehoek* (Government's Five-Year Management Plan].

Moon, Young-Joo. and Song, Kyu-Jin. (2000) 'Sikminji chabonjuŭi ŭi wigi wa p'aguk' ('The Crisis of Colonial Capitalism'), in Man-Kil Kang (ed) *Han'guk chabonjuŭi ŭi Yŏksa* (*A History of Korean Capitalism*), pp. 141–91. Seoul: Yŏksa Pip'yŏngsa.

Moseley, F. (1991) *The Falling Rate of Profit in the Postwar United States Economy*. London: Macmillan.

Mosley, L. (2005) 'Globalisation and the State: Still Room to Move?', *New Political Economy* 10(3): 355–62.

Müller, W. and Neusüss, C. (1978) 'Illusion of State Socialism and the Contradiction between Wage Labour and Capital', in J. Holloway and S. Picciotto (eds) *State and Capital: A Marxist Debate*, pp. 32–9. London: Edward Arnold.

Nem Singh, J. and Ovadia, J. S. (2018) 'The Theory and the Practice of Building the Developmental State in the Global South', Special Issue *Third World Quarterly* 39(6): 1033–55.

Nodongja Chŏnsŏn (Labour Frontier). (2017) 'Mun Jae-in chŏngkwon ŭi sŏnggyŏk kwa taeŭng panghyang' ('The Nature of the Moon Jae-In Government and How to Counter it'), *Left Daegu* 13: 10–20.

Oberdorfer, D. (1997) *The Two Koreas: Contemporary History*. Reading, MA: Addison-Wesley.

OECD. www.OECD.org.(accessed April 20, 2008; October 20, 2018; April 1, 2019).

Ogle, E. G. (1990) *South Korea: Dissent within the Economic Miracle*. London: Zed Books.

Oh, Gil-Bo. (2002) 'Kabo nongmin chŏngjaeng kwa tonghak' ('The Kabo Peasant War and Donghak'), *Tongkak Yŏn'gu* (*Donghak Association of Korea*) 12: 259–87.

Ooh, Seok-Hoon. and Park, Kweon-Hl. (2008) *88-manwŏn sedae* (*The 88,000KW [US$ 800] Generation*). Seoul: Redian Media.

Palais, J. (1975) *Politics and Policy in Traditional Korea*. Cambridge, MA: Harvard University Press.

Panitch, L. (1994) 'Globalization and the State', *Socialist Register* 30: 60–93.

Panitch, L. and Gindin, S. (2005) 'Finance and American Empire', *Socialist Register* 41: 46–81.

Park, Hyeong-Joon. and Jeong, Kwan-Yong. (1989) 'Han'guk posu yadang ŭi kyegŭpjŏk sŏnggyŏk kwa chŏngch'ijŏk wishang' ('Class Characteristics and Political Status of the Korean Conservative Opposition Parties'), *Ch'angjak kwa Pip'yŏng* (*Creations and Criticism*) 64: 212–38.

Park, Jeong-Soo. (2008) 'Sinjayujuŭi wa yokmang ŭi anbo ch'eje' ('Neoliberalism and the New Regime of Social Control'), *alterRevoluation* 2: 136–55.

Park, No-Ja. (2006) *Tangsindŭl ŭi taehan min'guk* (*Your Republic of Korea*). Seoul: Hangyŏrae.

Park, No-ja. (2014) *Bigul ŭi sidae* (*The Age of Servility*). Seoul: Hangyŏrae.

Park, No-ja. (2016) *Taehan min'guk chusik hoesa* (*The Korean Republic Limited Company*). Seoul: Hangyŏrae.

Park, Sang-Young. (2015) 'Paljŏnjuŭi wa sinjayujuŭi ŭi honjaesŏng e taehan koch'al' – 90-nyŏndae ihu han'guk paljŏn kukka ŭi pyŏnwha wa honjaesŏng ŭi tayangsŏng' ('An Analysis of the Cohabitation of Developmentalism and Neoliberalism in Korea – Varieties of Developmental-Neoliberal Mixes since the 1990s'), *Atae Yŏn'gu* (*Journal of Asia-Pacific Studies*) 22(4): 5–40.

Park, Seong-Ho. (2013) 'Pak Chŏng-hŭi nŭn kyŏngje paljŏn ŭi kongnoja inga' – '"sanŏpwha, minjuhwa" tamron kwa "konggwaron" ŭi hamjŏng' ('Is Park Chung-Hee a contributor to economic development? – the discourses around "industrialisation, democratisation" and the problems of the thesis of "merits and demerits"'), *Naeil ŭl yŏnŭn yŏksa* (*History Opening Tomorrow*) 52: 79–97.

Park, Soon-Won. (1999) 'Colonial Industrial Growth and the Emergence of Korean Working Class', in Gi-Wook Shin and Michael Robinson (eds) *Colonial Modernity in Korea*, pp. 128–60. Cambridge, MA: Harvard University Press.

Park, Tae-Gyun. (2010) 'Panil ŭl t'onghan tto tarŭn ilbon toegi – Yi Sŭng-man taet'ongnŏng ŭi taeil insik' ('Becoming Another Japan through Anti-Japanism: Rhee Syngman's Perception of Japan'), *Ilbon Pip'yŏng* (*Korean Journal of Japanese Studies*) 3: pp. 98–119.

Pashukanis, E. B. (1989[1924]) *Law and Marxism: A General Theory*. Worcester: Pluto Press.

Patnaik, U. (2005) 'Lenin and the Agrarian Question', in K. S. Zomo (ed) *The Pioneers of Development Economics*, pp. 74–92. London and New York: Zed Books.

Payer. C. (1975) 'Pushed into the Debt Trap: South Korea's Export Miracle', *Journal of Contemporary Asia* 5(2): 153–64.

Phillips, N. (2005) 'The State Debate in Political Economy: Bringing the Comparative/International Divide in the Study of the State', *New Political Economy* 10(3): 335–43.

Pirie, I. (2005) 'The New Korean State', *New Political Economy* 90(1): 27–44.

Pirie, I. (2006) 'Economic Crisis and the Construction of a Neo-Liberal Regulatory Regime in Korea', *Competition and Chang* 10(1): 49–71.

Pirie, I. (2008) *The Korean Developmental State, From Dirigisme to Neo-Liberalism*. London: Routledge.

Pirie, I. (2012a) 'A comparative Analysis of the Impact of the 1997 Asian Crisis and the Contemporary Global Economic Crisis on the Korean Political Economy'. *Contemporary Politics* 18(4): 416–33.

Pirie, I. (2012b) 'The New Korean Political Economy: Beyond the Models of Capitalism Debate', *The Pacific Review* 25(3): 365–86.

Pirie, I. (2018) 'Korea and Taiwan: The Crisis of Investment-led Growth and the End of the Developmental State', *Journal of Contemporary Asia* 48(1): 133–58.

Podoler, G. (2016) '"Who Was Park Chung-hee?" The Memorial Landscape and National Identity Politics in South Korea', *East Asia, an International Quarterly* 33(4): 271–88.

Polanyi, K. (1957) *The Great Transformation*. Boston: Beacon Press.

Postone, M. (1993) *Time, Labour and Social Domination: A Reinterpretation of Marx's Critical Theory*. Cambridge: Cambridge University Press.

Postone, M. (2004) 'Critique and Historical Transformation', *Historical Materialism* 12(3): 53–72.

Poulantzas, N. (1969) 'The Problem of the Capitalist State', *New Left Review* 58: 67–78.

Poulantzas, N. (1976) 'The Capitalist State: A Reply to Miliband and Laclau', *New Left Review* 95: 63–83.

Pressian. (2008) *Samsŏng wangguk ŭi gerilladŭl* (*Guerrillas in the Samsung Republic*). Seoul: Woongin.

Ra, Jong Yil. (1992) 'Political Crisis in Korea, 1952: The Administration, Legislature, Military and Foreign Powers', *Journal of Contemporary History* 27(2): 301–18.

Radelet, S. and Sachs, J. (1998) 'The East Asian Financial Crisis: Diagnosis, Remedies and Prospects', *Brookings Paper on Economic Activity* 1: 1–90.

Radice, H. (2008) 'The Developmental State under Global Neoliberalism', *Third World Quarterly* 29(6): 1153–74.

Rahnema, M. and Bawtree, V. (1997) *The Post-Development Reader*. London: Zed Books.

Robinson, M. and White, G. (1998) *The Democratic Developmental State*. Oxford: Oxford University Press.

Roh, Joong-Ki. (2009) 'Lee Myŏng-bak chŏngbu ch'ulbŏm 1-yŏn ŭi nodong chŏngch'aek' ('Labour Policy in the First Year of the Lee Myong-Bak Government'), *Kyŏngje wa Sahoe* (*Economy and Society*) 81: 131–56.

Rosenberg, J. (2000) *The Follies of Globalisation Theory*. London: Vevso.

Rude, C. (2005) 'The Role on Financial Discipline in Imperial Strategy', *Socialist Register* 41: 82–107.

Rueschemeyer, D. and Evans, P. B. (1985) 'The State and Economic Transformation: Towards an Analysis of the Conditions Underlying Effective Intervention', in P. B. Evans, D. Rueschemeyer and T. Skocpol (eds) *Bringing the State Back In*, pp. 44–77. Cambridge: Cambridge University Press.

Saad-Filho, A. and Johnston, D. (eds). (2004) *Neoliberalism: A Critical Reader*. London: Pluto Press.

Scholte, A. J. (2000) *Globalisation, a Critical Introduction*. New York: Palgrave.

Selwyn, B. (2009) 'An Historical Materialist Appraisal of Friedrich List and His Modern-Day Followers', *New Political Economy* 14(2): 157–80.

Seo, Joong-Seok. (1995a) 'Pak chŏngkwon ŭi taeil chase wa p'ahaengjŏk hanil kwangye' ('The Park Chung-Hee Regime's Policy against Japan and Distorted Korea-Japan Relations'), *Yŏksa Pip'yŏng* (*Critical Review of History*) 30: 38–56.

Seo, Joong-Seok. (1995b) 'Hanil hyŏpjŏng ŭi hyŏnjaejŏk ŭimi' ('Present Meanings of Korea-Japan Diplomatic Normalisation'), *Hyŏndaesa Yŏn'gu* (*Modern History Research*) 6: 156–73.

Seo, Joong-Seok. (2011) 'Yi Sŭng-man kwa 3·15 puchŏng sŏngŏ' ('Rhee Syngman and 3.15 Unfair Elections'), Yŏksa Pip'yŏng (*Critical Review of History*) 96: 7–33.

Seo, Jung-Min. and Kim, Hyeon-Jin. (2013) 'Sinjayujuŭi taehan min'guk? – kyŏngjaengnyŏk innŭn kukka – kwanyŏm kwa han'kuk ŭi chŏngch'i kyŏngje' ('Neoliberal Korea? The Idea of Competitive Nation-State and Korean Political Economy'), *Hyŏndae Chŏngch'i Yŏn'gu* (*Journal of Contemporary Politics*) 6(2): 157–86.

Shaefedin, M. (2005) 'Friedrich List and the Infant Industry Argument', in K. S. Jomo (ed) *The Pioneers of Development Economics*, pp. 42–61. London: Zed.

Shaikh, A. (1979) 'Foreign Trade and the Law of Value: Part I', *Science & Society* 43(4): 281–302.

Shaikh, A. (1980) 'Foreign Trade and the Law of Value: Past II', *Science & Society* 44(1): 27–57.

Shaikh, A. and Tonak, E. (1994) *Measuring the Wealth of Nations: The Political Economy of National Accounts*. Cambridge: Cambridge University Press.

Shin, Gi-Wook. (2006) *Ethnic Nationalism in Korea*. Stanford: Stanford University Press.

Shin, Gi-Wook. and Han, Do-Hyun. (1999) 'Colonial Corporatism: The Rural Revitalization Campaign, 1932–1940', in Gi-Wook Shin and Michael Robinson (eds) *Colonial Modernity in Korea*, pp. 70–96. Cambridge, MA: Harvard University Press.

Shin, Gi-Wook. and Robinson, M. (1999) 'Rethinking Colonial Korea', in Gi-Wook Shin and Michael Robinson (eds) *Colonial Modernity in Korea*, pp. 1–18. Cambridge, MA: Harvard University Press.

Shin, Kwang-Young. (1999) *Tongasia ŭi sanŏphwa wa minjuhwa* (*Industrialisation and Democratisation in East Asia*). Seoul: Munhak kwa Chisŏngsa.

Shin, Kwang-Young. (2004) *Han'guk ŭi kyegŭp kwa pulp'yŏngdŭng* (*Class and Inequity in Korea*). Seoul: Eulyoo.

Shin, Wook-Hee. (2004) 'Yi Sŭng-man yŏkhal insik kwa 1950-yŏndae huban ŭi hanmi kwangye' ('The Rhee Syngman's Recognition of His Role and the ROK-US relation in the late 1950s'), *Han'kuk Chŏngch'I Oegyosa Nonchong* (*Journal of Korean Political and Diplomatic History*) 26(1): 37–61.

Shin, Yong-Ok. (1998) 'Pak Hyŏn-ch'ae ŭi minjok kyŏngjeron kwa chungjin chabonjuŭi' ('Park Hyeon-Chae's National Economy Theory and Mid-Capitalism'), *Yŏksa Pip'yŏng* (*Critical Review of History*) 43: 243–60.

Shin-Yong-Ok. (2000) '1950-yŏndae wŏnjo ŭijon kyŏngje ch'eje wa chongsokjŏk sanŏpwha' ('The Aid-Dependent Economic System and Dependent Industrialisation in the 1950s'), in Man-Kil Kang (ed.) *Han'guk chabonjuŭi ŭi Yŏksa* (*A History of Korean Capitalism*), pp. 249–308. Seoul: Yŏksa Pip'yŏngsa.

Shin, Yong-Ok. (2001) 'Wŏnjo ka kongjja ka anin iyu' ('Why US Aids Aren't Free'), *Naeil ŭl yŏnŭn yŏksa* (*History Opening Tomorrow*) 6: 108–18.

Shin, Yong-Ok. (2002) 'Pak Chŏng-hŭi, naengjŏn kwa pangong ŭi kŭmdan e kach'in suin' ('Park Chung-Hee, trapped in the Cold War and Anti-Communism'), *Naeil ŭl yŏnŭn yŏksa* (*History Opening Tomorrow*) 9: 56–75.

Shin, Yong-Ok. (2008) 'Chehŏn hŏnpŏp mit 2-ch'a hŏnpŏp ŭi kyŏngje chilsŏ e taehan insik kwa kŭ chihyang' ('Th Evaluation of the Economic Order in the ROK Constitution and the Direction of the Second Amendment'), *Sahak Yŏn'gu* (*Review of Korean History*) 89: 159–214.

Silver, B. J. and Arrighi, G. (2001) 'Workers North and South', *Socialist Register* 37: 53–76.

Skocpol, T. (1977) 'Wallerstein's World Capitalist System: A Theoretical and Historical Critique', *American Journal of Sociology* 82(5): 1075–90.

Skocpol, T. (1979) *States and Social Revolutions*. Cambridge: Cambridge University Press.

Skocpol, T. (1985) 'Bringing the State Back In: Strategies of Analysis in Current Research', in P. B. Evans, D. Rueschemeyer and T. Skocpol (eds) *Bringing the State Back In*, pp. 3–37. Cambridge: Cambridge University Press.

Soh, Byeon-Hee. (1997) 'Chaebŏl ŭi kongkwa: p'yŏngga wa apŭro ŭi kwaje' ('The Evaluation and Prospect of the *Chaebol*'), *Sasang* (*Thought*) 32: 242–60.

Song, Hae-Yung. (2011) 'Theorising the Korean State beyond Institutionalism: Class Content and Form of "National" Development', *New Political Economy* 16(3): 281–302.

Song, Hae-Yung (2013a) 'Democracy against Labour: The Dialectic of Democratisation and De-democratisation in Korea', *Journal of Contemporary Asia* 43(2): 338–62.

Song, Hae-Yung (2013b) 'Marxist Critiques of the Developmental State and the Fetishism of National Development', *Antipode* 45(5): 1254–76.

Song, Hae-Yung (2015) 'Re-orienting the Critique of the Capitalist-System beyond the Dichotomy of Trade vs. Production Relations', Review Symposium on André Guner Frank's ReOrienting the 19th Century, *Journal of World-Systems Research* 21(1): 174–83. http://jwsr.pitt.edu/ojs/index.php/jwsr/article/view/533 (accessed January 15, 2018).

Sonn, Ho-Chul. (1989a) 'Sinsik kukdokja/Sinsik p'asijŭmnon ŭi ironjŏk kwajedŭl' ('Theoretical Problems of Theories of Neo-Colonial State Monopoly Capitalism/ Neo-Colonial Fascism'), *Kyŏngje wa Sahoe* (*Economy and Society*) 3: 158–77.

Sonn, Ho-Chul. (1989b) 'Bŭrŭsŭ Cŏmingsŭ ŭi han'guk hyŏndaesa yŏn'gu pip'an' ('A Critique of Bruce Cuming's Approach to Korean Modern History: Theoretical and Methodological Problems'), *Silch'ŏn Munhak* (*Intervention Literature*) 15: 295–330.

Sonn, Ho-Chul. (1991) '5·16 kuteta rŭl ŏttŏk'e pyŏnga hal kŏsinga' ('How to Evaluate the 5/16 [Park's] coup?'), *Yŏksa Pip'yŏng* (*Critical Review of History*) 15: 161–77.

Sonn, Ho-Chul. (1993) 'Pak Chŏng-hŭi chŏngkwon ŭi chŏngch'ijŏk sŏngkyŏk' ('The Political Characteristics of the Park Chung-Hee Regime'), *Yŏksa Pip'yŏng* (*Critical Review of History*) 25: 34–47.

Sonn, Ho-Chul. (2004) *Hyŏndae han'guk chŏngch'i: iron kwa yŏksa 1945–2003* (*Modern Korean Politics: Theories and Histories 1945–2003*). Seoul: Sahoe P'yŏngnon.

Sonn, Ho-Chul. (2006) *Haebang 60-yŏnŭi han'guk chŏngch'i 1945–2005* (*Korean Politics in the Last 60 Years 1945–2005*). Seoul: Imagine.

Sonn, Nak-Goo. (2008) *Pudongsan kyegŭp sahoe* (*Estate Class Society*). Seoul: Humanitas.

Sorensen, C. (1999) 'National Identity and the Creation of the Category "Peasant" in Colonial Korea', in Gi-Wook Shin and Michael Robinson (eds) *Colonial Modernity in Korea*, pp. 288–310. Cambridge, MA: Harvard University Press.

Starosta, G. (2004) 'Editorial Introduction: Rethinking Marx's Mature Social Theory', *Historical Materialism* 12(3): 43–52.

Stiglitz (1999) 'What We Have Learned from the Recent Crises: Implications for Banking Regulation', *Federal Reserve Bank of Chicago Proceedings* (No. 632).

Stiglitz, J. (2000) 'Capital Market Liberalization, Economic Growth, and Instability', *World Development* 28(6): 1075–86.

Stoetzler, M. (2004) 'Postone's Marx: A Theorist of Modern Society, Its Social Movements and Its Imprisonment by Abstract Labour', *Historical Materialism* 12(3): 261–283.

Stoetzler, M. (2017) *Classical Social Theory, Beginning*. Manchester: Manchester University Press.

Strange, S. (1988) (2nd ed.) *States and Markets*. London and New York: Continuum.

Stubbs, R. (2009) 'What Ever Happened in the East Asian Developmental State? The Unfolding Debate', *The Pacific Review* 22(1): 1–22.

Stubbs, R. (2011) 'The East Asian Developmental State and the Great Recession: Evolving Contesting Coalitions', *Contemporary Politics* 17(2): 151–66.

Stuenkel, O. (2016) *Post Western World*. Cambridge: Polity Press.

Suh, Jae-Jin. (1988a) 'Han'guk sanŏp chabonga ŭi sahoejŏk kiwŏn' ('The Social Origins of the Korean Industrial Capitalists'), *Sahoe wa Yŏksa* (*Society and History*) 14: 12–39.

Suh, Jae-Jin. (1988b) 'Han'guk chabonga kyegŭp ŭi sahoejŏk · chŏngch'ijŏk yŏnjul mang yŏn'gu' ('A Study on the Social and Political Network of the Korean Capitalist Class'), *Han'guk Sahoehak* (*Korean Journal of Sociology*) 22: 46–67.

Suh, Jae-Jin. (1989) 'Han'guk chabonga kyegŭp ŭi kyegŭp kigu ŭi hyŏngsŏng kwa sŏnggyŏk' ('The Formation and Characteristics of Class Apparatus of the Korean Capital Class'), *Sahoe wa Yŏksa* (*Society and History*) 16: 169–97.

Suh, Jae-Jin. (1990) 'Han'guk chabonga kyegŭp ŭi ideologi punsŏk ŭl t'ong haesŏ pon chabonga kyegŭp, nodong kyegŭp, kukkawa ŭi kwange yŏn'gu' ('A Study on

Capital-Labour-State Relations through an Analysis of Capitalist Class Ideology'), *Han'guk Sahoehak* (*Korean Journal of Sociology*) 23: 75–96.

Sung, Doo-Hyun. (2016) 'Chinbo chŏngch'i, chinbo undoing chŏnban i mollakhan iyu' ('Reasons for Progressive Politics and Movements Have Collapsed'), *Left Daegu* 11: 10–25.

Sunoo, H. H. (1978) 'Economic Development and Foreign Control in South Korea', *Journal of Contemporary Asia* 8(3): 322–39.

Tabb, K. W. (1998) 'The East Asian Financial Crisis', *Monthly Review* 50(2): 24–38.

Thelen, K. and Steinmo, S. (1992) 'Historical Institutionalism in Comparative Politics', in S. Steinmo, K. Thelen and F. Longstreth (eds) *Structuring Politics: Historical Institutionalism in Comparative Perspective*, pp. 1–32. New York: Cambridge University Press.

von Braunmühl, C. (1978) 'On the Analysis of the Bourgeois Nation State within the World Market Content. An Attempt to Develop a Methodological and Theoretical Approach', in J. Holloway and S. Picciotto (eds) *State and Capital: Marxist Debate*, pp. 160–79. London: Edward Arnold.

Wade, R. (1983) 'South Korea's Agricultural Development: The Myth of the Passive State', *Pacific Viewpoint* 24(1): 11–28.

Wade, R. (1990) *Governing the Market: Economic Theory and the Role of Government in East Asian Industrialization*. Princeton, NJ: Princeton University Press.

Wade, R. (1998a) 'From "Miracle" to "Cronyism": Explaining the Great Asian Slump', *Cambridge Journal of Economics* 22(6): 693–706.

Wade, R. (1998b) 'The Asian Debt-and-Development Crisis of 1997-?: Causes and Consequences', *World Development* 26(8): 1535–53.

Wade, R. (2006) 'Choking the South', *New Left Review* 38: 115–27.

Wade, R. (2010) 'After the Crisis: Industrial Policy and the Developmental State in Low-income Countries', *Global Policy* 1(2): 150–61.

Wade, R. and Veneroso, F. (1998a) 'The Asian Crisis: The High Debt Model Versus the Wall Street-Treasury-IMF Complex', *New Left Review* 228: 3–24.

Wade, R. and Veneroso, F. (1998b) 'The Gathering World Slump and the Battle Over Capital Controls', *New Left Review* 231: 13–42.

Wallerstein, I. (1974) 'The Rise and Future Demise of the World Capitalist System: Concepts for Comparative Analysis', *Comparative Studies in Society and History* 16(4): 387–415.

Wallerstein, I. (1979) *The Capitalist World-Economy: Essays*. Cambridge: Cambridge University Press.

Wallerstein. I. (1984) The *Politics of the World Economy: The States, the Movements and the Civilization*. Cambridge: Cambridge University Press.

Wallerstein, I. (1995) *After Liberalism*. New York: The New Press.

Wallerstein, I. (1996) *Historical Capitalism with Capitalist Civilisation*. London: Verso.

Wallerstein, I. (2004) *The World-System Analysis*. Durham, NC and London: Duke University Press.

Wang, Hyeon-Jong. (2010) 'Taehan chegukki kojong ŭi hwangje kwon kangwha wa kaehyŏk nonli' ('Gojong's Reinforcement of Emperor's Power and His argument for Reform during the Daehan Empire Period'), *Yŏksa Hakbo* (*Korean Historical Review*) 208: 1–34.

Wang, Hyeon-Jong. (2014) '1894-yŏn nongmin kun ŭi p'yejŏng kaehyŏk ch'ujin kwa kabo kyehyŏk ŭi kwangye' ('A Study of the Relationship between the Peasant

Reform and Gabo Reform in the Peasant War of 1894'), *Yŏksa Yŏn'gu* (*Journal of History*) 27: 149–67.

Wang, Hyeon-Jong. (2015) 'Haebang ihu "Tonghaksa"' ŭi pip'anjŏk suyong kwa nongmin chŏngjeang yŏn'gu' ('A Study of Critical Reception of the History of Donghak and the Peasant War in Post-Colonial Korea'), *Yŏksa Kyoyuk* (*Korean History Education Review*) 133: 157–91.

Weiss, L. (1998) *The Myth of the Powerless State: Governing the Economy in a Global Era*. Cambridge: Polity Press.

Weiss, L. (2000) 'Developmental States in Transition: Adapting, Dismantling, Innovating, Not Normalizing', *The Pacific Review* 13(1): 21–55.

Weiss, L. (2003) *States in the Global Economy: Bringing Domestic Institutions Bank In*. Cambridge: Cambridge University Press.

Weiss, L. (2005) 'The State-Augmenting Effects of Globalisation', *New Political Economy* 10(3): 345–53.

Weiss, L. and Hobson, J. M. (1995) *States and Economic Development: A Comparative Historical Analysis*. Cambridge: Polity Press.

Wells, K. M. (1995) *South Korea's Minjung Movement: The Culture and Politics of Dissidence*. Honolulu: University of Hawaii Press.

Wong, J. (2005) 'Re-Marking the Developmental State in Taiwan: The Challenges of Biotechnology', *International Political Science Review* 26(2): 169–91.

Woo, Jung-En. (1991) *Race to the Swift*. New York: Colombian University Press.

Woo-Cumings, M. (1997) 'Slouching towards the Market: The Politics of Financial Liberalization in South Korea', in M. M. Loriaux et al. *Capital Ungoverned: Liberalizing Finance in Interventionist States*, pp. 57–91. Ithaca, NY: Cornell University Press.

Woo-Cumings, M. (1999a) 'Introduction: Chalmers Johnson and the Politics of Nationalism and Development', in M. Woo-Cumings (ed) *The Developmental State*, pp. 1–31. Ithaca, NY and London: Cornell University Press.

Woo-Cumings, M. (1999b) 'The State, Democracy, and the Reform of the Corporate Sector in Korea', in T. J. Pempel (ed) *The Politics of Asian Economic Crisis*, pp. 116–42. Ithaca, NY: Cornell University Press.

Woo-Cumings, M. (2003) 'South Korean Anti-Americanism', *Japan Policy Research Institute Working Paper* (No. 93). www.jpri.org/publications/workingpapers/wp93.html (accessed September 9, 2019).

Wood, E. M. (1995) *Democracy against Capitalism: Renewing Historical Materialism*. Cambridge: Cambridge University Press.

Wood, E. M. (2003) *Empire of Capital*. London and New York: Verso.

World Bank. (1987) *World Development Report 1987*. Oxford and New York: Oxford University Press.

World Bank. (1993) *The East Asian Miracle: Economic Growth and Public Policy*. Oxford and New York: Oxford University Press.

Yang, Dong-Man. (2008) 'Yi Sŭng-man kwa taehan min'guk kŏn'guk' ('Rhee Syngman and Making of the Republic of Korea'), *Chŏngsin Munwha Yŏn'gu* (*Korean Studies Quarterly*) 31(3): 41–70.

Yang, Woo-Jin. (2005) 'Two Key Historical Moments of the Early 1960s: A Preliminary Reconsideration of 4.19 and 5.16', *Journal of Korean Studies* 10(1): 121–43.

Yeung, W-c, H. (2017) 'State-led Development Reconsidered: The Political Economy of State Transformation in East Asia since the 1990s', Special Issue *Cambridge Journal of Regions, Economy and Society* 10(1): 83–98.

Yi, Man-Yeol. (1997) 'Ilche sikminji kŭndaehwaron munje kŏmt'o' ('A Critique of the Japanese Colonial Modernization of Korea'), *Han'guk Tokrip Undongsa Yŏn'guso* (*Institute of Korean Independence Movement Studies*) 11: 301–28.

Yoon, Sang-Woo. (2009) 'Oewhanwigi ihu han'guk ŭi paljŏnjuŭijŏk sinjayujuŭiwha' ('Internalising Neoliberal Globalisation in Korea – A Case for 'Developmental Neoliberalisation'), *Kyŏngje wa Sahoe* (*Economy and Society*) 83: 40–68.

You, Jong-Sung. (2017) 'Demystifying the Park Chung-Hee Myth: Land Reform in the Evolution of Korea's Developmental State', *Journal of Contemporary Asia* 47(4): 535–56.

Zakaria, F. (2011) *The Post-American World and the Rise of the Rest*. London: Penguin Books.

Zimbauer, D. (2001) 'From NeoClassical Economics to New Institutional Economics and Beyond – Prospects for an Interdisciplinary Research Programme?' *London School of Economics, Development Studies Institute Working Paper Series* (No. 01–12): 1–19.

Index

Note: Page numbers followed by "n" refer to notes.

For Product Safety Concerns and Information please contact our EU representative GPSR@taylorandfrancis.com
Taylor & Francis Verlag GmbH, Kaufingerstraße 24, 80331 München, Germany

www.ingramcontent.com/pod-product-compliance
Ingram Content Group UK Ltd.
Pitfield, Milton Keynes, MK11 3LW, UK
UKHW022014180926
475701UK00003B/354

9781032087672